STOCKS
for the
LONG
RUN

FIFTH EDITION

STOCKS
for the
LONG
RUN

THE DEFINITIVE GUIDE TO FINANCIAL MARKET
RETURNS & LONG-TERM INVESTMENT STRATEGIES

JEREMY J. SIEGEL

Russell E. Palmer Professor of Finance
The Wharton School
University of Pennsylvania

Mc
Graw
Hill
Education

New York   Chicago   San Francisco
Athens   London   Madrid   Mexico City
Milan   New Delhi   Singapore   Sydney   Toronto

Copyright © 2014, 2008, 2002, 1998, 1994 by Jeremy J. Siegel. All rights reserved. Printed in the United States of America. Except as permitted under the United States Copyright Act of 1976, no part of this publication may be reproduced or distributed in any form or by any means, or stored in a database or retrieval system, without the prior written permission of the publisher.

1 2 3 4 5 6 7 8 9 0   QFR/QFR   1 9 8 7 6 5 4 3

ISBN   978-0-07-180051-8
MHID   0-07-180051-4

eISBN 978-0-07-180052-5
eMHID   0-07-180052-2

This publication is designed to provide accurate and authoritative information in regard to the subject matter covered. It is sold with the understanding that neither the author nor the publisher is engaged in rendering legal, accounting, futures/securities trading, or other professional service. If legal advice or other expert assistance is required, the services of a competent professional person should be sought.

—From a Declaration of Principles jointly adopted by a Committee of the American Bar Association and a Committee of Publishers

McGraw-Hill Education books are available at special quantity discounts to use as premiums and sales promotions or for use in corporate training programs. To contact a representative, please visit the Contact Us pages at www.mhprofessional.com.

CONTENTS

Chapter 7

Stock Indexes
Proxies for the Market   **105**

Chapter 8

The S&P 500 Index
More Than a Half Century of U.S. Corporate History   **119**

Chapter 9

The Impact of Taxes on Stock and Bond Returns
Stocks Have the Edge   **133**

Chapter 10

Sources of Shareholder Value
Earnings and Dividends   143

Chapter 11

Yardsticks to Value the Stock Market   157

PART III

HOW THE ECONOMIC ENVIRONMENT IMPACTS STOCKS

Chapter 14

Gold, Monetary Policy, and Inflation   209

Chapter 15

Stocks and the Business Cycle   229

Chapter 16

When World Events Impact Financial Markets   241

Chapter 17

Stocks, Bonds, and the Flow of Economic Data   257

PART IV

STOCK FLUCTUATIONS IN THE SHORT RUN

Chapter 18
Exchange-Traded Funds, Stock Index Futures, and Options   271

Chapter 24

Structuring a Portfolio for Long-Term Growth   373

Notes   379

Index   405

FOREWORD

In July 1997 I called Peter Bernstein and said I was going to be in New York and would love to lunch with him. I had an ulterior motive. I greatly enjoyed his book *Capital Ideas: The Improbable Origins of Modern Wall Street* and the *Journal of Portfolio Management*, which he founded and edited. I hoped there might be a slim chance he would consent to write the preface to the second edition of *Stocks for the Long Run*.

His secretary set up a date at one of his favorite restaurants, Circus on the Upper East Side. He arrived with his wife Barbara and a copy of the first edition of my book tucked under his arm. As he approached, he asked if I would sign it. I said "of course" and responded that I would be honored if he wrote a foreword to the second edition. He smiled; "Of course!" he exclaimed. The next hour was filled with a most fascinating conversation about publishing, academic and professional trends in finance, and even what we liked best about Philly and New York.

I thought back to our lunch when I learned, in June 2009, that he had passed away at the age of 90. In the 12 years since our first meeting, Peter had been more productive than ever, writing three more books, including his most popular, *The Remarkable Story of Risk*. Despite the incredible pace he maintained, he always found time to update the preface of my book through the next two editions. As I read through his words in the fourth edition, I found that his insights into the frustrations and rewards of being a long-term investor are as relevant today as they were when he first penned them nearly two decades ago. I can think of no better way to honor Peter than to repeat his wisdom here.

> Some people find the process of assembling data to be a deadly bore. Others view it as a challenge. Jeremy Siegel has turned it into an art form. You can only admire the scope, lucidity, and sheer delight with which Professor Siegel serves up the evidence to support his case for investing in stocks for the long run.
>
> But this book is far more than its title suggests. You will learn a lot of economic theory along the way, garnished with a fascinating history of both the capital markets and the U.S. economy. By using history to maximum effect, Professor Siegel gives the numbers a life and meaning they would never enjoy in a less compelling setting. Moreover, he boldly does battle with all historical episodes that could contradict his thesis and emerges victorious—and this includes the crazy years of the 1990s.

With this fourth edition, Jeremy Siegel has continued on his merry and remarkable way in producing works of great value about how best to invest in the stock market. His additions on behavioral finance, globalization, and exchange-traded funds have enriched the original material with fresh insights into important issues. Revisions throughout the book have added valuable factual material and powerful new arguments to make his case for stocks for the long run. Whether you are a beginner at investing or an old pro, you will learn a lot from reading this book.

Jeremy Siegel is never shy, and his arguments in this new edition demonstrate he is as bold as ever. The most interesting feature of the whole book is his twin conclusions of good news and bad news. First, today's globalized world warrants higher average price/earnings ratios than in the past. But higher P/Es are a mixed blessing, for they would mean average returns in the future are going to be lower than they were in the past.

I am not going to take issue with the forecast embodied in this viewpoint. But similar cases could have been made in other environments of the past, tragic environments as well as happy ones. One of the great lessons of history proclaims that no economic environment survives the long run. We have no sense at all of what kinds of problems or victories lie in the distant future, say, 20 years or more from now, and what influence those forces will have on appropriate price/earnings ratios.

That's all right. Professor Siegel's most important observation about the future goes beyond his controversial forecast of higher average P/Es and lower realized returns. "Although these returns may be diminished from the past," he writes, "there is overwhelming reason to believe stocks will remain the best investment for all those seeking steady, long-term gains.

"[O]verwhelming reason" is an understatement. The risk premium earned by equities over the long run must remain intact if the system is going to survive. In the capitalist system, bonds cannot and should not outperform equities over the long run. Bonds are contracts enforceable in courts of law. Equities promise their owners nothing—stocks are risky investments, involving a high degree of faith in the future. Thus, equities are not inherently "better" than bonds, but we demand a higher return from equities to compensate for their greater risk. If the long-run expected return on bonds were to be higher than the long-run expected return on stocks, assets would be priced so that risk would earn no reward. That is an unsustainable condition. Stocks must remain "the best investment for all those seeking steady, long- term gains" or our system will come to an end, and with a bang, not a whimper.

—Peter Bernstein

PREFACE

The fourth edition of *Stocks for the Long Run* was written in 2007. During the last several years, as many of my colleagues my age had slowed the pace of their research, I was often asked why I was working so hard on yet another edition of this book. With a serious face I responded, "I believe that a few events of significance have occurred over the past six years."

A few events indeed! The years 2008 and 2009 witnessed the deepest economic recession and market collapse since the Great Depression of the 1930s. The disruptions were so extensive that I put off writing this edition until I gained better perspective on the causes and consequences of the financial crisis from which we still have not completely recovered.

As a result, this edition is more thoroughly rewritten than any of the previous editions were. This is not because the conclusions of the earlier editions needed to be changed. Indeed the rise of U.S. equity markets to new all-time highs in 2013 only reinforces the central tenet of this book: that stocks are indeed the best long-term investment for those who learn to weather their short-term volatility. In fact, the long-term real return on a diversified portfolio of common stocks has remained virtually identical to the 6.7 percent reported in the first edition of *Stocks for the Long Run*, which examined returns through 1992.

CONFRONTING THE FINANCIAL CRISIS

Because of the severe impact of the crisis, I felt that what transpired over the last several years had to be addressed front and center in this edition. As a result I added two chapters that described the causes and consequences of the financial meltdown. Chapter 1 now previews the major conclusions of my research on stocks and bonds and traces how investors, money managers, and academics regarded stocks over the past century.

Chapter 2 describes the financial crisis, laying blame where blame is due on the CEOs of the giant investment banks, the regulators, and Congress. I lay out the series of fatal missteps that led Standard and Poor's, the world's largest rating agency, to give its coveted AAA rating to subprime mortgages, foolishly declaring them as safe as U.S. Treasury bonds.

Chapter 3 analyzes the extraordinary impact of the financial crisis on the financial markets: the unprecedented surge of the "libor spread" that measured cost of capital to the banks, the collapse of stock prices that wiped out two-thirds of their value, and, for the time since the dark days of the 1930s, Treasury bill yields falling to zero and even below.

Most economists believed that our system of deposit insurance, margin requirements, and financial regulations rendered the above events virtually impossible. The confluence of forces that led to the crisis were remarkably similar to what happened following the 1929 stock market crash, with mortgage-back securities replacing equities as the main culprit.

Although the Fed failed miserably at predicting the crisis, Chairman Ben Bernanke took unprecedented measures to keep financial markets open by flooding the financial markets with liquidity and guaranteeing trillions of dollars of loans and short-term deposits. These actions ballooned the Fed's balance sheet to nearly $4 trillion, 5 times its precrisis level, and raised many questions about how the Fed would unwind this unprecedented stimulus.

The crisis also changed the correlation between asset classes. World equity markets became much more correlated, reducing the diversifying gains from global investing, while U.S. Treasury bonds and the dollar became "safe haven" assets, spurring unprecedented demand for federally guaranteed debt. All commodities, including gold, suffered during the worst stages of the economic downturn, but precious metals rebounded on fear that the central bank's expansionary policies would generate high inflation.

Chapter 4 addresses longer-run issues impacting our economic well-being. The economic downturn saw the U.S. budget deficit soar to $1.3 trillion, the highest level relative to GDP since World War II. The slowdown in productivity growth generated fears that increase in living standards will slow markedly or even grind to a halt. This raises the question of whether our children will be the first generation whose standard of living will fall below that of their parents.

This chapter updates and extends the results of earlier editions by using new data provided by the U.N. Population Commission and productivity forecasts provided by the World Bank and the IMF. I now calculate the distribution of world output of the major countries and regions of the world to the end of the twenty-first century. This analysis strongly suggests that although the developed world must increase the age at which social security and medical benefits are offered by the government, such increases will be moderate if productivity growth in the emerging economies remains strong.

OTHER NEW MATERIAL IN THE FIFTH EDITION

Although the financial crisis and its aftermath are front and center in this fifth edition, I have made other significant changes as well. Not only have all the charts and tables been updated through 2012, but the chapter on the valuation of equities has been expanded to analyze such important new forecasting models such as the CAPE ratio and the significance of profit margins as a determinant of future equity returns.

Chapter 19, "Market Volatility," analyzes the "Flash Crash" of May 2010 and documents how the volatility associated with the financial crisis compares with the banking crisis of the 1930s. Chapter 20 shows that, once again, following a simple technical rule such as the 200-day moving average would have avoided the worst part of the recent bear market.

This edition also addresses whether the well-known calendar anomalies, such as the "January effect, the "small stock effect," and the "September effect," have survived over the two decades since they were described in the first edition of this book. I also include for the first time a description of "liquidity investing" and explain how it might supplement the "size" and "value" effects that have been found by researchers to be important determinants of individual stocks' return.

CONCLUDING REMARKS

I am both honored and flattered by the tremendous reception that *Stocks for the Long Run* has received. Since the publication of the first edition nearly 20 years ago, I have given hundreds of lectures on the markets and the economy around the world. I have listened closely to the questions that audiences pose, and I have contemplated the many letters, phone calls, and e-mails from readers.

To be sure, there have been some extraordinary events in the capital markets in recent years. Even those who still believed in the long-term superiority of equities were put to severe test during the financial crisis. In 1937 John Maynard Keynes stated in *The General Theory of Employment, Interest and Money*, "Investment based on genuine long-term expectation is so difficult today as to be scarcely practicable." It is no easier 75 years later.

But those who have persisted with equities have always been rewarded. No one has made money in the long run from betting against stocks or the future growth of our economy. It is the hope that this latest edition will fortify those who will inevitably waver when pessimism once again grips economists and investors. History convincingly demonstrates that stocks have been and will remain the best investment for all those seeking long-term gains.

Jeremy J. Siegel
November 2013

ACKNOWLEDGMENTS

It is never possible to list all the individuals and organizations that have praised *Stocks for the Long Run* and encouraged me to update and expand past editions. Many who provided me with data for the first four editions of *Stocks for the Long Run* willingly contributed their data again for this fifth edition. David Bianco, Chief U.S. Equity Strategist at Deutsche Bank, whose historical work on S&P 500 earnings and profit margins was invaluable for my chapter on stock market valuation, and Walter Lenhard, senior investment strategist at Vanguard, once again obtained historical data on mutual fund performance for Chapter 23. My new Wharton colleague, Jeremy Tobacman, helped me update the material on behavioral finance.

This edition would not have been possible without the hard work of Shaun Smith, who also did the research and data analysis for the first edition of *Stocks for the Long Run* in the early 1990s. Jeremy Schwartz, who was my principal researcher for *The Future for Investors*, also provided invaluable assistance for this edition.

A special thanks goes to the thousands of financial advisors from dozens of financial firms, such as Merrill Lynch, Morgan Stanley, UBS, Wells Fargo, and many others who have provided me with critical feedback in seminars and open forums on earlier editions of *Stocks for the Long Run*.

As before, the support of my family was critical in my being able to write this edition. Now that my sons are grown and out of the house, it was my wife Ellen who had to pay the whole price of the long hours spent revising this book. I set a deadline of September 1 to get my material to McGraw-Hill so we could go on a well-deserved cruise from Venice down the Adriatic. Although I couldn't promise her that this would be the last edition, I know that completing this project has freed some very welcome time for both of us.

I

STOCK RETURNS
Past, Present, and Future

The Case for Equity

Historical Facts and Media Fiction

The "new-era" doctrine—that "good" stocks (or "blue chips") were sound investments regardless of how high the price paid for them—was at the bottom only a means of rationalizing under the title of "investment" the well-nigh universal capitulation to the gambling fever.

—BENJAMIN GRAHAM AND DAVID DODD,
SECURITY ANALYSIS[1]

Investing in stocks has become a national hobby and a national obsession. To update Marx, it is the religion of the masses.

—ROGER LOWENSTEIN, "A COMMON MARKET:
THE PUBLIC'S ZEAL TO INVEST"[2]

Stocks for the Long Run by Siegel? Yeah, all it's good for now is a doorstop.

—INVESTOR CALLING INTO CNBC, MARCH, 2009[3]

"EVERYBODY OUGHT TO BE RICH"

In the summer of 1929, a journalist named Samuel Crowther interviewed John J. Raskob, a senior financial executive at General Motors, about how the typical individual could build wealth by investing in stocks. In August of that year, Crowther published Raskob's ideas in a

Ladies' Home Journal article with the audacious title "Everybody Ought to Be Rich."

In the interview, Raskob claimed that America was on the verge of a tremendous industrial expansion. He maintained that by putting just $15 per month into good common stocks, investors could expect their wealth to grow steadily to $80,000 over the next 20 years. Such a return—24 percent per year—was unprecedented, but the prospect of effortlessly amassing a great fortune seemed plausible in the atmosphere of the 1920s bull market. Stocks excited investors, and millions put their savings into the market, seeking quick profit.

On September 3, 1929, a few days after Raskob's plan appeared, the Dow Jones Industrial Average hit a historic high of 381.17. Seven weeks later, stocks crashed. The next 34 months saw the most devastating decline in share values in U.S. history.

On July 8, 1932, when the carnage was finally over, the Dow Industrials stood at 41.22. The market value of the world's greatest corporations had declined an incredible 89 percent. Millions of investors' life savings were wiped out, and thousands of investors who had borrowed money to buy stocks were forced into bankruptcy. America was mired in the deepest economic depression in its history.

Raskob's advice was ridiculed and denounced for years to come. It was said to represent the insanity of those who believed that the market could rise forever and the foolishness of those who ignored the tremendous risks in stocks. Senator Arthur Robinson of Indiana publicly held Raskob responsible for the stock crash by urging common people to buy stock at the market peak.[4] In 1992, 63 years later, *Forbes* magazine warned investors of the overvaluation of stocks in its issue headlined "Popular Delusions and the Madness of Crowds." In a review of the history of market cycles, Forbes fingered Raskob as the "worst offender" of those who viewed the stock market as a guaranteed engine of wealth.[5]

Conventional wisdom holds that Raskob's foolhardy advice epitomizes the mania that periodically overruns Wall Street. But is that verdict fair? The answer is decidedly no. Investing over time in stocks has been a winning strategy whether one starts such an investment plan at a market top or not. If you calculate the value of the portfolio of an investor who followed Raskob's advice in 1929, patiently putting $15 a month into the market, you find that his accumulation exceeded that of someone who placed the same money in Treasury bills after less than 4 years. By 1949 his stock portfolio would have accumulated almost $9,000, a return of 7.86 percent, more than double the annual return in bonds. After 30 years the portfolio would have grown to over $60,000, with an annual return rising to 12.72 percent. Although these returns were not as high as Raskob had projected, the total return of the stock portfolio over 30 years was more than eight times the accumulation in bonds and more than nine times that in Treasury bills. Those who never bought stock, citing the Great Crash as the vindication of their caution, eventually found themselves far behind investors who had patiently accumulated equity.[6]

The story of John Raskob's infamous prediction illustrates an important theme in the history of Wall Street. Bull markets and bear markets lead to sensational stories of incredible gains and devastating losses. Yet patient stock investors who can see past the scary headlines have always outperformed those who flee to bonds or other assets. Even such calamitous events as the Great 1929 Stock Crash or the financial crisis of 2008 do not negate the superiority of stocks as long-term investments.

Asset Returns Since 1802

Figure 1-1 is the most important chart in this book. It traces year by year how real (after-inflation) wealth has accumulated for a hypothetical investor who put a dollar in (1) stocks, (2) long-term government bonds, (3) U.S. Treasury bills, (4) gold, and (5) U.S. currency over the last two centuries. These returns are called *total real returns* and include income distributed from the investment (if any) plus capital gains or losses, all measured in constant purchasing power.

These returns are graphed on a *ratio*, or *logarithmic* scale. Economists use this scale to depict long-term data since the same vertical distance anywhere on the chart represents the same percentage change. On a logarithmic scale the slope of a trendline represents a constant after-inflation rate of return.

The compound annual real returns for these asset classes are also listed in the figure. Over the 210 years I have examined stock returns, the real return on a broadly diversified portfolio of stocks has averaged 6.6 percent per year. This means that, on average, a diversified stock portfolio, such as an index fund, has nearly doubled in *purchasing power* every decade over the past two centuries. The real return on fixed-income investments has averaged far less; on long-term government bonds the average real return has been 3.6 percent per year and on short-term bonds only 2.7 percent per year.

The average real return on gold has been only 0.7 percent per year. In the long run, gold prices have remained just ahead of the inflation rate, but little more. The dollar has lost, on average, 1.4 percent per year

FIGURE 1–1

Total Real Returns on U.S. Stocks, Bonds, Bills, Gold, and the Dollar, 1802–2012

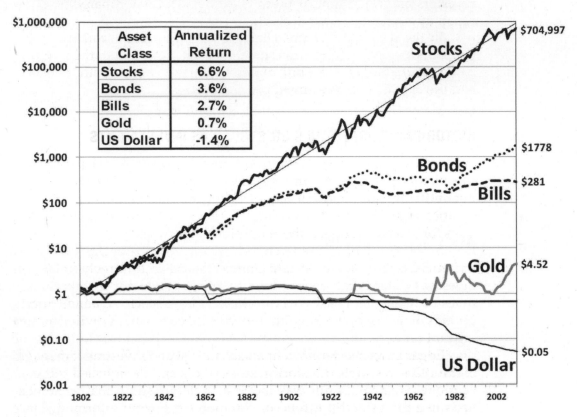

Asset Class	Annualized Return
Stocks	6.6%
Bonds	3.6%
Bills	2.7%
Gold	0.7%
US Dollar	-1.4%

of purchasing power since 1802, but it has depreciated at a significantly faster rate since World War II. In Chapter 5 we examine the details of these return series and see how they are constructed.

I have fitted the best statistical trendline to the real stock returns in Figure 1-1. The stability of real returns is striking; real stock returns in the nineteenth century do not differ appreciably from the real returns in the twentieth century. Note that stocks fluctuate both below and above the trendline but eventually return to the trend. Economists call this behavior *mean reversion*, a property that indicates that periods of above-average returns tend to be followed by periods of below-average returns and vice versa. No other asset class—bonds, commodities, or the dollar—displays the stability of long-term real returns as do stocks.

In the short run, however, stock returns are very volatile, driven by changes in earnings, interest rates, risk, and uncertainty, as well as psychological factors, such as optimism and pessimism as well as fear and greed. Yet these short-term swings in the market, which so preoccupy investors and the financial press, are insignificant compared with the broad upward movement in stock returns.

In the remainder of this chapter, I examine how economists and investors have viewed the investment value of stocks over the course of history and how the great bull and bear markets impact both the media and the opinions of investment professionals.

HISTORICAL PERSPECTIVES ON STOCKS AS INVESTMENTS

Throughout the nineteenth century, stocks were deemed the province of speculators and insiders but certainly not conservative investors. It was not until the early twentieth century that researchers came to realize that equities might be suitable investments under certain economic conditions for investors outside those traditional channels.

In the first half of the twentieth century, the great U.S. economist Irving Fisher, a professor at Yale University and an extremely successful investor, believed that stocks were superior to bonds during inflationary times but that common shares would likely underperform bonds during periods of deflation, a view that became the conventional wisdom during that time.[7]

Edgar Lawrence Smith, a financial analyst and investment manager of the 1920s, researched historical stock prices and demolished this conventional wisdom. Smith was the first to demonstrate that accumulations in a diversified portfolio of common stocks outperformed bonds not only when commodity prices were rising but also when prices were falling. Smith published his studies in 1925 in a book entitled *Common Stocks as Long-Term Investments*. In the introduction he stated:

> These studies are a record of a failure—the failure of facts to sustain a pre-conceived theory, . . . [the theory being] that high-grade bonds had proved to be better investments during periods of [falling commodity prices].[8]

Smith maintained that stocks should be an essential part of an investor's portfolio. By examining stock returns back to the Civil War, Smith discovered that there was a very small chance that an investor would have to wait a long time (which he put at 6 to, at most, 15 years) before being able to sell his stocks at a profit. Smith concluded:

> We have found that there is a force at work in our common stock holdings which tends ever toward increasing their principal value. . . . [U]nless we

have had the extreme misfortune to invest at the very peak of a noteworthy rise, those periods in which the average market value of our holding remains less than the amount we paid for them are of comparatively short duration. Our hazard even in such extreme cases appears to be that of time alone.[9]

Smith's conclusion was right not only historically but also prospectively. It took just over 15 years to recover the money invested at the 1929 peak, following a crash far worse than Smith had ever examined. And since World War II, the recovery period for stocks has been even better. Even including the recent financial crisis, which saw the worst bear market since the 1930s, the longest it has ever taken an investor to recover an original investment in the stock market (including reinvested dividends) was the five-year, eight-month period from August 2000 through April 2006.

The Influence of Smith's Work

Smith wrote his book in the 1920s, at the outset of one of the greatest bull markets in our history. Its conclusions caused a sensation in both academic and investing circles. The prestigious weekly *The Economist* stated, "Every intelligent investor and stockbroker should study Mr. Smith's most interesting little book, and examine the tests individually and their very surprising results."[10]

Smith's ideas quickly crossed the Atlantic and were the subject of much discussion in Great Britain. John Maynard Keynes, the great British economist and originator of the business cycle theory that became the paradigm for future generations of economists, reviewed Smith's book with much excitement. Keynes stated:

> The results are striking. Mr. Smith finds in almost every case, not only when prices were rising, but also when they were falling, that common stocks have turned out best in the long-run, indeed, markedly so. . . . This actual experience in the United States over the past fifty years affords prima facie evidence that the prejudice of investors and investing institutions in favor of bonds as being "safe" and against common stocks as having, even the best of them, a "speculative" flavor, has led to a relative over-valuation of bonds and under-valuation of common stocks.[11]

Common Stock Theory of Investment

Smith's writings gained academic credibility when they were published in such prestigious journals as the *Review of Economic Statistics* and the

Journal of the American Statistical Association.[12] Smith acquired an international following when Siegfried Stern published an extensive study of returns in common stock in 13 European countries from the onset of World War I through 1928. Stern's study showed that the advantage of investing in common stocks over bonds and other financial investments extended far beyond America's financial markets.[13] Research demonstrating the superiority of stocks became known as the *common stock theory of investment.*[14]

The Market Peak

Smith's research also changed the mind of the renowned Yale economist Irving Fisher, who saw Smith's study as a confirmation of his own long-held belief that bonds were overrated as safe investments in a world with uncertain inflation. In 1925 Fisher summarized Smith's findings with these prescient observations of investors' behavior:

> It seems, then, that the market overrates the safety of "safe" securities and pays too much for them, that it overrates the risk of risky securities and pays too little for them, that it pays too much for immediate and too litt for remote returns, and finally, that it mistakes the steadiness of mon income from a bond for a steadiness of real income which it does not p sess. In steadiness of real income, or purchasing power, a list of diversi common stocks surpasses bonds.[15]

Irving Fisher's "Permanently High Plateau"

Professor Fisher, cited by many as the greatest U.S. economist a father of capital theory, was no mere academic. He actively ar and forecast financial market conditions, wrote dozens of newsle topics ranging from health to investments, and created a highly ful card-indexing firm based on one of his own patented in Although he hailed from a modest background, his personal n the summer of 1929 exceeded $10 million, which is over $100 un in today's dollars.[16]

Irving Fisher, as well as many other economists in the 1920s, believed that the establishment of the Federal Reserve System in 1913 was critical to reducing the severity of economic fluctuations. Indeed the 1920s were a period of remarkably stable growth, as the instability in such economic variables as industrial production and producer prices was greatly reduced, a factor that boosted the prices of risky assets such as stocks. As we shall see in the next chapter, there was a remarkable similarity between the stability of the 1920s and the decade that preceded the recent 2008 financial crisis. In both periods not only had the business cycle moderated, but there was great confidence—later shattered—that the Federal Reserve would be able to mitigate, if not eliminate, the business cycle.

The 1920s bull market drew millions of Americans into stocks, and Fisher's own financial success and reputation as a market seer gained him a large following among investors and analysts. The market turbulence in early October 1929 greatly increased interest in his pronouncements.

Market followers were not surprised that on the evening of October 14, 1929, when Irving Fisher arrived at the Builders' Exchange Club in New York City to address the monthly meeting of the Purchasing Agents Association, a large number of people, including news reporters, pressed into the meeting hall. Investors' anxiety had been rising since early September when Roger Babson, businessman and market seer, predicted a "terrific" crash in stock prices.[17] Fisher had dismissed Babson's pessimism, noting that Babson had been bearish for some time. But the public sought to be reassured by the great man who had championed stocks for so long.

The audience was not disappointed. After a few introductory remarks, Fisher uttered a sentence that, much to his regret, became one of the most-quoted phrases in stock market history: "Stock prices," he proclaimed, "have reached what looks like a permanently high plateau."[18]

On October 29, two weeks to the day after Fisher's speech, stocks crashed. His "high plateau" turned into a bottomless abyss. The next three years witnessed the most devastating market collapse in history. Despite all of Irving Fisher's many accomplishments, his reputation—and the thesis that stocks were a sound way to accumulate wealth—was shattered.

A RADICAL SHIFT IN SENTIMENT

The collapse of both the economy and the stock market in the 1930s left an indelible mark on the psyches of investors. The common stock theory of investment was attacked from all angles, and many summarily dismissed the idea that stocks were fundamentally sound investments. Lawrence Chamberlain, an author and well-known investment banker, stated, *"Common stocks, as such, are not superior to bonds as long-term investments, because primarily they are not investments at all. They are speculations."*[19]

In 1934, Benjamin Graham, an investment fund manager, and David Dodd, a finance professor at Columbia University, wrote *Security Analysis*, which became the bible of the value-oriented approach to analyzing stocks and bonds. Through its many editions, the book has had a lasting impact on students and market professionals alike.

Graham and Dodd clearly blamed Smith's book for feeding the bull market mania of the 1920s by proposing plausible-sounding but fallacious theories to justify the purchase of stocks.

They wrote:

> The self-deception of the mass speculator must, however, have its element of justification. . . . In the new-era bull market, the "rational" basis was the record of long-term improvement shown by diversified common-stock holdings. [There is] a small and rather sketchy volume from which the new-era theory may be said to have sprung. The book is entitled *Common Stocks as Long-Term Investments* by Edgar Lawrence Smith, published in 1924.[20]

THE POSTCRASH VIEW OF STOCK RETURNS

Following the Great Crash, both the media and analysts trashed both the stock market and those who advocated stocks as investments. Nevertheless, research on indexes of stock market returns received a big boost in the 1930s when Alfred Cowles III, founder of the Cowles Commission for Economic Research, constructed capitalization-weighted stock indexes back to 1871 of all stocks traded on the New York Stock Exchange. His total-return indexes included reinvested dividends and are virtually identical to the methodology that is used today to compute stock returns. Cowles confirmed the findings that Smith reached before the stock crash and concluded that most of the time stocks were undervalued and enabled investors to reap superior returns by investing in them.[21]

After World War II, two professors from the University of Michigan, Wilford J. Eiteman and Frank P. Smith, published a study of the investment returns of actively traded industrial companies and found that by regularly purchasing these 92 stocks without any regard to the stock market cycle (a strategy called *dollar cost averaging*), stock investors earned returns of 12.2 percent per year, far exceeding those in fixed-income investments. Twelve years later they repeated the study, using the same stocks they had used in their previous study. This time the returns were even higher despite the fact that they made no adjustment for any of the new firms or new industries that had surfaced in the interim. They wrote:

> If a portfolio of common stocks selected by such obviously foolish methods as were employed in this study will show an annual compound rate of return as high as 14.2 percent, then a small investor with limited knowledge of market conditions can place his savings in a diversified list of common stocks with some assurance that, given time, his holding will provide him with safety of principal and an adequate annual yield.[22]

Many dismissed the Eiteman and Smith study because the period studied did not include the Great Crash of 1929 to 1932. But in 1964, two professors from the University of Chicago, Lawrence Fisher and James H. Lorie, examined stock returns through the stock crash of 1929, the Great Depression, and World War II.[23] Fisher and Lorie concluded that stocks offered significantly higher returns (which they reported at 9.0 percent per year) than any other investment media during the entire 35-year period, 1926 through 1960. They even factored taxes and transaction costs into their return calculations and concluded:

> It will perhaps be surprising to many that the returns have consistently been so high. . . . The fact that many persons choose investments with a substantially lower average rate of return than that available on common stocks suggests the essentially conservative nature of those investors and the extent of their concern about the risk of loss inherent in common stocks.[24]

Ten years later, in 1974, Roger Ibbotson and Rex Sinquefield published an even more extensive review of returns in an article entitled "Stocks, Bonds, Bills, and Inflation: Year-by-Year Historical Returns (1926–74)."[25] They acknowledged their indebtedness to the Lorie and Fisher study and confirmed the superiority of stocks as long-term investments. Their summary statistics, which are published annually in yearbooks, are frequently quoted and have often served as the return benchmarks for the securities industry.[26]

THE GREAT BULL MARKET OF 1982–2000

The 1970s were not good years for either stocks or the economy. Surging inflation and sharply higher oil prices led to negative real stock returns for the 15-year period from the end of 1966 through the summer of 1982. But as the Fed's tight money policy quashed inflation, interest rates fell sharply and the stock market entered its greatest bull market ever, a market that would eventually see stock prices appreciate by more than tenfold. From a low of 790 in August 1982, stocks rose sharply, and the Dow Industrial Average surged past 1,000 to a new record by the end of 1982, finally surpassing the 1973 highs it had reached nearly a decade earlier.

Although many analysts expressed skepticism that the rise could continue, a few were very bullish. Robert Foman, president and chairman of E.F. Hutton, proclaimed in October 1983 that we are "in the dawning of a new age of equities" and boldly predicted the Dow Jones average could hit 2,000 or more by the end of the decade.

But even Foman was too pessimistic, as the Dow Industrials broke 2,000 in January 1987 and surpassed 3,000 just before Saddam Hussein invaded Kuwait in August 1990. The Gulf War and a real estate recession precipitated a bear market, but this one, like the stock crash of October 1987, was short lived.

Iraq's defeat in the Gulf War ushered in one of the most fabulous decades in stock market history. The world witnessed the collapse of communism and the diminished threat of global conflict. The transfer of resources from military expenditures to domestic consumption enabled the United States to increase economic growth while keeping inflation low.

As stocks moved upward, few thought the bull market would last. In 1992, *Forbes* warned investors in a cover story "The Crazy Things People Say to Rationalize Stock Prices" that stocks were in the "midst of a speculative buying panic" and cited Raskob's foolish advice to invest at the market peak in 1929.[27]

But such caution was ill advised. After a successful battle against inflation in 1994, the Fed eased interest rates, and the Dow subsequently moved above 4,000 in early 1995. Shortly thereafter, *BusinessWeek* defended the durability of the bull market in an article on May 15, 1995, entitled "Dow 5000? Don't Laugh." The Dow quickly crossed that barrier by November and then reached 6,000 eleven months later.

By late 1995, the persistent rise in stock prices caused many more analysts to sound the alarm. Michael Metz of Oppenheimer, Charles Clough of Merrill Lynch, and Byron Wien of Morgan Stanley expressed strong doubts about the underpinnings of the rally. In September 1995, David Shulman, chief equity strategist for Salomon Brothers, wrote an article entitled "Fear and Greed," which compared the current market climate with that of similar stock market peaks in 1929 and 1961. Shulman claimed intellectual support was an important ingredient in sustaining bull markets, noting Edgar Smith's and Irving Fisher's work in the 1920s, the Fisher-Lorie studies in the 1960s, and my *Stocks for the Long Run*, published in 1994.[28] But these bears had little impact as stocks continued upward.

Warnings of Overvaluation

By 1996, price/earnings ratios on the S&P 500 Index reached 20, considerably above its average postwar level. More warnings were issued. Roger Lowenstein, a well-known author and financial writer, asserted in the *Wall Street Journal*:

> Investing in stocks has become a national hobby and a national obsession. People may denigrate their government, their schools, their spoiled sports stars. But belief in the market is almost universal. To update Marx, it is the religion of the masses.[29]

Floyd Norris, lead financial writer for the *New York Times*, echoed Lowenstein's comments by penning an article in January 1997, "In the Market We Trust."[30] Henry Kaufman, the Salomon Brothers guru whose pronouncements on the fixed-income market had frequently rocked bonds in the 1980s, declared that "the exaggerated financial euphoria is increasingly conspicuous," and he cited assurances offered by optimists equivalent to Irving Fisher's utterance that stocks had reached a permanently high plateau.[31]

Warnings of the end of the bull market did not emanate just from the media and Wall Street. Academicians were increasingly investigating this unprecedented rise in stock values. Robert Shiller of Yale University and John Campbell of Harvard wrote a scholarly paper showing that the market was significantly overvalued and presented this research to the Board of Governors of the Federal Reserve System in early December 1996.[32]

With the Dow surging past 6,400, Alan Greenspan, chairman of the Federal Reserve, issued a warning in a speech before the annual dinner for the American Enterprise Institute in Washington on December 5, 1996. He asked, "How do we know when *irrational exuberance* has unduly escalated asset values, which then become subject to unexpected and prolonged contractions as they have in Japan over the past decade? And how do we factor that assessment into monetary policy?"

His words had an electrifying effect, and the term *irrational exuberance* became the most celebrated utterance of Greenspan's tenure as Fed chairman. Asian and European markets fell dramatically as his words were flashed across computer monitors, and the next morning Wall Street opened dramatically lower. But investors quickly regained their optimism, and stocks closed in New York with only moderate losses.

The Late Stage of the Great Bull Market, 1997–2000

From there it was onward and upward, with the Dow breaking 7,000 in February 1997 and 8,000 in July. Even *Newsweek*'s cautious cover story "Married to the Market," depicting a Wall Street wedding between America and a bull, did nothing to quell investor optimism.[33]

The market became an ever-increasing preoccupation of middle- and upper-income Americans. Business books and magazines proliferated, and the all-business cable news stations, particularly CNBC, drew huge audiences. Electronic tickers and all-business TV stations were broadcast in lunchrooms, bars, and even lounges of the major business schools throughout the country. Air travelers flying 35,000 feet above the sea could view up-to-the-minute Dow and Nasdaq averages as they were flashed from monitors on phones anchored to the backs of the seats facing the travelers.

Adding impetus to the already surging market was the explosion of communications technology. The Internet allowed investors to stay in touch with markets and with their portfolios from anywhere in the world. Whether it was from Internet chat rooms, financial websites, or e-mail newsletters, investors found access to a plethora of information at their fingertips. CNBC became so popular that major investment houses made sure that all their brokers watched the station on television or their desktop computers so that they could be one step ahead of clients calling in with breaking business news.

The bull market psychology appeared impervious to financial and economic shocks. The first wave of the Asian crisis sent the market down a record 554 points on October 27, 1997, and closed trading temporarily. But this did little to dent investors' enthusiasm for stocks.

The following year, the Russian government defaulted on its bonds, and Long-Term Capital Management, considered the world's premier hedge fund, found itself entangled in speculative positions measured in the trillions of dollars that it could not trade. These events sent the Dow Industrials down almost 2,000 points, or 20%, but three quick Fed rate cuts sent the market soaring again. On March 29, 1999, the Dow closed above 10,000, and it then went on to a record close of 11,722.98 on January 14, 2000.

The Top of the Market

As has happened so many times, at the peak of the bull market the discredited bears retreat while the bulls, whose egos have been reinforced by the continued upward movement of stock prices, become even bolder. In 1999, two economists, James Glassman and Kevin Hassett, published a book entitled *Dow 36,000*. They claimed that the Dow Jones Industrial Average, despite its meteoric rise, was still grossly undervalued, and its true valuation was three times higher at 36,000. Much to my surprise, they asserted that the theoretical underpinning for their analysis came from my book *Stocks for the Long Run*! They claimed that since I showed that bonds were as risky as stocks over long horizons, then stock prices must rise threefold to reduce their returns to those of bonds, ignoring that the real comparison should be with the Treasury inflation-protected bonds, whose yield was much higher at that time.[34]

Despite the upward march of the Dow Industrials, the real action in the market was in the technology stocks that were listed on the Nasdaq, which included such shares as Cisco, Sun Microsystems, Oracle, JDS Uniphase, and other companies as well as the rising group of Internet stocks. From November 1997 to March 2000, the Dow Industrials rose 40 percent, but the Nasdaq index rose 185 percent, and the dot-com index of 24 online firms soared nearly tenfold from 142 to 1,350.

The Tech Bubble Bursts

The date March 10, 2000, marked the peak not only of the Nasdaq but also of many Internet and technology stock indexes. Even I, a longtime bull, wrote that the technology stocks were selling at ridiculous prices that presaged a collapse.[35]

When technology spending unexpectedly slowed, the bubble burst, and a severe bear market began. Stock values plunged by a record $9 trillion, and the S&P 500 Index declined by 49.15 percent, eclipsing the 48.2 percent decline in the 1972 to 1974 bear market and the worst since the Great Depression. The Nasdaq fell 78 percent and the dot-com index by more than 95 percent.

Just as the bull market spawned the irrational optimists, the collapsing stock prices brought back the bears in droves. In September 2002, with the Dow hovering around 7,500 and just a few weeks before the bear market low of 7,286, Bill Gross, the legendary head of the PIMCO, home of the world's largest mutual fund, came out with a piece entitled "Dow 5,000" in which he stated that despite the market's awful decline, stocks were still nowhere near as low as they should be on the basis of economic fundamentals. It was startling that within a period of two years, one well-regarded forecaster claimed the right value for the Dow was as high as 36,000, while another claimed it should fall to 5,000!

The bear market squelched the public's fascination with stocks. Televisions in public venues were no longer tuned to CNBC but instead switched on sports and Hollywood gossip. As one bar owner colorfully put it, "People are licking their wounds and they don't want to talk about stocks anymore. It's back to sports, women, and who won the game."[36]

The declining market left many professionals deeply skeptical of stocks, and yet bonds did not seem an attractive alternative, as their yields had declined below 4 percent. Investors wondered whether there might be attractive investments beyond the world of stocks and bonds.

David Swenson, chief investment officer at Yale University since 1985, seemed to provide that answer. At the peak of the bull market, he wrote a book, *Pioneering Portfolio Management: An Unconventional Approach to Institutional Investment*, that espoused the qualities of "nontraditional" (and often illiquid) assets, such as private equity, venture capital, real estate, timber, and hedge funds. As a result, hedge funds, pools of investment money that can be invested in any way the fund managers see fit, enjoyed a boom.[37] From a mere $100 billion in 1990, assets of hedge funds grew to over $1.5 trillion by 2007.

But the surge of assets into hedge funds drove the prices of many unconventional assets to levels never before seen. Jeremy Grantham, a successful money manager at GMO and a onetime big booster of unconventional investing, stated in April 2007, "After these moves, most diversifying and exotic assets are badly overpriced."[38]

RUMBLINGS OF THE FINANCIAL CRISIS

From the ashes of the technology bust of 2000–2002, the stock market almost doubled from its low of 7,286 on October 9, 2002, to an all-time high of 14,165 exactly five years later on October 9, 2007. In contrast to the peak of the technology boom, when the S&P 500 was selling for 30 times earnings, there was no general overvaluation at the 2007 market peak; stocks were selling for a much more modest 16 times earnings.

But there were signs that all was not well. The financial sector, which in the bull market had become the largest sector of the S&P 500 Index, peaked in May 2007, and the price of many large banks, such as Citi and BankAmerica, had been falling all year.

More ominous developments came from the real estate market. Real estate prices, after having nearly tripled in the previous decade, peaked in the summer of 2006 and were heading downward. All of a sudden, subprime mortgages experienced large delinquencies. In April 2007 New Century Financial, a leading subprime lender, filed for bankruptcy, and in June Bear Stearns informed investors that it was suspending redemptions from its High-Grade Structured Credit Strategies Enhanced Leverage Fund, a fund whose name is as complex as the securities that it held.

At first the market ignored these developments, but on August 9, 2007, BNP Paribas, when France's largest bank, halted redemptions in its mortgage funds, world equity markets sold off sharply. Stocks recovered when the Fed lowered the Fed funds rate 50 basis points in an emergency meeting in August and another 50 basis points at its regular September meeting.

Yet 2008 brought no relief from subprime troubles. Bear Stearns, which had to take an increasing volume of subprime mortgages back on its own balance sheets, began to experience funding problems, and the price of its shares plummeted. On March 17, 2008, the Federal Reserve, in an effort to shield Bear from imminent bankruptcy, arranged an emergency sale of all of Bear Stearns's assets to JPMorgan at a price of $2 (later raised to $10) a share, almost 99 percent below its high of $172.61 reached in January of the prior year.

Beginning of the End for Lehman Brothers

But Bear Stearns was only the appetizer for this bear market, and the main dish was not far behind. Lehman Brothers, founded in the 1850s, had a storied history that included bringing such great companies as Sears, Woolworth's, Macy's, and Studebaker public. Its profitability soared after the firm went public in 1994, and in 2007 the firm reported its fourth consecutive year of record profitability as net revenues reached $19.2 billion and the number of employees neared 30,000.

But Lehman Brothers, like Bear Stearns, was involved in the subprime market and other leveraged real estate investments. Its price had sunk from over $40 to $20 a share when Bear was merged into JPMorgan in March. Lehman was well known for financing large real estate deals, booking significant fees as investors sold and refinanced commercial real estate at ever higher prices. In July, Blackstone, another large investment house that went public in July 2007, had purchased Sam Zell's

Equity Office Property for $22.9 billion, collecting high fees for placing almost all of the properties before the market collapsed.

Lehman felt confident despite the chaos enveloping the subprime market. Many analysts were convinced that commercial real estate did not suffer from the overbuilding that plagued the residential sector. In fact, commercial real estate prices continued to rise well after the general market peaked. Reacting favorably to lower interest rates, the Dow Jones REIT Index of all publicly traded real estate investment trusts peaked in February 2008, four months after the general market and more than a year after the major commercial banks hit their highs.[39]

In May, just after commercial real estate prices reached their peak, Lehman financed a huge $22 billion stake in Archstone-Smith Trust, hoping to flip the properties to buyers, just as Blackstone did a few months earlier.[40] But as in the child's game of musical chairs, the music stopped in the summer of 2008. Blackstone got the very last chair in the real estate closing room, but Lehman was left standing. On September 15, 2008, as Lehman CEO Richard Fuld thrashed about to find a last-minute buyer, Lehman Brothers, an investment firm that had thrived for more than a century and a half, filed for bankruptcy. It was the largest in U.S. history, and Lehman listed a record $613 billion in liabilities. Just as the Great Crash of 1929 launched the Great Depression of the 1930s, the fall of Lehman Brothers in 2008 precipitated the greatest financial crisis and deepest economic contraction that the world had seen in nearly a century.

The Great Financial Crisis of 2008

Its Origins, Impact, and Legacy

Regarding the Great Depression. You're right, we did it. We're very sorry. But thanks to you, we won't do it again.

—BEN BERNANKE, NOVEMBER 8, 2002,
ON THE NINETIETH BIRTHDAY CELEBRATION
FOR MILTON FRIEDMAN

THE WEEK THAT ROCKED WORLD MARKETS

It was only Wednesday, September 17, but I had already had an exhausting week trying to make sense of the upheaval in the financial markets. On Monday, stocks surprised investors by opening higher despite the Sunday night news of the bankruptcy of Lehman Brothers, the largest bankruptcy filing in U.S. history. With no government aid forthcoming, Lehman Brothers, a 150-year-old investment firm that had survived the Great Depression, had no chance this time.

But that hopeful opening was quickly countered by rumors that key firms would not clear trades for Lehman customers, throwing markets into a state of anxiety.[1] As Monday morning's gains turned into losses, fear enveloped the financial markets. Investors wondered: What assets were safe? Which firm would be the next to fail? And could this crisis be contained? Risk premiums soared as lenders backed away from all credit markets except U.S. Treasury bonds.[2] By the end of the day, the Dow Industrials had fallen more than 500 points.

The following day, speculators attacked AIG, the world's largest and most profitable insurance company. AIG's stock price, which had reached nearly $60 a share a year earlier, plunged below $3, down from its closing price of over $10 the previous Friday. AIG's collapse sent stocks sharply lower; but some traders speculated, correctly as it turned out, that the Fed could not risk letting another major financial firm go under, and the market stabilized later in the day. Indeed, after the close of trading, the Fed announced that it had loaned $85 billion to AIG, avoiding another market-shaking bankruptcy. The Fed's decision to bail out AIG was a dramatic turnaround, as Chairman Ben Bernanke had rejected the giant insurer's request for a $40 billion loan just a week earlier.

But the crisis was far from over. After the markets closed on Tuesday, the $36 billion Reserve Primary Money Market Fund made a most ominous announcement. Because the Lehman securities that the money fund held were marked down to zero, Reserve was going to "break the buck" and pay investors only 97 cents on the dollar.[3]

Although other money funds reassured investors that they held no Lehman debt and that they were honoring all withdrawals at full value, it was clear that these declarations would do little to calm investor anxiety. Bear Stearns had repeatedly reassured investors that everything was fine before the Fed forced the failing firm to merge into JPMorgan six months earlier. Similarly Lehman CEO Richard Fuld told investors just a week before filing for bankruptcy that all was well and blamed short sellers for driving down the price of his stock.

COULD THE GREAT DEPRESSION HAPPEN AGAIN?

I returned to my office after lunch that Wednesday and looked at my Bloomberg screen. Yes, stocks were down again, and that didn't surprise me. But what caught my attention was the yield on U.S. Treasury bills. A Treasury auction of three-month bills conducted that afternoon was so heavily oversubscribed that buyers sent the interest rate down to 6 hundredths of 1 percent.

I had monitored markets closely for almost 50 years, through the savings and loan crises of the 1970s, the 1987 stock market crash, the Asian crisis, the Long-Term Capital Management crisis, the Russian default, the 9/11 terrorist attack, and many other crises. But I had never seen investors rush to Treasuries like this. The last time Treasury bill yields had fallen toward zero was during the Great Depression, 75 years earlier.[4]

My eyes returned to the screen in front of me, and a chill went down my spine. Was this a replay of a period that we economists thought was dead and gone? Could this be the start of the second "Great Depression"? Can policy makers prevent a repeat of that financial and economic catastrophe?

In the ensuing months the answers to these questions started to emerge. The Federal Reserve did implement aggressive programs to prevent another Depression. But the credit disruptions that followed the Lehman bankruptcy caused the world's deepest economic contraction and the deepest decline in equity prices since the Great Depression. And the recovery from the "Great Recession," as the economic downturn became known, was one of the slowest in U.S. history, causing many to question whether the future of the U.S. economy could ever be as bright as it appeared when the Dow Industrials crossed 14,000 in October 2007.

THE CAUSE OF THE FINANCIAL CRISIS

The Great Moderation

The economic backdrop for the financial crisis of 2008 was the "Great Moderation," the name that economists gave to the remarkably long and stable economic period that preceded the Great Recession. The volatility of key economic variables, such as the quarterly changes in real and nominal GDP, fell by about one-half during the 1983–2005 period compared with the average levels that existed since World War II.[5] Although part of this stability was ascribed to the increase in the size of the service sector and advances in inventory control that moderated the "inventory cycle," many attributed the reduction of economic volatility to the increasing effectiveness of monetary policy, primarily as practiced during the tenure of Alan Greenspan as Fed chairman from 1986 through 2006.

As one might expect, risk premiums on many financial instruments declined markedly during the Great Moderation as investors believed that prompt central bank action would counteract any severe shock to the economy. Indeed, the 2001 recession reinforced the market's opinion that the economy was more stable. That recession was very mild by historical standards despite the popping of the huge tech bubble in 2000 and the consumer retrenchment that followed the 9/11 terrorist attacks.

The unusual economic stability that preceded the Great Recession was very similar to the 1920s, a period of calm that preceded the 1929 stock crash and the Great Depression. The standard deviation of changes in industrial production from 1920 to 1929 was less than one-half of what it was in the preceding 20 years, similar to what occurred during the Great Moderation. During the 1920s, many economists, including the influential Irving Fisher of Yale University, attributed the increased stability to the Federal Reserve, as did economists before the recent financial crisis. And in the 1920s, investors also believed that the Federal Reserve, created in the preceding decade, would "backstop" the economy in the case of a crisis, moderating any downturn.

Unfortunately, the increased appetite for risky assets during a stable economic environment may set the stage for a more severe crisis to follow. A slowdown in business activity, which under normal times would be well tolerated, can easily overwhelm highly leveraged borrowers who have too little cushion to insulate them from a market decline.

Some economists believe that the cycle of falling risk premiums and rising leverage is the major cause of economic fluctuations. Hyman Minsky, an economics professor from Washington University in St. Louis, formulated the "financial instability hypothesis,"[6] in which he believed long periods of economic stability and rising asset prices drew in not only speculators and "momentum" investors but also swindlers who engage in Ponzi schemes that trap ordinary investors who wish to ride the market's upward breaks. Minsky's theories never gained much currency with mainstream economists because he did not formulate them in a rigorous form. But Minsky had a strong impact on many, including the late Charles Kindleberger, an economics professor at MIT whose five editions of *Manias, Panics, and Crashes: A History of Financial Crises* have drawn a large following.

Subprime Mortgages

In contrast to 1929, where rampant lending against a soaring stock market contributed to the financial crisis, the primary cause of the 2008 financial crisis was the rapid growth of subprime mortgages and other real estate securities that found their way into the balance sheets of very large and highly leveraged financial institutions. When the real estate market reversed direction and the prices of these securities plunged, firms that had borrowed money were thrown into a crisis that sent some into bankruptcy, others into forced mergers with stronger firms, and still others to the government for capital to ensure their survival.[7]

Many investors welcomed these higher-yielding mortgage securities, believing that the Great Moderation and a Federal Reserve "safety net" had significantly reduced their risks of default. But the proliferation of these securities accelerated when the major rating agencies, such as Standard & Poor's and Moody's, gave these subprime mortgages their highest ratings. This allowed hundreds of billions of dollars of mortgage-based securities to be marketed worldwide to pension funds, municipalities, and other organizations that demanded only the highest-quality fixed-income investments. And it also lured many Wall Street firms that were seeking higher yields to buy, attracted by their AAA ratings.

Although some assume that the investment banks pressured the rating agencies to give these securities investment-grade ratings so that the banks could enlarge the pool of potential buyers, in fact these securities were rated by statistical techniques very similar to those used to evaluate other securities. Unfortunately, these techniques were ill suited to analyze default probabilities in a housing market where real estate prices soared far above fundamentals.

The Crucial Rating Mistake

Figure 2-1 is a yearly plot of housing prices from the end of World War II, measured both before and after inflation. The period from 1997 through 2006 was marked by an accelerating pace of real estate appreciation, in both real and nominal terms. Over these years, nominal home prices, as measured by the Case-Shiller Index of 20 metropolitan communities, nearly tripled, and real home prices increased 130 percent, well exceeding the increase during the 1970s and topping the previous record-breaking increases that immediately followed World War II.

Before the housing price boom, conventional mortgages were based on an 80 percent loan-to-market ratio, and the creditworthiness of the borrower was important to the lender. This is because the price of an individual home, or even the average price of homes in specific geographic regions, could fall more than 20 percent and thus impair the value of the lender's collateral.

But what if mortgages from many diverse localities could be bundled together to form a security that would greatly reduce the risk of local real estate fluctuations? Then the price of the underlying assets backing the security should look more like the nominal home price series shown in Figure 2-1, which—until 2006—showed very little downside movement. In fact, prior to 1997 there were only three years when the nominal national home index had declined: two of these declines were less than 1.0 percent, and the third, from the second quarter of 1990 to the second quarter of 1991, was 2.8 percent. Therefore,

F I G U R E   2-1

Nominal and Real U.S. Home Prices 1950–2012

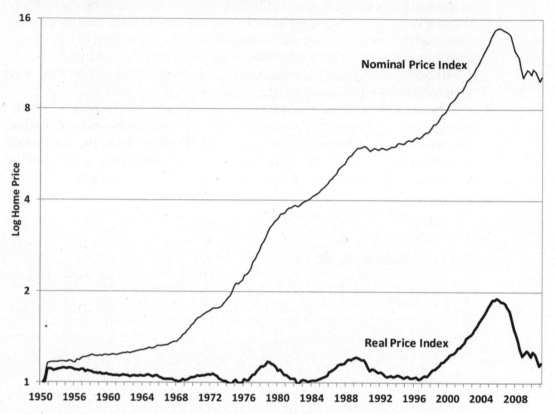

based on postwar historical data, there would have been no period when the nationwide real estate price index even began to approach the 20 percent decline necessary to cut into the collateral of the standard mortgage.[8,9]

Standard & Poor's, as well as Moody's and other rating agencies, analyzed these historical home price series and performed the standard statistical tests that measure the risk and return of these securities. On the basis of these studies, they reported that the probability that collateral behind a nationally diversified portfolio of home mortgages would be violated was virtually zero. The risk management departments of many investment banks agreed with this conclusion.

An equally important conclusion reached by this analysis was that as long as the real estate behind the mortgage was virtually always going to be worth more than the mortgage, the creditworthiness of the borrower should not be important to the lender. If the borrower defaults, the lender can take over the property and sell it for more than the value of the loan. The rating agencies therefore stamped "AAA" on these securities, ignoring the creditworthiness of the home buyer. This assumption provided the impetus for the sale of hundreds of billions of dollars of subprime and other "nonconventional" mortgages backed by little or no credit documentation as long as the loan was collateralized by a pool of geographically diversified mortgages.

Some rating agencies knew that the high credit ratings for these mortgages depended on the continued appreciation and negligible downside risk of home prices. This was illustrated by the following exchange between an associate of First Pacific Advisors, a California-based investment advisory firm, and the Fitch rating agency in June 2007, as reported by First Pacific CEO Robert Rodriguez:

> My associate asked [Fitch], "What are the key drivers of your rating model?"
>
> They [Fitch] responded, FICO [credit] scores and home price appreciation of low single digit or mid single digit range, as appreciation has been for the past 50 years.
>
> My associate then asked, "What if home-price appreciation was flat for an extended period of time?"
>
> They responded that their model would start to break down.
>
> He then asked, "What if home prices were to decline 1% to 2% for an extended period of time?"
>
> They responded that their models would break down completely.
>
> He then asked, "With 2% depreciation, how far up the rating's scale would it harm?"
>
> They responded that it might go as high as the AA or AAA tranches.[10]

It should be noted that by the time this exchange took place, homes prices had already fallen 4 percent from a year earlier, a greater decline than any previous postwar period, so that a scenario of falling home prices became highly likely. Yet this likelihood was not built into the credit ratings of these securities.

As Fitch predicted in the previous exchange, as home prices declined, the ratings of these top mortgage securities deteriorated rapidly. In April 2006, a few months before the peak of housing prices, Goldman Sachs sold investors 12 mortgage bonds, of which 10 were originally rated investment grade and 3 were rated AAA. By September 2007, seven of the original ten investment-grade tranches were downgraded to junk status, and four were totally wiped out.[11]

The Real Estate Bubble

What should have alerted the rating agencies that the sustained increase in housing prices could not continue can be found in Figure 2-2. The ratio of housing prices to median family income remained in a tight range between 2.5 and 3.1 from 1978 to 2002 but then moved sharply higher and eventually surpassed 4.0 in 2006, nearly 50 percent above previous levels.

But even when the price of an asset moves beyond its economic fundamentals, this does not guarantee that there is a "bubble." Investors should recognize that there could be structural changes that justify the price rise. Indeed there have been periods in history when prices have moved away from fundamentals but were fully justified on the basis of changes in the economic environment. One such episode that I will describe in Chapter 11 is the relationship between the dividend yield on

FIGURE 2–2

Ratio of U.S. Home Prices to Median Family Income 1978–2012

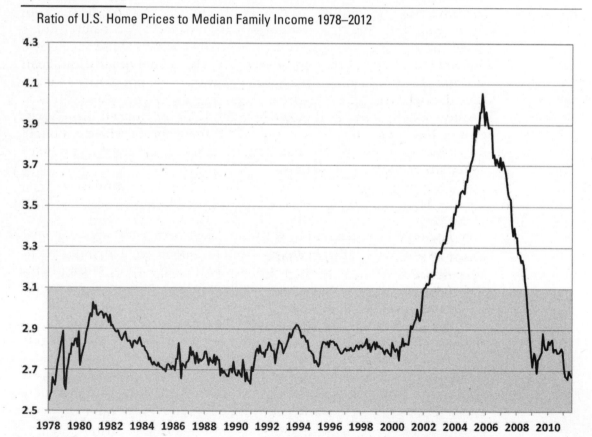

stocks and the interest rate on long-term Treasury bonds. Between 1871 and 1956 the dividend yield was always above the bond yield, and this was thought to be necessary since stocks were seen as riskier than bonds. The strategy of selling stocks when the spread narrowed and buying them when the spread widened was profitable for many decades.

But when the United States left the gold standard, chronic inflation began to be factored into the interest rate, and in 1957 rates rose above the dividend yield on stocks and remained that way for more than a half century. Those who sold stocks and bought bonds in 1957 when this fundamental-based indicator flashed "Sell!" experienced poor returns, as stocks proved to be a much better hedge against inflation and provided far greater returns than fixed-income investments.

In a similar vein, there were plausible reasons why real estate prices rose above their historical relation to median family income in the early 2000s. First there were significant declines in both nominal and real interest rates that made the cost of home financing extremely low. Second, there was the proliferation of new mortgage instruments, such as subprime and "full-funding" mortgages, which loaned up to—and in some cases more than—the purchase price of the home. These mortgages opened the door to borrowers who previously did not qualify for a loan and greatly expanded the demand for housing. The popularity of these full-funding mortgages was driven home by the National Association of Realtors (NAR) when in January 2006 the NAR announced that 43 percent of first-time home buyers purchased their homes with no-money-down loans and that the median down payment was a mere 2 percent of a median-priced $150,000 home.[12]

There were well-known and highly respected economists, such as Charles Himmelberg, senior economist of the Federal Reserve Bank of New York, Chris Mayer, director of the Center for Real Estate at Columbia University Business School, and Todd Sinai, an associate professor of real estate at the Wharton School, who argued that the lower interest rates justified the high level of real estate prices.[13] Some also pointed to the boom in second homes, a factor that many thought would persist for many years as the baby boomers entered retirement.[14]

But many others questioned the sustainability of the housing price increase. Professor Robert Shiller of Yale University and his colleague Karl Case, who developed the Case-Shiller residential housing indexes that have become the benchmark for the profession, first warned about the bubble of real estate in a 2003 *Brookings Papers* article entitled, "Is There a Housing Bubble?"[15] Dean Baker, codirector of the Center for Economic and Policy Research in Washington, also had written and lectured extensively about the dangers of the housing bubble in 2005 and early 2006.[16, 17] The disagreement among experts about whether a real estate bubble actually existed should have alerted the rating agencies to refrain from rating these securities as if there were essentially no probability that they could default.[18]

Regulatory Failure

Despite these warnings, regulatory bodies in general, and the Federal Reserve in particular, did not believe the house price inflation posed a threat to the economy, and they did not question the high ratings given to the subprime mortgage securities. Furthermore, they did not monitor the buildup of risky mortgage-related securities in the balance sheet of key financial institutions. These failures leave a serious blot on the record of the U.S. Monetary Authority.

It is especially tragic that Federal Reserve Chairman Alan Greenspan, by far the most influential public official in economic affairs, did not warn the public of the increasing risks posed by the unprecedented rise in housing prices. Greenspan should have been aware of the burgeoning subprime debt and the potential threat that it posed to the economy since one of his fellow governors at the Federal Reserve, Edward Gramlich, wrote extensively about these subprime instruments and published a book entitled *Subprime Mortgages: America's Latest Boom and Bust* in June 2007.[19]

Some have maintained that the Fed lacked oversight over nonbank financial institutions and that the impact of higher real estate prices was outside its purview. But why then did Greenspan worry sufficiently about the rise in *stock prices* a decade earlier to fashion his famous "irrational exuberance" speech before the Economic Club in Washington, D.C., in December 1996? All matters impacting the stability of the financial sector are the responsibility of the Federal Reserve, whether they originate in banks or not. Greenspan's lack of concern about the buildup of risky assets in the balance sheets of financial firms was revealed when he declared before congressional committees in October 2008 that he was in a state of "shocked disbelief" that the leading lending institutions did not take measures to protect shareholders' equity against a housing meltdown, nor had they neutralized their exposure to risk by using financial derivatives or credit default swaps.[20, 21]

Although Greenspan failed to foresee the financial crisis, I do not, contrary to others,[22] hold him responsible for creating the housing bubble. That is because the Fed's policy of slowly raising interest rates was not the primary force driving real estate values upward. The fall in long-term interest rates, driven by slowing of economic growth, the switch from equities to bonds in corporate pension funds, the huge buildup of reserves in Asian countries, particularly China, and the proliferation of subprime and full-funding mortgages, were far more important in propelling real estate prices higher than the level of the Fed funds rate set by Greenspan and the Federal Open Market Committee. Furthermore, the forces pushing real estate prices upward asserted themselves on a worldwide basis and in currencies of nations with completely independent central banks. For example, housing prices soared in Spain and Greece, countries whose monetary policy was set by the European Central Bank.

Overleverage by Financial Institutions in Risky Assets

It is unlikely that the rise and fall in real estate prices and the related mortgage-backed securities *by itself* would have caused either the financial crisis or a severe recession had it not been for the buildup of these securities in the balance sheets of key financial firms. The total value of subprime, alt-A (slightly higher-quality debt than subprime), and jumbo mortgages reached $2.8 trillion by the second quarter of 2007.[23] Even if the price of all these securities went to zero, the loss in value would be less than the decline in the value of technology stocks during the crash of the dot-com boom that occurred seven years earlier. And that stock market collapse, even when followed by the economic disruptions that occurred after the devastating 9/11 terrorist attacks, caused only a mild recession.

The big difference between the two episodes is that at the peak of the tech boom, brokerage houses and investment banks did not hold large quantities of speculative stocks whose price was set to plummet. This is because investment firms had sold off virtually all their risky technology holdings to investors before the dot-com bubble burst.

In sharp contrast, at the peak of the real estate market, Wall Street was up to its ears in housing-related debt. As noted earlier, in a declining interest rate environment, investors were hungry for yield, and these mortgage-based securities carried interest rates that were higher than comparably rated corporate and government debt. This tempted investment banks, such as Bear Stearns, to sell these bonds to investors with the promise of higher yield with comparable safety.[24] Although many investment banks held these bonds for their own account, their holdings of subprime debt grew substantially when they were forced to take back the faltering subprime funds they sold to investors because of complaints that investors were not fully informed of their risks.[25]

Risks to the financial system were compounded when AIG, the world's largest insurance company, offered to insure hundreds of billions of dollars of these mortgages against default through an instrument called the *credit default swap*. When the prices of these mortgages fell, AIG had to come up with billions of dollars of reserves that it did not have. At the same time, the investment banks that had borrowed heavily to purchase these mortgages found that their funding had dried up when creditors called their loans that were pledged against these assets. The decline in the value of these real estate–related securities precipitated the financial crisis. It is likely that had investment banks held the tech stocks on margin when prices collapsed in late 2000, a similar liquidity crisis would have occurred at that time. But they did not.

THE ROLE OF THE FEDERAL RESERVE IN MITIGATING THE CRISIS

Lending is the lifeblood, the oil that lubricates all large economies. In a financial crisis, institutions that were once believed to be safe and trustworthy are suddenly viewed with suspicion. When Lehman failed, fears spread that many other financial institutions were also in difficulty. This prompted lenders to call their loans and cut their lines of credit at the same time investors sold risky assets and attempted to increase the level of "safe" assets in their portfolios.

But there is only one entity that can provide such liquidity in the time of crisis, and that is the central bank—an institution that Walter Bagehot, a nineteenth-century English journalist, dubbed "the Lender of Last Resort."[26] The central bank creates liquidity by crediting reserves to banks that either borrow from or sell securities to the central bank. Banks can, on demand, turn these reserves into central bank notes or "currency," the ultimate liquid asset. In this way the central banks can respond to a "run on a bank," or the desire of depositors to withdraw their deposits in the form of currency, by loaning such banks any quantity of reserves against their assets, whether or not the quality or price of these assets had declined.

The Lender of Last Resort Springs to Action

After the Lehman bankruptcy, the Fed did provide the liquidity the market desired. On September 19, three days after the Reserve Primary Fund announced it would break below a dollar, the Treasury announced that it was insuring all participating money market funds to the full amount of the investor's balance. The Treasury indicated that it was using the money in its Exchange Stabilization Fund, normally used for foreign exchange transactions, to back its insurance plan. But since the Treasury had only $50 billion in its fund, less than 2 percent of the assets in money market funds, the Treasury would have had to rely on an unlimited line of credit to the Fed to make good on its pledge. The Fed itself created a credit facility to extend nonrecourse loans to banks buying commercial paper from mutual funds,[27] and a month later the Money Market Investor Funding Facility was established.

On September 29, 2008, the Federal Deposit Insurance Corporation, or FDIC, announced that it had entered into a loss-sharing arrangement with Citigroup on a $312 billion pool of loans, with Citigroup absorbing the first $42 billion of losses and the FDIC absorbing losses beyond that. The Fed provided a nonrecourse loan on the remaining $270 billion of the plan. This was followed in January by a similar agreement at about one-third the size with Bank of America. In return, Citigroup issued the FDIC $12 billion in preferred stock and warrants. On September 18 the Fed entered into a $180 billion swap arrangement with leading world central banks to improve liquidity within the global financial markets.

In addition to the money market mutual fund guarantees announced immediately following the Lehman bankruptcy, the FDIC announced on October 7 an increase in deposit insurance coverage to $250,000 per depositor, which was authorized by the Emergency Economic Stabilization Act of 2008 that Congress had passed four days earlier. On October 14 the FDIC created a new Temporary Liquidity Guarantee Program to guarantee the senior debt of all FDIC-insured institutions and their holding companies, as well as deposits in non-interest-bearing deposit accounts.[28] In effect, the government's guarantee of senior debt effectively guaranteed all deposits since deposits have prior claim in the bankruptcy code.

The only way the FDIC was able to guarantee the funds provided through these policy initiatives was with the full backing of the Federal Reserve. The FDIC does have a trust fund, but its size is a tiny fraction of the deposits it insures.[29] The credibility of the FDIC to make good on its promises, like that of the Exchange Stabilization Fund used to "insure" the money market accounts, depends on an unlimited line of credit that the agency has with the Federal Reserve.

Why did the Federal Reserve and Chairman Bernanke take all these bold actions to ensure sufficient liquidity to the private sector? Because of the lessons that he and other economists learned from what the central banks did *not* do during the Great Depression.

Every macroeconomist has studied the 1963 work *The Monetary History of the United States* written by the University of Chicago Nobel-winning economist Milton Friedman. His research built a damning case against the Federal Reserve for failing to provide reserves to the banking system during the Great Depression. It was certain that Ben Bernanke, who received his Ph.D. in economics with a specialty of monetary theory and policy at the Massachusetts Institute of Technology, was acutely aware of Friedman's research and was determined to avoid repeating the Fed's mistakes.[30] In a speech delivered at Milton Friedman's ninetieth birthday celebration in 2002, six years before the financial crisis, Bernanke, addressing Professor Friedman, said, "Regarding the Great Depression. You're right, we did it. We're very sorry. But thanks to you, we won't do it again."[31]

Should Lehman Brothers Have Been Saved?

Although the Federal Reserve sprang into action *following* the demise of Lehman Brothers, economists and policy analysts will debate for years whether the central bank should have bailed out the ailing investment bank in the first place. Despite denials by the Federal Reserve that it did not have full legal authority to rescue Lehman, the facts dictate otherwise. In 1932 Congress amended the original Federal Reserve Act of 1913 by adding Section 13 (3), which stated:

> In unusual and exigent circumstances, the Board of Governors of the Federal Reserve System, by the affirmative vote of not less than five members, may authorize any Federal reserve bank, during such periods as the said board may determine, . . . to discount for any individual, partnership, or corporation, notes, drafts, and bills of exchange when [they] are secured to the satisfaction of the Federal Reserve bank: *Provided*, that before discounting . . . the Federal Reserve bank shall obtain evidence that such individual, partnership, or corporation is unable to secure adequate credit accommodations from other banking institutions.[32]

There is no doubt that on the weekend before Lehman Brothers declared bankruptcy, it qualified for Fed lending, as Lehman was clearly "unable to secure adequate credit accommodations from other banking institutions."

The reason that the Fed did not bail out Lehman was more about politics than economics. Earlier government bailouts of Bear Stearns, Fannie Mae, and Freddie Mac garnered considerable criticism from the public and particularly Republicans. After the March bailout of Bear Stearns, the word went out from the Bush administration: "No More Bailouts." Secretary of Treasury Henry Paulson told Lehman Brothers shortly after the Bear bailout that it should get its house in order and that it should not expect help from the Fed. Just days before Lehman filed, the Fed had rejected a $40 billion loan request from the firm. Treasury Secretary Paulson and the Fed hoped that with so much advance notice, a Lehman failure would be digested by the financial markets without significant disruption.[33]

But the truth of the matter was that in March when Treasury warned Lehman to clean up its balance sheet, it was already too late. Lehman not only had borrowed heavily to buy subprime mortgages but had recently, with the Bank of America, lent $17 billion to Tishman Speyer to buy the Archstone-Smith Trust for $22.2 billion. Lehman was hoping to sell the debt to new buyers for hefty fees, much as Blackstone did when it sold Sam Zell's properties at the peak of the market. But Lehman was left with $5 billion in unsold real estate in what some describe as the worst deal Lehman Brothers ever made.[34] Although CEO Richard Fuld continued to insist that Lehman was solvent, traders knew that because of the falling real estate market, Lehman had little chance to survive. The path to bankruptcy had been irrevocably set after Lehman plunged into mortgage-related securities and the overheated property market.

The Fed's decision to bail out AIG was necessitated by the unexpected financial chaos that immediately followed the Lehman bankruptcy. The Fed and the Treasury, shocked by investors' sudden rush to cash and the surging risk premiums in international money markets, believed that another bankruptcy that threw hundreds of billions of dollars of bonds and credit default swaps into question would likely bring down the global financial system. Despite the fact that AIG, as an insurance company, was arguably further from the Federal Reserve's sphere of responsibility than Lehman, the Fed saved the insurance giant.[35] I have little doubt that had AIG failed first, the ensuing financial panic would have forced the Fed to bail out Lehman the next day.

TARP, or the Troubled Asset Relief Program, described in detail in the next chapter, was not at all essential in staving off the financial crisis. That is because all the funds authorized by TARP, and even more, could have been supplied by the Federal Reserve under existing legislation without Congressional approval. TARP was pushed by Bernanke and Paulson to gain political cover. They knew that the bailouts would be very unpopular, and they wanted Congress to approve the actions that they had taken.

Fed historian Allan Meltzer, an economics professor at Carnegie-Mellon University, claimed that the Fed blundered by setting up expectations that it would bail out systemic institutions, such as Bear Stearns, whose failure threaten the financial system, but then standing aside and letting Lehman collapse.[36] This is echoed by Charles Plosser, president of the Federal Reserve Bank of Philadelphia, who believed that a Bear Stearns failure in March could have been absorbed by the market and would have prompted other firms to increase their liquidity, stemming further damage.

But I believe that it is far more likely that had Bear been allowed to fail, it would have greatly accelerated the run on Lehman, precipitating the crisis in March rather than September. It is inconceivable that financial firms took the Fed's rescue of Bear Stearns as a signal to "lever up" with more risky assets because the Fed would rescue those firms in trouble. It should be noted that even the "rescue" of Bear meant breaking up the firm and giving shareholders a tiny fraction of their book value. The owners of AIG are still litigating the near total takeover of the insurance giant by the federal government when it was rescued from certain bankruptcy. In 2008, it was already too late for regulators to stem the crisis. Regulators needed to take action years earlier, when the rating firms were stamping AAA on subprime mortgages and banks, seeking higher yields, began to increase their leverage in these securities.

Reflections on the Crisis

The overleveraging that took place prior to the financial crisis was motivated by the decline in risk that took place during the long period of financial stability that preceded the financial crisis, the misrating of mortgage-related securities by the rating agencies, the approval by the political establishment of the expansion of homeownership, and the lack of oversight by critical regulatory organizations, particularly the Federal Reserve. But it was the management of many of these financial firms who should be held most accountable. They were unable to grasp the threats that would befall their firms once the housing boom ended, and they abdicated responsibility for assessing risks to technicians running faulty statistical programs.

The financial crisis also punctured the myth that grew during Greenspan's tenure as Fed chairman that the Federal Reserve could fine-tune the economy and eliminate the business cycle. Nevertheless, despite having failed to see the crisis brewing, the Federal Reserve acted quickly to assure liquidity and prevented the recession from becoming far more severe than it turned out to be.

The financial crisis of 2008 is illustrated by the following analogy. There is no doubt that the improvements in engineering have made the passenger car safer than it was 50 years ago. But that does not mean that the automobile is safe at any speed. A small bump on the road can flip the most advanced passenger car speeding 120 mph today just as surely as an older model traveling 80 mph. During the Great Moderation, risks were indeed lower, and financial firms rationally leveraged their balance sheets in response. But their leverage became too great, and all that was needed was an unexpected increase in the default rate on subprime mortgages—that "bump on the road"—to catapult the economy into a crisis.

3

The Markets, the Economy, and Government Policy in the Wake of the Crisis

You don't ever want a serious crisis to go to waste. It's an opportunity to do important things that you otherwise couldn't get done.
—RAHM EMANUEL, WHITE HOUSE CHIEF
OF STAFF UNDER PRESIDENT OBAMA,
NOVEMBER 2008

The credit shock, sharply falling real estate prices, and plunging stock markets precipitated the deepest recession in the developed world economies since World War II. In the United States, real GDP declined 4.3 percent from the fourth quarter of 2007 through the second quarter of 2009, eclipsing the previous record of 3.1 percent during the 1973–1975 recession by a wide margin. The 18-month recession, which lasted from December 2007 to June 2009, was also the longest since the 43-month Great Depression of the early 1930s as unemployment reached 10.0 percent in October 2009. Although this was 0.8 percentage points below the record postwar level of 10.8 percent set in November 1982, the jobless rate remained above 8 percent for three years, more than twice as long as the 1981–1982 recession.

As Figure 3-1 shows, though the crisis originated in the United States, the decline in U.S. GDP was less than in most of the developed

FIGURE 3–1

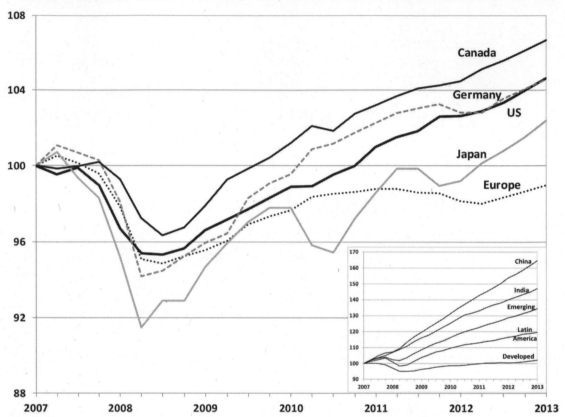

International Comparisons of GDP Through the Financial Crisis and Great Recession (2007 Q4 = 100)

world: output declined 9.14 percent in Japan, 5.50 percent in the Eurozone, and 6.80 percent in Germany, Europe's largest economy. Canada, whose banks never became as overleveraged in real estate assets as in the United States, experienced the mildest downturn.

    Figure 3-1 also shows that the emerging economies withstood the economic shock much better than the developed world; real GDP growth slowed but did not decline in fast-growing countries such as China and India. For emerging economies as a whole, GDP declined only 3 percent; and by the second quarter of 2009, their output had surpassed their previous high. In contrast, it was not until the end of 2011 that the United States regained the output lost, while Japan just reached its peak output by the end of 2013 while Europe was still below its peak.

AVOIDING DEFLATION

Despite the severity of the Great Recession, its depth in no way compares with the decline in economic activity that occurred during the Great Depression of the 1930s. Real GDP in the United States fell 26.3 percent between 1929 and 1933, more than 5 times the decline in the Great Recession, and unemployment soared to between 25 and 30 percent.[1, 2] One reason for the difference between the Great Depression of 1929–1933 and the Great Recession of 2007–2009 was the behavior of the price level. Consumer prices declined by 27 percent between September 1929 and March 1933, while the maximum decline of the consumer price index during the Great Recession was 3.5 percent.[3] By March 2010, the CPI surpassed its precrisis peak, while it took 14 years for consumer prices to recover to their 1929 level following the Great Depression.

Deflation worsens a business cycle, since a fall in wages and prices increases the burden of debt, which increases in real value as prices decline. Consumers were already burdened by record debt levels in 2007 before the financial crisis. Had wages and prices fallen as they did in the Great Depression, the burden of consumer and mortgage debt would have been more than one-third larger in real terms, greatly increasing the number of insolvencies.[4] That is the reason that stabilization of the price level was a priority for the Federal Reserve and is a major reason why consumer and business spending did not decline as much in the 2007–2009 recession compared with what happened in the 1930s.[5]

The Federal Reserve was able to avoid deflation by stabilizing the money supply. In the Great Depression, the money supply, measured as the sum of demand and savings deposits (M2), fell by 29 percent between August 1929 and March 1933.[6] In contrast, the money supply actually rose during the 2008 financial crisis as the Federal Reserve increased the total reserves by over $1 trillion. This action provided sufficient reserves so that banks were not forced to call in loans as they were forced to in the 1930s. Although one can certainly question whether the later injections of reserves (called *quantitative easing*) aided the economy, there was little doubt that the initial provisions of liquidity were critical to stabilizing the financial markets and preventing the downturn from becoming substantially worse.

REACTION OF THE FINANCIAL MARKETS TO THE FINANCIAL CRISIS

Stocks

Despite the actions taken by the Federal Reserve to moderate the economic contraction, the credit disruption that followed the Lehman bankruptcy had a devastating impact on the equity markets, which suffered their worst decline in 75 years. In the 9 weeks following September 15, the S&P 500 Index fell 40 percent to an intraday low of 740 on November 21. Ultimately this broad-based benchmark sank to a 12-year low of 676 on March 9, 2009, nearly 57 percent below its closing peak reached 1½ years earlier. Although the decline in the benchmark index exceeded the previous postwar record of 48 percent that occurred between January 1973 and October 1974, it did not approach the decline that ushered in the Great Depression, when stocks fell by more than 87 percent.[7] From the market high of October 2007 through March 2009, U.S. stock market wealth had declined $11 trillion, a sum of more than 70 percent of U.S. GDP.

The volatility of stock prices increased sharply, as it always does in bear markets. The VIX volatility index, which measures the premium built into put and calls on the stock market (in effect measuring the cost of "insuring" a stock portfolio), soared from under 10 in March 2007, before the crisis began, to nearly 90 immediately following the Lehman bankruptcy. This level exceeded any other in the postwar period except that immediately following the October 19, 1987, stock market crash.[8]

Another measure of volatility, the number of days that the stock market rose or fell by 5 percent or more, increased sharply to levels not reached since the early 1930s. Between the Lehman bankruptcy on September 15 and December 1, there were 9 days when the Dow Industrials dropped by at least 5 percent and 6 days when it rose by 5 percent or more. Except for the 1930s when a record 78 days saw changes of 5 percent or more, these 15 days of changes of 5 percent or more exceeded the total for any other decade since 1890.[9]

The plunge in the U.S. equity markets was echoed abroad. Around the world, approximately $33 trillion of stock market wealth was lost, about half the world's annual GDP.[10] In local currency, the Morgan Stanley EAFE Index for non-U.S. developed markets declined by nearly the same magnitude as in the United States, but because the dollar appreciated during the period, the total decline was 62 percent in dollar terms. The emerging market stocks fell 64 percent in dollar terms, although they fell less in the local currency as the currencies of almost all emerging markets, except for the Chinese yuan, depreciated against the dollar.[11]

The decline in the emerging stock markets was nearly identical to the decline suffered during the Asian financial crisis in 1997–1998. But the emerging market indexes at their 2009 lows remained well above the levels reached at the bottom of the 2002 bear market. This contrasted with the United States and most other developed markets that fell below their 2002 bear market lows.

FIGURE 3–2

The S&P 500 and the LIBOR—Fed Funds Spread Through the Financial Crisis, January 2007 – June 2013

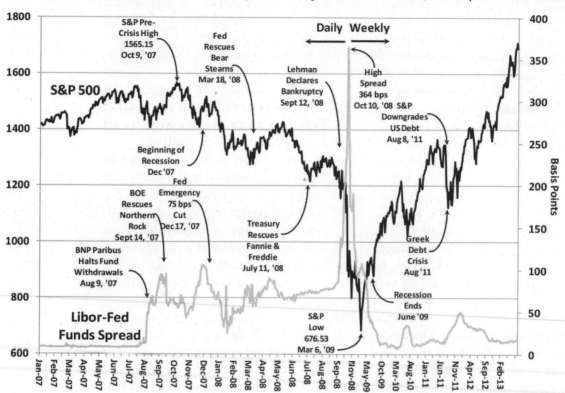

Certain equity sectors that held up well in the early stages of the market decline fell sharply as credit markets froze. Real estate investment trusts (REITs) are a case in point. Buying them for their yield, investors at first flocked to these stocks as interest rates fell and REITs actually rallied in the week after Lehman went under. But when investors feared that lenders would pull credit lines, REITs lost on average an astounding two-thirds of their value in the next 10 weeks and fell a total of 75 percent by the time the bear market ended in March 2009. Real estate trusts that were funded by short-term loans or that took on extra leverage during the boom in an effort to boost yields to investors were hit particularly hard.[12]

The financial sector of the S&P 500 declined 84 percent from its peak in May 2007 to its trough in March 2009, wiping out about $2.5 trillion of equity. The percentage decline exceeded the 82.2 percent decline in the S&P 500 technology sector that occurred from 2000 to 2002, but since the tech sector had valuations at the peak more than three times that of the financial sector, the equity values lost in the tech crash were a much higher $4 trillion.[13] Nevertheless, while the tech crash wiped out the previous 5 years of total stock market gains, the financial crisis wiped out 17 years, sending equity prices down to 1992 levels.

Many financial firms declined much more than the 84 percent average for the sector. Peak to trough, Bank of America lost 94.5 percent of the market value of its equity, Citibank lost 98.3 percent, and AIG lost an astounding 99.5 percent.[14] The equity holders of Lehman Brothers, Washington Mutual, and a large number of smaller financial institutions lost everything, while shareholders of Fannie Mae and Freddie Mac, the giant government-sponsored enterprises that went public in the early 1980s, hold on to a sliver of hope that they might recover some of their capital.[15] Many international banks fared just as poorly as U.S. banks. From peak to trough, Barclays fell 93 percent, BNP Paribas 79 percent, HSBC 75 percent, and UBS 88 percent. The Royal Bank of Scotland, which needed a loan from the Bank of England to survive, fell 99 percent.

The percentage fall in the S&P 500 Index exceeded the decline in operating earnings of firms in the index. S&P 500 operating earnings declined 57 percent from a record $91.47 in the 12 months ending on June 30, 1997, to $39.61 in the 12 months ending September 30, 2009. But the decline in reported earnings was much greater: as a result of the record $23.25 *loss* for S&P 500 firms in the fourth quarter of 2008, the S&P 500 12-month reported earnings fell from a high of $84.92 in 1997 to only $6.86 for the 12 months ending March 31, 2009. This 92 percent decline in earnings exceeds the 83 percent decline in earnings that took place in the Great Depression from 1929 through 1932.[16]

The huge write-downs by the financial firms were the main cause of the devastating earnings drop of the S&P 500 in 2008 and 2009. When calculating earnings on the S&P 500 Index, it is the policy of Standard & Poor's to sum all the profits and losses of each firm dollar for dollar and to compare the aggregate earnings with the aggregate value of the S&P 500 portfolio in order to compute the P/E ratio of the index. The $61 billion fourth-quarter 2008 loss of AIG, which had a weight of less than 0.2 percent in the index, more than wiped out the total profits of the 30 most profitable firms in the S&P 500, which composed almost half the index value. S&P's method of aggregating firms' earnings dollar for dollar understates the earnings and vastly overstates the P/E ratio of the index during recessions when a few firms report very large losses.[17] In fact, after-tax aggregate corporate profits taken from the national income and product accounts fell by only 24 percent for the 12-month period ending in June 30, 2007, to the year ending March 31, 2009.

Real Estate

I noted that the buildup of real estate and real estate–related assets in the portfolios of highly leveraged financial institutions was the primary cause of the financial crisis. The Federal Reserve reported in its quarterly Flow of Funds Report that from the third quarter of 2007 through the first quarter of 2009, the value of residential real estate fell from $24.2 trillion to $17.6 trillion, a decline of 27 percent. The price index of residential real estate declined by 26 percent as measured by the Case-Shiller Index of 20 metropolitan areas,[18] and commercial real estate prices fell by 41 percent from October 2007 through November 2009.[19]

Fluctuations in real estate prices have a significant impact on the economy. It has been estimated that consumers spent between 25 and 30 percent of the home equity borrowings during the real estate boom between 2002 and 2006.[20] Given that such borrowings averaged 2.8 percent of GDP, the spending boost powered by the rise in home equity values contributed about a ¾ percentage point, or one quarter of the annual growth rate of the U.S. economy during that period. After 2008, the fall in real estate prices reduced consumption and contributed significantly to the slow recovery from the Great Recession.

Treasury Bond Markets

After the Lehman bankruptcy, the rush to safety sent the yield on Treasury bills to zero and even lower. On December 4, 2008, the 90-day-bill rate fell to an all-time low of minus 1.6 basis points.[21] The huge demand for Treasury securities extended to the long end, as the 10-year U.S. Treasury notes fell to near 2 percent at the end of 2008. The yield on Treasury long bonds continued to fall for four more years, with the 10-year bond reaching its low of 1.39 percent in July 2012.

During the crisis, the Federal Reserve not only provided liquidity to the markets but also sharply lowered the fed funds rate. The Fed lowered the funds target rate from 2 to 1.5 percent in an emergency meeting on October 23, 2008 and lowered it further to 1 percent at its regular November meeting. On December 16, as conditions continued to worsen, the Federal Open Market Committee reduced the federal funds rate to an all-time low of between zero and 0.25 percent; and at the end of 2013, the funds rate remains at this level, the longest period since World War II that the rate has remained unchanged.

Even though the Federal Reserve guarantees on bank deposits and money market funds stopped the liquidity panic, the Fed could not prevent the shock waves that reverberated through the credit markets. While long-term Treasury rates fell substantially, interest rates on non-Treasury debt rose. The spread between the lowest investment-grade corporate bond and the 10-year Treasury reached 6.1 percent in November 2008, the highest since the record 8.91 percent spread in May 1932 that was reached near the bottom of the Great Depression. The spread between lower-rated 30-year B-rated industrial bonds and Treasury bonds widened from 4 percentage points to nearly 8 percentage points after the rescue of Bear Stearns and to a record 15.1 percentage points in the first week of January 2009.

The LIBOR Market

One of the most watched spreads in the money market is that between the rate set by the Federal Reserve in the fed funds market (a market to facilitate the borrowing and lending of reserves between U.S. banks) and the interbank lending rates outside the United States, called the London Interbank Offered Rate, or LIBOR.

There are literally hundreds of trillions of dollars of loans and financial instruments around the world that are based on the LIBOR, including almost one-half of all adjustable-rate mortgages. The history of the LIBOR goes back to the 1960s, when the market for overseas dollar lending grew dramatically after the U.S. government put restrictions on dollar outflows in a futile attempt to reverse its balance-of-payments deficit and staunch its gold outflow. The LIBOR rate is computed for 15 time periods from one day to one year in duration and for 10 different currencies. By far, the dollar LIBOR is the most important of these fixings.

Return to Figure 3-2. Before the financial crisis, the LIBOR stayed very close (usually within 10 basis points) to the federal funds target. The first rumblings of trouble in the banking sector came in August 2007 when the LIBOR–fed funds spread jumped above 50 basis points in response to the BNP Paribas announcement of stopping fund redemptions and the problems at Northern Rock in the United Kingdom. Over the next 12 months, as the subprime crisis grew, the LIBOR-funds spread remained mostly between 50 and 100 basis points. But the LIBOR spread soared after the Lehman bankruptcy, and on October 10 the difference between the LIBOR and the fed funds rate reached an unheard-of 364 basis points.

It was extraordinarily frustrating to policy makers that the interest rate upon which so many loans were based actually rose at the same time the Fed was aggressively lowering the fed funds rate. After the Federal Reserve flooded the financial system with reserves, the LIBOR spread finally came down, but it did not fall decisively under 100 basis points until the stock market began to recover from its bear market low in March 2009, three months before the National Bureau of Economic Research called the recession over.

For all its importance in setting loan rates, the LIBOR does not represent actual transactions but what a bank *expects* the cost of its own noncollateralized borrowing to be, even if it does not borrow any funds. Following the Lehman crisis, fears for the solvency of banks skyrocketed, and the interbank lending market between banks effectively froze. But banks were still obligated to submit LIBOR rates to the British Bankers Association although they had little actual data on which to base such submissions. Mervyn King, governor of the Bank of England, told the U.K. Parliament in November 2008 that "[the LIBOR rate] is, in many ways, the rate at which banks do not lend to each other."[22]

Many regulatory agencies, in both the United States and United Kingdom, strongly suspected that several banks underreported their cost of borrowing to avoid signaling to the market that creditors feared for their solvency. Nevertheless, it was not until July 2012 that the British government announced that it had fined Barclays bank $453 million for submitting false interbank interest rates and intimated that other banks also submitted false rates.[23] The outcry over the scandal raised the call to reform this multitrillion-dollar market, an effort that would require a total restructuring of the way this benchmark rate is calculated or a shift to alternative instruments.

Commodity Markets

In the early stages of the subprime crisis, the prices of commodities rose rapidly as the emerging economies continued to grow strongly. Oil (West Texas Intermediate) rose from $40 a barrel in January 2007 to an all-time high of $147.27 in July 2008, and the Commodity Research Bureau Index of 18 actively traded commodities rose by over 60 percent. But following the Lehman crisis, the decline in economic activity sent commodity prices down sharply. Oil fell to $32 a barrel in December, and the CRB Index fell by 58 percent to its lowest level since 2002.

It is remarkable that the commodity price decline measured by the CRB Index was almost the same magnitude as the decline in world stock markets. Investors who believed that commodities provided them a hedge against a severe stock market decline were wrong. As we explore later in this chapter, virtually no asset, except for long-term U.S. Treasury bonds, served as an effective hedge against the sudden and sharp decline in asset values that took place during the financial crisis. Even gold, which had peaked just below $1,000 per ounce in July 2008, fell below $700 after the Lehman bankruptcy.

Foreign Currency Markets

After hitting a 15-year high in the summer of 2001, the dollar declined steadily against the currencies of the major developed countries and continued to do so in the early stages of the financial crisis. In the immediate wake of the Bear Stearns merger into JPMorgan, the dollar reached its all-time low on March 17, 2008, a full 23 percent below its precrisis high in November 2005 and 41 percent below its 25-year high reached in 2001. But as the financial crisis worsened, the dollar regained its "safe-haven" status, and foreign investors switched back to dollar securities. This caused the greenback to rise by over 26 percent against developed world currencies, reaching its high on March 4, 2009, just a week before the U.S. equity market reached its bear market low. Only the Japanese yen advanced against the dollar during the financial crisis, as the market tumult caused investors to unwind their "carry trade," the name given to the strategy of borrowing from Japan at the world's lowest interest rates in order to invest in riskier, higher-yielding currencies elsewhere. As the crisis eased and the equity markets began to recover, the dollar lost some of its safe-haven premium, and its price fell.

Impact of the Financial Crisis on Asset Returns and Correlations

One of the principal conclusions of financial theory is that to attain the best return for a given risk, investors should seek to diversify their holdings not only within an asset class but also among asset classes. For that reason investors put a premium on assets whose prices are negatively correlated with the market, and discount assets that are positively correlated with the market.

Figure 3-3 shows the correlations of various asset classes with the S&P 500 over all five-year windows from 1970 through 2012. One can see that the financial crisis had a significant impact on the correlation between asset classes, in most cases accelerating trends that had taken place before the crisis. The correlation between both developed economies' equity markets

FIGURE 3–3

Monthly Correlations of S&P 500 and Various Assets Classes from 1970–2012

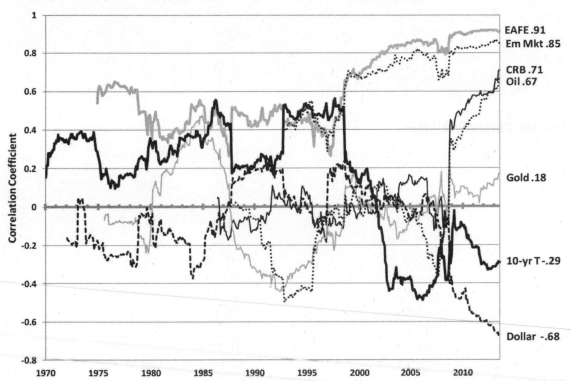

(EAFE) and emerging economies' equity markets (EM) with the U.S. stock market has grown significantly, reaching 0.91 for EAFE and 0.85 for EM.

There are good economic reasons why the correlation between stock markets has become greater over recent years. First, there is an increase in the economic interdependence as world trade constitutes an ever greater share of world output. The second is that traders and investors operate in many different markets simultaneously so that market sentiment is much less likely to be isolated to a given market. And third, most of the shocks to the financial and commodity markets since 2008 have been global in nature, overwhelming idiosyncratic shocks that impact one country or one market.

Not only has the correlation between equity markets increased, but Figure 3-3 shows the correlation between the equity markets and commodities, measured by either the CRB Index of commodity prices or the price of oil, has increased sharply since the financial crisis.[24] Commodity prices are impacted by demand factors, such as the growth in the world economy, and supply factors, such as weather (for crops) and political developments (for oil). Fluctuations in demand cause a positive correlation between stock prices and commodity prices, while fluctuations in supply induce a negative correlation. If the major source of disturbances to the price of commodities arises from supply fluctuations, then holding commodities will serve as a good hedge against stocks. But when global demand shocks predominate, then commodity prices will move in tandem with stock prices, and commodities will serve as poor diversifiers against equity fluctuations.

There are good reasons why the correlation between commodity and equity prices may continue to be high. Recent developments in the energy markets mean that OPEC is not likely to have as great an impact on the supply of oil as in the past. Alternative sources of oil and gas from non-OPEC countries arising from shale exploration, fracking, and other extractive techniques are becoming more important. These developments mean that fluctuations in demand may take an upper hand in determining the price of energy, leading to a positive correlation between stock and commodity prices. And this means that commodities will likely decline as an effective hedge against stocks.

Some argue that the increased correlation between world stock markets reduces or even eliminates the incentive to diversify one's portfolio. If international stocks move in tandem, the proponents of the argument maintain, then investing in foreign markets will do little to offset the fluctuations in one's home market. But correlations are usually calculated over relatively short periods of time, say one week or one month. Long-term correlations between asset returns are significantly lower than short-term correlations. This means that long-term investors should continue to diversify even though such diversification does not lead to significant reductions in the short term volatility of portfolio returns.

Decreased Correlations

In contrast to commodities, which have increased their correlation with stocks since the financial crisis, there are two notable asset classes whose returns have become significantly less correlated with equities: U.S. Treasury bonds and the U.S. dollar.

The price of a dollar in foreign exchange markets is impacted by the strength of the U.S. economy and the safe-haven status that international investors accord the U.S. dollar. The first factor leads to a positive correlation between U.S. equities and the exchange rate: good or bad news about the economy will impact stock prices and the exchange rate in the same direction.

But the safe-haven status of the U.S. dollar leads to the opposite correlation: bad economic news, particularly emanating from outside the United States, will elicit a flight to the dollar, raising its value at the same time that the news sends world and U.S. stock prices lower. Since the onset of the financial crisis and particularly the European monetary crisis, the safe-haven status of the U.S. dollar has increased dramatically. Bad news about Europe negatively impacts world stock markets but drives the euro downward and therefore the dollar higher in exchange markets. The European crisis has led to a record negative correlation between the U.S. dollar and U.S. stocks, as seen in Figure 3-3.

U.S. Treasury bonds have also enjoyed enhanced safe-haven status since the financial crisis. Bad news, originating either within or outside the United States, has prompted investors to purchase Treasury bonds and has led to a strong negative correlation between Treasury bond prices and stock prices. This negative correlation enhances the attractiveness of Treasury bonds to investors wishing to hedge their equity portfolios and has no doubt supported the high prices and correspondingly low yields on long-term U.S. Treasury securities during and immediately following the financial crisis.

The ability of long-term U.S. Treasury bonds to hedge equity risk is even stronger for the non-dollar-based investor. For non-dollar investors, bad news increases the demand for dollar-denominated assets and in particular Treasury bonds. This leads to an even higher negative correlation of U.S. Treasury bonds and stock markets measured in non-dollar currencies. Long-term Treasuries have de facto become the world's ultimate "hedge" asset, and this explains why so many sovereign wealth funds hold a high percentage of their assets in Treasury bonds despite their very low yields and expected returns.

The single asset class whose *correlation* with the equity markets has not been impacted by the financial crisis is gold. The rise in the price of gold after the financial crisis has been caused by the increased fear of hyperinflation and financial collapse, but the correlation with the equity markets has remained near zero over the past 50 years. By early 2013 the price of gold had increased markedly since 2008, although it never was as high, after inflation, as it was at the top of the 1980 bubble when it reached $850 per ounce, or $2,545 in 2013 prices.

The positive correlations of equity markets with commodities and oil and the negative correlation with Treasury bonds and the dollar have given rise to the term *risk-on/risk-off* market. A risk-on market occurs when good news about the economy entices investors to buy stocks and go long commodities and sell the U.S. dollar and Treasury bonds. In such markets, stocks and commodity prices rise while U.S. Treasury bond prices and the dollar fall. Risk-off markets are the opposite, where bad economic news entices investors to buy U.S. Treasuries and the dollar while selling commodities and stocks. Gold prices can either rise or fall on these days.

But as Figure 3-3 shows, the correlation between asset classes has not been stable. In particular, the correlation between stock prices and Treasury bonds in the 1970s and 1980s was positive, not negative. This is because the major threat to the economy in those years was inflation, and lower inflation was good for both stocks and bond prices. It is only when inflation is not a threat and the financial stability of the private sector is in question that the Treasury bonds take on safe-haven status and become negatively correlated with equity prices.

Certainly under current monetary policy, the risk that inflation will once again be a concern for policy makers is high. In that situation, Treasury bonds will cease to be a hedge asset, and bond prices could fall substantially since investors will require much higher yield for an asset that no longer acts as a diversifier to the equities in their portfolios. The unprecedented bull market in Treasury bonds, supported by the belief that Treasury bonds are "insurance policies" in the case of financial collapse, could end as badly as the bull market in technology stocks did at the turn of the century. When economic growth increases, Treasury bondholders will receive the double blow of rising interest rates and loss of safe-haven status.

One of the prime lessons learned from long-term analysis is that no asset class can stay permanently detached from fundamentals. Stocks had their comeuppance when the technology bubble burst and the financial system crashed. It is quite likely that bondholders will suffer a similar fate as the liquidity created by the world's central banks turns into stronger economic growth and higher inflation.

Legislative Fallout from the Financial Crisis

Just as the Great Depression generated a host of legislation such as the Securities and Exchange Act, which created the SEC, the Glass-Steagall Act, which separated commercial and investment banks, and establishment of the Federal Deposit Insurance Corporation, the financial crisis of 2008 spurred legislators to design laws to prevent a repeat of the financial collapse. The result was embodied in a massive 849-page piece of legislation crafted by Senator Christopher Dodd (D-Conn) and Representative Barney Frank (D-Mass), called the Dodd-Frank Wall Street Reform and Consumer Protection Act, which was signed into law by President Obama in July 2010. The act's powers range from establishing the fees for debit cards, to setting the regulations of hedge funds, restricting "predatory lending," addressing compensation of CEOs and other employees, and formulating measures designed to stabilize the economy and financial system. The act comprises 16 titles and requires that regulators create 243 rules, conduct 67 studies, and issue 22 periodic reports.[25]

The three most important parts of the law that impact the overall economy are (1) the "Volcker rule," which limits the proprietary trading of commercial banks, (2) Title II, which provides for the liquidation of large financial firms not under the purview of the Federal Deposit Insurance Corporation, and (3) Title XI, which adds responsibilities but also places new restrictions on the Federal Reserve.

The Volcker rule was named after Paul Volcker, former chairman of the Federal Reserve and chair of President Obama's President's Economic Recovery Advisory Board, who argued that financial stability required that Congress sharply limit the ability of banks to trade for their own accounts. Such a provision was not in the original bill submitted to Congress but inserted later. Originally the Volcker proposal specifically prohibited a bank or an institution that owns a bank from engaging in proprietary trading that is not at the behest of its clients and from owning or investing in a hedge fund or private equity fund. However, this proposal was later modified to allow up to 3 percent of the capital of banks to go into proprietary trading and exempts hedging operations as well as trading in U.S. Treasury debt. The Volker rule was designed to restore the separation between investment banks and commercial banks that was first mandated by the Glass-Steagall Act of 1933 but was effectively repealed by Congress in 1999 in the Gramm-Leach-Bliley Act.

But would the Volcker amendment, had it been law in 2007, have prevented the 2008 financial crisis? The financial crisis was caused by the overleveraging of real estate–related securities in Bear Stearns and Lehman Brothers, which were investment banks and would not have fallen under the purview of the Volcker amendment. Nor would it have applied to the insurance giant AIG, which the Fed chose to save after seeing the turmoil unleashed by the Lehman bankruptcy. Furthermore, banks that obtained loans from the Fed, specifically Citibank and Bank of America, ran into trouble because of bad real estate loans, not proprietary trading. Given this history, it is dubious that the Volcker amendment, had it been in effect in 2007, would have changed the course of the financial crisis.

Title II of the Dodd-Frank Act permits the government to dismantle expeditiously financial firms that become a threat to the stability of the financial system in order to minimize the risk of a financial crisis. Although the Federal Deposit Insurance Corporation has rules for the liquidation of commercial banks and the Securities Investor Protection Corporation has powers to liquidate the assets of brokerage houses, the government had no guidelines for dismantling investment banks, such as Bear Stearns and Lehman, nor insurance companies such as AIG. Under the usual bankruptcy laws, a determination of order of claims may take months or years, far too long to calm the waters in a crisis.

Title II specifies that financial firms submit to the government the order that assets should be liquidated if a firm cannot meet its financial obligations and prohibits the government from taking equity positions in the firm being dismembered. The law also specifies measures to avoid exposing taxpayers to undue losses that can be absorbed by other creditors to the firm. This part of the bill would have prohibited the Federal Reserve taking the equity stakes that it did in AIG, Citibank, or any other financial firm.

Title XI restricts the actions of the Federal Reserve by basically abolishing the Section 13(3) amendments to the Federal Reserve Act that gave the central bank virtually unlimited power to lend to any financial firm in crisis. Under the new law, the Federal Reserve cannot lend to individual firms, although it can use its powers to provide broad-based liquidity to the financial system as long as it gets the approval of the secretary of treasury. Furthermore the act requires that the Federal Reserve disclose which financial firms are receiving assistance within seven days of authorizing an emergency facility.[26]

Whether these restrictions prove to be detrimental in the next financial crisis remains to be seen. Most of these restrictions were inserted to buy Republican support for passage of the bill, since a vast majority of Republicans opposed both the Fed's and Congress's bailout of the financial institutions. Many were particularly unhappy about the Troubled Asset Recovery Program, or TARP, signed into law on October 3, 2008, that provided up to $700 billion to financial institutions but also was used to provide funds to General Motors.[27]

The $700 billion TARP was a very controversial piece of legislation, first proposed by Treasury Secretary Paulson and Fed Chairman Bernanke just days after the Lehman bankruptcy. Although supported by President Bush, the Republicans in the House voted down the legislation on September 29, 2008, sending the Dow Industrials to a 777-point (6.98 percent) loss. After minor changes were made (and undoubtedly quite a few phone calls to Republican legislators from agitated investors), many House Republicans reversed themselves and passed the legislation four days later.

As noted in the last chapter, Bernanke did not need Congress to pass TARP to extend credit to either financial or nonfinancial firms stressed by credit developments, because Section 13(3) of the Federal Reserve Act provided him with the authority to do so. But having taken the heat for the Fed's previous interventions, Bernanke and Paulson felt they needed congressional approval to proceed. Had the restrictions in the Dodd-Frank Act been in effect in 2008, the Fed would not have the ability to lend to individual firms like AIG, an action that stanched the crisis.

Yet the Fed will still likely have enough flexibility to act in order to calm the markets. Under Dodd-Frank the Federal Reserve can, with Treasury approval, establish liquidity facilities for classes of institutions, such as investment banks or even insurance companies. Certainly Treasury Secretary Henry Paulson worked closely with Ben Bernanke throughout all the stages of the financial crisis, and the two men developed a good working relationship. Bernanke would have most likely obtained approval by Paulson of the general lending facilities that the Fed established to provide liquidity to the market.

Nevertheless, the relationship between the treasury secretary and the Fed chairman may not always be so cordial. There have been times at which the administration has been critical of the Fed, and although the treasury secretary can be removed by the president at any time, the chairman of the Fed is appointed for a four-year term and can only be removed by impeachment by the Senate.

Time will tell how effective—or harmful—the provisions of the Dodd-Frank Act turn out to be. Most of the rules and regulations are yet to be written by committees and groups of "experts" chosen by the government to craft the rulebooks and procedures. It has often been said that the devil is in the details, and most of those details have yet to be formulated.

Concluding Comments

The financial crisis and subsequent recession spawned the deepest bear market in stocks and the greatest bull market in Treasury bonds since the

Great Depression of the 1930s. And the sharp downturn in economic activity that followed caused record peacetime government budget deficits, one of the slowest economic recoveries in our nation's history, and a growing pessimism about the future of America.

But debt, deficits, and slow economic growth need not be the legacy of the Great Recession. The next chapter peers into the future to identify those trends that will dominate the economic landscape over the remainder of this century and explains why there is significant cause for optimism about the future of the U.S. and world economy.

The Entitlement Crisis

Will the Age Wave Drown the Stock Market?

Demography is Destiny

—AUGUSTE COMTE

The Great Recession led to record peacetime government budget deficits in the United States, Europe, and Japan and highlighted the unsustainability of the generous and increasingly costly entitlement programs that had been enacted years earlier. Furthermore, the housing and stock market collapse erased trillions of dollars of wealth from consumer balance sheets, leaving many with insufficient assets to realize the comfortable retirement that they had once expected.

Against this backdrop of declining economic fortunes, pollsters detected a marked loss of confidence in America's future. In 2010 less than half of the Americans responded yes to the question, "Do you think that your children will be better off than you are?"[1] The faith in an ever-rising standard of living, which served as a core belief for American families and a beacon for millions of immigrants throughout the country's history, was fading.

This chapter examines whether this pessimism is justified. Is it true that our children, for the first time in our country's history, have a bleaker future than their parents, or are there forces that might renew the American Dream and restore economic growth?

THE REALITIES WE FACE

Two conflicting forces will impact the world economy over the coming decades. The first force, which gives rise to rising government budget deficits and strains private and public pension programs, is the "age wave," or the unprecedented rise in the number of individuals in the developed world who will enter retirement. The age wave poses two fundamental questions: Who will produce the goods and services that the retirees will consume, and who will buy their assets that they plan on selling to finance their retirement? It can be shown that if the developed world must rely solely on its own population to produce these goods, then the age that people will be able to retire must increase significantly.

The second offsetting force is the strong growth of emerging economies, particularly in India, China, and the rest of Asia, that will soon produce the bulk of the world's output. Is it possible that emerging economies will be productive enough to produce the goods and generate enough saving to purchase the assets of these new retirees? This chapter answers these questions and reveals what is ahead for the United States and world economy.

THE AGE WAVE

August Comte's famous quotation "Demography is Destiny" reminds us how important the age wave is to the world's future. After World War II, population increased rapidly, as those who had delayed childbearing during the Great Depression and war envisioned a future bright enough to take on the burdens of parenthood. Between 1946 and 1964, birthrates rose significantly above the average of the previous two decades, spawning a cohort dubbed "the baby boom generation."

But the baby boom was followed by the baby bust. The *fertility* rate, the number of children born to a woman, fell dramatically in the mid-1960s; and in most of the developed world, it has remained below the 2.1 level that stabilizes the population. The fertility rate in Europe fell from more than 2.5 in 1960 to 1.8 in 2010, and in some countries, such as Spain, Portugal, Italy, and Greece, fertility rates have fallen to well below 1.5. The fertility rate fell even more in many Asian economies and is now 1.3 in Japan and South Korea, 1.1 in Taiwan, and below 1 in Shanghai. In 2011 the U.S. fertility rate fell below 2.0, and the *birthrate* (number of births per 1,000 women aged 15–44) fell to an all-time low of 63.2, nearly one-half the level that prevailed in 1957.

RISING LIFE EXPECTANCY

The period since World War II has also been marked by rising life expectancy. When the United States passed the Social Security Act in 1935, which provided income benefits beginning at the age of 65, life expectancy for males, who made up the vast majority of the workforce, was only 60. By 1950, life expectancy of males reached 66.6; and in 2010 male life expectancy hit 76.2; and reached 81.1 for females.[2]

James Vaupel and James Oeppen of Cambridge University have determined that since 1840 life expectancy in the developed world has increased at a remarkably constant rate of 2.5 years per decade, a trend that shows only slight signs of abating.[3] But until the middle of the twentieth century, life expectancy rose primarily because infant and childhood deaths declined. Between 1901 and 1961, male life expectancy at birth rose by more than 20 years, but the life expectancy for men age 60 rose by less than 2 years.

But in the last half century, the life expectancy of the elderly is being extended significantly by medical advances. Throughout most of history, there have been more young than old, as disease, wars, and natural forces depleted the population. But the drop in the mortality rate among the baby boomers combined with the reduction in fertility rates has dramatically changed the age distribution of the world's developed countries. By the middle of this century, the age profiles of Japan and many of the southern European countries, such as Greece, Spain, and Portugal, will be "inverted"; i.e., instead of the normal pattern of more young than old that has ruled through most of history, the most heavily populated age bracket will consist of those well into their seventies and eighties, and the number of those over 80 will outnumber children below age 15.

FALLING RETIREMENT AGE

Despite the increase in life expectancy, the retirement age continued to fall in the developed world. In 1935 when social security was instituted to give income benefits to individuals 65 and older, the average retirement age was 67. In the postwar period, the fall in the retirement age accelerated in 1961 when Congress allowed social security recipients to begin collecting reduced benefits at age 62.

In Europe the decline in the retirement age was even greater than in the United States. In the early 1970s many European governments lowered the minimum retirement age from 65 to 60 and in many cases to 55.[4] In contrast to the United States, where social security payments are increased if you continue to work, few if any incentives were created in Europe for those considering a later retirement. In France, from 1970 to 1998, the proportion of the men in the workforce from age 60–64 fell from about 70 percent to under 20 percent, and in West Germany it fell from over 70 percent to 30 percent, while in the United States it remained well above 50 percent.[5]

The twin forces of rising life expectancy and falling retirement age resulted in a dramatic increase in the number of years the average worker was retired, a period that I call the *retirement period*. In the United States between 1950 and 2010, life expectancy increased from age 69 to 78, while the average age of retirement fell from 67 to 62. As a result, the retirement period increased more than eightfold, from 1.6 to 15.8 years, and the increase was even larger in Europe.

The rapid increase in the retirement period is an extremely significant change in the lifestyle of the average worker. Before World War II, very few workers enjoyed a lengthy retirement, and even fewer did so in good health. Now there are millions in the United States, Europe, and Japan who are enjoying retirement with generous health and income benefits provided either by the state or through corporate retirement plans.

THE RETIREMENT AGE MUST RISE

But this golden trend of increasing life expectancy and falling retirement age cannot continue. As Figure 4-1A shows, in 1950 there were 14 retired persons for every 100 workers in the United States. This ratio rose to 28 retirees per 100 workers in 2013, and by 2060 it is expected to rise to 56. In Japan the number of retirees will rise from 49 per 100 workers today to 113 in 2060, while Europe's ratio will rise to 75. And these ratios are apt to understate the number of retirees, as they assume a retirement age of 65, above that in the United States and Japan and well above the level now in Europe.

Even though the demographic trends in Japan and Europe are more severe than in the United States, the spending in those countries impacts all retirees, no matter where they reside. Since goods and services are traded in global markets, the future demands by the European and Japanese retirees will drive up world prices and adversely influence Americans as well.

FIGURE 4–1

Ratio of Retirees to Workers in Developed and Emerging Economies 1950–2060

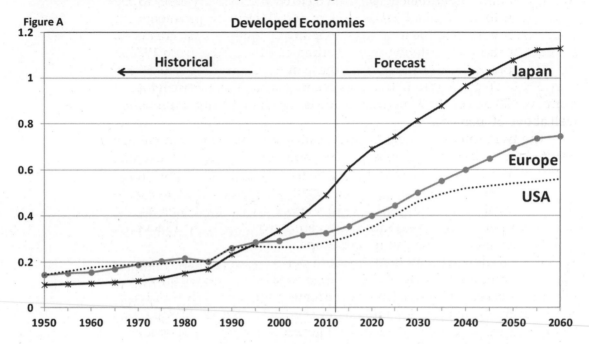

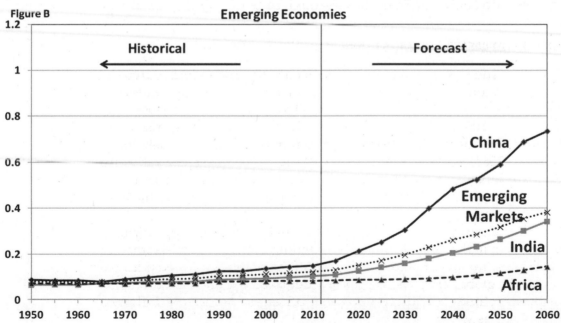

But the impact of the age wave reaches beyond raising the prices of the goods and services that are traded on world markets. The age wave also has a negative impact on the value of assets that workers accumulate to enable them to consume during retirement. This is because the value of stocks and bonds, like the value of any good, is determined by supply and demand. The buyers are savers, and the savers are the workers who consume less than they earn, using the money they save to accumulate assets that they can, in turn, sell in their retirement. The sellers of assets are the retirees who need to generate funds to consume during the period when they do not earn income from working.

An increase in the number of retirees generates an excess of sellers over buyers, a situation that could depress asset prices substantially. Lower asset prices are the market's way of saying that the economy cannot accommodate retirees' expectations of early retirement and generous health and income benefits. As the value of their assets falls, baby boomers will have to work longer and retire later than they had planned.

But how much longer will that be? The impact of the baby boomers on the retirement age in the United States can be seen by referring to Figure 4-2. Scenario A is the case where the developed world must rely on the output produced by its own workers and not on increased imports from abroad to supply the goods demanded by the retirees.

The impact on the retirement age is dramatic. The retirement age must increase from the current age of 62 to 77 by the middle of this century, a 15-year rise that easily outstrips the increase in life expectancy. This scenario will reduce the retirement period from the current level of 15.8 years to 7 years, a reduction of more than 50 percent, and will reverse most of the gains made by retirees in the postwar period.[6]

WORLD DEMOGRAPHICS AND THE AGE WAVE

It is analyses such as these that have led to the pessimistic forecasts of asset returns by those evaluating the aging of the population. Some researchers have used the specific demographics of each country to predict country asset returns based on these demand and supply conditions.[7]

But viewing the future through the lens of each country's demographics is wrong. One must envision the world as one economy and not as separate nations where each tries to match its own consumption to its own production. In a world of expanding global trade, the young of the developing nations can produce goods for—and buy assets from—the retirees of the world's developed nations.

FIGURE 4–2

Life Expectancy and Retirement Age Under Different Growth Scenarios 1950–2060

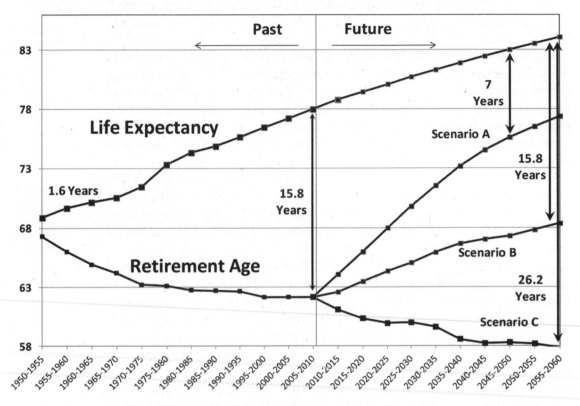

The reason that this could be significant is that although the developed world has a marked "age wave," the rest of the world does not. Outside Japan, Europe, and the United States, the emerging economies have very young populations.

Figure 4-1B plots the retiree-to-worker ratio of the developing countries. To be sure, the ratio of retirees to workers rises in almost all countries. But with the exception of China, the rise in the number of retirees in the emerging economies is much more gradual than in the developing countries. From 2013 to 2033 when the majority of baby boomers in developed countries retire, the number of retirees per 100 workers rises from 11 to only 18 in the emerging economies, far less than the United States, where the ratio increases from 27 to 45. For Africa, the number of retirees per 100 workers is virtually unchanged at the extremely low level of 7.5. And even for China, the most rapidly aging emerging economy because of its one-child policy, the number of retirees per 100 workers rises from 14 to 30 over the next 20 years, and its retiree ratio does not eclipse that of the United States until 2060.

FUNDAMENTAL QUESTION

The question is, can the workers in the emerging markets produce enough goods to provide for the retirees of the developed world, and can these workers save enough income to purchase the assets that must be sold by the developed-world retirees to finance their retirement? Right now, the answer is no. Although 80 percent of the world's population lives in the developing countries, those economies only produce about one-half of the world's output.

But that proportion is changing rapidly. In 1980 in China, Deng Xiaoping altered the course of the Chinese economy, opened it to market forces, and launched the country into a period of rapid and sustained growth. Per capita income, measured in terms that equate the purchasing power of the U.S. and Chinese currencies, has risen from only 2.1 percent of the U.S. level in 1980 to 16.1 percent in 2010. Since China has nearly four times the population as the United States, China will be the world's largest economy when its per capita income reaches 25 percent of that of the United States, which is forecast to occur around 2016. And the economy of China will become twice the size of the U.S. economy in 2025 if both countries' per capita income continues to grow at recent rates.

A decade after China began its rapid growth, a similar transformation occurred in India. Prime Minister Narasimha Rao, along with his finance minister Manmohan Singh, initiated the economic liberalization of India in 1991. The reforms did away with many bureaucratic requirements, reduced tariffs and interest rates, and ended many public monopolies. Since that time, India has begun growing more rapidly, and although current growth is less than that of China, India's total GDP will likely exceed that of the United States in the 2030s and eventually exceed China's output.

Figure 4-3 shows how the distribution of world GDP will evolve based on IMF and OECD forecasts of productivity growth and U.N. forecasts of population growth in each country. In 1980, the developed world produced three-quarters of the world output, with the United States producing one-quarter. Currently, the developed world produces about one-half of the world's GDP. In 20 years that will shrink to one-third, and by the end of this century, it will fall to one-quarter. By contrast, the output of the emerging economies will increase to three-quarters of the world GDP by the end of this century.

FIGURE 4–3

World GDP 1980-2100 Based on IMF, OECD, and U.N. Forecasts

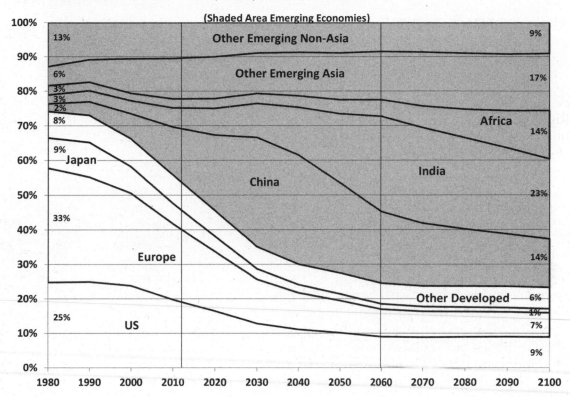

The GDP growth of China and India is particularly noteworthy. China has grown from only 2 percent of world output in 1980 to 16 percent today and is forecast to reach a maximum of 32 percent of world output in 2032 before falling back to 14 percent by the end of the century. This decline is due to China's one-child policy plus the fact that as its per capita GDP nears that of developed countries, its growth will slow. India has grown from 3 percent of world GDP in 1980 to 6 percent today and is forecast to be 11 percent of world GDP by 2032. By 2060, India's economy is projected to be larger than China's because of its greater population growth. India is forecast to produce about one-quarter of world GDP from 2040 through the rest of this century.

Africa remains a small part of the world economy until 2070, when it begins to expand rapidly, reaching 14 percent, the same size as the economy of China, by the end of the century. The assumptions used to project Africa's growth are quite conservative and will likely understate the importance of Africa in the second half of this century. It is very difficult to determine when and whether an underdeveloped economy will take off, as China's did in the 1980s and India's did one decade later. Current IMF assumptions assume a 5 percent growth rate for sub-Saharan Africa, greater than that of the developed world but far below what Asia has achieved. Since Africa is forecast to house nearly one-third of the world's population by the end of this century (and that assumes that the fertility rate of Africa will decline markedly over this period), if this continent can achieve rapid growth, it could potentially overtake Asia as the world's largest producer.

Other researchers have confirmed the importance of the emerging nations to the world economy. Homi Khara, of the OECD Development Centre, has estimated that the "middle class," defined as those earning between $3,650 and $36,500 per year, will increase by more than 3 billion, or 170 percent, between 2009 and 2030.[8] And their spending will increase by 150 percent, rising by over $34 trillion, more than twice the current size of the U.S. economy. More than 80 percent of that growth is projected to occur in Asia. In contrast, total spending in Western Europe and the United States will barely increase over that time.

The growth of the emerging economies has profound implications for developed countries. First, many of the goods that will be demanded by the retirees in the developed world will be produced by the workers in the emerging world. And the income earned from selling those goods will be used to increase not only the workers' consumption but also their saving. Asians are naturally high savers; even rich and aged countries like Japan have national saving ratios of nearly 25 percent, well above that of most Western economies and more than double that of the United States.

The growth in savings by investors in the emerging economies suggests that the financial markets in the developed world may not be overwhelmed by assets sold by the aging boomers. If the growth of productivity in the emerging markets can average 4.5 percent a year over the next half century, which is equal to the average since 1990, then the future retirement age in the United States will follow Scenario B in Figure 4-2.

To be sure, Scenario B does not allow for a further decline in the retirement age, nor does it stabilize the retirement *age* at its current level of 62. But it does stabilize the number of years an average worker will live in retirement—by increasing the retirement age at the same rate as the increase in life expectancy.

Figure 4-4 shows the past and future projected rates of productivity growth in developed and developing countries from 1980 through 2035. Productivity growth has averaged nearly 5 percent over the past 20 years in the emerging economies, a period that includes the Great Recession.

Is it possible that the retirement age in the developed world could continue to fall? Scenario C presents the extremely optimistic prospects that would prevail if all the emerging economies can grow as fast as the 9 percent rate that China has grown over the past 20 years. In that case there will be so many goods produced that the demands of the baby boomers in the developed world will be completely offset by the surge in production of goods and services by the developing world. The retirement age in the United States would continue to decline and lead to a retirement period that would exceed 26 years by 2060.

FIGURE 4–4

Historical and Forecast Productivity Growth of Developed and Emerging Economies 1980–2035

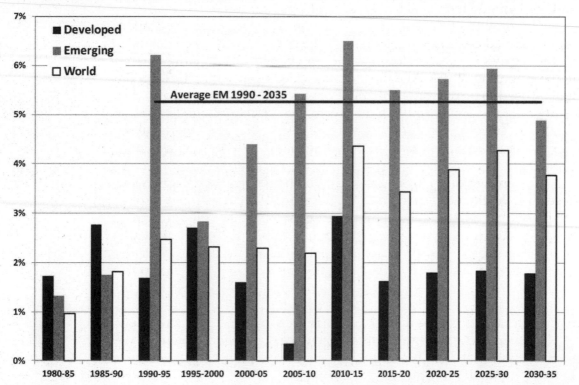

EMERGING ECONOMIES CAN FILL THE GAP

At the beginning of the chapter, I posed the question: Who will produce the goods that the retirees will consume, and who will buy the assets that they must sell to finance that consumption?

We now know the answer is the workers and investors from the developing countries. As they sell their output to the developed economies, they will be paid by the proceeds for selling the stocks and bonds that are now held by the baby boom population. The extent to which they can mitigate the age wave is directly linked to their economic growth. If they continue to grow rapidly, it is likely that most of the stocks and bonds issued by firms in the United States, Europe, and Japan will be owned by investors in the developing world. By the middle of this century, Chinese, Indians, and other investors from these young economies will gain majority ownership of most of the large global corporations.

Some may question why investors from emerging economies will buy Western assets when their countries are growing so rapidly. The answer is that in a global environment, firms' prospects are no longer tied to their country of origin. The growth of the emerging markets generates huge opportunities for Western firms marketing to the new middle class. And growth in the emerging economies also puts tremendous demands on their infrastructure. Infrastructure spending in emerging economies is estimated to be between 2 and 3 percent of global GDP over the next 20 years. This amounts to over \$2 trillion per year, and U.S. firms are leading beneficiaries of this spending.[9]

There is little doubt that consumers in rapidly expanding economies are attracted to brand names, and Western brand names hold a special appeal. This is illustrated by the 2013 Best Global Brands report from Interbrand, a consulting company owned by the Omnicom Group. The report ranks what it deems the 100 most valuable global brands on criteria that include financial performance, the role the brand plays in influencing the choices made by consumers, and the brand's ability to help its parent's earnings. U.S.-headquartered firms own the top 7 brands (Apple, Google, Coca-Cola, IBM, Microsoft, GE, and McDonald's) and 14 of the top 20.

What happens if Western firms do not compete effectively in the global marketplace? In that case, one can be certain that foreign competitors will step up to fill the void. But those Western firms with brand-name recognition are more likely to be bought by foreign investors who will supply the expertise needed to sell in these foreign markets.

CAN PRODUCTIVITY GROWTH KEEP PACE?

Productivity growth drives our standard of living.[10] The rapid productivity growth in the emerging economies is based on borrowing and using the technology that has already been developed by the most advanced economies.

But productivity growth in the developed countries must rely on innovation and invention since these economies are already operating at the frontier of technological know-how. Historically, productivity in the developed world has increased at a remarkably steady 2 to 2½ percent per year, which means that every 35 years the standard of living doubles.[11]

But some economists, such a Professor Robert Gordon of Northwestern University, believe that productivity growth is due to fall dramatically in the United States.[12] He cites the aging of the population, growing income inequality, and faltering educational achievement, among others factors, as the reasons for the decline. Except for the top 1 percent of the income distribution, Gordon predicts the vast majority of the U.S. population will experience growth of only 0.5 percent per year, less than one-quarter the long-term average.

Others have echoed Professor Gordon's pessimism and complain that discoveries today have not changed people's lives as fundamentally as they did a century ago. Tyler Cowen, an economist at George Mason University and author of *The Great Stagnation*, has voiced his belief that the developed world is on a technological plateau and that all the low-hanging fruit has already been discovered.[13]

Indeed, look at Table 4-1. It shows the most important life-changing inventions of the past 100 years. Those that took place in the first half of that period appear far more important than those of the second half in transforming the life of the average individual.[14]

There are some in Silicon Valley who also believe that the United States is in a downtrend. Peter Thiel, founder of PayPal, has claimed that innovation in America is "somewhere between dire straits and dead."[15] This downbeat view has spread to many in the investment community. Bill Gross and Mohammed El-Erian, heads of the giant investment firm PIMCO, coined the term *new normal* in 2009 to describe a condition where U.S. economic growth will sink to 1 to 2 percent, well below the 3+ percent that it has averaged in the post–World War II period.[16] Other investment managers have also embraced the concept.[17]

Even if growth is slower in the United States, this does not mean that growth rates will decline around the world. Although the life-changing innovations cited in the first column of Table 4-1 have long existed in the

TABLE 4–1

Life-Changing Inventions of the Past 100 Years

1910–1960	1960–2010
Electricity	Birth control
Indoor plumbing	Mobile phone
Washing machine	Internet
Refrigeration	Personal computer
Automobile	
Telephone	
Television/movies	
Large computers	
Air travel	
Antibiotics/vaccines	
Atomic energy	

developed world, the developing world is just beginning to acquire the conveniences of advanced economies. In 2006 the United Nations Human Development Report estimated that 2.6 billion people, or 40 percent of the world's population, had no indoor plumbing. Electrification, refrigeration, and basic healthcare still elude billions of people. Indeed, a large part of the increase in the world's income and wealth over the next several decades involves the developing world acquiring the lifestyle that the developed world has long possessed.

I do not believe that even the developed world's productivity is necessarily on a downward path. The digitization and instant availability of information will combine to spur faster productivity growth.

When we study history, we find that inventions that hastened communication, such as Ts'ai Lun's discovery of paper in the first century and Johannes Guttenberg's invention of the printing press in the fifteenth century, preceded periods of rapid discovery and innovation.[18] In the nineteenth and twentieth centuries, the telegraph and then the telephone spurred growth by enabling the first instant communication between distant individuals.

But no recent discovery has as much potential to foster innovation as the Internet. Soon virtually everything that has ever been written and recorded—on tape, on film, in print, or digitally—will be instantly accessible online. For the first time in human history, there is the real prospect of virtually free and unlimited connectivity of every researcher to the world's body of knowledge on any subject.

Professor Charles Jones of Stanford University has conducted extensive research on productivity growth and claims that 50 percent of U.S. growth between 1950 and 1993 can be attributed to the rise in worldwide—not just country specific—research intensity. His paper "Sources of U.S. Economic Growth in a World of Ideas" claims that a significant determination of productivity growth is "the implementation of ideas that are discovered throughout the world . . . which in turn is proportional to the total population of innovating countries."[19]

It is, indeed, the growth in the number of the "innovating countries" that paints a bright picture for our future. In the past century over 90 percent of the Nobel Prize winners in the scientific discipline were European and American, even though they constituted only a small fraction of the world's population. That is set to change radically. The opening of China and India alone has more than doubled those with access to the world's research. And language barriers are disappearing as technology enables instant translation. This implies that productivity growth will not decline but will actually rise in the coming decades.[20]

CONCLUSION

If most high-income countries, including the United States, have to rely on their own workers to produce goods and services for their aging population, there must be a dramatic rise in the retirement age, an increase that would far outstrip the expected increase in life expectancy. But as productivity rises in the world's developing economies, there will likely be enough workers to produce the goods and sufficient savers to buy the assets of the retiring boomers with only moderate increases in the retirement age. This growth will enable the future returns on equities to be near their historical levels.

Clearly this favorable scenario may not come to pass. Trade wars, restrictions on the flow of capital, and a pullback from the pro-growth policies in Asia and elsewhere will have a negative impact on both the economy and equity returns. Yet there are also good reasons why productivity may advance more rapidly, not only in the developing world, but also in developed economies. The communications revolution has enabled researchers to collaborate on a scale unthinkable just a few years ago. And collaboration drives discovery, innovation, and invention. As Fed Chairman Ben Bernanke stated in his 2013 graduation address at Bard College at Simon's Rock, "Both humanity's capacity to innovate and the incentives to innovate are greater today than at any other time in history."[21]

PART II

THE VERDICT
OF HISTORY

Stock and Bond Returns Since 1802

I know of no way of judging the future but by the past.
—PATRICK HENRY, 1775 SPEECH IN THE VIRGINIA
CONVENTION, MARCH 23, 1775

FINANCIAL MARKET DATA FROM 1802 TO THE PRESENT

This chapter analyzes the returns on stocks, bonds, and other assets classes over the last two centuries. U.S. history is divided here into three subperiods. In the first subperiod, from 1802 through 1870, the United States made a transition from an agrarian to an industrialized economy, comparable to the changes that many "emerging markets" of Latin America and Asia are making today. In the second subperiod, from 1871 through 1925, the United States became the foremost political and economic power in the world. The third subperiod, from 1926 to the present, covers the Great Depression, the postwar expansion, the tech bubble, and the 2008 financial crisis.

These time periods are chosen not only because they are historically significant, but because they also mark breaks in the quality and comprehensiveness of the historical data on stock returns. The most difficult stock returns to collect were those from 1802 through 1871 because few dividend data were available from that period. In prior editions of *Stocks for the Long Run* I used a stock price index based on the research of Professor William Schwert.[1] But his research did not include dividends, so I estimated a dividend yield using dividend data and macroeconomic information from the second subperiod. The dividend yields I obtained for the first period were consistent with other historical information that had been published about early-period dividend yields.[2]

In 2006, two of the prominent researchers in the field of U.S. stock returns, Bill Goetzmann and Roger Ibbotson of Yale University, published the most thoroughly documented research on stock returns before 1871.[3] Their research, which took more than a decade to complete, determined monthly price and dividend data on more than 600 individual securities over more than a century of stock data. The 6.9 percent annual stock return that I use in this volume for the 1802–1871 period is based on this Goetzmann-Ibbotson research and is only 0.2 percentage points below my earlier estimates of early-nineteenth-century stock returns.[4]

For the years 1871 through 1925, the returns on stocks are calculated using a capitalization-weighted index of all NYSE stocks (including reinvested dividends) and are taken from the well-regarded indexes compiled by the Cowles Foundation and reported in Shiller.[5] The data from the third period, from 1925 to the present, are the most thoroughly researched and are taken from the Center for Research in Security Prices. These returns represent a capitalization-weighted index of all New York Stock Exchange stocks and, starting in 1962, all American and Nasdaq stocks. The behavior of stock and bond returns since 1925 has also been researched by Roger Ibbotson, who has published yearbooks that have become benchmarks for U.S. asset returns since 1972.[6] All the stock and bond returns reported in this volume, including those from the early nineteenth century, are free from "survivorship bias," a bias that arises from only using the returns from firms that have survived and ignoring the lower returns from firms that have disappeared over time.

TOTAL ASSET RETURNS

The story of these assets is told in Figure 5-1. It depicts the total nominal (*not* inflation adjusted) return indexes for stocks, long- and short-term government bonds, gold, and commodities from 1802 through 2012. *Total return* includes changes in the capital value plus interest or dividends and assumes that all these cash flows are automatically reinvested in the asset over time.

It can be easily seen that over the last two centuries the total return on equities dominates all other assets. The amount of $1 invested in a capitalization-weighted portfolio in 1802, with reinvested dividends, would have accumulated to almost $13.5 million by the end of 2012.

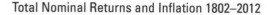

FIGURE 5–1

Total Nominal Returns and Inflation 1802–2012

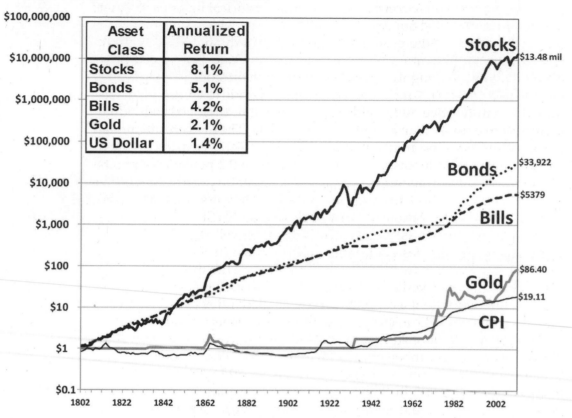

Even the cataclysmic stock crash of 1929, which caused a generation of investors to shun stocks, appears as a mere blip in the total stock return index. Bear markets, which so frighten those who hold equity investments, pale in the context of the upward thrust of stock returns.

It is important to understand that the total return on stocks depicted in Figure 5-1 does *not* represent the growth in the total value of the U.S. stock market. The wealth in stocks increases at a rate significantly slower than that of total stock return. The reason that total return grows faster than stock wealth is because investors consume most of the dividends paid by stocks, and therefore these dividends are not reinvested and cannot be used by firms to create capital. It would take only $1.33 million invested in the stock market in 1802 to grow, with dividends reinvested, to about $18 trillion, the total value of U.S. stocks, by the end of 2012. The sum of $1.33 million in 1802 is equivalent to roughly

$25 million in today's purchasing power, an amount far less than the value of the stock market at that time.[7]

Although financial theory (and government regulations) require that total return be calculated with reinvested dividends (or other cash flows), it is rare for anyone to accumulate wealth for long periods of time without consuming part of his or her return. The longest period of time investors typically hold onto assets without touching the principal and income occurs when they are accumulating wealth in pension plans for their retirement or in insurance policies that are passed on to their heirs. Even those who bequeath fortunes untouched during their lifetimes must realize that these accumulations are often dissipated in the next generation or spent by the foundations to which the money is bequeathed. The stock market has the power to turn a single dollar into millions by the forbearance of generations—but few will have the patience or desire to endure the wait.

THE LONG-TERM PERFORMANCE OF BONDS

Fixed-income investments are the largest and most important financial asset competing with stocks. Bonds promise fixed monetary payments over time. In contrast to equity, the cash flows from bonds have a maximum monetary value set by the terms of the contract. Except in the case of default, bond returns do not vary with the profitability of the firm.

The bond series shown in Figure 5-1 are based on long- and short-term U.S. Treasury bonds, when available; if they were not available, as occurred in some of the early years of our sample, the highest-grade municipal bonds were chosen. Default premiums were estimated and removed from the interest rates of riskier securities in order to obtain a comparable high-grade sample over the entire period.[8]

The interest rates on long-term bonds and short-term bonds (called *bills*), over the 210-year period, are displayed in Figure 5-2. Interest rate fluctuations during the nineteenth and early twentieth centuries remained within a narrow range. But from 1926 to the present, the behavior of both long- and short-term interest rates changed dramatically. During the Great Depression of the 1930s, short-term interest rates fell to nearly zero, and in October 1941 the yield on the 20-year Treasury bond fell to a record low of 1.82 percent. In order to finance record wartime borrowings, the government maintained extraordinarily low rates during World War II and the early postwar years.

The 1970s marked an unprecedented change in the behavior of interest rates. Inflation reached double-digit levels, and interest rates

FIGURE 5–2

U.S. Long- and Short-Term Interest Rates 1800–2012

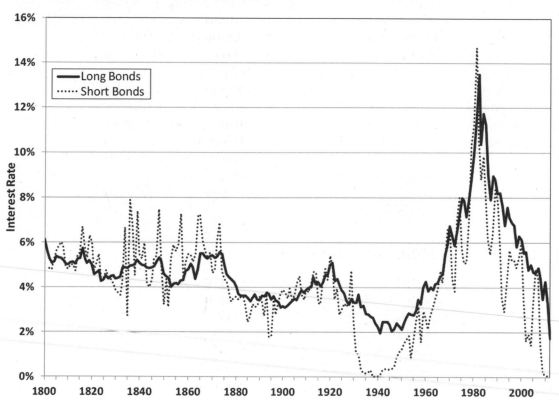

soared to heights that had not been seen since the debasing of the continental currency in the early years of the republic. Never before had inflation, and therefore interest rates, been so high for so long.

The public clamored for government action to slow rising prices. That cry was answered by Paul Volcker, chairman of the Federal Reserve System since 1979, who sent interest to near 20 percent and eventually brought inflation and interest rates down to moderate levels. The change in the behavior of interest rates is directly related to the changes in the determinants of the price level.

GOLD, THE DOLLAR, AND INFLATION

Consumer prices in the United States and the United Kingdom over the past 200 years are depicted in Figure 5-3. In each country, the price level

FIGURE 5-3

U.S. and U.K. Consumer Price Index 1800–2012

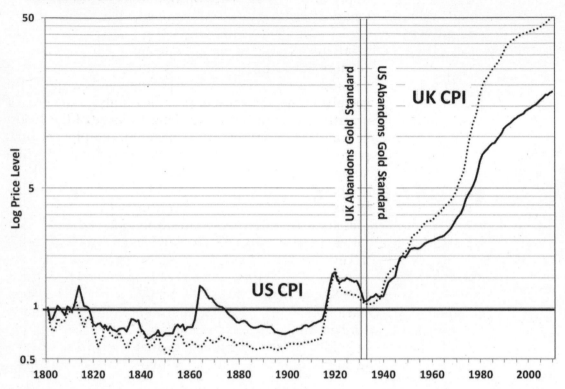

at the beginning of World War II was essentially the same as it was 150 years earlier. But after World War II, the nature of inflation changed dramatically. The price level rose almost continuously after the war, often gradually, but sometimes at double-digit rates, as in the 1970s. Excluding wartime, the 1970s witnessed the first rapid and sustained inflation ever experienced in U.S. or British history

The dramatic changes in the inflationary trend can be explained by the change in the monetary standard. During the nineteenth and early twentieth centuries, the United States, the United Kingdom, and the rest of the industrialized world were on a gold standard. As shown in Figure 5-1, the price of gold and the price level were very closely linked during this period. That is because the gold standard restricts the supply of money and hence the inflation rate. But from the Great Depression through World War II, the world shifted to a paper money standard. Under a paper money standard there is no legal constraint on the issuance of money, so inflation is subject to political as well as economic forces. Price stability depends on the desire of central banks to limit the growth of the supply of money in order to counteract deficit spending and other inflationary forces that result from government spending and regulation.[9]

The chronic inflation that the United States and other developed economies have experienced since World War II does not mean that the gold standard was superior to the current paper money standard. The gold standard was abandoned because of its inflexibility in the face of economic crises, particularly during the banking collapse of the 1930s. The paper money standard, if properly administered, can prevent runs on banks and severe depressions that plagued the gold standard while maintaining inflation at low to moderate levels.

But monetary policy was not well run. Gold prices soared to $850 per ounce in January 1980, following the rapid inflation of the 1970s. When inflation was finally brought under control, gold prices fell, but they rose again after the 2008 financial crisis when the flood of credit issued by central banks stoked fears of inflation. By the end of 2012, the price of gold reached $1,675 per ounce, and $1 of gold bullion purchased in 1802 was worth $86.40 at the end of 2012, while the price level itself increased by a factor of 19.12. Nevertheless, although gold protects investors against inflation, the yellow metal offers little more. Whatever hedging property gold possesses, this precious metal will likely exert a considerable drag on the return of a long-term investor's portfolio.[10]

TOTAL REAL RETURNS

The focus of long-term investors should be the growth of purchasing power of their investment—that is, the creation of wealth adjusted for the effects of inflation. Figure 5-4 reproduces Figure 1-1 in Chapter 1 and is constructed by taking the dollar returns shown in Figure 5-1 and correcting (or "deflating") them by the changes in the price level. The annualized real returns for the various asset classes are found in the upper left corner of the graph.

The compound annual real return on stocks is approximately 6.6 percent per year after inflation. Despite the addition of 20 years of stock market data since the first edition of *Stocks for the Long Run*, this return is just one-tenth of a percentage point lower than the 6.7 percent return that I reported in 1994.[11]

Some have maintained that this return is not sustainable since it is almost double the 3.0 to 3.5 percent growth rate of real GDP.[12] But that is

FIGURE 5-4

Total Real Returns on U.S. Stocks, Bonds, Bills, Gold, and the Dollar, 1802–2012

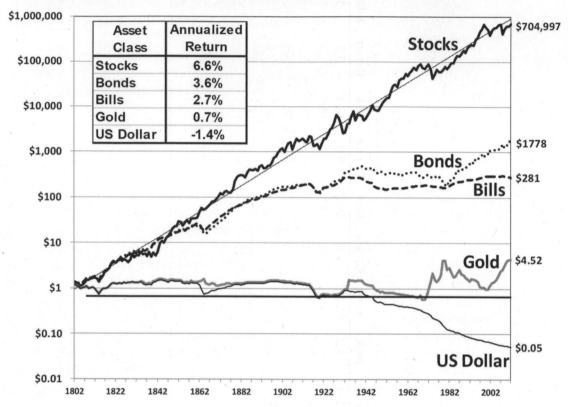

incorrect. Even if the economy is not growing at all, capital will receive a positive return because it is a scarce resource, just as labor will be paid positive wages and land will be paid positive rents. As noted earlier, the total real return on stocks assumes that all dividends and capital gains are reinvested into the market, and this sum grows far faster than total stock wealth or GDP.[13]

The annual returns on U.S. stocks over various time periods are summarized in Table 5-1. Note the extraordinary stability of the real return on stocks over all major subperiods: 6.7 percent per year from 1802 through 1870, 6.6 percent from 1871 through 1925, and 6.4 percent per year from 1926 through 2012. Even since World War II, during which all the inflation that the United States has experienced over the past 200 years occurred, the average real rate of return on stocks has been 6.4 percent per year. This is virtually identical to the real return on stocks during the previous 125 years, which saw no overall inflation. Stocks

TABLE 5-1

Real Returns on Stocks, Gold, and Inflation 1802–2012

		Total Nominal Return		Nominal Capital Appreciation		Dividend Yield	Total Real Return %		Real Capital Appreciation		Real Gold Return	Price Inflation
		Return	Risk	Return	Risk		Return	Risk	Return	Risk		
	1802–2012	8.1	17.6	2.9	17.2	5.1	6.6	18.0	1.5	17.4	0.7	1.4
	1871–2012	8.7	18.9	4.1	18.4	4.4	6.5	19.1	2.0	18.5	1.0	2.0
Major Sub-Periods	I 1802–1870	6.9	14.5	0.4	14.0	6.4	6.7	15.4	0.3	14.8	0.2	0.1
	II 1871–1925	7.3	16.5	1.9	15.9	5.3	6.6	17.4	1.3	16.9	–0.8	0.6
	III 1926–2012	9.6	20.3	5.5	19.6	3.9	6.4	20.2	2.5	19.6	2.1	3.0
Postwar Periods	1946–2012	10.5	17.5	6.8	16.9	3.5	6.4	17.8	2.9	17.2	2.0	3.9
	1946–1965	13.1	16.5	8.2	15.7	4.6	10.0	18.0	5.2	17.2	–2.7	2.8
	1966–1981	6.6	19.5	2.6	18.7	3.9	–0.4	18.7	–4.1	18.1	8.8	7.0
	1982–1999	17.3	12.5	13.8	12.4	3.1	13.6	12.6	10.2	12.6	–4.9	3.3
	2000–2012	2.7	20.6	0.8	20.1	1.9	0.3	19.9	–1.6	19.4	11.8	2.4

Return = compound annual return
Risk = standard deviation of arithmetic returns
All data in percent (%)

represent real assets, which in the long run appreciate at the same rate as inflation, so that real stock returns are not adversely affected by changes in the price level.

The long-term stability of stock returns has persisted despite the dramatic changes that have taken place in our society during the last two centuries. The United States evolved from an agricultural to an industrial economy and then to the postindustrial, service- and technology-oriented economy it is today. The world shifted from a gold-based standard to a paper money standard. And information, which once took weeks to cross the country, can now be instantaneously transmitted and simultaneously broadcast around the world. Yet despite mammoth changes in the basic factors generating wealth for shareholders, equity returns have shown an astounding stability.

But stability in the long-run returns on stocks in no way guarantees stability in the short run. From 1982 through 1999 during the greatest bull market in U.S. history, stocks offered an extraordinary after-inflation return of 13.6 percent per year, more than double the historical average. These superior returns followed the dreadful returns realized in stocks the previous 15 years, from 1966 through 1981, when stock returns fell behind inflation 0.4 percent per year. Nevertheless, this great bull market carried stocks too high, and the valuation of the market reached record levels, which in turn led to the poor returns of the following decade. The subsequent bear market and financial crisis plunged stocks once again well below trend as real stock returns have fallen to a mere +0.3 percent in the 12 years following the bull market peak of 2000.

REAL RETURNS ON FIXED-INCOME ASSETS

As stable as the long-term real returns have been for equities, the same cannot be said of fixed-income assets. As Table 5-2 indicates, the real return on Treasury bills has dropped precipitously from 5.1 percent in the early part of the nineteenth century to a bare 0.6 percent since 1926, a return only slightly above inflation.

The real return on long-term bonds has shown a similar, but more moderate, decline. Bond returns fell from a generous 4.8 percent in the first subperiod to 3.7 percent in the second and then to only 2.6 percent in the third. The decline in real yield on government bonds over time can be partly explained by certain factors that boosted their demand: the greatly improved liquidity of bonds and the fact that these bonds satisfy many fiduciary requirements that other fixed-income assets do not. These demand-boosting factors raised the prices of government bonds

TABLE 5–2

Real Returns on Bonds and Inflation 1802–2012

		Long-Term Governments				Short-Term Governments			
			Nominal Return		Real Return		Nominal	Real Return		Price
		Coupon Rate	Return	Risk	Return	Risk	Rate	Return	Risk	Inflation
	1802–2012	4.7	5.1	6.7	3.6	9.0	4.2	2.7	6.0	1.4
	1871–2012	4.7	5.2	7.9	3.0	9.3	3.6	1.6	4.4	2.0
Major Sub-Periods	I 1802–1870	4.9	4.9	2.8	4.8	8.3	5.2	5.1	7.7	0.1
	II 1871–1925	4.0	4.3	3.0	3.7	6.4	3.8	3.1	4.8	0.6
	III 1926–2012	5.1	5.7	9.7	2.6	10.8	3.6	0.6	3.9	3.0
	1946–2012	5.8	6.0	10.8	2.0	11.5	4.3	0.4	3.2	3.9
Postwar Periods	1946–1965	3.1	1.5	5.0	–1.2	7.1	2.0	–0.8	4.3	2.8
	1966–1981	7.2	2.5	7.1	–4.2	8.1	6.8	–0.2	2.1	7.0
	1982–1999	8.5	12.1	13.8	8.5	13.6	6.3	2.9	1.8	3.3
	2000–2012	4.5	9.0	11.7	6.5	11.6	2.2	–0.2	1.8	2.4

Return = compound annual return
Risk = standard deviation of arithmetic returns
All data in percent (%)

and therefore reduced their yields. The real returns on longer-term bonds were also reduced by the unexpected inflation that investors experienced in the post–World War II period.

The short-run volatility of stock returns from decade to decade is not unexpected. What may surprise investors is that the volatility of the real returns on government bonds is also quite large. For the 35-year-period from 1946 through 1981, the real return on Treasury bonds was negative. In other words, the coupon on the bonds did not offset the decline in bond prices brought about by rising interest rates and inflation. As we shall see in the next chapter, there never has been even a 20-year period, not to speak of a 35-year period, where real stock returns were negative.

The decline in real returns on bonds since 1926 would have been much greater if it were not for the stellar bond returns of the past three decades. Since 1981, the decline in inflation and interest rates has pushed bond prices upward and greatly improved bondholder returns. Although bond returns fell well short of equities during stocks' mega bull market from 1981 through 1999, bonds easily outpaced stocks in the following decade. In fact, for the entire three decades that followed the peak in bond yields in the early 1980s, bond returns virtually matched those of equities.

THE CONTINUING DECLINE IN FIXED-INCOME RETURNS

But those spectacular bond returns cannot continue. Prospective real returns for Treasury bonds became far easier to determine when, in January 1997, the U.S. Treasury introduced TIPS, or Treasury inflation-protected securities. The coupons and principal from these bonds, backed by the full faith and credit of the U.S. government, are linked to the U.S. consumer price index, so that the yield on these bonds is a *real*, inflation-adjusted yield, shown in Figure 5-5.

The steady decline in the yields on these bonds is readily apparent. When these bonds were first issued, their yield was just short of 3.5 percent. That is almost identical to the historical real return on government bonds that I had found in my research analyzing data dating from 1802. After issuance, the yield on TIPS increased, reaching a high of 4.40 per-

F I G U R E   5–5

Real Yield on 10-Year Treasury Inflation-Protected Securities (TIPS) 1997–2012

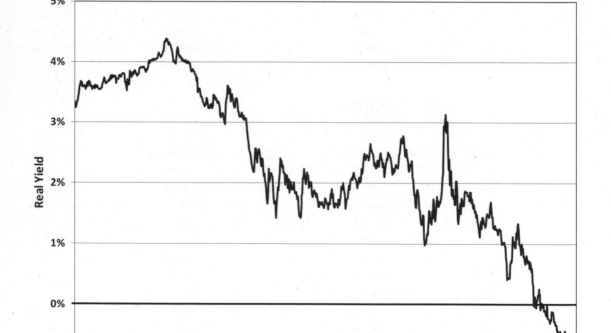

cent in January 2000, the month that also marked the peak of the tech and Internet bubble.

From that date, the yield on TIPS began a relentless decline. From 2002 through 2007 the yield fell to 2 percent. As the financial crisis deepened, the yield continued to decline and sank below zero in August 2011, reaching nearly –1 percent by December 2012.[14] This negative real yield was similar to the implied after-inflation yields on the standard Treasury bonds. The yield on the 10-year Treasury bond fell to a 75-year low of 1.39 percent in July 2012, well below the ongoing and forecast rate of inflation.

The real yield on Treasury bonds is determined by many factors, such as the state of the economy, fears of inflation, and the risk attitudes of investors. But in almost all economic models, the most important factor influencing the real return on bonds is economic growth. Indeed, the 3.4 percent yield set at the first TIPS auction was almost exactly equal to real GDP growth in the 1990s. As real economic growth slowed to about 2 percent from 2002 through 2007, the yields on TIPS fell accordingly.

But no forecaster in 2012 predicted real economic growth over the next decade would be negative, as the yield on TIPS suggested. Only extreme risk aversion can explain why investors were willing to accept negative after-inflation returns on government bonds even though other assets, such as equities, have consistently delivered long-term real returns of 6 to 7 percent per year.

THE EQUITY PREMIUM

The excess return of stocks over bonds (either long or short) is referred to as the *equity risk premium*, or simply the *equity premium*. It can be measured historically, as shown in Figure 5-6, or prospectively, on the basis of current bond yields and stock valuations. Subtracting stock and bond returns from Tables 5-1 and 5-2 shows that the equity premium has averaged 3.0 percent against Treasury bonds and 3.9 percent against Treasury bills over the entire 210 years.

Because of the extraordinary returns on long-term bonds over the past 30 years, the historical equity premium of stocks over bonds has shrunk to zero. But the forward-looking equity premium at the end of 2013 is far higher since the prospective real yields on long bonds have fallen so low. If forward-looking equity returns match their historical average, the forward-looking equity premium in 2013 could be 6 percent or more.[15]

FIGURE 5–6

The Equity Premium: Difference between 30 Year Return on Stocks and Bonds and Stocks and Bills 1831–2012

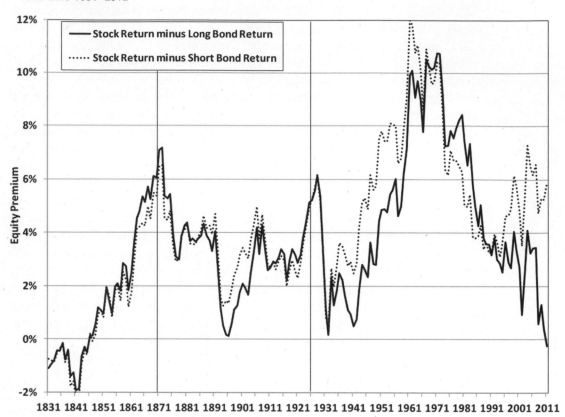

WORLDWIDE EQUITY AND BOND RETURNS

When I published *Stocks for the Long Run* in 1994, some economists questioned whether my conclusions, drawn from data from the United States, might overstate historical equity returns measured on a worldwide basis. They claimed that U.S. stock returns exhibited *survivorship bias*, a bias caused by the fact that returns are collected from successful equity markets, such as the United States, but ignored in countries where stocks have faltered or disappeared outright, such as in Russia or Argentina.[16] This bias suggested that stock returns in the United States, a country that over the last 200 years has been transformed from a small British colony into the world's greatest economic power, are unique and that historical equity returns in other countries would be lower.

Prodded by this question, three U.K. economists examined the historical stock and bond returns from 19 countries since 1900. Elroy Dimson and Paul Marsh, professors at the London Business School, and Mike Staunton, director of the London Share Price Database, published their research in 2002 in a book entitled *Triumph of the Optimists: 101 Years of Global Investment Returns*.[17] This book provides a rigorous yet readable account of worldwide financial market returns in 19 different countries.

Updated returns from this study are given in Figure 5-7, which shows the average historical real stock, bond, and bill returns of all 19 countries analyzed from 1900 through 2012. Despite the major disasters visited on many of these countries, such as war, hyperinflation, and depression, every one of them exhibited substantially positive after-inflation stock returns.

FIGURE 5–7

International Real Returns on Stocks, Bonds, and Bills 1900–2012

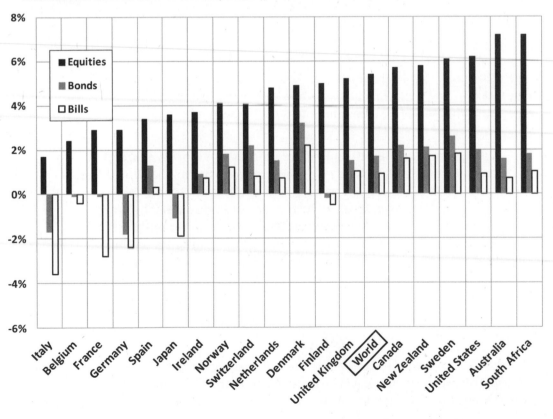

Real equity returns ranged from a low of 1.7 percent in Italy to a high of 7.2 percent in Australia and South Africa. Stock returns in the United States, although quite good, were not exceptional. The simple arithmetic mean of the returns of the 19 countries is 4.6 percent, and a portfolio that put a single dollar in each of those countries' stock markets in 1900 would have produced a compound real return of 5.4 percent, very close to the 6.2 percent that is found in the United States. And those countries that had lower stock returns also had lower fixed-income returns, so that the average equity premium against bonds was 3.7 percent and against bills was 4.5 percent, actually higher than found in the United States.

When all the information was analyzed, the authors concluded:

> . . . that the US experience of equities outperforming bonds and bills has been mirrored in all sixteen countries examined. . . . Every country achieved equity performance that was better than that of bonds. Over the 101 years as a whole, there were only two bond markets and just one bill market that provided a better return than our *worst* performing equity market.

Furthermore:

> While the US and the UK have indeed performed well, . . . there is no indication that they are hugely out of line with other countries. . . . Concerns about success and survivorship bias, while legitimate, may therefore have been somewhat overstated [and] investors may have not been materially misled by a focus on the US.[18, 19]

This last statement is significant. More studies have been made of the U.S. markets than the markets of any other country in the world. Dimson, Marsh, and Staunton are saying that the results found in the United States have relevance to all investors in all countries. The title they chose for their book suggests their conclusions: it is the optimists, not the pessimists, who take positions in the equity market, and they have decidedly triumphed over more cautious investors over the last century. International studies have reinforced, not diminished, the case for equities.

CONCLUSION: STOCKS FOR THE LONG RUN

Over the past 210 years, the compound annual real return on a diversified portfolio of common stock has been between 6 and 7 percent in the United States, and it has displayed a remarkable constancy over time.

Certainly the returns on stocks are dependent on the quantity and quality of capital, productivity, and the return to risk taking. But the ability to create value also springs from skillful management, a stable political system that respects property rights, and the capacity to provide value to consumers in a competitive environment. Swings in investor sentiment resulting from political or economic crises can throw stocks off their long-term path, but the fundamental forces producing economic growth have always enabled equities to regain their long-term trend. Perhaps that is why stock returns have displayed such stability despite the radical political, economic, and social changes that have impacted the world over the past two centuries.

Yet one must be aware of the political, institutional, and legal framework in which these returns were generated. The superior performance of stocks over the past two centuries might be explained by the growing dominance of nations committed to free market economics. Few expected the triumph of market-oriented economies during the dark days of the Great Depression and World War II. But if history is any guide, government bonds in our paper money economies may fare far worse than stocks in any political or economic upheaval. As the next chapter shows, even in stable political environments, the risks in government bonds actually outweigh those in stocks for long-term investors.

APPENDIX 1: STOCKS FROM 1802 TO 1870

The first actively traded U.S. stocks, floated in 1791, were issued by two banks: the Bank of New York and the Bank of the United States.[20] Both offerings were enormously successful and were quickly bid to a premium. But they collapsed the following year when Alexander Hamilton's assistant at the Treasury, William Duer, attempted to manipulate the market and precipitated a crash. It was from this crisis that the antecedents of the New York Stock Exchange were born on May 17, 1792.

Joseph David, an expert on the eighteenth-century corporation, claimed that equity capital was readily forthcoming not only for every undertaking likely to be profitable but also, in his words, "for innumerable undertakings in which the risk was very great and the chances of success were remote."[21] Although over 300 business corporations were chartered by the states before 1801, fewer than 10 had securities that traded on a regular basis. Two-thirds of those chartered before 1801 were connected with transportation: wharves, canals, turnpikes, and bridges. But the important stocks of the early nineteenth century were financial institutions: banks and, later, insurance companies. Banks and insurance companies held loans and equity in many of the manufacturing firms that, at that time, did not have the financial standing to issue equity. The fluctuations in the stock prices of financial firms in the nineteenth century reflected the health of the general economy and the profitability of the firms to which they lent. One of the first large nonfinancial ventures was the Delaware and Hudson Canal, issued in 1825, which also became an original member of the Dow Jones Industrial Average 60 years later.[22] In 1830, the first railroad, the Mohawk and Hudson, was listed; and for the next 50 years, railroads dominated trading on the major exchanges.

6

Risk, Return, and Portfolio Allocation

Why Stocks Are Less Risky Than Bonds in the Long Run

> *As a matter of fact, what investment can we find which offers real fixity or certainty income? . . . As every reader of this book will clearly see, the man or woman who invests in bonds is speculating in the general level of prices, or the purchasing power of money.*
>
> —IRVING FISHER, 1912[1]

MEASURING RISK AND RETURN

Risk and return are the building blocks of finance and portfolio management. Once the risk, expected return, and correlations between asset classes are specified, modern financial theory can help investors allocate their portfolios. But the risk and return on stocks and bonds are not physical constants, like the speed of light or gravitational force, waiting to be discovered in the natural world. Investors cannot, as in the physical sciences, run repeated controlled experiments, holding all other factors constant, and home in on the "true" value of each variable. As Nobel laureate Paul Samuelson was fond of saying, "We have but one sample of history."

This means that despite the overwhelming quantity of historical data, one can never be certain that the underlying factors that generate asset prices have remained unchanged. Indeed we saw in Chapter 3 that the correlations between assets classes change substantially over time

Yet one must start by analyzing the past in order to plan for the future. The last chapter showed that not only have fixed-income returns lagged substantially behind those on equities, but because of the uncertainty of inflation, bonds can be quite risky for long-term investors. In this chapter investors will see that uncertain inflation will make their portfolio allocations depend crucially on their planning horizon.

RISK AND HOLDING PERIOD

For many investors, the most meaningful way to describe risk is by portraying a worst-case scenario. The best and worst after-inflation returns for stocks, bonds, and bills from 1802 over holding periods ranging from 1 to 30 years are displayed in Figure 6-1. Here stock returns are measured, as before, by dividends plus capital gains or losses on a broad-based capitalization-weighted index of U.S. stocks. Note that the height of the bars, which measures the difference between best and worst returns, declines far more rapidly for equities than for fixed-income securities as the holding period increases.

Stocks are unquestionably riskier than bonds or Treasury bills over one- and two-year periods. However, in every five-year period since 1802, the worst performance in stocks, at –11.9 percent per year, has been only slightly worse than the worst performance in bonds or bills. And for 10-year holding periods, the worst stock performance has actually been *better* than that for bonds or bills.

For 20-year holding periods, stock returns have never fallen below inflation, while returns for bonds and bills once fell as much as 3 percent per year below the inflation rate. During that inflationary episode, the real value of a portfolio of Treasury bonds, including all reinvested coupons, fell by nearly 50 percent. The worst 30-year return for stocks remained comfortably ahead of inflation by 2.6 percent per year, a return that is not far below the *average* performance of fixed-income assets.

It is very significant that stocks, in contrast to bonds or bills, have never delivered to investors a negative real return over periods lasting 17 years or more. Although it might appear to be riskier to accumulate wealth in stocks rather than in bonds over long periods of time, for the preservation of purchasing power, precisely the opposite is true: the

FIGURE 6–1

Highest and Lowest Real Returns on Stocks, Bonds, and Bills over 1-, 2-, 5-, 10-, 20-, and 30-Year Holding Periods 1802–2012

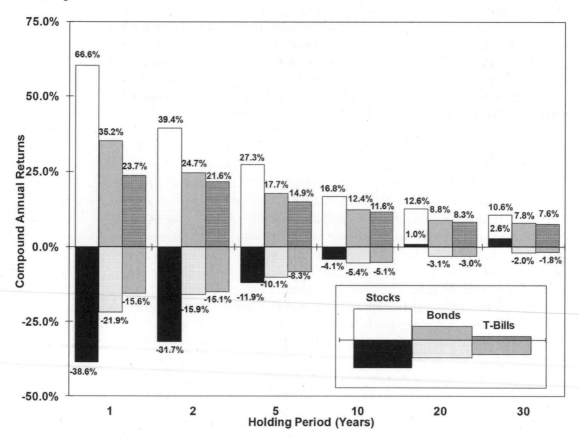

safest long-term investment has clearly been a diversified portfolio of equities. There is no doubt that inflation-protected U.S. Treasury bonds safeguard investors from unexpected inflation. But as noted in Chapter 5, the real yields on those securities, even for maturities as long as 20 years, fell below zero in 2012 and remain very low. Stocks, in contrast, have never given investors a negative real return over a 20-year horizon.

Some investors question whether holding periods of 20 or 30 or more years are relevant to their planning horizon. But one of the greatest mistakes that investors make is to underestimate their holding period. This is because many investors think about the holding periods of a particular stock, bond, or mutual fund. But the holding period that is relevant for portfolio allocation is the length of time the investors hold *any* stocks or bonds, no matter how many changes are made among the individual issues in their portfolio.

The percentage of times that stock returns outperform bond or bill returns over various holding periods is shown in Table 6-1. As the holding period increases, the probability that stocks will outperform fixed-income assets increases dramatically. For 10-year horizons, stocks beat bonds about 80 percent of the time; for 20-year horizons, about 90 percent of the time; and over 30-year horizons, nearly 100 percent of the time.

In the first four editions of *Stocks for the Long Run*, I noted that the last 30-year period when the return on long-term bonds beat stocks ended in 1861, at the onset of the U.S. Civil War. That is no longer true. Because of the large drop in government bond yields over the past decade, the 11.03 percent annual return on long-term government bonds just surpassed the 10.98 percent on stocks for the 30-year period from January 1, 1982, through the end of 2011. This striking event caused some

TABLE 6–1

Percentage of Time Stocks Outperform Bonds and Bills over Various Holding Periods

Holding Period	Stocks Outperform Time Period	Stocks Outperform Bonds	T-Bills
1 Year	1802–2012	58.8	62.1
	1871–2012	61.3	66.9
2 Year	1802–2012	60.5	62.9
	1871–2012	64.1	70.4
3 Year	1802–2012	67.2	70.2
	1871–2012	68.7	73.3
5 Year	1802–2012	67.6	68.6
	1871–2012	69.0	74.6
10 Year	1802–2012	72.3	73.3
	1871–2012	78.2	83.8
20 Year	1802–2012	83.9	87.5
	1871–2012	95.8	99.3
30 Year	1802–2012	91.2	91.2
	1871–2012	99.3	100.0

researchers to conclude that stock returns can no longer be counted on to surpass bond returns.[2]

But a closer look at why bonds outperformed stocks during this period shows that it is almost impossible for bonds to repeat that feat in the coming decades. In 1981 the interest rate on 10-year U.S. Treasury bonds reached 16 percent. As interest rates fell, bondholders benefited from both high coupons and capital gains on their bonds. This resulted in a real return on bonds of 7.8 percent per year from 1981 to 2011, approximately the same real return as on stocks. A 7.8 percent real return is only about 1 percentage point above the stocks' 210-year average, but it is more than double the average historical real return on bonds and more than 3 times its return over the last 75 years.

As interest rates have fallen to historic lows, bondholders face a wholly different situation. At the end of 2012, the yield on nominal bonds was about 2 percent. The only way that bonds could generate a 7.8 percent real return is if the consumer price index *fell* by nearly 6 percent per year over the next 30 years. Yet a deflation of this magnitude has never been sustained by any country in world history. In contrast, stocks can easily repeat their performance over the last three decades and are likely to do so given their favorable valuation at the end of 2012. As noted in the last chapter, the prospective returns of stocks over bonds will likely exceed their historical average by a wide margin.

Although the dominance of stocks over bonds is readily apparent in the long-run data, it is also important to note that over one- and even two-year periods, stocks outperform bonds or bills only about three out of every five years. This means that nearly two out of every five years a stockholder's return will fall behind the return he or she would get on Treasury bills or bank certificates. The high probability that bonds and even bank accounts will outperform stocks in the short run is the primary reason why it is so difficult for many investors to stay in stocks.[3]

STANDARD MEASURES OF RISK

The risk—defined as the standard deviation of average real annual returns—for stocks, bonds, and bills based on the historical sample of over 200 years is displayed in Figure 6-2. Standard deviation is the measure of risk used in portfolio theory and asset allocation models.

Although the standard deviation of stock returns is higher than for bond returns over short-term holding periods, once the holding period increases to between 15 and 20 years, stocks become less risky than bonds. Over 30-year periods, the standard deviation of the return on a

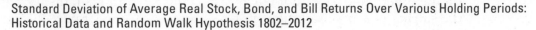

FIGURE 6–2

Standard Deviation of Average Real Stock, Bond, and Bill Returns Over Various Holding Periods:
Historical Data and Random Walk Hypothesis 1802–2012

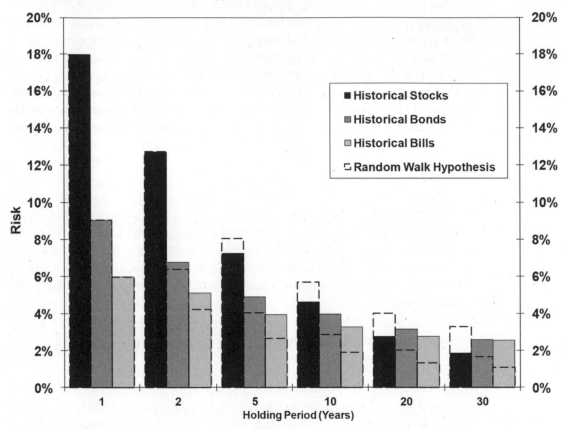

portfolio of equities falls to less than three-fourths that of bonds or bills.
The standard deviation of average returns falls nearly twice as fast for
stocks as for fixed-income assets as the holding period increases.

If asset returns follow a random walk, the standard deviation of
each asset class will fall by the square root of the holding period. A *random walk* is a process whereby future returns are completely independent of past returns. The dashed bars in Figure 6-2 show the decline in
risk predicted under the random walk assumption.

But the historical data show that the random walk hypothesis cannot be maintained for equities. This occurs since the actual risk of average stock returns declines far faster than predicted by the random walk
hypothesis because of the mean reversion of equity returns.

The standard deviation of average returns for fixed-income assets, on the other hand, does not fall as fast as the random walk theory predicts. This is a manifestation of *mean aversion* of bond returns. Mean aversion implies that once an asset's return deviates from its long-run average, there is an increased chance that it will deviate further, rather than return to more normal levels. Mean aversion of bond returns is especially characteristic of hyperinflations, where price changes proceed at an accelerating pace, rendering paper assets worthless. But mean aversion is also present in the more moderate inflations that have impacted the United States and other developed economies. Once inflation begins to accelerate, the inflationary process becomes cumulative, and bondholders have virtually no chance of making up losses in their purchasing power. In contrast, stockholders who hold claims on real assets rarely suffer a permanent loss due to inflation.

Note that I am not claiming that the risk on a portfolio of stocks *falls* as we extend the time period. The standard deviation of *total* stock returns rises with time, but it does so at a diminishing rate. On the other hand, because of uncertain inflation, the standard deviation of real bond returns increases at an accelerating rate as the investment horizon increases, and eventually bonds become riskier than a diversified portfolio of common stocks.

VARYING CORRELATION BETWEEN STOCK AND BOND RETURNS

Even though the returns on bonds fall short of that on stocks, bonds may still serve to diversify a portfolio and lower overall risk. This will be particularly true if bond and stock returns are *negatively correlated*, which would happen if bond and stock prices move in the opposite direction.[4] The diversifying strength of an asset is measured by the correlation coefficient. The *correlation coefficient* ranges between −1 and +1 and measures the co-movement between an asset's return and the return of the rest of the portfolio. The lower the correlation coefficient, the better the asset serves as a portfolio diversifier. Assets with near-zero or especially negative correlations are particularly good diversifiers. As the correlation coefficient between the asset and portfolio returns increases, the diversifying quality of the asset declines.

In Chapter 3 we examined the changing correlation coefficient between the return on 10-year Treasury bonds and stocks, represented by the S&P 500 Index. Figure 6-3 displays the correlation coefficient between annual stock and bond returns for three subperiods between 1926 and 2012. From 1926 through 1965 the correlation was only slightly

FIGURE 6–3

Correlation of Real Bond and Stock Returns Over Various Historical Periods

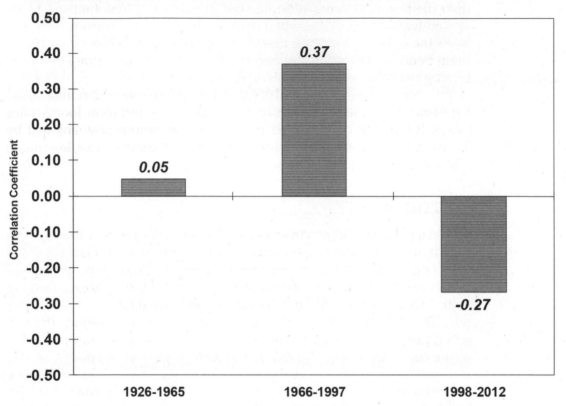

positive, indicating that bonds were fairly good diversifiers for stocks. Bonds were good diversifiers in this period because it contained the Great Depression, which was characterized by falling economic activity and consumer prices, a situation that was bad for stocks but good for U.S. government bonds.

However, under a paper money standard, bad economic times are more likely to be associated with *inflation*, not deflation. This was true from the mid-1960s through the mid-1990s, as the government attempted to offset economic downturns with expansionary monetary policy that was inflationary. Under these circumstances, stock and bond prices tend to move together, sharply reducing the diversifying qualities of government bonds.

But this positive correlation has switched again in recent decades. Since 1998, stock prices have once again become *negatively* correlated with government bond prices. The reason for this switch is twofold. In the early part of that period, the world markets were roiled by economic and currency upheavals in Asia, the deflationary economy in Japan, and then the terrorist events of September 11. Later the 2008 financial crisis stoked fears of the 1930s, when deflation ruled and government bonds were the only appreciating asset. These events led to the U.S. government bond market becoming once again a safe haven for those investors fearing more economic turmoil and lower stock prices.

Nevertheless, it is unlikely that Treasury bonds will remain good *long-term* diversifiers, especially if the specter of inflation looms once again. If inflation does indeed increase, the premium now enjoyed by Treasury bonds as a hedge against deflation will again be lost, leading to further losses for bondholders.

EFFICIENT FRONTIERS[5]

Modern portfolio theory describes how investors may alter the risk and return of a portfolio by changing the mix between assets. Figure 6-4 displays the risks and returns that result from varying the proportion of stocks and bonds in a portfolio over various holding periods ranging from 1 to 30 years based on 210 years of historical data.

The "blank" square at the bottom of each curve represents the risk and return of an all-bond portfolio, while the darkened square at the top of the curve represents the risk and return of an all-stock portfolio. The circle on the curve indicates the minimum risk achievable by combining a varying proportion of stocks and bonds. The curve that connects these points represents the risk and return of all blends of portfolios from 100 percent bonds to 100 percent stocks. This curve, called the *efficient frontier*, is the heart of modern portfolio analysis and is the foundation of asset allocation models.

Note that the allocation that achieves the minimum risk is a function of the investor's holding period. Investors with a 1-year horizon seeking to minimize their risk should hold almost their entire portfolio in bonds, and that is also true for those with the 2-year horizon. At a 5-year horizon, the allocation of stock rises to 25 percent in the minimum-risk portfolio, and it further increases to more than one-third when investors have a 10-year horizon. For 20-year horizons, the minimum-risk portfolio is over 50 percent in stock, and for a 30-year horizon it is 68 percent.

Given these striking differences, it might seem puzzling that the holding period has almost never been considered in standard portfolio theory. This is because modern portfolio theory was established when

FIGURE 6–4

Risk-Return Tradeoffs (Efficient Frontiers) for Stocks and Bonds Over Various Holding Period 1802–2012

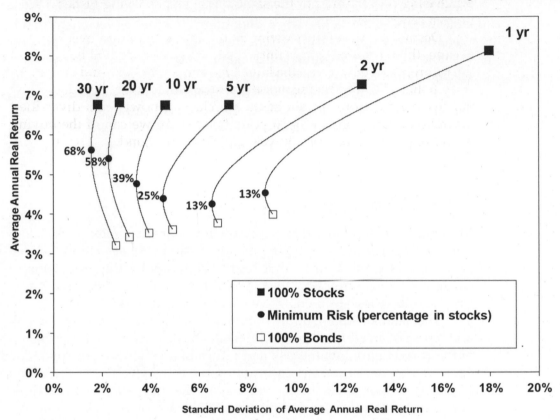

the vast majority of the academic profession supported the random walk theory of security prices. As noted earlier, when prices are a random walk, the risk over any holding period is a simple function of the risk over a single period, so that the *relative* risk of different asset classes does not depend on the holding period. In that case the efficient frontier is invariant to the time period, and asset allocation does not depend on the investment horizon of the investor. When security markets do not obey random walks, that conclusion cannot be maintained.[6]

CONCLUSION

No one denies that, in the short run, stocks are riskier than fixed-income assets. But in the long run, history has shown that stocks are actually safer than bonds for long-term investors whose goal is to preserve the purchasing power of their wealth. The inflation uncertainty that is inherent in a paper money standard means that "fixed income" and "fixed purchasing power" are not the same thing, just as Irving Fisher conjectured a century ago.

Despite the dramatic slowing in the rate of inflation over the past decade, there is much uncertainty about what a dollar will be worth in the future, especially given the large government deficits and easy monetary policy followed by the world's central banks. Historical data show that we can be more certain of the purchasing power of a diversified portfolio of common stocks 30 years hence than we can of the buying power of the principal on a 30-year U.S. Treasury bond.

Stock Indexes

Proxies for the Market

> *It has been said that figures rule the world.*
> —Johann Wolfgang Goethe, 1830

MARKET AVERAGES

"How's the market doing?" one stock investor asks another.

"It's having a good day—it's up over 100 points."

For those who follow the markets, no one would ask, "What's up 100 points?" The Dow-Jones Industrial Average is still the way many refer to how the market is doing, even though they well recognize the limitations of this index. This index, popularly called the Dow, is so renowned that the news media often called the Dow "the stock market." No matter how imperfectly the index describes the movement of share prices—and virtually no money manager pegs his or her performance to it—the Dow is the way that many investors describe the ups and downs of the stock market.

But today there are many other, far more inclusive indexes. The S&P 500, created in March 1957 by Standard & Poor's, now a division of the McGraw-Hill Financial, has become the uncontested benchmark index for large U.S. stocks. And the Nasdaq, an automated electronic market that began in 1971, has become the exchange of choice for technology companies. The Nasdaq Index measures the performance of such large technology firms as Microsoft, Intel, Google, and Apple.

Although the term *Industrials* conjures up old-line manufacturing companies, the Dow has become much more representative of firms that dominate today's landscape. In 1999, the Dow Industrials entered the technological age when, for the first time, the company selected two Nasdaq stocks—Microsoft and Intel—to join its venerable list of 30 stocks. Below is the story of these three very different indexes with three unique reflections of the stock market.

THE DOW JONES AVERAGES

Charles Dow, one of the founders of Dow Jones & Co.—the company that also publishes the *Wall Street Journal*—created the Dow Jones averages in the late nineteenth century. On February 16, 1885, he began publishing a daily average of 12 stocks (10 railroads and 2 industrials) that represented active and highly capitalized stocks. Four years later, Dow published a daily average based on 20 stocks—18 railroads and 2 industrials.

As industrial and manufacturing firms succeeded railroads in importance, the Dow Jones Industrial Average was created on May 26, 1896, comprising the original 12 stocks shown in Table 7-1. The old index created in 1889 was reconstituted and renamed the Rail Average on October 26, 1896. In 1916, the Industrial Average was increased to 20 stocks, and in 1928 the number was expanded to 30, its present size. The Rail Average, whose name was changed to the Transportation Average in 1970, is composed of 20 stocks, as it has been for over a century.

The early Dow firms were centered on commodities: cotton, sugar, tobacco, lead, leather, rubber, and so on. Six of the twelve companies have survived in much the same form, but only one—General Electric—has retained both its membership in the Dow Industrials and its original name.[1]

Almost all the original Dow stocks thrived as large and successful firms, even if they were eventually removed from the index (see the Appendix at the end of this chapter for historical details). The only exception was U.S. Leather Corp., which was liquidated in the 1950s. Shareholders received $1.50 plus one share of Keta Oil & Gas, a firm acquired earlier. But in 1955, the president, Lowell Birrell, who later fled to Brazil to escape U.S. authorities, looted Keta's assets. Shares in U.S. Leather, which in 1909 was the seventh-largest corporation in the United States, became worthless.

TABLE 7-1

Stocks in Dow Jones Industrials 1886–2013

1896	1916	1928	1965	2013
American Cotton Oil	American Sugar	Allied Chemical	Allied Chemical	3M Co.
American Sugar	American Can	American Can	Aluminum Co. of America	American Express
American Tobacco	American Car &	American Smelting	American Can	AT&T
Chicago Gas	Foundry	American Sugar	American Tel. & Tel.	Boeing
Distilling & Cattle	American Locomotive	American Tobacco	American Tobacco	Caterpillar
Feeding	American Smelting	Atlantic Refining	Anaconda Copper	Chevron
General Electric	American Sugar	Bethlehem Steel	Bethlehem Steel	Cisco Systems
Laclede Gas	American Tel. & Tel.	Chrysler	Chrysler	Coca-Cola
National Lead	Anaconda Copper	General Electric	DuPont	DuPont
North American	Baldwin Locomotive	General Motors	Eastman Kodak	Exxon Mobil
Tennessee Coal and Iron	Central Leather	General Railway Signal	General Electric	General Electric
U.S. Leather	General Electric	Goodrich	General Foods	Goldman Sachs
U.S. Rubber	Goodrich	International Harvester	General Motors	Home Depot
	Republic Iron & Steel	International Nickel	GoodYear	Intel
	Studebaker	Mack Trucks	International Harvester	IBM
	Texas Co.	Nash Motors	International Nickel	Johnson & Johnson
	U.S. Rubber	North American	International Paper Co.	JPMorgan Chase
	U.S. Steel	Paramount Publix	Johns-Manville	McDonald's
	Utah Copper	Postum, Inc.	Owens-Illinois Glass	Merck
	Westinghouse	Radio Corp.	Procter & Gamble	Microsoft
	Western Union	Sears, Roebuck	Sears, Roebuck	Nike
		Standard Oil (N.J.)	Standard Oil of California	Pfizer
		Texas Corp.	Standard Oil (N.J.)	Procter & Gamble
		Texas Gulf Sulphur	Swift & Company	Travelers
		Union Carbide	Texaco Incorporated	United Technologies
		U.S. Steel	Union Carbide	UnitedHealth
		Victor Talking Machine	United Aircraft	Verizon Comm.
		Westinghouse Electric	U.S. Steel	Visa
		Woolworth	Westinghouse Electric	WalMart
		Wright Aeronautical	Woolworth	Walt Disney

Computation of the Dow Index

The original Dow Jones averages were simply the sum of the prices of the component shares divided by the number of stocks in the index. However, this divisor had to be adjusted over time to prevent jumps in the index when there were changes in the companies that constituted the average or stock splits. In October 2013, the divisor was about 0.1557, so that a 1-point rise in any Dow stock caused the average to increase about 6½ points.[2]

The Dow Industrials is a *price-weighted index*, which means that the prices of the component stocks are added together and then divided by the number of firms in the index. As a result, proportional movements of high-priced stocks in the Dow averages have a much greater impact than movements of lower-priced stocks, regardless of the size of the company. In November 2013, Visa, with a market price of $200 a share, constitutes more than 8 percent of the index, while Cisco, the lowest-priced stock, has a weight of less than 1 percent.[3]

Price-weighted indexes are uncommon since the impact of the firm's stock price on the index is unrelated to the size of the company. This is in stark contrast to a capitalization-weighted index, such as Standard & Poor's 500 Index, in which each company's weight in the index is proportional to the market value of its shares. As of October 2013, the 30 Dow stocks were valued at $4.5 trillion, which is a bit less than one-quarter of the capitalization of the entire U.S. market. At the end of 2013, the Dow Industrials did not contain the world's largest market-value stock, Apple, nor did it contain Google, which was also one of the top 10 highest-market-value stocks.

Long-Term Trends in the Dow Jones Industrial Average

Figure 7-1 plots the monthly high and low of the Dow Jones Industrial Average from its inception in 1885, corrected for changes in the cost of living. The inset shows the Dow Industrial Average uncorrected for inflation.

A *trendline* and a *channel* are created by statistically fitting the Dow on a time trend. The upper and lower bounds are 1 standard deviation, or 50 percent, above and below the trend. The slope of the trendline, 1.94 percent per year, is the average compound rate at which the Dow stocks have appreciated after inflation, since 1885. The Dow Jones average, like most other popular averages, does not include dividends, so the appreciation of the rise in the index greatly understates the total return on the

FIGURE 7–1

Nominal and Real Dow-Jones Industrial Average 1885–2012

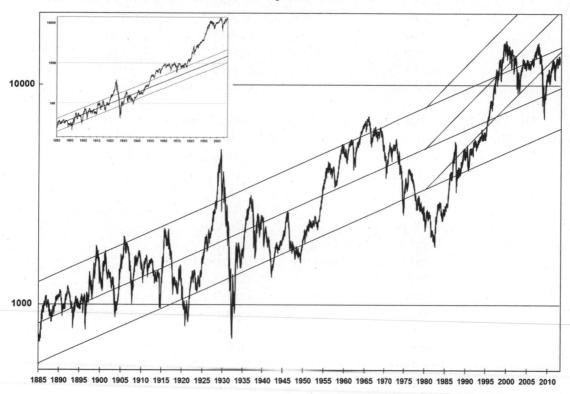

Dow stocks. Since the average dividend yield on all stocks was about 4.3 percent over this period, the total annual real compound return on the Dow stocks was about 6.2 percent per year over this period.[4]

The inflation-corrected Dow average has stayed within the channel about three-quarters of the time. When the Dow broke out of the channel to the upside, as it did in 1929, in the mid-1960s, and in 2000, stocks subsequently suffered poor short-term returns. Likewise, when stocks penetrated the channel on the downside, they subsequently experienced superior short-term returns. As of August 2013, the inflation-corrected all-time high of the Dow Industrials occurred in January 2000 at 16,130.

Beware the Use of Trendlines to Predict Future Returns

Using channels and trendlines to predict future returns, however tempting, can be misleading. Longstanding trends have been broken for good economic reasons. Uncorrected for inflation, the Dow Industrials broke and stayed above the trendline in the mid-1950s, as shown in the inset of Figure 7-1. This is because inflation, caused by the shift to a paper money standard, propelled nominal stock prices justifiably above their previous trend, established during noninflationary times. Those who used trend-line analysis and who failed to plot stock prices in *real* instead of nominal terms would have sold in 1955 and *never* reentered the market.[5]

But there is now another justification why the channel may again be penetrated on the upside. As noted above, stock indexes track only capital appreciation and therefore understate total returns, which include dividends. But firms have been paying an ever-lower fraction of their earnings as dividends, using the difference to buy back their shares and invest capital in their business. So in recent years a greater part of the return on stocks now comes through capital gains instead of dividend income. Because the average dividend yield on stocks has fallen 2.88 percentage points since 1980, a new channel has been drawn in Figure 7-1 with a slope that is 2.88 percentage points higher to represent the increase in the expected growth of capital gains. At the end of 2012, the real Dow Industrials were above the mean, uncorrected for the change in dividend yield but below the bottom of the dividend-corrected channel.

VALUE-WEIGHTED INDEXES

Standard & Poor's Index

Although the Dow Jones Industrial Average was published in 1885, it was certainly not a comprehensive index of stock values, covering at most 30 stocks. In 1906 the Standard Statistics Co. was formed, and in 1918 it began publishing the first index of stock values based on each stock's performance weighted by its capitalization, or market value, instead of its price as Dow-Jones did. Capitalization weighting is now recognized as giving the best indication of the return on the overall market, and it is almost universally used in establishing market benchmarks.[6] In 1939, Alfred Cowles, founder of the Cowles Commission for Economic Research, used Standard & Poor's market-weighting techniques to construct indexes of stock values back to 1871 that consisted of all stocks listed on the New York Stock Exchange.

The Standard & Poor's stock price index began in 1923, and in 1926 it became the Standard & Poor's Composite Index containing 90 stocks. The index was expanded to 500 stocks on March 4, 1957, and became the

S&P 500 Index. At that time, the value of the S&P 500 Index made up about 90 percent of the value of all NYSE-listed stocks. The 500 stocks contained exactly 425 industrial, 25 railroad, and 50 utility firms. Before 1988, the number of companies in each industry was restricted to these guidelines, but since that date, there are no industry restrictions on the firms selected.

A base value of 10 was chosen for the average value of the S&P Index from 1941 to 1943, so that when the index was first published in 1957, the average price of a share of stock (which stood between $45 and $50) was approximately equal to the value of the index. An investor at that time could easily identify with the changes in the S&P 500 Index since a 1-point change approximated the price change for an average stock.

The S&P 500 Index contains a few firms that are quite small, representing companies that have fallen in value and have yet to be replaced.[7] As of the end of 2012, the total value of all S&P 500 companies was about $13.6 trillion, but this constituted less than 75 percent of the value of all stocks traded in the United States, significantly less than the 90 percent share it constituted when the index was first formulated. A history of the S&P 500 Index, along with the insights that come from analyzing the stocks in this world-famous index, is described in the next chapter.

Nasdaq Index

On February 8, 1971, the method of trading stocks underwent a revolutionary change. On that date, an automated quotation system called the *Nasdaq* (an acronym for National Association of Securities Dealers Automated Quotations) provided up-to-date bid and asked prices on 2,400 leading over-the-counter stocks. Formerly, quotations for these unlisted stocks were submitted by the principal trader or by brokerage houses that carried an inventory. The Nasdaq linked the terminals of more than 500 market makers nationwide to a centralized computer system.

In contrast to the Nasdaq, stocks traded on the New York or American Stock Exchange are assigned to a Designated Market Maker (used to be called "specialist"), who is charged with maintaining an orderly market in that stock. The Nasdaq changed the way quotes were disseminated and made trading these issues far more attractive to both investors and traders.

At the time that the Nasdaq was created, it was clearly more prestigious to be listed with an exchange (and preferably the New York Stock Exchange) than be traded on the Nasdaq. Nasdaq stocks tended to be small or new firms that had recently gone public or did not meet the listing requirements of the larger exchanges. However, many young technology firms found the computerized Nasdaq system a natural home. Some, such as Intel and Microsoft, chose not to migrate to the Big Board, as the NYSE is termed, even when they qualified to do so.

The Nasdaq Index, which is a capitalization-weighted index of all stocks traded on the Nasdaq, was set at 100 on the first day of trading in 1971. It took almost 10 years to double to 200 and another 10 years to reach 500 in 1991. It reached its first major milestone of 1,000 in July 1995.

As the interest in technology stocks grew, the rise in the Nasdaq Index accelerated, and it doubled its value to 2,000 in just three years. In the fall of 1999, the technology stock boom sent the Nasdaq into orbit. The index increased from 2,700 in October 1999 to its all-time peak of 5,048.62 on March 10, 2000.

The increase in popularity of technology stocks resulted in a tremendous increase in volume on the Nasdaq. At the onset, the volume on this electronic exchange was a small fraction of that on the New York Stock Exchange. But by 1994 share volume on the Nasdaq exceeded that on the NYSE, and five years later dollar volume on the Nasdaq surpassed the NYSE as well.[8]

No longer was the Nasdaq the home of small firms waiting to qualify for Big Board membership. By 1998 the capitalization of the Nasdaq had already exceeded that of the Tokyo Stock Exchange. At the market peak in March 2000, the total market value of firms traded on the Nasdaq reached nearly $6 trillion, more than one-half that of the NYSE and more than any other stock exchange in the world. At the beginning of the millennium, Nasdaq's Microsoft and Cisco had the two largest market values in the world, and Nasdaq-listed Intel and Oracle were also among the top 10.

When the technology bubble burst, trading and prices on the Nasdaq sank rapidly. The Nasdaq Index declined from over 5,000 in March 2000 to 1,150 in October 2002 before rebounding to 3,000 at the end of 2012. Trading also fell off from an average of over 2.5 billion shares when prices peaked to approximately 2 billion shares in 2007. Despite the decline in the Nasdaq Index, the Nasdaq still trades in some of the world's most active stocks.

But the importance of individual exchanges and "floor trading" has declined precipitously, as the overwhelming percentage of shares listed on the New York Stock Exchange is now traded electronically. In 2008 the NYSE bought the American Stock Exchange, and in late 2012, the ICE, or Intercontinental Exchange, a 12-year-old Atlanta-based firm that trades futures contracts electronically, made an $8 billion bid to acquire the NYSE. Even though it may seem exciting for news reporters to broadcast from the floor of the New York Stock Exchange, the colonnaded building, built at Broad and Wall Street in 1903 to trade the world's largest and most important companies, may soon go dark.

Other Stock Indexes: The Center for Research in Security Prices

In 1959, Professor James Lorie of the Graduate School of Business of the University of Chicago received a request from the brokerage house Merrill Lynch, Pierce, Fenner & Smith. The firm wanted to investigate how well people had done investing in common stock, and it could not find reliable historical data. Professor Lorie teamed up with colleague Lawrence Fisher to build a database of securities data that could answer that question.

With computer technology in its infancy, Lorie and Fisher created the Center for Research in Security Prices (CRSP, pronounced "crisp") that compiled the first machine-readable file of stock prices dating from 1926 that was to become the accepted database for academic and professional research. The database currently contains all stocks traded on the New York and American Stock Exchanges and the Nasdaq.

At the end of 2012, the market value of the nearly 5,000 stocks in the database was near $19 trillion. The CRSP is the largest comprehensive index of U.S. firms.

Figure 7-2 shows the size breakdown and total market capitalization of the stocks in the CRSP. The top 500 firms, which closely mirror the S&P 500 Index, constitute 78.6 percent of the market value of all stocks. The top 1,000 firms in market value, which are virtually identical to the Russell 1000 and published by the Russell Investment Group, compose nearly 90 percent of the total value of equities. The Russell 2000 contains the next 2,000-largest companies, which adds an additional 9.6 percent to the market value of the total index. The Russell 3000, the sum of the Russell 1000 and 2000 indexes, composes 99.1 percent of all U.S. stocks. The remaining 1,788 stocks constitute 0.8 percent of the value of all stocks traded.[9]

RETURN BIASES IN STOCK INDEXES

Because stock indexes such as the S&P 500 Index constantly add new firms and delete old ones, some investors believe that the return calcu-

FIGURE   7–2

CRSP Total Market Index, 2012

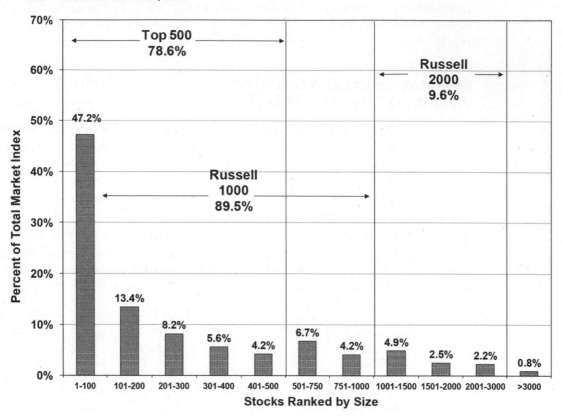

lated from these indexes will be higher than the return that can be achieved by investors in the overall market.

But this is not the case. It is true that the best-performing stocks will stay in the S&P 500 Index, but this index misses the powerful upside move of many small and mid-sized issues. For example, Microsoft was not added to the S&P 500 Index until June 1994, eight years after going public. And while small stock indexes are the incubators of some of the greatest growth stocks, they also contain those "fallen angels" that dropped out of the large-cap indexes and are headed downward.

An index is not biased if its performance can be replicated or matched by an investor. To replicate an index, the date of additions and deletions to the index must be announced in advance so that new stocks can be bought and deleted stocks can be sold. This is particularly important for issues that enter into bankruptcy: the postbankrupt price (which might be zero) must be factored into the index. All the major stock indexes, such as Standard & Poor's, Dow Jones, and the Nasdaq, can be replicated by investors.[10] Consequently, there is no statistical reason to believe that these indexes give a biased representation of the return on the market.

APPENDIX: WHAT HAPPENED TO THE ORIGINAL 12 DOW INDUSTRIALS?

Two stocks (General Electric and Laclede) retained their original name (and industry); five (American Cotton, American Tobacco, Chicago Gas, National Lead, and North American) became large public companies in their original industries; one (Tennessee Coal and Iron) was merged into the giant U.S. Steel; and two (American Sugar and U.S. Rubber) went private—both in the 1980s. Surprisingly, only one (Distilling & Cattle Feeding) changed its product line (from alcoholic beverages to petrochemicals), and only one (U.S. Leather) was liquidated. Here is a rundown of the original 12 stocks (market capitalizations as of December 2012):

- *American Cotton Oil* became Best Food in 1923, Corn Products Refining in 1958, and finally CPC International in 1969—a major food company with operations in 58 countries. In 1997, CPC spun off its corn-refining business as Corn Products International and changed its name to Bestfoods. Bestfoods was acquired by Unilever in October 2000 for $20.3 billion. Unilever (UN), which is headquartered in the Netherlands, has a current market value of $115 billion.

- *American Sugar* became Amstar in 1970 and went private in 1984. In September 1991 the company changed its name to Domino Foods, Inc., to reflect its world-famous Domino line of sugar products.

- *American Tobacco* changed its name to American Brands (AMB) in 1969 and to Fortune Brands (FO) in 1997, a global consumer products holding company with core businesses in liquor, office products, golf equipment, and home improvements. American Brands sold its American Tobacco subsidiary, including the Pall Mall and Lucky Strike brands, to one-time subsidiary B.A.T. Industries in 1994. In 2011 Fortune Brands changed its name to Beam Inc (BEAM), which operates as a distribution company in the spirits industry. The market value is $9 billion.

- *Chicago Gas* became Peoples Gas Light & Coke Co. in 1897 and then Peoples Energy Corp., a utility holding company, in 1980. Peoples Energy Corp. (PGL) was bought by WPS Resources and changed its name in 2006 to Integrys Energy Group (TEG). It has a market value of $4.1 billion. PGL was a member of the Dow Jones Utility Average until May 1997.

- *Distilling & Cattle Feeding* went through a long and complicated history. It changed its name to American Spirits Manufacturing and then to Distiller's Securities Corp. Two months after the passage of Prohibition, the company changed its charter and became U.S. Food Products Corp. and then changed its name again to National Distillers and Chemical. The company became Quantum Chemical Corp. in 1989, a leading producer of petro-chemicals and propane. Nearing bankruptcy, it was purchased for $3.4 billion by Hanson PLC, an Anglo-American conglomerate. It was spun off as Millennium Chemicals (MCH) in October 1996. Lyondell Chemical (LYO) bought Millennium Chemicals in November 2004. In 2007 Lyondell was taken over by the Dutch firm that renamed itself Lyondell Basell Industries (LYB). The current market value of Lyondell Basell is $28 billion.

- *General Electric (GE)*, founded in 1892, is the only original stock still in the Dow Industrials. GE is a huge manufacturing and broadcasting conglomerate that owns NBC and CNBC. Its market value of $218 billion is the third-highest capitalization stock in the United States.

- *Laclede Gas (LG)* changed its name to Laclede Group, Inc., and it is a retail distributor of natural gas in the St. Louis area. The market value is $900 million.

- *National Lead (NL)* changed its name to NL Industries in 1971, and it manufactures products relating to security and to precision ball bearings, as well as titanium dioxide and specialty chemicals. The market value is $520 million.

- *North American* became Union Electric Co. (UEP) in 1956, providing electricity in Missouri and Illinois. In January 1998, UEP merged with Cipsco (Central Illinois Public Service Co.) to form Ameren (AEE) Corp. The market value is $72 billion.

- *Tennessee Coal and Iron* was bought out by U.S. Steel in 1907, and it became USX-U.S. Steel Group (X) in May 1991. In January 2002, the company changed its name back to U.S. Steel Corp. U.S. Steel has a market value of $3 billion.

- *U.S. Leather*, one of the largest makers of shoes in the early part of this century, liquidated in January 1952, paying its shareholders $1.50 plus stock in an oil and gas company that was to become worthless.
- *U.S. Rubber* became Uniroyal in 1961, and it was taken private in August 1985. In 1990 Uniroyal was purchased by the French company Michelin Group, which has a market value of $15 billion.

The S&P 500 Index

More Than a Half Century of U.S. Corporate History

> *Most of the change we think we see in life is due to truths being in and out of favor.*
>
> —ROBERT FROST, "THE BLACK COTTAGE," 1914

Out of the three major U.S. stock market indexes, the Dow, the Nasdaq, and the S&P 500, only one became the world standard for measuring the performance for stocks. It was born on February 28, 1957, and it grew out of Standard & Poor's Composite Index, a capitalization-weighted index begun in 1926 that contained 90 large stocks. Ironically, the 1926 index excluded the largest stock in the world at that time, American Telephone and Telegraph, because S&P did not want to let the performance of such a large firm dominate the index. To correct this omission and to recognize the growth of new firms in the postwar period, Standard & Poor's compiled an index of 500 of the largest industrial, rail, and utility firms that traded on the New York Stock Exchange.

The S&P 500 Index made up nearly 90 percent of the total value of firms traded on the Big Board in 1957. It soon became the standard against which the performance of institutions and money managers

investing in large U.S. stocks was compared. The S&P 500 Index originally contained exactly 425 industrial, 25 rail, and 50 utility firms, but
these groupings were abandoned in 1988 in order to maintain, as
Standard & Poor's claimed, an index that included "500 leading companies in leading industries of the economy."

Since its creation, the index has been continually updated by adding
new firms that meet Standard & Poor's criteria for market value, earnings, and liquidity while deleting an equal number that fall below these
standards.[1] The total number of new firms added to the S&P 500 Index
from its inception in 1957 through 2012 was 1,159, an average of about 20
per year. On average, the new firms constitute about 5 percent of the market value of the index.

The highest number of new firms added to the index in a single
year occurred in 1976, when Standard & Poor's added 60 stocks including 15 banks and 10 insurance carriers. Until that year, the only financial
stocks in the index were consumer finance companies, because banks
and insurance companies were traded in the over-the-counter market
and because timely price data were not available to compute the index
until the Nasdaq exchange began in 1971. In 2000, at the peak of the technology bubble, 49 new firms were added to the index, the highest since
Nasdaq stocks were included in 1976. In 2003, the number of additions
fell to a record-tying low of 8.

SECTOR ROTATION IN THE S&P 500 INDEX

The evolution of the U.S. economy during the past half century has
brought about profound changes in its industrial landscape. Steel, chemical, auto, and oil companies once dominated our economy. Today healthcare, technology, finance, and other consumer services firms hold sway.

Increasingly, active investors are using sector analysis to allocate
their portfolios. The most popular industry classification system was
formulated in 1999 when Standard & Poor's joined Morgan Stanley to
create the Global Industrial Classification Standard (GICS). This system
arose from the earlier Standard Industrial Code (SIC) system devised by
the U.S. government that had grown less suited to our service-based
economy.[2]

The GICS divides the economy into 10 sectors: *materials* (chemicals,
papers, steel, and mining), *industrials* (capital goods, defense, transportation, and commercial and environmental services), *energy* (exploration, production, marketing, refining of oil and gas, and coal), *utilities*
(electric, gas, water, and nuclear generating or transmission firms),

telecommunication services (fixed line, cellular, wireless, and bandwidth), *consumer discretionary* (household durables, autos, apparel, hotels, restaurants, media, and retailing), *consumer staples* (food, tobacco, personal products, retailing, and hypermarkets), *healthcare* (equipment producers, healthcare providers, pharmaceuticals, and biotechs), *financial* (commercial and investment banking, mortgages, brokerage, insurance, and real estate [REITs]), and *information technology* (software services, Internet, home entertainment, data processing, computers, and semiconductors).

The share of the market value of each of these sectors in the S&P 500 Index from 1957 through 2012 is displayed in Figure 8-1. Many of the changes have been dramatic. The materials sector, by far the largest in 1957, had become one of the smallest (along with utilities and telecom) by the end of 2012. The materials and energy sectors made up almost one-half of the market value of the index in 1957, but by 2013 these two

FIGURE 8–1

Market Value of S&P 500 Sectors as a Percentage of Total S&P 500 1957–2012

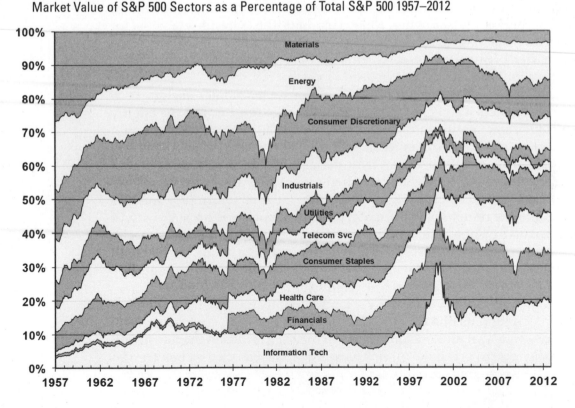

sectors together constituted only 14 percent of the index. On the other hand, the financial, healthcare, and technology sectors, which started off as the three smallest sectors and constituted only 6 percent of the index in 1957, commanded almost one-half of the market value of all S&P 500 firms by 2013.

It is important to realize that when measured over long periods of time, the rising or falling market shares do not necessarily correlate with rising or falling investor returns. That is because the change in sector shares often reflects the change in the *number* of firms, not just the change in the *value* of individual firms. This is especially true in the financial sector, as commercial and investment banks, insurance companies, brokerage houses, and government-sponsored enterprises such as Fannie Mae and Freddie Mac were added to the index.[3] The technology share has also increased primarily because of the addition of new firms. In 1957, IBM's weight was two-thirds of the technology sector; in 2013, IBM was only the third largest in a sector that contains 70 firms.

One can see in Figure 8-2 how little relation there is between the change in the market value of a sector and its return. The fastest-growing technology sector did have slightly above-average returns, but the second-fastest-growing financials had the second-worst sector returns. The weights of the financial and technology sectors increased primarily because many new firms had been added to the sector, not because individual stocks increased in value.

It is true that the healthcare and consumer staples sectors both increased their weights and had above-average returns; but the energy sector shrank significantly from 20 to 11 percent in market weight, and yet its return of 11.76 percent was well above the S&P 500 Index. Statistical analysis shows that over the past 50 years only 10 percent of the return to a sector is related to whether the sector is expanding or contracting. This means that 90 percent of the investor return of a sector is based on the returns of the firms in the sector, not the relative growth of the industry. Rapidly expanding sectors often induce investors to pay too high a price, which results in lower returns. As a result, the best values are often found in stagnant or declining sectors that are ignored by investors and whose price is low relative to fundamentals.

The performance of the 20 largest companies that Standard & Poor's put into its first list in 1957 is shown in Table 8-1. One feature that stands out is that all 9 oil companies on the list finished in the top 10 and that the returns on all the oil companies beat the S&P 500 by between 96 and 275 basis points *per year*.

FIGURE 8–2

Relation Between Change in Sector Weight and Sector Return for S&P 500, 1957–2012

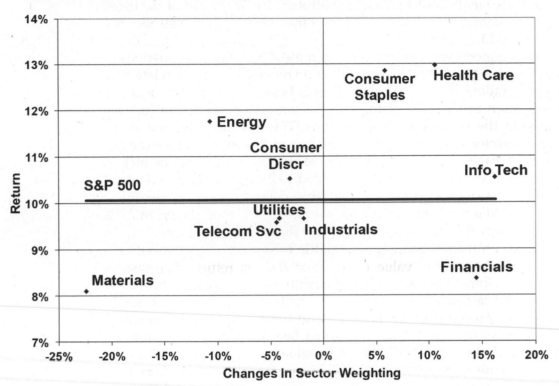

The top-performing firm of the original 20 largest stocks in the S&P 500 Index was Royal Dutch Petroleum, a firm founded in the Netherlands and one of the companies that Standard & Poor's deleted from its index in 2002 when it purged all foreign-based firms. The second-best-performing stock was Socony Mobil Oil, which dropped the "Socony" (which stood for Standard Oil Company of New York) in 1966 and merged with Exxon in 1999. Third-ranking Gulf Oil, sixth-ranking Standard Oil of California, and eighth-ranking Texas Co (Texaco) eventually merged to form ChevronTexaco, whose name was shortened to Chevron. The fourth-best-performing stock was Shell Oil, a U.S.-based company that was purchased by Royal Dutch in 1985 and is no longer in the S&P 500 Index. The fifth-best performer was Standard Oil of New Jersey, which changed its name to Exxon in 1972 and currently vies with Apple as the world's largest market-value stock. Ninth-ranked Standard Oil of Indiana merged into BP Amoco in 1998, and tenth-ranking Phillips

T A B L E   8–1

Returns of 20 Largest original S&P 500 Firms, 1957-2012

Return Rank	1957 Name	1957–2012 Return	1957 Market Cap Rank
1	Royal Dutch Petroleum	12.82%	12
2	Socony Mobil Oil	12.76%	13
3	Gulf Oil	12.46%	6
4	Shell Oil	12.40%	14
5	Standard Oil Co NJ	12.28%	2
6	Standard Oil Co CA	12.02%	10
7	IBM	11.57%	11
8	Texaco	11.43%	8
9	Standard Oil Co Ind	11.26%	16
10	Phillips Petroleum	11.03%	20
11	AT&T	9.76%	1
12	Union Carbide	9.75%	7
13	General Electric	9.65%	5
14	Sears, Roebuck	8.04%	15
15	Du Pont	7.42%	4
16	Eastman Kodak	6.09%	19
17	USX Corp.	6.00%	9
18	Aluminum Co. Of America	4.24%	17
19	General Motors	3.71%	3
20	Bethlehem Steel	—	18
	Average Top 10	12.09%	
	Average Top 20	10.94%	
	S&P 500	10.07%	

Petroleum merged with Conoco (Continental Oil Co.) to form ConocoPhillips in 2002.

The only firm to beat any oil firm is IBM, incorporated in 1911 as C-T-R (Computer-Tabulating-Recording) Company. IBM had the highest weight in the S&P 500 Index (at over 6 percent) from 1983 through 1985 and in 2013 is still one of the top 10 most valuable companies.

Ten of the original twenty largest companies lagged the performance of the S&P 500 Index. U.S. Steel, AT&T, and General Motors were at one time the largest corporations in the world. U.S. Steel and AT&T have gone through tortuous paths of industrial changes and corporate divestments and at one time had shrunk to a tiny fraction of their former size.

Yet both have come back, and as of 2013, AT&T is the thirteenth-largest company by market value in the United States.

U.S. Steel was formed in 1901 from the merger of 10 steel companies, led by Andrew Carnegie and financed by J. P. Morgan. After the merger, it was the first billion-dollar-sales company in history, and it controlled two-thirds of the U.S. market. To cushion itself against rising energy costs, it bought Marathon Oil Company in 1982 and renamed itself USX Corporation. In 1991, U.S. Steel was spun off as a separate firm, and in 2003, the value of its shares sank to just over $1 billion, the same size as it was a century earlier. Aggressive cost cutting has brought U.S. Steel back, and it is now the second-largest U.S. steel producer behind Mittal Steel USA, which purchased, among other steel firms, the bankrupt assets from Bethlehem Steel, the eighteenth-largest company in the S&P 500 Index in 1957.

American Telephone and Telegraph Co. was the largest company in the world when it joined the S&P 500 Index in 1957, and it remained that way until 1975. The company boasted a market value of $11.2 billion in 1957, a capitalization that would rank in the bottom half of the S&P 500 firms in 2012. The telephone monopoly known as "Ma Bell" was broken up in 1984, giving birth to the "Baby Bell" regional providers. But the stripped-down AT&T was bought by one of its children, SBC Communications, in 2005, and through other acquisitions, it worked itself back to the top 20 in market value in the United States by 2007. The 55-year return on AT&T, had you also held all the Baby Bells when Ma Bell spun them off 23 years ago, would have given you a 9.76 percent annual return, virtually matching the index.

General Motors, which was formed by the consolidation of 17 auto companies in 1908, was destined to become the largest auto producer in the world. But the impact of foreign competition and mounting healthcare obligations forced GM into bankruptcy in 2009 during the Great Recession. The company, however, has reemerged and vies with Toyota as the largest auto manufacturer in the world. Although GM stock went to zero, the value of Delphia, Raytheon, and Electronic Data Systems that the giant automaker spun off before the bankruptcy gave shareholders a meager 3.71 percent annual return since 1957. A slightly better return was offered by Eastman Kodak, which declared bankruptcy in January 2012, but because it had spun off its holdings in the highly successful Eastman Chemical Company in 1994, the parent company managed to offer its shareholders since 1957 about a 6 percent return. This was not the case for stockholders of Bethlehem Steel. The world's second-largest steel company went bankrupt in 2001, and the original stockholders have no assets to show for it. The remaining three firms belong to the materials industry: the returns of Union Carbide (now part of Dow Chemical) have slightly lagged the market, while the returns of DuPont and Alcoa have fallen significantly behind the Index.

TOP-PERFORMING FIRMS

The 20 best-performing firms of the original S&P 500 that have survived with their corporate structure intact are shown in Table 8-2, along with their annual return, sector, and total return per dollar invested. Table 8-3 lists the 20 best-performing firms whether they have survived intact or have been merged into another firm.[4]

By far the best-performing stock is Philip Morris, which in 2003 changed its name to Altria Group and in 2008 spun off its international division (Philip Morris International).[5] Philip Morris introduced the

TABLE 8–2

Returns of 20 Best Performing Original and Surviving S&P 500 Firms 1957–2012

Rank	1957 Name	2012 Name	Ticker	Return	Sector	Accum of $1
1	Philip Morris	Altria Group Inc	MO	19.47%	Consumer staples	$ 19,737.35
2	Abbott Labs	Abbott Laboratories	ABT	15.18%	Healthcare	$ 2,577.27
3	Coca-Cola	Coca Cola Co.	KO	14.68%	Consumer staples	$ 2,025.91
4	Colgate-Palmolive	Colgate Palmolive Co.	CL	14.64%	Consumer staples	$ 1,990.55
5	Bristol-Myers	Bristol Myers Squibb Co.	BMY	14.40%	Healthcare	$ 1,768.50
6	Pepsi-Cola Co.	Pepsico Inc.	PEP	14.13%	Consumer staples	$ 1,547.44
7	Merck & Co.	Merck & Co. Inc. New	MRK	13.95%	Healthcare	$ 1,419.26
8	Heinz	Heinz H J Co.	HNZ	13.80%	Consumer staples	$ 1,317.34
9	Melville Corp.	C V S Caremark Corp.	CVS	13.65%	Consumer staples	$ 1,224.81
10	Sweets Co.	Tootsie Roll Inds.	TR	13.57%	Consumer staples	$ 1,178.92
11	Crane Co.	Crane Co.	CR	13.57%	Industrials	$ 1,178.44
12	Hershey Foods	Hershey Co.	HSY	13.53%	Consumer staples	$ 1,154.02
13	Pfizer Inc.	Pfizer Inc.	PFE	13.38%	Healthcare	$ 1,072.61
14	Equitable Gas	E Q T Corp.	EQT	13.16%	Energy	$ 964.47
15	General Mills	General Mills Inc.	GIS	13.12%	Consumer staples	$ 947.03
16	Oklahoma Nat Gas	Oneok Inc. New	OKE	13.04%	Utilities	$ 907.42
17	Procter & Gamble	Procter & Gamble Co.	PG	13.00%	Consumer staples	$ 890.97
18	Deere & Co.	Deere & Co.	DE	12.86%	Industrials	$ 833.05
19	Kroger Co.	Kroger Company	KR	12.70%	Consumer staples	$ 768.88
20	McGraw-Hill Co.	McGraw Hill Co. Inc.	MHP	12.58%	Consumer discretionary	$ 725.52

TABLE 8–3

Returns of 20 Best Performing Original S&P 500 Firms 1957–2012

Rank	Original Company	Surviving Company	Ann. return
1	Philip Morris	Altria Group, Philip Morris International	19.56%
2	Thatcher Glass	Altria Group, Philip Morris International	18.43%
3	Lane Bryant	Limited Group	17.84%
4	National Can	Privatized	17.71%
5	Dr. Pepper	Privatized	17.09%
6	General Foods	Altria Group, Philip Morris International	17.03%
7	Del Monte Corp.	Altria Group, Philip Morris International	16.51%
8	Standard Brands	Altria Group, Philip Morris International	16.41%
9	National Dairy	Altria Group, Philip Morris International	16.30%
10	Celanese Corp.	Privatized	16.19%
11	RJ Reyonolds Tobacco	Altria Group, Philip Morris International	15.78%
12	National Biscuit	Altria Group, Philip Morris International	15.78%
13	Penick & Ford	Altria Group, Philip Morris International	15.64%
14	Flintkote	British American Tobacco	15.60%
15	Lorillard	Loews Corp	15.29%
16	Abbott Labs	Abbott Labs	15.12%
17	Columbia Pictures	Coca-Cola	14.85%
18	Coca-Cola	Coca-Cola	14.66%
19	Colgate-Palmolive	Colgate-Palmolive	14.64%
20	Bristol-Myers	Bristol-Myers	14.59%

world to the Marlboro Man, one of the world's most recognized icons, two years before the formulation of the S&P 500 Index. Marlboro cigarettes subsequently became the world's best-selling brand and propelled Philip Morris stock upward.

The average annual return on Philip Morris over the past half century, at 19.47 percent per year, almost doubled the 10.07 percent annual return on the S&P 500 Index. This return means that $1,000 invested in Philip Morris on March 1, 1957, would have accumulated to almost $20 million by the end of 2102, more than 100 times the $191,000 accumulation in the S&P 500 Index.

Philip Morris's outstanding performance does not just date from midcentury. Philip Morris was also the best-performing stock since 1925, the date when comprehensive returns on individual stocks were first compiled. From the end of 1925 through the end of 2012, Philip Morris delivered a 17.3 percent compound annual return, 7.7 percent greater than the market indexes. Had your grandmother bought 40 shares (cost of $1,000) of Philip Morris in 1925 and joined its dividend investment plan, her shares would have been worth over $1 *billion* dollars by the end of 2012!

Philip Morris's bounty did not extend to only its own stockholders. Philip Morris eventually became the owner of *10* other original S&P 500 firms. Many investors became enormously wealthy because the shares of their firms were exchanged with shares of successful companies such as Philip Morris. Riding on the coattails of such winners is an unexpected bounty for many stockholders.

HOW BAD NEWS FOR THE FIRM BECOMES GOOD NEWS FOR INVESTORS

Some readers may be surprised that Philip Morris is the top performer for investors in the face of the onslaught of governmental restrictions and legal actions that have cost the firm tens of billions of dollars and at one time threatened the cigarette manufacturer with bankruptcy.

But in the capital markets, bad news for the firm often can be good news for investors who hold onto the stock and reinvest their dividends. If investors become overly pessimistic about the prospects for a stock, the low price enables stockholders who reinvest their dividends to buy the company on the cheap. These reinvested dividends have turned its stock into a pile of gold for those who stuck with Philip Morris.

TOP-PERFORMING SURVIVOR FIRMS

Philip Morris is not the only firm that has served investors well. The return on the other 19 best-performing surviving companies listed in Table 8-2 has beaten the return on the S&P 500 Index by between 2½ and 5 percentage points per year. Of the top 20 firms, 15 belong to two industries: consumer staples, represented by internationally well-known consumer brand-name companies, and healthcare, particularly large pharmaceutical firms. Hershey chocolate, Heinz ketchup, and Tootsie Roll, as well as Coca-Cola and Pepsi-Cola, have built up wide brand equity and consumer trust.

Three other winners are Crane, a manufacturer of engineered industrials products founded in 1855 by Richard Crane; Deere, a manufacturer of agricultural and construction machinery, established in 1840 by John Deere; and McGraw-Hill (now McGraw Hill Financial), a global information provider, founded by James H. McGraw in 1899 and now the owner of Standard & Poor's. In the last five years, this top 10 list has been joined by gas producers EQT, formerly Equitable Gas (founded in 1888 in Pittsburgh), and ONEOK Inc., formerly Oklahoma Natural Gas (founded in 1906).

One firm of particular note is CVS Corporation, which in 1957 entered the S&P 500 Index as Melville Shoe Corp., a company whose name was taken from the founder, Frank Melville, who started a shoe company in 1892 and incorporated as Melville Shoe in 1922. Shoe companies have been among the worst investments over the past century, and even Warren Buffett bemoans his purchase of Dexter Shoe in 1991. But Melville Shoe was fortunate enough to buy the Consumer Value Store chain in 1969, specializing in personal health products. The chain quickly became the most profitable division of the company, and in 1996 Melville changed its name to CVS. So a shoe manufacturer, destined to be a bad investment, turned to gold as a result of the management's fortuitous purchase of a retail drug chain.

There are similar stories for the firms in Table 8-3, which, as noted earlier, lists the 20 best-performing stocks whether they have survived in their original corporate form or have been merged into another firm. Thatcher Glass was the second-best performing of all the original S&P 500 stocks behind Philip Morris and was the leading milk bottle manufacturer in the early 1950s. But as the baby boom turned into the baby bust and glass bottles were replaced by cardboard cartons, Thatcher's business sank. Fortunately for Thatcher shareholders, in 1966 the firm was purchased by Rexall Drug, which became Dart Industries, which merged with Kraft in 1980 and was eventually bought by Philip Morris in 1988. An investor who purchased 100 shares of Thatcher Glass in 1957 and reinvested the dividends would have owned 140,000 shares of Philip Morris stock and an equal number of shares of Phillip Morris International, worth more than $16 million at the end of 2012.

OTHER FIRMS THAT TURNED GOLDEN

As the medical, legal, and popular assault on smoking accelerated through the 1980s, Philip Morris, as well as the other giant tobacco manufacturer, RJ Reynolds, diversified into brand-name food products. In 1985 Philip Morris purchased General Food, and in 1988 it purchased Kraft Foods for $13.5 billion, which had originally been called National Dairy Products and was an original member of the S&P 500 Index. Philip Morris completed its food acquisitions with Nabisco Group Holdings in 2000.

Nabisco Group Holdings was the company that Kohlberg Kravis Roberts & Co. (KKR) spun off in 1991 after taking RJR Nabisco private in 1989 for $29 billion, at that time the largest leveraged buyout in history. Under our methodology for computing long-term returns, if a firm is taken private, the cash from the buyout is assumed to be invested in an S&P 500 Index fund until the company is spun off, at which point the shares are repurchased in the new IPO.[6] RJ Reynolds Tobacco Co. had previously absorbed six original S&P companies: Penick & Ford, California Packing, Del Monte Foods, Cream of Wheat (purchased in 1971 by Nabisco), Standard Brands, and finally National Biscuit Co. in 1985. All these companies became top-20 performers in large part because of their ultimate purchase by Philip Morris.

OUTPERFORMANCE OF ORIGINAL S&P 500 FIRMS

One of the most remarkable aspects of these original 500 firms is that the investor who purchased the original portfolio of 500 stocks and never bought any of the more than 1,000 additional firms that have been added by Standard & Poor's in the subsequent 50 years would have outperformed the dynamic updated index. The return of the original 500 firms is more than 1 percentage point higher than the updated index's 10.07 percent annual return.[7]

Why did this happen? How could the new companies that fueled our economic growth and made America the preeminent economy in the world underperform the older firms? The answer is straightforward. Although the earnings and sales of many of the new firms grew faster than those of the older firms, the price that investors paid for these stocks was simply too high to generate good returns.

Stocks that qualify for entry into the S&P 500 Index must have sufficient market value to be among the 500 largest firms. But a market value this high is often reached because of unwarranted optimism on the part of investors. During the energy crisis of the early 1980s, firms such as Global Marine and Western Co. were added to the energy sector, and they subsequently went bankrupt. In fact, 12 of the 13 energy stocks that were added to the S&P 500 Index during the late 1970s and early 1980s did not subsequently match the performance of either the energy sector or the S&P 500 Index.

About 30 percent of the 125 firms that have been added to the technology sector of the S&P 500 Index since 1957 were added in 1999 and 2000. Needless to say, most of these firms have greatly underperformed the market. The telecommunications sector added virtually no new firms from 1957 through the early 1990s. But in the late 1990s, firms such as WorldCom, Global Crossing, and Quest Communications entered the index with great fanfare, only to collapse afterward.

Of all 10 industrial sectors, only the consumer discretionary sector has added firms that have outperformed the original firms put into the index. This sector was dominated by the auto manufacturers (GM, Chrysler, and then Ford), their suppliers (Firestone and Goodyear), and large retailers, such as JCPenney and Woolworth's.

CONCLUSION

The superior performance of the original S&P 500 firms surprises most investors. But value investors (as described in Chapter 12) know that growth stocks often are priced too high, and excitement over their prospects often induces investors to pay too high a price. Profitable firms that do not catch investors' eyes are often underpriced. If investors reinvest the dividends of such firms, they are buying undervalued shares that will add significantly to their return.

The study of the original 500 companies also gives you an appreciation of the dramatic changes that the U.S. economy has undergone in the past half century. Although, many of the top performers are producing the same brands that they did 50 years earlier, most have aggressively expanded their franchise internationally. Brands such as Heinz ketchup, Coca-Cola, Pepsi-Cola, and Tootsie Roll are as profitable today as they were when these products were launched, some over a hundred years ago.

But we also see that many companies make good investments by being merged into a stronger company. And four of the top-performing original companies—Dr. Pepper, Celanese, National Can, and Flintkote—are now owned by foreign companies. In fact, it is more likely than not that many of the future winners will not be headquartered in the United States. As we noted in Chapter 4, foreign firms, clearly of secondary importance when the S&P 500 Index was founded in 1957, are apt to be the ultimate owners of many of today's top firms.

The Impact of Taxes on Stock and Bond Returns

Stocks Have the Edge

In this world nothing is certain but death and taxes.
—BENJAMIN FRANKLIN[1]

The power to tax involves the power to destroy.
—JOHN MARSHALL[2]

For all long-term investors, there is only one objective—maximum total real return after taxes.
—JOHN TEMPLETON[3]

John Templeton's objective to maximize total real return after taxes is an essential investment strategy. And stocks are very well suited to this purpose. In contrast to fixed-income investments, both capital gains and dividends are treated favorably by the U.S. tax code. So in addition to having superior before-tax returns, stocks often hold an even larger after-tax advantage over bonds.

HISTORICAL TAXES ON INCOME AND CAPITAL GAINS

Figure 9-1 plots the historical marginal tax rate at three income levels: the highest tax bracket, the tax rate for income of $150,000, and the tax

FIGURE 9–1

Federal Tax Rates on Interest and Dividend Income and Capital Gains 1913–2012

Figure A

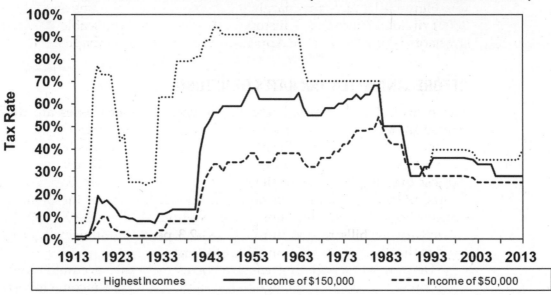

Tax Rates on Interest Income (and Dividends before 2003)

Figure B

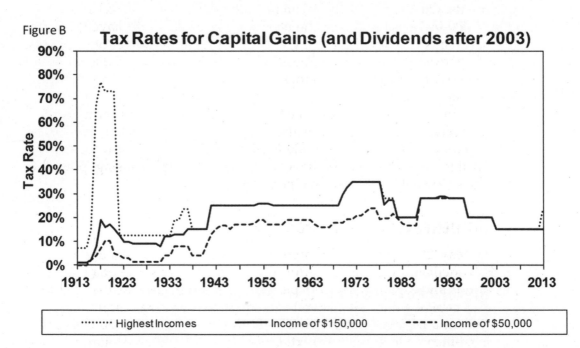

Tax Rates for Capital Gains (and Dividends after 2003)

rate for real income of $50,000 all adjusted to 2012 dollars. Figure 9-1A is the tax rate for ordinary income (including interest income) from 1913, when the federal income tax was established, and for dividends until 2003, when the dividend tax was set at the same rate as the capital gains tax. Figure 9-1B plots the marginal tax rate for capital gains and (since 2003) dividend income. A history of the tax code applicable to stock investors is provided in the Appendix at the end of this chapter.

BEFORE- AND AFTER-TAX RATES OF RETURN

The historical real after-tax returns for various asset classes are displayed in Table 9-1 for four tax brackets. Since 1913, when the federal income tax was instituted, the after-tax real return on stocks has ranged from 6.1 percent for untaxed investors to 2.7 percent for investors in the highest bracket who realize their capital gains each year. For taxable bonds, the real annual return ranges from 2.2 percent for the untaxed investor to –0.3 for the investor in the maximum tax bracket, while the real return on bills ranges from 0.4 to –2.3 percent. Municipal bonds have realized a 1.3 percent annual real return since 1913.

Despite the debilitating effect of taxes on equity accumulations, taxes cause the greatest damage to the returns on fixed-income investments. On an after-tax basis, an investor in the top tax bracket who put $1,000 in Treasury bills at the beginning of 1946 would have $138 after taxes and after inflation today, a *loss* in purchasing power of more than 86 percent. Instead, a highest-bracket investor would have turned $1,000 into over $5,719 in stocks, a 470 percent increase in purchasing power.

In fact, for someone in the highest tax bracket, short-term Treasury bills have yielded a negative after-tax real return since 1871, even lower if state and local taxes are taken into account. In contrast, top-bracket taxable investors would have increased their purchasing power in stocks 288-fold over the same period.

THE BENEFITS OF DEFERRING CAPITAL GAINS TAXES

In May 2003 President George W. Bush signed the Jobs and Growth Reconciliation Act, which reduced the highest tax rate on qualified dividends and capital gains to 15 percent. This is the first time that dividend and capital gains taxes have been equalized for a significant length of time at a preferential rate. In 2013 both taxes were set at 20 percent for high-income investors. Nevertheless, *effective* taxes on capital gains are

After-Tax Real Returns on Stocks, Bonds, and Bills for Various Income Levels, 1802–2012

		Stocks Tax Bracket				Bonds Tax Bracket				Bills Tax Bracket				Muni Bds	Gold	CPI
		$0	$50K	$150K	Max	$0	$50K	$150K	Max	$0	$50K	$150K	Max			
Period	1802–2012	6.6	5.7	5.4	5.0	3.6	2.9	2.7	2.4	2.7	2.2	1.7	1.4	3.1	0.7	1.4
	1871–2012	6.5	5.2	4.7	4.1	3.0	2.0	1.7	1.2	1.6	0.8	0.1	-0.4	2.2	1.0	2.0
	1913–2012	6.1	4.2	3.6	2.7	2.2	0.8	0.3	-0.3	0.4	-0.7	-1.6	-2.3	1.3	1.2	3.2
Major Sub-Periods	I 1802–1870	6.7	6.7	6.7	6.7	4.8	4.8	4.8	4.8	5.1	5.1	5.1	5.1	5.0	0.2	0.1
	II 1871–1925	6.6	6.6	6.5	6.2	3.7	3.7	3.6	3.4	3.1	3.1	3.0	2.7	3.3	-0.8	0.6
	III 1926–2012	6.4	4.4	3.7	2.8	2.6	1.0	0.4	-0.2	0.6	-0.6	-1.7	-2.2	1.5	2.1	3.0
	1946–2012	6.4	4.0	3.3	2.8	2.0	0.0	-0.5	-1.0	0.4	-1.1	-2.4	-3.1	1.1	2.0	3.9
Postwar Periods	1946–1965	10.0	7.0	5.2	3.9	-1.2	-2.0	-2.7	-3.5	-0.8	-1.5	-2.3	-2.7	-0.6	-2.7	2.8
	1966–1981	-0.4	-2.2	-3.0	-3.3	-4.2	-6.2	-7.0	-7.5	-0.2	-3.0	-5.2	-6.1	-1.0	8.8	7.0
	1982–1999	13.6	9.4	9.1	9.1	8.5	5.0	4.5	4.5	2.9	0.8	-0.8	-1.7	2.7	-4.9	3.3
	1982–2012	7.8	5.5	5.3	5.3	7.6	4.8	4.4	4.3	1.6	0.1	-1.0	-1.7	3.4	1.8	2.9

*Federal income tax only. Assume 1-year holding period for capital gain portion of return.

still lower than on dividends since taxes on capital gains are paid only when the asset is sold, not as the gain is accrued. The advantage of this tax deferral is that the return from capital gains accumulates at the higher before-tax rates rather than the after-tax rates, as would be the case from reinvested dividends. I call the advantage of capital gains over dividend income the "deferral benefit."

For long-term investors the advantage of the deferral benefit can be substantial. For example, take two stocks, one yielding 10 percent per year in dividend income and the other yielding 10 percent per year solely in capital gains. Assume an investor is taxed 20 percent on dividends and capital gains. For an untaxed investor, both investments would yield identical 10 percent returns. But the after-tax yield on the dividend-paying stock is 8.0 percent per year, while, if the investor waits for 30 years before selling the capital gains–paying stock, the after-tax return is 9.24 percent per year. This is only 76 basis points less than the return of an untaxed investor.

Therefore, from a tax standpoint, there is still a motivation for firms to deliver capital gains as opposed to dividend income. This is unfortunate since, as we shall note in Chapter 12, dividend-paying stocks generally yield better before- and after-tax returns than non-dividend-paying stocks. The government can put dividends on the same tax basis as capital gains if the tax authorities allow investors to obtain a tax deferral on reinvested dividends until the stock is sold.

INFLATION AND THE CAPITAL GAINS TAX

In the United States, capital gains taxes are paid on the difference between the price of an asset when it is purchased (its *nominal price*) and the value (price) of that asset when it is sold, with no adjustment made for inflation. This nominally based tax system means that an asset that appreciates by less than the rate of inflation—resulting in a loss of purchasing power—will nevertheless be taxed upon sale.

Although the appreciation of stock prices generally compensates investors for increases in the rate of inflation, especially in the long run, a tax code based on *nominal* prices penalizes investors in an inflationary environment. For a given real return, even a moderate inflation rate of 3 percent causes an investor with a five-year average holding period to lose 60 basis points per year compared with the after-tax return that would result if the inflation rate were zero. If the inflation rate rises to 6 percent, the decline in annual return rises to 112 basis points per year. I call this effect the "inflation tax." The inflation tax for various inflation

rates and various holding periods under the current tax system is displayed in Figure 9-2.[4]

The inflation tax has a far more devastating effect on after-tax real
returns when the holding period is short than when it is long. This is
because the more frequently an investor buys and sells assets, the more
frequently the government can tax the nominal capital gain, which
might not be a real, after-inflation gain at all.

There is considerable support, both inside and outside government, to make some adjustment for inflation in the tax system. In 1986,
the U.S. Treasury proposed the indexation of capital gains, but this provision was never enacted into law. In 1997, the House of Representatives
included capital gains indexation in its tax law, but it was removed by
House-Senate conferees under threat of a presidential veto. Under these
plans, investors would pay taxes on only that portion of the gain (if any)

FIGURE 9–2

Real After-Tax Return and Inflation for Various Holding Periods Under 2013 Tax Law

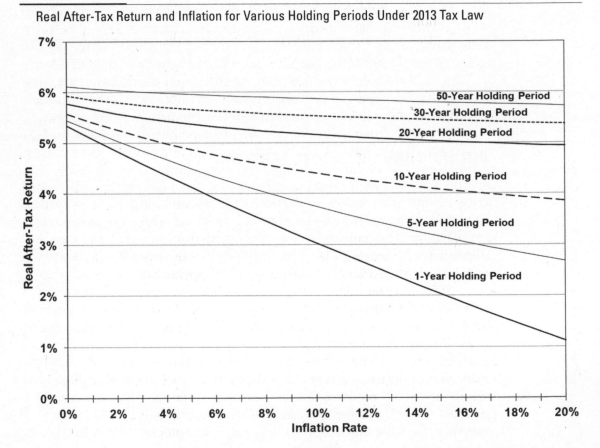

that exceeded the increase in the price level over the holding period of the asset. Since inflation has remained low in recent years, there is less pressure to adjust the capital gains tax for inflation, and legislation to correct this defect is dormant.

INCREASINGLY FAVORABLE TAX FACTORS FOR EQUITIES

Despite the passage of the American Taxpayer Relief Act of 2012, which raised the top rate on dividends and capital gains to 20 percent (23.8 percent if the Medicare tax is included), there have been some very favorable tax developments for stockholders over the last several decades. They include the following:

1. A reduction in the capital gains tax rate from a maximum of 35 percent in 1978 to 23.8 percent and comparable reductions for lower-bracket taxpayers[5]
2. Lower inflation, which reduces the inflation tax imposed on nominal capital gains
3. A switch to capital gains from dividends, which increases the deferral benefit

Until 2003, when the tax rate on dividends was for the first time decoupled from the tax rate on ordinary income, the tax rate on dividends ranged as high as 90 percent in the immediate postwar period.

As noted above, since the tax law is based on only nominal values unadjusted for inflation, inflation imposes an additional tax on capital gains. The inflation rate has fallen from double-digit levels in 1979 to the 2 to 3 percent level in the past decade. Since tax brackets are indexed to inflation, the tax rate on dividends is not directly affected by inflation. Furthermore, since the capital gains tax is based on realizations instead of accruals, firms have been buying back shares, in lieu of paying dividends, and generating more capital gains income. As a result, the average dividend yield has fallen from about 5 percent before 1980 to only 2 percent in more recent years.

It can be calculated that all these factors have increased the real after-tax return on stocks by about 2 percentage points over the past 30 years for a *given* before-tax return. Although the real after-tax return on bonds has also increased as a result of the drop in the tax rates on ordinary income, the increase in the real return on stocks has been greater. In any equilibrium model of asset pricing, the favorable tax factors for equities suggest that stocks should be priced at a higher multiple of earnings, an issue that will be discussed in Chapter 10.

STOCKS OR BONDS IN TAX-DEFERRED ACCOUNTS?

The most important savings vehicles for many individuals are their tax-deferred accounts (TDAs) such as Keogh, IRA, and 401(k) plans. Many investors hold most of their stock (if they hold any at all) in their tax-deferred accounts, while they hold primarily fixed-income assets in their taxable accounts.

Yet many of the recent changes in the tax laws argue that investors should do the opposite. Dividends will enjoy the lower tax rates, and appreciation on shares will gain the lower capital gains tax advantage only if they are held in taxable accounts. This is because when a tax-deferred account is cashed out at retirement, an individual pays the full ordinary income tax on the entire withdrawal regardless of how much of the accumulation has been realized through capital gains and how much through dividend income.

The above counsel, however, ignores two factors. First, if you are an active trader or buy mutual funds that actively trade, then there may be significant capital gains realized, some short run, that would be best kept in a tax-deferred account. Trading in tax-deferred accounts also does not require complicated tax computations since no taxes are paid until money is withdrawn and the source of the profits is of no consequence.

Second, although the government taxes capital gains and dividends at ordinary rates when withdrawn from a TDA, the government also shares more of the risk. If you realize a capital loss in a taxable account, the government limits your ability to offset this loss against ordinary income. However, when funds are withdrawn from a tax-deferred account, the full withdrawal is treated as taxable income, so that all losses become totally deductible from taxable income. Therefore, there is less after-tax risk by putting one's savings in tax-deferred accounts.

When all the factors are considered, it is better for most investors to hold stocks in their taxable accounts, unless they are active traders. If you have a long horizon, the possibility that you will have a loss in your stock accounts is minimal, so the loss-sharing aspect of TDAs is less important. It is advisable, though, to hold stocks that do not pay tax-qualified dividends, such as REITs and other income trusts, in your tax-deferred account to avoid current taxes. However, some risk-averse investors who are reluctant to hold stocks in their personal accounts because of short-term volatility find it easier to hold stocks in their retirement accounts where they have a longer-term perspective and may be better able to tolerate short-term losses.

CONCLUSION

Tax planning is important to maximize returns from financial assets. Because of favorable dividend and capital gains tax rates and the potential to defer those capital gains taxes, stocks hold a significant tax advantage over fixed-income assets. These advantages have risen in recent years, as capital gains and dividend taxes have been reduced, inflation has remained low, and firms have repurchased shares to increase capital gains. These favorable developments have increased the after-tax return of equities by about 2 percentage points over the average after-tax return of the past 50 years. As favorable as stocks are over bonds for long-term investors, the tax advantage of equities is even greater.

APPENDIX: HISTORY OF THE TAX CODE

Federal income tax was first collected under the Revenue Act of 1913, when the Sixteenth Amendment to the U.S. Constitution was ratified. Until 1921 no tax preference was given to capital gains income. When tax rates were increased sharply during World War I, investors refrained from realizing gains and complained to Congress about the tax consequences of selling their assets. Congress was persuaded that such "frozen portfolios" were detrimental to the efficient allocation of capital, and so in 1922 a maximum tax rate of 12.5 percent was established on capital gains income. This rate became effective when taxable income reached $30,000, which is equivalent to about $240,000 in today's dollars.

In 1934, a new tax code was enacted that, for the first time, excluded a portion of capital gains from taxable income. This exclusion allowed middle-income investors, and not just the rich, to enjoy the tax benefits of capital gains income. The excluded portion of the gain depended on the length of time that the asset was held; there was no exclusion if the asset was held 1 year or less, but the exclusion was increased to 70 percent if the asset was held more than 10 years. Since marginal tax rates ranged up to 79 percent in 1936, the effective maximum tax on very long-term gains was reduced to about 24 percent.

In 1938, the tax code was amended again to provide for a 50 percent exclusion of capital gains income if an asset was held more than 18 months, but in no case would the tax exceed 15 percent on such capital gains. The maximum rate on capital gains income was raised to 25 percent in 1942, but the holding period was reduced to 6 months. Except for a 1 percent surtax that raised the maximum rate to 26 percent during the Korean War, the 25 percent rate held until 1969.

In 1969, the maximum tax rate on capital gains in excess of $50,000 was phased out over a number of years, so ultimately the 50 percent exclusion applied to all tax rates. Since the maximum rate on ordinary income was 70 percent, this meant the maximum tax rate on capital gains rose to 35 percent by 1973. In 1978, the exclusion was raised to 60 percent, which lowered the effective maximum tax rate on capital gains to 28 percent. When the maximum tax rate on ordinary income was reduced to 50 percent in 1982, the maximum tax rate on capital gains was again reduced to 20 percent.

In 1986, the tax code was extensively altered to reduce and simplify the tax structure and ultimately eliminate the distinction between capital gains and ordinary income. By 1988, the maximum tax rates for capital gains and ordinary income were identical, at 33 percent. For the first time since 1922, there was no preference for capital gains income. In 1990, the top rate was lowered to 28 percent on both ordinary and capital gains income. In 1991, a slight wedge was reopened between capital gains and ordinary income: the top rate on the latter was raised to 31 percent, while the former remained at 28 percent. In 1993, President Clinton raised tax rates again, increasing the top rate on ordinary income to 39.6 percent while keeping the capital gains tax unchanged. In 1997, Congress lowered the maximum capital gains tax to 20 percent for assets held more than 18 months and the following year returned to the 12-month capital gains period. Starting in 2001, investors could take advantage of a new 18 percent top capital gains rate for assets held at least 5 years.

In 2003 President Bush signed into law legislation that lowered the top rate on capital gains and qualified dividend income to 15 percent. Qualified dividend income must come from taxable enterprises, not "flow-through" organizations such as real estate investment trusts or investment companies. In 2013 the top bracket on capital gains was raised to 20 percent for married couples earning over $450,000, and for the first time a Medicare surtax of 3.8 percent was applied to investment income for couples earning more than $250,000. The tax rates on qualified dividend income were set equal to the new capital gains tax rates.

Sources of Shareholder Value

Earnings and Dividends

> *The importance of dividends for providing wealth to investors is self-evident. Dividends not only dwarf inflation, growth, and changing valuations levels individually, but they also dwarf the combined importance of inflation, growth, and changing valuation levels.*
>
> —Robert Arnott, 2003[1]

It is just after 4 p.m. eastern time, and the major U.S. stock exchanges have just closed. The anchorperson of one of the major financial networks excitedly proclaims: "Intel just out with its earnings! It 'beat the Street' by 20 cents, and its price has jumped $2 in after-hours trading."

Earnings drive stock prices, and their announcements are eagerly awaited by Wall Street. But exactly how should we calculate earnings, and how do firms turn these earnings into stockholder value? This chapter addresses those questions.

DISCOUNTED CASH FLOWS

The fundamental source of asset values derives from the expected cash flows that can be obtained from owning that asset. For stocks these cash flows come from dividends or from cash distributions resulting from earnings or the sale of the firm's assets. Stock prices also depend on the rate at which these future cash flows are discounted. Future cash flows are *discounted* because cash received in the future is not valued as highly as cash received in the present. The reasons investors discount the future are (1) the existence of a *risk-free rate*, a yield on a safe alternative asset such as government or other AAA-rated securities, which allows investors the ability to transform a dollar invested today into a greater sum tomorrow; (2) *inflation*, which reduces the purchasing power of cash received in the future, and (3) the risk associated with the *magnitudes* of expected cash flows, which induces investors of risky assets, such as stocks, to demand a premium to that on safe securities. The sum of these three factors—the risk-free rate, the inflation premium, and the equity risk premium—determines the discount rate for equities. This discount rate is also called the *required return on equity* or the *cost of equity*.

SOURCES OF SHAREHOLDER VALUE

Earnings are the source of cash flows to shareholders. *Earnings* (also called *profits* or *net income*) are the difference between the revenues to the firm and the costs of production. The costs of production include all labor and material costs, interest on debt, taxes, and allowances for depreciation.

Firms can transform these earnings into cash flows to shareholders in a number of ways. The first and historically the most important is *payment of cash dividends*.

Earnings that are not used to pay dividends are called *retained earnings*. Retained earnings create value by raising future cash flows through:

- Retirement of debt, which reduces interest expense
- Investment in securities or other assets, including the acquisition of other firms
- Investment in capital projects designed to increase future profits
- Repurchase of the firm's own shares (which is known as a *buyback*)

If a firm retires its debt, it reduces its interest expense and therefore increases the profits available to pay dividends. If a firm buys assets, the income from these assets is available to pay future dividends. Retained earnings can be used to expand the capital of the firm in order to generate higher future revenues and/or reduce costs and thereby increase future cash flows to shareholders. Finally, if a firm repurchases its shares, it reduces the number of shares outstanding and thus increases *per share* earnings and permits an increase in per share dividends.

The last source of value, buybacks, deserves some elaboration. Clearly shareholders who sell their shares to the company receive cash for their stock. But those shareholders who do not sell will realize greater *per share* earnings and *per share* dividends in the future as the firm's earnings are divided among a smaller number of shares. It should be noted that at the time of the buyback, there is no change in the price of shares as one asset is exchanged for another. But *over time* buybacks increase the growth in per share earnings, and this increases the price of shares, generating capital gains that replace the dividends the shareholders would have received.

HISTORICAL DATA ON DIVIDENDS AND EARNINGS GROWTH

Figure 10-1 plots real per share reported earnings and real per share dividends in the United States from 1871 through 2012 for the S&P 500 Index and aggregate real corporate profits, which come from the national income and product accounts (NIPA), which were first calculated for 1929. Table 10-1 summarizes these data. Over the whole period, dividends are by far the most important source of shareholder return. From 1871 the real return on stocks has averaged 6.48 percent, composed of an average dividend yield of 4.40 percent and real capital gains of 1.99 percent. The capital gains have been generated almost entirely by the growth of per share earnings, which have increased at an annual rate of 1.77 percent over the past 140 years.[2]

Table 10-1 also shows that there has been a significant change in the mix of dividends and earnings since World War II. The growth rate of per share earnings has increased, while the dividend payout ratio and the dividend yield have decreased. Before World War II, firms paid two-

T A B L E   10–1

Dividends, Earnings, and Payout Data for Various Historical Periods

Summary	Reported EPS Growth	Dividend Growth	Dividend Yield	Capital Gains	Stock Returns	Payout Ratio	NIPA Profits
1871–2012	1.77%	1.35%	4.40%	1.99%	6.48%	61.3%	
1871–1945	0.69%	0.77%	5.26%	1.03%	6.61%	71.8%	
1946–2012	2.97%	1.99%	3.43%	3.07%	6.35%	49.6%	4.08%
1929–2012	1.85%	1.20%	3.85%	2.09%	5.69%	55.6%	3.22%

FIGURE   10–1

Real per Share Reported Earnings, Dividends, and NIPA (National Income and Product Account) Profits 1871–2012

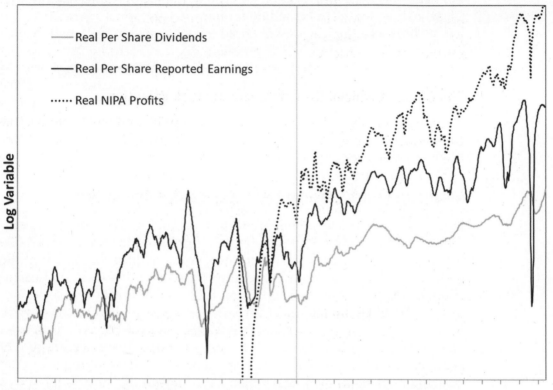

thirds of their earnings as dividends. Since retained earnings were too small to fund expansion, firms issued more shares to obtained needed capital, thereby reducing per share earnings growth. However, in the postwar period, firms reduced dividends and generated sufficient earnings so that the need to issue new shares to finance growth declined. This is why in the postwar period per share earnings growth increased significantly.

As noted earlier, from 1929 on, we have data on corporate profits from NIPA.[3] These profits grow significantly faster than earnings per share because over time firms increase the number of shares to finance capital expansion.

There are several reasons why firms have reduced the dividend payout ratio since World War II. After the war, tax rates on dividends increased sharply. Even when the tax rate on dividends is set equal to the rate on capital gains, there is still a disadvantage since capital gains taxes can be deferred while dividend taxes cannot. Second, since options are based on share price alone, it is in the interest of management who receive such options to follow a low-dividend policy, which boosts share prices. These changes have reduced the share of dividends in the total return to shareholders.

The Gordon Dividend Growth Model of Stock Valuation

To show how dividend policy impacts the price of a stock, we use the *Gordon dividend growth model* developed by Roger Gordon in 1962.[4] Since the price of a stock is the present value of all future dividends, it can be shown that if future dividends per share grow at a constant rate g, then the price per share of a stock P, which is the discounted value of all future dividends, can be written as follows:

$$P = d/(1 + r) + d(1 + g)/(1 + r)^2 + d(1 + g)^2/(1 + r)^3 + \ldots$$

or

$$P = d/(r - g)$$

where d is the dividend per share, g is the rate of growth of future dividends per share, and r is the required return on equity, which is the sum of the risk-free rate, the expected rate of inflation, and the equity risk premium.

Since the Gordon model formula is a function of the per share dividend and the per share dividend growth rate, it appears that dividend policy is crucial to determining the value of the stock. But as long as one specific condition holds—*that the firm earns the same return on its retained earnings as its required return on equity*—then future dividend policy does not impact the price of the stock or the market value of the firm.[5] This is because dividends not paid today become retained earnings that generate higher dividends in the future, and it can be shown that the present value of those dividends is unchanged, no matter when they are paid.

The management can, of course, influence the time path of dividends. The lower the *dividend payout ratio*, which is the ratio of dividends to earnings, the smaller the dividends will be in the near future. But because a lower dividend today increases retained earnings, future dividends will rise and eventually exceed the level of dividends that would have prevailed if the dividend payout ratio was not cut. Assuming the firm earns the same return on its retained earnings as it does on its equity capital, the present value of these dividend streams will be identical no matter what payout ratio is chosen.

This equivalence can be shown by using the Gordon dividend growth model. Let us assume that the discount rate r is 10 percent, that there is no growth ($g = 0$), that the dividend d is \$10 per share, and that the firm pays out all its earnings as dividends. In this case the price of the shares would be \$100. Now assume that the firm lowered its dividend payout ratio from 100 percent to 90 percent, thereby reducing its per share dividend (d) to \$9 and increasing its retained earnings by \$1.

If the firm earns 10 percent on its retained earnings, then earnings per share next year will be \$10.10, and the dividend, at a 90 percent payout ratio, will be \$9.09. If the firm maintains this payout ratio, the growth rate in per share dividends will be 1 percent. Setting $g = 0.01$ and $d = \$9$ into the Gordon growth model yields the same \$10 price of the stock as before. As long as r remains at 10 percent, the price per share of the stock will rise at 1 percent a year, identical to the growth of per share earnings and per share dividends, and the total return to shareholders will remain at 10 percent, with 9 percentage points of the return coming from the dividend yield and 1 percentage point coming from stock appreciation. The firm can choose any proportion of the return that comes from dividends and capital gains by varying the dividend payout ratio from zero to 100 percent, but the return to stockholders remains at 10 percent.

The exact same result would hold if the firm used its retained earnings to buy back shares. In the case above, the \$1 not used to pay dividends would be used to purchase 1 percent of the shares per year. The 1 percent reduction in the number of shares would mean that *per share* dividends (and *per share* earnings) will rise by 1 percent per year.

This theory is borne out by the long-run data shown in Table 10-1. Before World War II, the average dividend payout ratio was 71.8 percent, and since then, it has fallen to 49.6 percent. This reduced the dividend yield from 5.26 to 3.43 percent, almost 2 percentage points. But capital gains have risen by about 2 percentage points, so that the total returns before and after World War II are approximately equal. The lower dividend yield has resulted in an acceleration of per share earnings growth from 0.69 to 2.8 percent.

It should be noted that although the rate of growth of the forward-looking dividend per share increases after the dividend payout ratio is cut, the rate of growth of dividends will for many years be less than the growth rate of dividends if measured from a time period before the dividend cut. This is indeed what the historical data show in Table 10-1, as the rate of growth of dividends per share has lagged behind that of per share earnings or price appreciation However, if the dividend payout ratio does not continue to fall, theory dictates that the dividend growth rate will accelerate in coming years.

Discount Dividends, Not Earnings

Although earnings determine the amount of dividends paid by the firm, the price of the stock is always equal to the present value of all future *dividends* and not the present value of future earnings. Earnings not paid to investors can have value only if they are paid as dividends or other cash disbursements at a later date. Valuing stock as the present discounted value of future *earnings* is manifestly wrong and greatly overstates the value of a firm.[6]

John Burr Williams, one of the greatest investment analysts of the early part of the last century and the author of the classic *Theory of Investment Value*, argued this point persuasively in 1938:

> Most people will object at once to the foregoing formula for valuing stocks by saying that it should use the present worth of future earnings, not future dividends. But should not earnings and dividends both give the same answer under the implicit assumptions of our critics? If earnings not paid out in dividends are all successfully reinvested at compound interest for the benefit of the stockholder, as the critics imply, then these earnings should produce dividends later; if not, then they are money lost. Earnings are only a means to an end, and the means should not be mistaken for the end.[7]

EARNINGS CONCEPTS

Clearly dividends cannot be paid on a sustained basis unless the firm is profitable. As a result, it is critical that a definition of earnings be developed that gives investors the best possible measure of the sustainable cash that the firm can generate for the payment of dividends.

Earnings, which, as we noted, are also called *net income* or *profit*, are the difference between revenues and costs. But the determination of earnings is not just a "cash-in minus cash-out" calculation, since many costs and revenues, such as capital expenditures, depreciation, and contracts for future delivery, extend over many years. Furthermore, some expenses and revenues are onetime or "extraordinary" items, such as capital gains and losses or major restructurings, and they do not add meaningfully to the picture of the ongoing profitability or sustainability of earnings that are so important in valuing a firm. Because of these issues, there is no single "right" concept of earnings.

Earnings Reporting Methods

There are two principal ways that firms report their earnings. *Net income* or *reported earnings* are those earnings sanctioned by the Financial Accounting Standards Board (FASB), an organization founded in 1973 to establish accounting standards. These standards are called the *generally accepted accounting principles* (GAAP), and they are used to compute the earnings that appear in the annual report and are filed with government agencies.[8]

The other, often more generous, concept of earnings is called *operating earnings*, which often exclude onetime events such as restructuring charges (expenses associated with a firm's closing a plant or selling a division), investment gains and losses, inventory write-offs, expenses associated with mergers and spin-offs, and depreciation or impairment of "goodwill," among others. But the term *operating earnings* is not defined by FASB, and this gives firms latitude to interpret what is and what is not excluded. There are circumstances where the same specific type of charge may be included in operating earnings for one company and omitted from another.

There are two principal versions of operating earnings. Standard & Poor's calculates a very strict version that differs from GAAP reported earnings only by excluding asset impairments (including inventory write-downs) and severance pay associated with such impairments. However, when firms report their earnings, they frequently exclude many more items, such as litigation costs, pension costs associated with changing market rates or return assumptions, stock option expenses, etc. We shall call the earnings that are reported by firms *firm operating earnings*, although the terms *non-GAAP earnings*, *pro forma earnings*, and *earnings from continuing operations* are also used.

Table 10-2 summarizes items that are included and excluded from earnings for nonfinancial companies.[9] For financial companies, virtually all these items are included in both S&P operating earnings and the earnings reported by the firms, as well as GAAP earnings. Figure 10-2 plots these GAAP, S&P, and firm operating earnings for S&P 500 companies from 1967 to the present.

From 1988 forward, when all three earnings series were available, S&P operating earnings averaged 16.5 percent above reported (GAAP) earnings, and firm-reported operating earnings averaged 3.2 percent above S&P operating earnings. During recessions, and particularly the 2007–2009 Great Recession, the gaps between these earnings concepts

TABLE 10–2

Dividends, Earnings, and Payout Data for Various Historical Periods

	GAAP EPS	S&P Operating EPS	Non-GAAP EPS
Asset Impairments (incl. inventory write-down)	Included	Excluded	Excluded
Severance costs	Included	Excluded*	Excluded
Cash plant closing costs	Included	Included	Excluded
Litigation	Included	Included	Excluded
Pension fair value charges	Included	Included	Excluded
Stock option expense	Included	Included	Usually Included*

* Except when associated with asset impairment

FIGURE 10–2

Three Measures of Earnings Per Share: GAAP, S&P Operating, and Firm Operating, 1975–2012

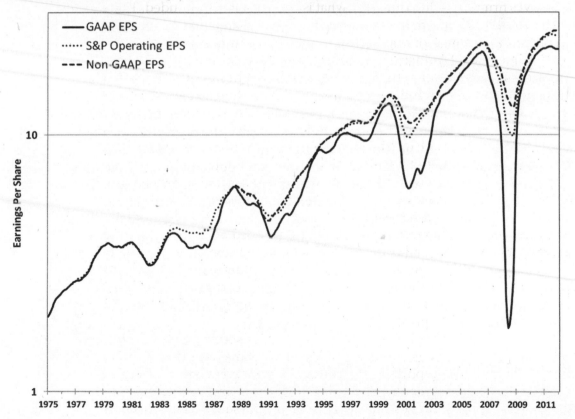

widened significantly. In 2008, firm operating earnings were $50.84, and S&P reported earnings were $39.61, while GAAP reported earnings fell to $12.54.

It is often assumed that "reported earnings" better represent the true earnings of a firm than operating earnings. But that is not necessarily true. In fact, the increasing conservatism of FASB standards, especially as related to the required write-down of asset values, has resulted in severe downward biases to reported earnings. These write-downs were mandated by SFAS (Statement of Financial Account Standard) Rules 142 and 144, issued in 2001, which required any impairments to the value of property, plant, equipment, and other intangibles (such as goodwill acquired by purchasing stock above book value) be marked to market, and previously by Rule 115, issued in 1993, which stated that securities of financial institutions held for trading or "available for sale" were required to be carried at fair market value.[10] These new standards required firms to "write down" asset values regardless of whether the asset was sold or not. These rules are especially severe in economic downturns when market prices are depressed.[11] On the other hand, firms are not allowed to write tangible fixed assets back up, even if they recover from a previous markdown, unless they are sold and recorded as "capital gains" income.[12]

A striking example of earnings distortion is Time Warner's purchase of America Online (AOL) for $214 billion in January 2000 at the peak of the Internet boom. AOL, a member of the S&P 500 Index at that time, registered a huge capital gain for shareholders when the firm was acquired by Time Warner, also an S&P 500 member, as the purchase price was far above book value. But that capital gain was never recorded in the S&P earnings data. In 2002, after the Internet bubble popped, Time Warner was forced to write down its investment in AOL by $99 billion, at that time the largest loss ever recorded by an American corporation. The combined profits and market value of AOL and Time Warner were not materially different after the tech bubble than before, but because the capital gain on AOL shares was never included as earnings, the aggregate earnings of the S&P 500 Index fell dramatically when AOL's market price tumbled. Many other firms during that period also took large write-downs on acquired assets while the profits realized by the acquired firm upon purchase were never recorded.

Operating Earnings and NIPA Profits

Looking back at Figure 10-1, we can see that the outsized declines in S&P reported earnings during the two most recent recessions differed sharply not only from the behavior of the S&P in previous recessions but also from the behavior of after-tax corporate profits reported by the Bureau of Economic Analysis (BEA), which computes NIPA. In every recession before 1990 except 1937–1938, the decline in S&P reported earnings was *less than* the decline in NIPA profits. In fact, the average magnitude of the decline in S&P reported earnings in recessions before 1990 averaged just slightly over one-half that reported by NIPA profits. But in the last three recessions, S&P reported profits fell by more than twice as much as NIPA profits. In the 1990 recession, S&P reported profits fell 43 percent while NIPA fell only 4 percent; in the 2001 recession, S&P reported profits fell 55 percent while NIPA declined 24 percent; and in the Great Recession, NIPA fell 53 percent while S&P reported earnings declined 92 percent. It is particularly striking that the decline in S&P reported earnings in the 2008–2009 recession, where the maximum decline in GDP was just over 5 percent, was much greater than the 63 percent decline in S&P's recorded earnings in the Great Depression, which was five times as deep. In fact, NIPA corporate profits were negative in 1931 and 1932, which is not surprising given the severity of the economic decline. These disparities suggest that recent FASB rulings have resulted in much lower earnings, particularly in economic downturns.[13]

But recent FASB rulings are not the only reason GAAP often *understates* the true profitability of firms. Research and development costs are routinely expensed, although there is good reason to capitalize these expenditures and then depreciate them over time.[14] This means that the earnings of firms with a high level of R&D expenditures, such as the pharmaceutical industry, may understate their economic earnings.

For example, Pfizer, one of the world's largest pharmaceutical firms, spent about $8 billion in 2012 on research and development and about $1.5 billion on plant and equipment. Governed by current accounting rules, Pfizer subtracted from its earnings only 5 percent of the money it spent on plant and equipment as depreciation, and the remainder would be deducted over the useful life of these "brick-and-mortar" assets.

But 100 percent of the $8 billion Pfizer spent on research and development must be subtracted from its earnings. This is because Pfizer's R&D is not considered an asset under GAAP accounting rules, and it must be expensed. This treatment also applies to the technology sector. The tangible, depreciable assets of Google and Facebook are a tiny fraction of their market value. For many industries whose products are the result of research and development and patentable innovations, all standard earnings measures will understate the true earnings potential of these firms.

Inflation also distorts GAAP earnings. As inflation rises, so do interest rates. Nevertheless, all interest expenses are deducted from corporate earnings even though inflation often causes an equal if not greater reduction in the real value of corporate debt. In inflationary times the impact of rising prices on fixed corporate liabilities can be substantial and can give rise to sharply lower accounting earnings than true earnings of firms.

It is true that inflation also creates some upward biases to firms' profits. Depreciation is based on historical prices, and hence in inflationary times the charges taken for depreciation may be insufficient to cover the cost of replacing and upgrading the capital. Also the capital gains that firms earn on their inventories during inflation do not represent an increase in earnings capability.[15] That is why NIPA makes an adjustment for depreciation and inventory profits when computing the profits earned by corporations, although it doesn't make any adjustment for the change in the real value of the debt. When all factors are taken into consideration, reported corporate profits during inflationary times likely understate the true earnings of corporations.

The Quarterly Earnings Report

The difference between the operating earnings a firm reports and what traders expect is what drives stock prices during the "earnings season," which occurs primarily in the three-week period following the end of each quarter. When we hear that XYZ Corporation "beat the Street," it invariably means that its earnings came in above the consensus forecast of *operating* earnings.[16]

But the published consensus estimates do not always match the expectations built into the price of the stock at the time the announcements are made. This is because analysts and traders who monitor companies closely often come up with estimates that differ from the consensus. These estimates, frequently referred to as the *whisper estimates* because they are not widely disseminated, are the ones built into the price of the stock. More often than not, these whisper estimates are higher than the ones that circulate as the consensus, particularly for technology stocks, which often have to beat the Street by a wide margin to send their stock prices higher.

One reason whisper estimates are higher than consensus estimates is that a firm's *earnings guidance* to analysts is often tilted to the pessimistic side, so that the firm can "surprise" the Street on the upside and "beat the consensus" in its quarterly reports. How else can one explain that over the past 10 years approximately 65 percent of the quarterly earnings reports beat the consensus estimate?[17] Furthermore, a large number of firms beat the Street by exactly one penny, far higher than one would calculate on a statistical basis.

Earnings, although very important, are not the only data that traders act on in the quarterly reports. Revenue is generally considered the next most important indicator of a firm's prospects and is considered even more important than earnings by some traders. When the revenue data are combined with the earnings data, one can compute the profit margin on sales, another important piece of data.

But the earnings and revenue data are cut from different pieces of cloth. Earnings are quoted on a *per share* basis, while revenue is not. It is perfectly possible for firms to fall short of revenue estimates and fail to meet their margin expectations, yet still beat on per share earnings because over the past quarter the firm has reduced the number of shares outstanding through corporate buybacks. Per share earnings can continue to grow even if overall revenues are stagnant.

Finally, investors are influenced by any earnings guidance that firms give over the next quarter or year. Forward guidance below earlier forecasts will certainly influence the stock price negatively. Years ago, management would often tip off analysts when unexpected good or bad news impacted the firm. But after tough new fair disclosure laws were adopted by the SEC in 2000, such selected disclosure is no longer permitted. The quarterly conference call is an ideal time for management to release any and all important information to shareholders.

CONCLUSION

The fundamental determinant of stock values is the future expected cash flows to investors. These cash flows, called dividends, are derived from the earnings. If a firm earns the same rate of return on its retained earnings that it does on the rest of its corporate capital, then the dividend policy of a firm will not influence the current stock price, although it will influence the future growth rate of per share earnings and dividends.

There are many earnings concepts. Firm operating earnings are what are calculated and forecast by analysts and are the most important data in the quarterly reports. These operating earnings are almost always higher than reported or GAAP earnings. But recent rulings by the FASB have led to a downward bias in reported earnings, especially during recessions when firms are required to record unrealized capital losses in their earnings reports. The implications of these earnings data for the valuation of the stock market are the subject of our next chapter.

Yardsticks to Value
the Stock Market

Even when the underlying motive of purchase [of common stocks] is
mere speculative greed, human nature desires to conceal this unlovely
impulse behind a screen of apparent logic and good sense.
—BENJAMIN GRAHAM AND DAVID DODD, 1940[1]

AN EVIL OMEN RETURNS

In the summer of 1958, an event of great significance took place for those
who followed long-standing yardsticks of the stock market valuation.
For the first time in history, the interest rate on long-term government
bonds rose decidedly above the dividend yield on common stocks.

BusinessWeek noted this event in an August 1958 article entitled
"An Evil Omen Returns," warning investors that when yields on stocks
approached those on bonds, a major market decline was in the offing.[2]
The stock market crash of 1929 occurred in a year when stock dividend
yields fell to the level of bond yields. The stock crashes of 1891 and 1907
also followed episodes when the yield on bonds came within 1 percent
of the dividend yield on stocks.

Until 1958, as Figure 11-1 indicates, the yearly dividend yield on
stocks had always been higher than long-term interest rates, and
investors thought that this was the way it was supposed to be. Stocks
were riskier than bonds and therefore should yield more in the marketplace. Under this criterion, whenever stock prices went too high and
sent dividend yields below the yields on bonds, it was time to sell.

FIGURE 11–1

Dividend Yield and Nominal Bond Yield 1870–2012

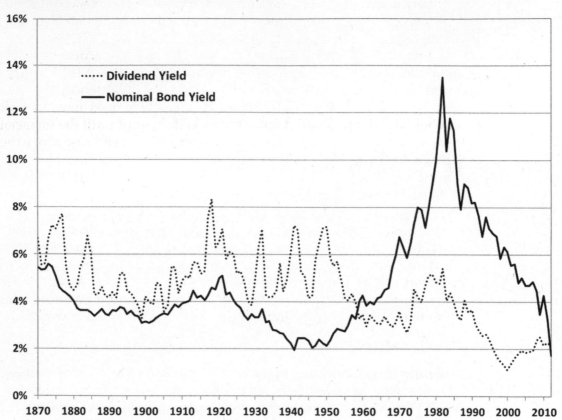

But things did not work that way in 1958. Stocks returned over 30 percent in the 12 months after dividend yields fell below bond yields, and stocks continued to soar into the early 1960s.

It is now understood that there were good economic reasons why this well-respected valuation indicator fell by the wayside. Inflation increased the yield on bonds to compensate lenders for rising prices, while investors bought stocks because they were claims on real assets. As early as September 1958, *BusinessWeek* noted, "The relationship between stock and bond yields was clearly posting a warning signal, but investors still believe inflation is inevitable and stocks are the only hedge against it."[3]

Yet many on Wall Street were troubled by the "great yield reversal." Nicholas Molodovsky, vice president of White, Weld & Co. and editor of the *Financial Analysts Journal*, observed:

Some financial analysts called [the reversal of bond and stock yields] a financial revolution brought about by many complex causes. Others, on the contrary, made no attempt to explain the unexplainable. They showed readiness to accept it as a manifestation of providence in the financial universe.[4]

Imagine the investor who followed this well-regarded indicator and pulled all her money out of the stock market in August 1958, putting it into bonds and vowing never to buy stocks until dividend yields rose once again above bond yields. Such an investor would have to wait another 50 years to get back into stocks, as it was not until the financial crisis in 2009 that the dividend yield on stocks once again rose above the yield on long-term Treasury bonds. Yet over that half century, real stock returns averaged over 6 percent per year and overwhelmed the returns on fixed-income securities.

This example illustrates that valuation yardsticks are valid only as long as underlying economic and financial conditions do not change. The chronic postwar inflation, resulting from a switch to a paper money standard, changed forever the way investors judged the investment merits of stocks and bonds. Stocks were claims on real assets whose prices rose with inflation, while bonds were not. Those investors who clung to the old ways of valuing equity never participated in one of history's greatest bull markets.

HISTORICAL YARDSTICKS FOR VALUING THE MARKET

Many yardsticks have been used to evaluate whether stock prices are overvalued or undervalued. Most of these measure the market value of the shares outstanding relative to economic *fundamentals*, such as earnings, dividends, or book values, or to some economic variable, such as GDP or interest rates.

Price/Earnings Ratio and the Earnings Yield

The most basic and fundamental yardstick for valuing stocks is the *price/earnings ratio* (or *P/E ratio*). The P/E ratio of a stock is simply the ratio of its price to its earnings. The P/E ratio of the market is the ratio of the aggregate earnings of the market to the aggregate value of the market. The P/E ratio measures how much an investor is willing to pay for a dollar's worth of current earnings.

Figure 11-2 shows the historical P/E ratio of the market from 1871 through December 2012, based on the last 12 months of S&P reported

FIGURE 11–2

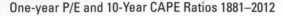

One-year P/E and 10-Year CAPE Ratios 1881–2012

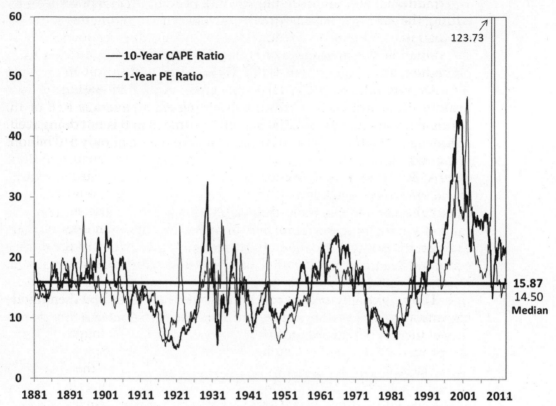

earnings and an alternative P/E ratio based on the last 10 years of earnings, called the CAPE ratio, that will be discussed later in this chapter. The P/E ratio based on 12-months earnings is marked by a large spike, reaching 123.73 in the 2009 recession. This spike was not caused by high stock prices but by extremely low aggregate earnings that were caused by large losses concentrated in a few firms. A smaller spike, also caused by a few firms reporting large losses, occurred in the 2000 recession. The median value of the P/E ratio, in contrast to the arithmetic average, reduces the impact of these spikes and gives a better guide to the historical valuation of the market. From 1871 through 2012, the median P/E ratio based on the last 12 months of earnings is 14.50, and based on the next 12 months of earnings, it is 15.09.

The Aggregation Bias

The traditional way of calculating the P/E of an index or a portfolio is by adding the earnings of each firm in the index and dividing this sum into the total market value of the index. Normally this gives a good picture of the valuation. But when one or more firms reports a large loss, such a procedure can give a very distorted view of the index's valuation.

As a simple example, take two firms, A and B. Assume A is a healthy firm earnings $10 billion and selling for an average P/E of 15, giving it a market value of $150 billion. Assume firm B is not doing well, reporting a $9 billion loss and having a market value of only $10 billion. A capitalization weighted portfolio consists of approximately 94% of firm A ($150 billion/$160 billion) and 6% of firm B. Yet using the traditional way of computing the P/E ratio of this portfolio would compute the total earnings of the two firms of $1 billion and divide this into the market value of these firms of $160 billion. This yields an extraordinarily high P/E ratio of 160, even though over 94% of the portfolio is concentrated in a firm that has a P/E of 15. I call this distortion in index P/E ratios the *aggregation bias*.

The reason why adding together profits and losses and then dividing into aggregate market value is wrong is that losses in one firm do not cancel the profits of another firm. Equity holders have unique rights to the profits of their firms, unsullied by the losses in others.

The aggregation bias was particularly operative in the 2001–2002 recession and the recent financial crisis. The big dip in earnings in 2001 was caused by the bust in the tech sector, and the large write-down that some firms, such as Time Warner, were forced to take on their portfolio investments. In 2009 the large losses were in the financial industry, as Citibank, BankAmerica, and particularly AIG took outsized losses that absorbed most of the earnings from the profitable firms in the S&P 500 Index.

There is no easy fix to the aggregation bias. One method is to weight the profits and losses of each firm by its market weight in the index.[5] During normal periods when most firms are profitable and losses of other firms are small, the aggregation bias is very small. When a few firms experience large losses, the aggregation bias becomes significant.

The Earnings Yield

Another variable of importance is the reciprocal of the P/E ratio, which is called the *earnings yield*. The earnings yield is analogous to the dividend yield and measures the earnings generated per dollar of stock market value.[6]

A median P/E ratio of approximately 15 for the U.S. market means the median earnings yield is 1/15, or 6.67 percent, a value that is strikingly close to the long-run real return on stocks. This is not a coincidence and is indeed what would be predicted by finance theory. Stocks, in contrast to bonds, whose coupons and principal remain unchanged during inflation, are claims on real assets, and real assets will rise in value with an increase in the general level of prices. Therefore the earnings yield on stocks is a *real* yield and should match the average real return that shareholders receive for holding equities.

The CAPE Ratio

In 1998, Robert Shiller and his coauthor John Campbell published a path-breaking article, "Valuation Ratios and the Long-Run Stock Market Outlook."[7] This article, following up on some of their earlier work on stock market predictability, established that long-term stock market returns were not random walks but could be forecast by a valuation measure called the *cyclically adjusted price/earnings ratio*, or *CAPE ratio*.[8] The CAPE ratio was calculated by taking a broad-based index of stock market prices, such as the S&P 500, and dividing by the average of the last 10 years of aggregate earnings, all measured in real terms. Its purpose is to smooth out temporary fluctuations in profits caused by business cycles. The CAPE ratio was then regressed against the future 10-year real returns on stocks, establishing that this ratio was a significant variable predicting long-run stock returns.[9] The CAPE ratio is plotted along with the one-year P/E ratio in Figure 11-2. Because the CAPE ratio is based on 10-year average earnings, it does not display the spikes that appear when plotting the one-year P/E ratio.

The ability of the CAPE ratio to predict real stock returns implied that long-term equity returns were "mean reverting." When the CAPE ratio is above its long-run average, the model predicts below-average real stock returns and above-average returns when the CAPE ratio is below its average. The forecast and actual 10-year real stock returns for the CAPE model are plotted in Figure 11-3.[10]

The CAPE ratio gained attention when Campbell and Shiller presented a preliminary version of their work to the Board of Governors of the Federal Reserve on December 3, 1996, and warned that stock prices in the late 1990s were running well ahead of earnings. Greenspan's "irrational exuberance speech," delivered one week later, was said to have

FIGURE   11–3

CAPE Forecast and Realized 10-Year Real Stocks Returns 1881–2012

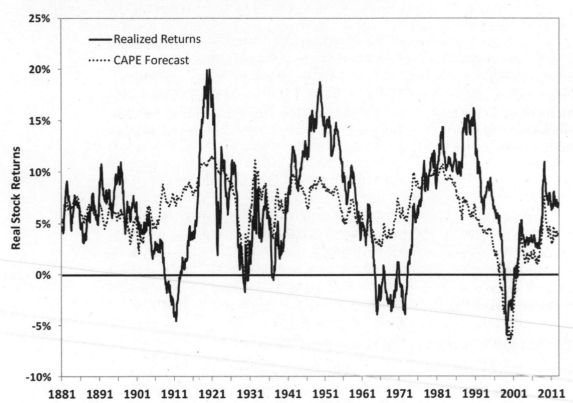

been based, in part, on their research.[11] At the top of the bull market in 2000, the CAPE ratio hit an all-time high of 43, more than twice its historical average, and correctly forecast the poor equity returns over the next decade.

In January 2013, the CAPE ratio reached 20.68, about 30 percent above its long-term average, and predicted a 10-year future annual real stock return of 4.16 percent, about 2½ percentage points below its long-run average. Although forecast stock returns were still significantly higher than what was available at that time in the bond market, the bearish CAPE prediction created concern among many stock market forecasters that the stock market at the end of 2012 had become overvalued and that another bear market might be forthcoming.

But closer analysis suggests that the CAPE ratio based on S&P 500 reported earnings may be too bearish. There have been only 9 months since January 1991 when the CAPE ratio has been below its long-term average, but in 380 of the 384 months from 1981 through 2012, the actual 10-year real returns in the stock market have exceeded forecasts using the CAPE model.

The unwarranted bearishness of the CAPE model can be attributed to several sources: the most significant one is the distorted level of earnings reported by Standard & Poor's for its benchmark S&P 500 Index.[12] As discussed in the last chapter, new FASB rulings have depressed S&P reported earnings, particularly in recessions. Furthermore the aggregation bias makes the S&P methodology of determining the valuation of the market particularly unrepresentative when a few firms report extremely large losses. The outsized decline in S&P reported earnings in 2009 will bias the CAPE ratio upward until that year drops out of the ten-year average in 2019.

When S&P operating earnings or adjusted real corporate profits from NIPA are substituted for S&P reported earnings, a very different picture emerges.[13] Figure 11-4 displays the CAPE ratio relative to its long-run average using S&P reported and operating earnings and NIPA corporate profits. With these alternative measures, the overvaluation of the stock market in recent years is eliminated or significantly reduced.

The Fed Model, Earnings Yields, and Bond Yields

In early 1997, in response to Federal Reserve Chairman Alan Greenspan's increasing concern about the impact of the rising stock market on the economy, three researchers from the Federal Reserve produced a paper entitled "Earnings Forecasts and the Predictability of Stock Returns: Evidence from Trading the S&P."[14] This paper documented the remarkable correspondence between the earnings yields on stocks and the 30-year government bond rates.

Greenspan supported the results of this paper and suggested that the central bank regarded the stock market as "overvalued" whenever this earnings yield fell below the bond yield and "undervalued" whenever the reverse occurred. The analysis showed that the market was most overvalued in August 1987, just before the October 1987 stock market crash, and most undervalued in the early 1980s, when the great bull market began.

The basic idea behind the Fed model is similar to comparing the dividend yield to the bond yield discussed at the onset of this chapter but, recognizing that firms pay out only a fraction of their earnings as dividends, uses the earnings yield and not the dividend yield. When the bond yields rise above the earnings yields, stock prices fall because

FIGURE 11–4

CAPE Ratios Based on Reported Earnings, Operating Earnings, and NIPA Profits 1987–2012

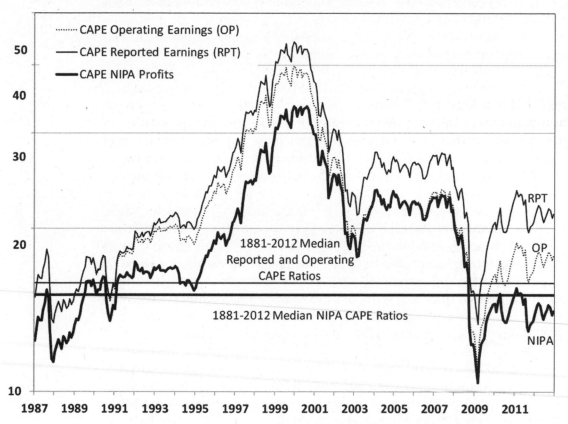

investors shift their portfolio holdings from stocks to bonds. On the other hand, when the bond yields fall below the earnings yields, investors shift to stocks from bonds.

But this model has the same shortcoming as the dividend yield–bond yield yardstick described at the beginning of this chapter. Government bonds have ironclad guarantees to pay a specified number of dollars over time but bear the risk of inflation. Stocks, on the other hand, are real assets whose prices will rise with inflation, but they bear the risk of the uncertainty of earnings. The reason why the Fed model worked is that the market rated these two risks as approximately equal during this period.

But these two risks are not equal when inflation is low or when deflation threatens. In those circumstances, bonds (especially U.S. government bonds) will do very well, but deflation undermines firms' pricing power and is bad for corporate profits. The Fed model did not do a good job of predicting stock returns before inflation became a major concern in the 1970s, nor has it done well in recent years as deflation became a real concern following the financial crisis. For these reasons, the Fed model has rightfully received less attention in recent years.

Corporate Profits and GDP

Another indicator of stock market valuation is the ratio of aggregate corporate profits to GDP. The rise in this ratio in recent years has alarmed some stock market analysts, who worry that if the share of profits to national income falls to its long-term average, earnings and hence stock prices will suffer.

However, closer examination of the data put those fears to rest. Figure 11-5 displays the ratio of after-tax corporate profits and after-tax profits plus proprietors' income, beginning in 1929. Proprietors' income is profits of nonincorporated businesses, including profits to partnerships and individual owners.

One can see that although the ratio of corporate profits is high relative to GDP, the ratio of corporate profits plus proprietor's income to GDP is only 24.3 percent, less than 4 percentage points above its historical average. Over this time span, many brokerage houses, investment banks, and other firms became publicly traded corporations, moving from the proprietor's income category to corporate profits. This has boosted the corporate share of profits but not the total share of profits to all capital, corporate and non-corporate.

Another factor raising the share of corporate profits is the increasing fraction of earnings that come from abroad. In 2011, over 46 percent of the sales of S&P 500 companies were foreign. As the U.S. economy shrinks relative to the size of the world economy, the corporate profits of U.S. multinational corporations should rise relative to U.S. GDP. This is another reason why the rising share of corporate profits to US GDP is not a cause for alarm.

Book Value, Market Value, and Tobin's Q

The *book value* of a firm has often been used as a valuation yardstick. The book value is the value of a firm's assets minus its liabilities, evaluated at historical costs. The use of aggregate book value as a measure of the overall value of a firm is severely limited because book value uses *his*-

FIGURE 11–5

Corporate and Proprietor's Income as a Percentage of GDP 1929–2012

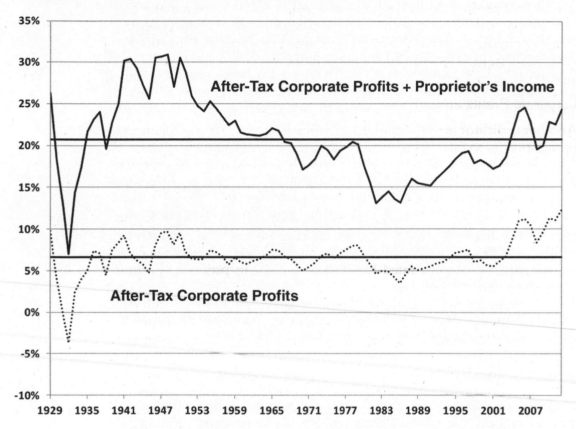

torical prices and thus ignores the effect of changing prices on the value of the assets or liabilities. If a firm purchased a plot of land for $1 million that is now worth $10 million, examining the book value will not reveal this. Over time, the historical value of assets becomes less reliable as a measure of current market value.

To help correct these distortions, James Tobin, former professor at Yale University and a Nobel laureate, adjusted the book value for inflation and computed the "replacement cost" of the assets and liabilities on the balance sheets of U.S. corporations.[15] He proposed that the "equilibrium" or "correct" market price of a firm should equal its assets minus its liabilities adjusted for inflation. If the aggregate market value of a firm exceeds the cost of capital, it would be profitable to create more capital, sell shares to finance it, and reap a profit. If the market value falls below the replacement cost, then it would be better for a firm to dismantle and sell its capital or to stop investment and cut production.

Tobin designated the ratio of the market value to the replacement cost with the letter Q, and he indicated that its ratio should be unity if the stock market was properly valued. In 2000 Andrew Smithers and Stephen Wright of the United Kingdom published the book *Valuing Wall Street*,[16] which maintained that Tobin's Q was the best measure of value and that the U.S. markets as well as the U.K. and many other European markets were extremely overvalued by this criterion, a prediction also made by those who monitored the P/E ratio.

But there are critics of the Q theory. Capital equipment and structures lack a good secondary market, and hence there is no realistic way to value much of the capital stock independent of the value of the stock market. In July 2013 the United States revised its national income accounts to include research and development and other knowledge investment (such as entertainment, literary, and artistic originals) in the investment category. These changes added about $2 trillion to the capital stock and certainly improved the relevance of the Q theory. Nevertheless, book value is a construct of the past; market value derives from prospective earnings and looks to the future. These prospective earnings more accurately establish the basis of stock valuation than the historical costs at which the firms purchased these assets.

Profit Margins

Another ratio that has generated concern in recent years is the level of profit margins, the ratio of corporate profits to revenues. Figure 11-6 plots the profit margins on S&P 500 firms since 1967. One can see that profit margins have recently risen to the highest levels in 45 years. Many claim that these margins are "unsustainable" and that if the margins retreat, that could lead to a significant decline in corporate profits and hence stock prices.

But there are several reasons why corporate margins are high and are not likely to retreat.[17] One is the low leverage of American corporations, which reduces interest expenses and boosts margins. Second, about one-third of the increase in the profit margins since the 1990s is due to the increase in the share of profits coming from foreign sales. Margins on foreign sales are higher than on domestic sales because the foreign corporate tax rates abroad are almost all lower than in the United States. Finally, much of the increase in profit margin is due to the increase in the size of the technology sector, which has historically had

FIGURE   11–6

Profit Margin of S&P 500 Firms 1967–2012

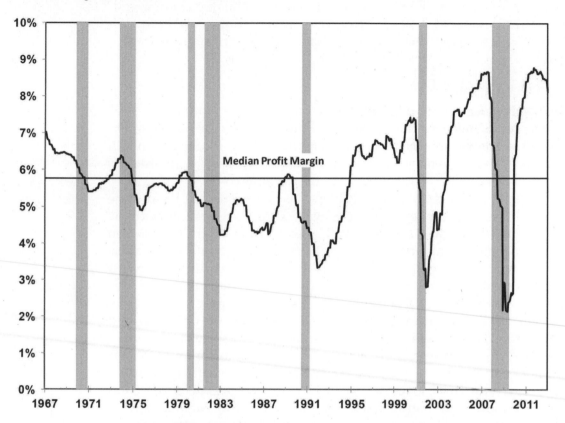

high margins. This is due to the large level of intellectual capital in tech-nology firms and the high level of foreign sales.

These higher margins on the S&P 500 are unlikely to fall signifi-cantly. Foreign sales will continue to contribute an increasing share of S&P profits. Firms would lower their profit margin by increasing their leverage, but with the interest rate so much lower than the earnings yield, such actions will significantly boost earnings per share. In fact, profit margins might rise further if the United States lowers its corporate tax rates, a measure that has support in both parties.

FACTORS THAT MAY RAISE FUTURE VALUATION RATIOS

We have noted that the historical real return on equity has been between 6 and 7 percent per year over long periods and that this has coincided with an average P/E ratio of approximately 15. But there have been changes in the economy and financial markets that may raise the P/E ratio in the future. These changes include a decrease in the cost of investing in equity indexes, a lower discount rate, and an increase in knowledge about the advantages of equity versus fixed-income investments.

A Fall in Transaction Costs

Chapter 5 confirmed that the real return on equity *as measured by stock indexes* was between 6 and 7 percent after inflation over the past two centuries. But over the nineteenth century and the early part of the twentieth century, it was extremely difficult, if not impossible, for an investor to replicate these stock returns because of transactions costs.

Charles Jones of Columbia University has documented the decline in stock trading costs over the last century.[18] These costs include both the fees paid to brokers and the bid-asked spread, or the difference between the buying and selling price for stocks. His analysis shows that the average one-way cost to either buy or sell a stock has dropped from over 1 percent of value traded as late as 1975 (before the deregulation of brokerage fees) to under 0.18 percent in 2002, and even lower today.

The fall in transaction costs implies that the price of obtaining and maintaining a diversified portfolio of common stocks, which is necessary to replicate index returns, could have easily cost investors from 1 to 2 percent per year over much of the nineteenth and early twentieth centuries. Because of these costs, investors in earlier years were less diversified and assumed more risk than implied by stock indexes. Alternatively, if investors attempted to buy all the stocks to replicate a broad-based index, their real returns could have been as low as 5 percent per year after deducting transaction costs. If the required real return on equity for investors is only 5 percent, then a P/E ratio of 20, corresponding to an earnings yield of 5 percent, will produce that return for today's investors.[19]

Lower Real Returns on Fixed-Income Assets

We have noted that the real returns on fixed-income assets have fallen dramatically over the past decade. When the 10-year TIPS were floated in January 1997, their real return was almost 3.5 percent, and their yield rose over 4 percent the following year. But since then, there has been a steady decline in their real yield, which became negative in 2011 and fell to almost −1 percent by the end of 2012. The implied real yield on standard Treasury bonds also fell below zero.

There are many reasons for the decline in real returns available to investors: the slowdown in economic growth, the aging of the population, and the desire of pension funds to buy bonds to match their liabilities to their retirees. Whatever the reasons, such a decline implies that the real return on equity need not be as high as it had been historically in order to attract buyers. We have noted that the historical premium (the equity premium) on holding stocks over bonds has been approximately 3 to 3 ½ percent. If we assume that the long-run real rate settles at 2 percent, about 1 to 1½ percent below its long-run average, then a 3 percent equity premium will require a 5 percent real return on stocks, which, as we noted above, arises from a 20 P/E multiple.

The Equity Risk Premium

The decline in transaction costs and the decline in discount rates may each be used to justify a higher P/E ratio. Yet another reason is that the equity risk premium itself may shrink. In 1985, economists Rajnish Mehra and Edward Prescott published a paper entitled "The Equity Premium: A Puzzle."[20] In their work they showed that given the standard models of risk and return that economists had developed over the years, one could not explain the large gap between the returns on equities and fixed-income assets found in the historical data. They claimed that economic models predicted that either the rate of return on stocks should be lower, or the rate of return on fixed-income assets should be higher, or both. In fact, according to their studies, an equity premium as low as 1 percent or less could be justified.[21]

There is much literature that attempts to justify the 3 to 3½ percent risk premium found in the historical data in the context of standard macroeconomic models. Some of these are based on very high aversion by individuals. Others are based on the myopic behavior of those who dislike taking short-term losses on their investments even when they have substantial long-run gains. Perhaps part of the explanation of the size of the equity premium lies with the ignorance of the investing public of the magnitude of the outperformance of equities.[22] If indeed the equity premium were fully recognized, the demand for stock would rise and P/E ratios would increase from historical levels. This was precisely the explanation that Professor Chelcie Bosland of Brown University had made more than 75 years ago. He stated in 1937 that one of the consequences of the spread of knowledge of superior stock returns, generated by Edgar Lawrence Smith's contributions, was the bull market of the 1920s and a narrowing of the equity premium:

Paradoxical though it may seem, there is considerable truth in the statement that widespread knowledge of the profitability of common stocks, gained from the studies that have been made, tends to diminish the likelihood that correspondingly large profits can be gained from stocks in the future. The competitive bidding for stocks which results from this knowledge causes prices at the time of purchase to be high, with the attendant smaller possibilities of gain in the principal and high yield. The discount process may do away with a large share of the gains from common stock investment and returns to stockholders and investors in other securities may tend to become equalized.[23]

CONCLUSION

Proper valuation of the equity market is necessary to project future stock returns. Although those who wait long enough will eventually recoup losses on a diversified portfolio of stocks, buying stocks at or below their historical valuation is the best way to guarantee superior returns. Nevertheless, there are persuasive reasons why the valuation of the market may in the future rise above the historical average. This will lead to lower long-term returns on stocks but higher returns during the transition to a higher valuation. Whether that transition takes place or not, stocks remain the most attractive asset class for long-term investors.

Outperforming the Market

The Importance of Size, Dividend Yields, and Price/Earnings Ratios

> *Security analysis cannot presume to lay down general rules as to the "proper value" of any given common stock. . . . The prices of common stocks are not carefully thought out computations, but the resultants of a welter of human reactions.*
> —BENJAMIN GRAHAM AND DAVID DODD, 1940[1]

STOCKS THAT OUTPERFORM THE MARKET

What criteria can investors use to choose stocks with superior returns that will outperform the market? Investors are inevitably drawn to firms able to generate high earnings and revenue growth. But empirical data show this pursuit of growth often leads to subpar returns. To illustrate how growth does not necessarily translate into superior returns, imagine for a moment that you are an investor in 1950, at the dawn of the computer age. You have $1,000 to invest and are given the choice of two stocks: Standard Oil of New Jersey (now ExxonMobil) or a much smaller, promising new company called IBM. You will instruct the firm you choose to reinvest all dividends paid back into new shares, and you will put your investment under lock and key for the next 62 years, to be distributed at the end of 2012 to your great-grandchildren or to your favorite charity.

Which firm should you buy? And why?

Let us assume that to help you with your decision, a genie presented you with Table 12-1, which displays the actual growth data of these two firms over the next 62 years.

Table 12.1A shows that IBM beat Standard Oil by wide margins in *every* growth measure that Wall Street uses to pick stocks: sales, earnings, dividends, and sector expansion. IBM's earnings per share growth, Wall Street's favorite stock-picking criterion, was more than 3 percentage points per year above the oil giant's earnings growth over the next six decades. As information technology advanced and technology became more important to our economy, the technology sector rose from 3 percent of the market to nearly 20 percent.

In contrast, the oil industry's share of the market shrank dramatically over this period. Oil stocks made up about 20 percent of the market value of all U.S. stocks in 1950 but fell to nearly half that value in 2012.

By these growth criteria, IBM stock should be a slam dunk to win investors' favor. But Standard Oil proved to be the best stock to buy.

TABLE 12–1

Growth, Valuation, and Returns on IBM and Standard Oil (NJ) 1950–2012

Table A

Growth Measures	IBM	Standard Oil of NJ	Advantage
Revenue per share	10.03%	8.31%	IBM
Dividends per share	10.73%	6.32%	IBM
Earnings per share	11.14%	7.90%	IBM
Sector growth*	16.10%	–9.11%	IBM

*Change in market share of technology and energy sectors 1957–2012

Table B

Valuation Measures	IBM	Standard Oil of NJ	Advantage
Price appreciation	8.95%	7.58%	IBM
Dividend return	2.17%	4.72%	Standard Oil of NJ
Total return	11.32%	12.66%	Standard Oil of NJ

Table C

Return Measures	IBM	Standard Oil of NJ	Advantage
Average price/earnings ratio	25.06	14.08	Standard Oil of NJ
Average dividend yield	2.17%	4.21%	Standard Oil of NJ

Returns measured year end 1957–2012

Although both stocks did well, investors in Standard Oil earned more than 1 percentage point per year over IBM, as shown in Table 12-1B. When your lockbox was opened 62 years later, the $1,000 you invested in the oil giant would be worth $1,620,000, more than twice as much as IBM.

Why did Standard Oil beat IBM when it fell far short in every growth category? One simple reason: *valuation*, the price you pay for the earnings and dividends you receive. The price investors paid for IBM was just too high. Even though the computer giant trumped Standard Oil on growth, Standard Oil trumped IBM on valuation, and valuation determines investor returns.

As you can see from Table 12.1C, the average price/earnings ratio of Standard Oil was almost half of IBM's ratio, and the oil company's average dividend yield was more than 2 percentage points higher.

Dividends are a critical factor driving investor returns. Because Standard Oil's price was low and its dividend yield much higher than that of IBM, those who bought its stock and reinvested the oil company's dividends accumulated 12.7 times the number of shares they started out with, while investors in IBM accumulated only 3.3 times their original shares. Although the price of Standard Oil's stock appreciated at a rate that was more than 2 percentage points lower than the price of IBM's stock, its higher dividend yield made the oil giant the winner for investors.

What Determines a Stock's Return?

What does finance theory say about the importance of earnings growth in determining investor returns? Finance theory has shown that if capital markets are "efficient" in the sense that known valuation criteria, such as earnings, dividends, cash flows, book values, and other factors are already factored into security prices, investing on the basis of these fundamentals factors will not improve returns. In an efficient market, the only way investors can consistently earn higher returns is to undertake higher "risk," where risk is defined as the correlation of an asset's return with the overall market, known as *beta*.[2] This is the fundamental conclusion of the *capital asset pricing model* (CAPM), developed in the 1960s by William Sharpe and John Lintner.[3]

Beta can be estimated from historical data and represents the risk of an asset's return that cannot be eliminated in a well-diversified portfolio; it is therefore the risk for which investors must be compensated. If beta is greater than 1, the stock requires a return greater than that offered by the overall stock market; and if it is less than 1, a lesser return is required. Risk that is not correlated to the market can be eliminated through diversification (called *diversifiable* or *residual risk*) and does not warrant a higher return. The *efficient market hypothesis* and the CAPM became the basis for stock return analysis in the 1970s and 1980s.

Unfortunately, as more data were analyzed, beta did not prove effective in explaining the differences in returns among individual stocks. In fact, the beta of Standard Oil of New Jersey was far lower than the beta of IBM, although Standard Oil's return was greater.[4] In 1992, Eugene Fama and Ken French wrote an article, published in the *Journal of Finance*, that showed that there are two factors, one relating to the market capitalization of the firm and the other to the valuation of stocks, that are far more important in determining a stock's return than the beta of a stock.[5]

After further analyzing returns, they claimed that the evidence against the CAPM was "compelling" and that "the average return anomalies . . . are serious enough to infer that the [CAPM] model is not a useful approximation" of a stock's return, and they suggested researchers investigate "alternative" asset pricing models or "irrational asset pricing stories."[6]

Fama and French's findings prompted financial economists to classify the stock universe along two dimensions: *size*, measured by the market value of the stock, and *valuation*, or the price relative to "fundamentals" such as earnings and dividends. The emphasis on valuation to gain an investment edge did not originate with Fama and French. Valuation formed the cornerstone of the principles that Benjamin Graham and David Dodd put forth more than 70 years ago in their investment classic *Security Analysis*.[7]

SMALL- AND LARGE-CAP STOCKS

Cracks in the capital asset pricing model's predictions of stock returns appeared well before Fama and French's research. In 1981, Rolf Banz, a graduate student at the University of Chicago, investigated the returns on stocks using the database that had been recently compiled by the Center for Research in Security Prices (CRSP) located at the university. He found that small stocks systematically outperformed large stocks, even after adjusting for risk as defined within the framework of the capital asset pricing model.[8]

To analyze this claim, the returns from 1926 through 2012 on 10 groups of more than 4,000 stocks, sorted by market capitalization, are shown in Table 12-2.

The compound annual return on the smallest decile of stock, at 17.03 percent per year, was more than 9½ percentage points over what

TABLE 12–2

Return on Size Deciles of U.S. Stocks, 1926–2012

Size Decile (Smallest to Largest)	Geometric Return	Beta Average	Arithmetic Return	Excess Return Over CAPM
1	17.03%	1.38	25.56%	9.58%
2	12.77%	1.35	19.17%	3.56%
3	11.29%	1.26	16.50%	1.86%
4	11.31%	1.24	15.92%	1.58%
5	10.97%	1.22	14.89%	0.70%
6	10.97%	1.21	14.82%	0.74%
7	11.16%	1.18	14.39%	0.76%
8	10.24%	1.12	12.94%	–0.09%
9	11.04%	1.09	13.41%	0.80%
10	9.28%	0.95	11.01%	–0.02%
Total market	9.67%	1.00	11.59%	0.00%

would be predicted by the CAPM. The return of the second-smallest decile of stocks, at 12.77 percent, was more than 3½ percentage points above the CAPM prediction.[9]

Trends in Small-Cap Stock Returns

Although the historical return on small stocks has outpaced large stocks since 1926, the magnitude of the small-cap stock outperformance has waxed and waned unpredictably over the past 86 years. A comparison of the cumulative returns on small stocks with those of the S&P 500 Index is shown in Figure 12-1.[10]

Small stocks, measured by the bottom quintile of market capitalization, recovered smartly from their beating during the Great Depression, but their performance only matched large stocks from 1926 to 1960. Even by the end of 1974, the average annual compound return on small stocks exceeded that of large stocks by only about 0.5 percent per year, not nearly enough to compensate most investors for their extra risk and trading costs.

But between 1975 and the end of 1983, small stocks exploded. During these years, small stocks averaged a 35.3 percent compound annual return, more than double the 15.7 percent return on large stocks. Cumulative returns in small stocks during these nine years exceeded

FIGURE 12–1

Returns to Small and Large Stocks 1926–2012 Including and Excluding 1975–1983 Period

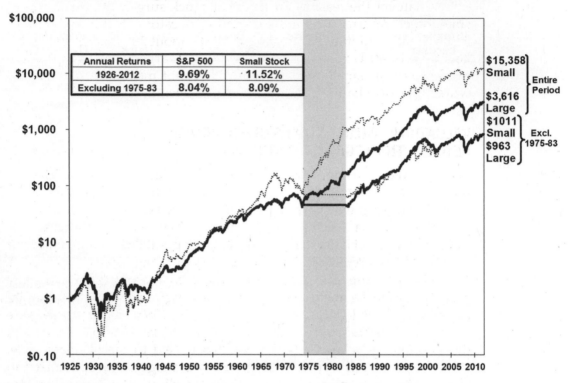

Annual Returns	S&P 500	Small Stock
1926-2012	9.69%	11.52%
Excluding 1975-83	8.04%	8.09%

$15,358 Small ⎫ Entire Period
$3,616 Large ⎭
$1011 Small ⎫ Excl. 1975-83
$963 Large ⎭

1,400 percent. Nevertheless, Figure 12-1 shows that if the nine-year period from 1975 through 1983 is eliminated, the total accumulation in large stocks over the entire period from 1926 through 2006 is virtually the same.

What caused the tremendous performance of small stocks during the 1975-to-1983 period? In the late 1970s and early 1980s, pension and institutional managers found themselves attracted to smaller stocks following the collapse of the large-growth stocks, known as the "Nifty Fifty," that were so popular in the preceding bull market. In addition, the enactment of the Employee Retirement Income Security Act by Congress in 1974 made it far easier for pension funds to diversify into small stocks, boosting their holdings of these issues.

After 1983, small stocks hit a long dry period that lasted 17 years, as they underperformed large stocks, especially in the late 1990s as the technology boom gained momentum. But when the technology bubble burst, small stocks strongly outperformed once again. From the March 2000 peak through 2012, despite the severe intervening bear market, small stocks enjoyed a 7.2 percent annual return, while large stocks, represented by the S&P 500 Index, returned less than 1 percent per year.

Whatever the reasons for the small stock surges, the trendiness of small stock returns does not mean that investors should avoid these firms. Small- and mid-cap stocks constitute about 20 percent of the market value of all U.S. stocks. One should be warned, however, that the existence of the small stock premium does not mean that small stocks will outperform large stocks every year, or even every decade.

VALUATION: "VALUE" STOCKS OFFER HIGHER RETURNS THAN "GROWTH" STOCKS

The second dimension along which stocks are classified is by *valuation*—that is, factors relating the price of the stock relative to some fundamental metric of firm worth, such as dividends, earnings, book values, and cash flows. Fama and French determined that, like small-cap stocks, stocks that were cheap relative to these fundamentals had higher returns than would be predicted by the capital asset pricing model.

Stocks whose prices are low relative to these fundamentals are called *value* stocks, while those with prices high relative to firm fundamentals are called *growth* stocks. Prior to the 1980s, value stocks were often called *cyclical stocks* because low-P/E stocks were often found in those industries whose profits were closely tied to the business cycle. With the growth of style investing, equity managers that specialized in these stocks were uncomfortable with the "cyclical" moniker and greatly preferred the term *value*.

Value stocks generally occur in such industries as oil, motor, finance, and utilities where investors have low expectations of future growth or believe that profits are strongly tied to the business cycle, while growth stocks are generally found in such industries as technology, brand-name consumer products, and healthcare where investors expect profits either to grow quickly or to be more resistant to the business cycle.

DIVIDEND YIELDS

Dividends have always been an important criterion for choosing stocks, as Graham and Dodd stated in 1940:

> Experience would confirm the established verdict of the stock market that a dollar of earnings is worth more to the stockholder if paid him in dividends than when carried to surplus. The common-stock investor should ordinarily require both an adequate earning power and an adequate dividend.[11]

Graham and Dodd's claim has been supported by subsequent research. In 1978, Krishna Ramaswamy and Robert Litzenberger established a significant correlation between dividend yield and subsequent returns.[12] And more recently, James O'Shaughnessy has shown that in the period 1951 through 1994, the 50 highest-dividend-yielding large-capitalization stocks had a return that was 1.7 percentage points higher than the market.[13]

The historical analysis of the S&P 500 Index supports the case for using dividend yields to achieve higher stock returns. On December 31 of each year from 1957 onward, I sorted the firms in the S&P 500 Index into five groups (or quintiles) ranked from the highest to the lowest dividend yields and then calculated the total returns over the next calendar year. The striking results are shown in Figure 12-2.

FIGURE 12–2

Returns to S&P 500 Stocks Ranked by Dividend Yield, 1957–2012

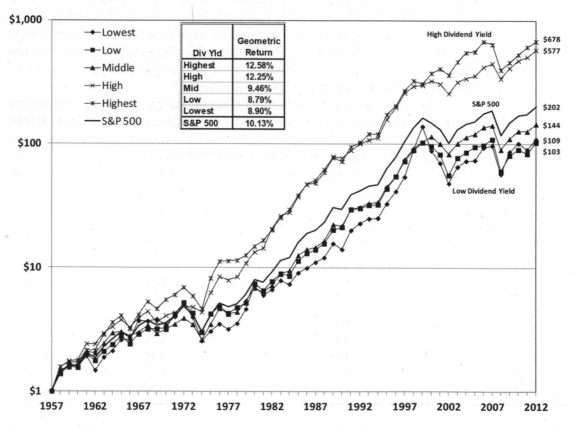

Div Yld	Geometric Return
Highest	12.58%
High	12.25%
Mid	9.46%
Low	8.79%
Lowest	8.90%
S&P 500	10.13%

The portfolios with higher dividend yields offered investors higher total returns than the portfolios of stocks with lower dividend yields. If an investor put $1,000 in an S&P 500 Index fund at the end of December 1957, she would have accumulated $201,760 by the end of 2012, for an annual return of 10.13 percent. An identical investment in the 100 highest dividend yielders accumulated to over $678,000, with a return of 12.58 percent.

The highest dividend yielders also had a beta below 1, indicating these stocks were more stable over market cycles, as shown in Table 12-3.

The lowest-dividend-yielding stocks not only had the lowest return but also the highest beta. The annual return of the 100 highest dividend yielders in the S&P 500 Index since the index was founded in 1957 was 3.42 percentage points per year above what would have been predicted by the efficient market model, while the return of the 100 lowest dividend yielders would have had a return that was 2.58 percentage points per year lower.

Other Dividend-Yield Strategies

There are other high-dividend-yield strategies that have outperformed the market. A well-known one is called the "Dogs of the Dow," or the "Dow 10" strategy, and is chosen from high-yielding stocks in the Dow Jones Industrial Average.

The Dow 10 strategy has been regarded by some as one of the simplest and most successful investment strategies of all time. James Glassman of the *Washington Post* claimed that John Slatter, a Cleveland investment advisor and writer, invented the Dow 10 system in the 1980s.[14] Harvey Knowles and Damon Petty popularized the strategy in their book

T A B L E   12–3

Return on S&P 500 Stocks Ranked by Dividend Yield, 1957–2012

Dividend Yield	Geometric Return	Arithmetic Return	Standard Deviation	Beta	Excess Return Over CAPM
Highest	12.58%	14.25%	19.34%	0.94	3.42%
High	12.25%	13.42%	16.26%	0.82	3.91%
Mid	9.46%	10.77%	16.64%	0.92	0.18%
Low	8.79%	10.64%	19.29%	1.07	−1.75%
Lowest	8.90%	11.62%	23.92%	1.23	−2.58%
S&P 500	10.13%	11.55%	17.15%	1.00	0.00%

The Dividend Investor, written in 1992, as did Michael O'Higgins and John Downes in *Beating the Dow*.

The strategy calls for investors at year-end to buy the 10 highest-yielding stocks in the Dow Jones Industrial Average and to hold them for the subsequent year and then repeat the process each December 31. These high-yielding stocks are often those that have fallen in price and are out of favor with investors—which is the reason the strategy is often called the Dogs of the Dow.

Another natural extension of the Dow 10 strategy is to choose the 10 highest-yielding stocks from among the 100 largest stocks in the S&P 500. The 100 largest stocks in the S&P 500 Index compose a much higher percentage of the entire U.S. market than the 30 stocks in the Dow Jones Industrial Average.

Indeed, both these strategies have excelled, as Figure 12-3 shows.[15] Since 1957, the Dow 10 strategy returned 12.63 percent per year, and the S&P 10 returned a dramatic 14.14 percent per year, consistently above their respective benchmarks. And both of these strategies have a lower beta than either the Dow Jones Industrial Average or the S&P 500 Index, as shown in Figure 12-3.

The worst year for both the Dow 10 and S&P 10 strategies relative to the benchmark indexes was 1999, when the high-capitalization tech stocks reached their bubble peak. The Dow 10 underperformed the S&P 500 Index by 16.72 percent that year, and the S&P 10 underperformed by over 17 percentage points. It is during the later stages of a bull market, when growth stocks catch the eye of speculative investors, that these value-based strategies will underperform capitalization-weighted strategies.

But these strategies have gained these losses back—and more—during subsequent bear markets. The Dow 30 was down by 26.5 percent, and the S&P 500 Index was down 37.3 percent during the 1973-to-1974 bear markets. But the S&P 10 strategy fell only 12 percent, while the Dow 10 strategy actually gained 2.9 percent in these two years.

These dividend-based strategies also resisted the 2000-to-2002 bear market. From the end of 2000 through the end of 2002, when the S&P 500 Index fell by more than 30 percent, the Dow 10 strategy fell by only less than 10 percent, and the S&P 10 strategy fell by less than 5 percent. In the bear market that followed the financial crisis, the Dow 10 and S&P 10 strategies did not cushion investors, as such high-profile dividend-paying stocks as General Motors filed for bankruptcy. But over the entire market cycle from 2007 through 2012, they only slightly underperformed their respective benchmarks and did not significantly reduce their long-term outperformance.

FIGURE 12–3

Returns to S&P 500 and Dow Industrials and Their 10 Highest Yielding Stocks, 1957–2012

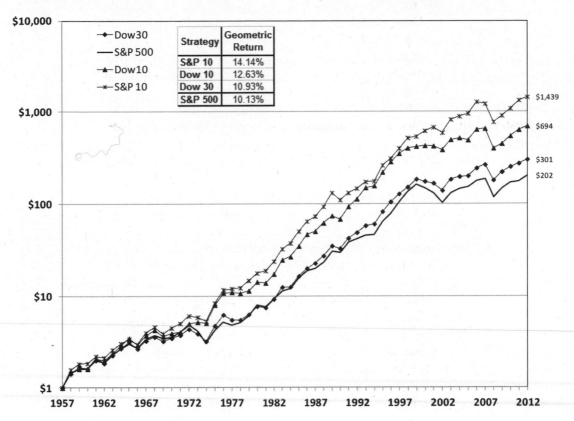

Strategy	Geometric Return
S&P 10	14.14%
Dow 10	12.63%
Dow 30	10.93%
S&P 500	10.13%

PRICE/EARNINGS RATIOS

Another important metric of value that can be used to formulate a winning strategy is the P/E ratio—the price of a stock relative to its earnings. The research into P/E ratios began in the late 1970s, when Sanjoy Basu, building on the work of S. F. Nicholson in 1960, discovered that stocks with low price/earnings ratios have significantly higher returns than stocks with high price/earnings ratios, even after accounting for risk.[16]

Again, these results would not have surprised the value investors Graham and Dodd, who, in their classic 1934 text *Security Analysis*, stated the following:

Hence we may submit, as a corollary of no small practical importance, that people who habitually purchase common stocks at more than about 16 times their average earnings are likely to lose considerable money in the long run.[17, 18]

In a manner analogous to the research on dividend yields among S&P 500 stocks, I computed the P/E ratios for all 500 firms in the index on December 31 of each year by dividing the last 12 months of earnings by the year-end prices. I then ranked these firms by P/E ratios and divided them into five quintiles, computing their subsequent return over the next 12 months.[19] The results of this research are similar to that reported on the dividend yield and are shown in Figure 12-4.

Stocks with high P/Es (or low earnings yields) are, on average, overvalued and have given lower returns to investors. A $1,000 portfolio of the highest-P/E stocks has accumulated to $64,116 by the end of 2012, earning an annual return of 7.86 percent, while the lowest-P/E stocks had a return of 12.92 percent and accumulated to almost $800,000.

FIGURE   12–4

Returns to S&P 500 Stocks Ranked by P/E Ratio, 1957–2012

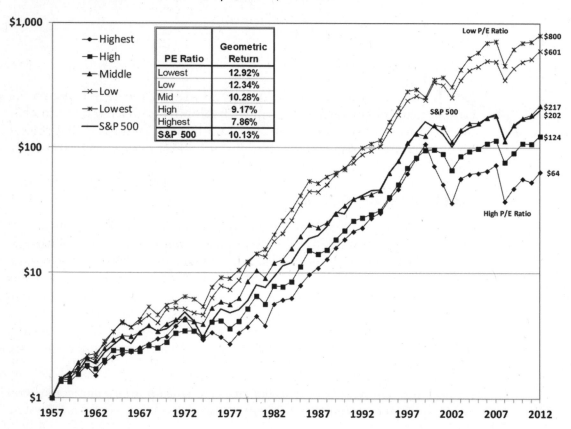

PE Ratio	Geometric Return
Lowest	12.92%
Low	12.34%
Mid	10.28%
High	9.17%
Highest	7.86%
S&P 500	**10.13%**

TABLE 12-4

Return on S&P 500 Stocks Ranked by P/E Ratio 1957–2012

PE Ratio	Geometric Return	Arithmetic Return	Standard Deviation	Beta	Excess Return Over CAPM
Lowest	12.92%	14.20%	16.59%	0.71	6.01%
Low	12.34%	13.54%	16.23%	0.65	6.05%
Mid	10.28%	11.45%	15.67%	0.69	3.46%
High	9.17%	10.30%	15.49%	0.73	1.85%
Highest	7.86%	9.86%	19.84%	0.92	–0.78%
S&P 500	10.13%	11.55%	17.15%	1.00	0.00%

In addition to a higher yield, the standard deviation of low-P/E stocks was lower, and the beta was much lower, than that of the S&P 500 Index stocks, as shown in Table 12-4. In fact, the return on the 100 lowest-P/E stocks in the S&P 500 Index was more than 6 percentage points per year above what would have been predicted on the basis of the capital asset pricing model.

PRICE/BOOK RATIOS

Price/earnings ratios and dividend yields are not the only value-based criteria. A number of academic papers, beginning with Dennis Stattman's in 1980 and later supported by Fama and French, suggested that price/book ratios might be even more important than price/earnings ratios in predicting future cross-sectional stock returns.[20]

Just as they did with P/E ratios and dividend yields, Graham and Dodd considered book value to be an important factor in determining returns:

> [We] suggest rather forcibly that the book value deserves at least a fleeting glance by the public before it buys or sells shares in a business undertaking. . . . Let the stock buyer, if he lays any claim to intelligence, at least be able to tell himself, first, how much he is actually paying for the business, and secondly, what he is actually getting for his money in terms of tangible resources.[21]

Although Fama and French found that the ratio of book to market value was a slightly better value metric than the dividend yield or P/E ratio in explaining cross-sectional returns in their 1992 research, there are conceptual problems with using book value as a value criterion.

Book value does not correct for changes in the market value of assets, nor does it capitalize research and development expenditures. In fact, over the time period 1987 through 2012, our studies showed that book value underperformed either dividend yields, P/E ratios, or cash flows in explaining returns.[22] Since it is likely that an increasing fraction of a firm's worth will be captured by intellectual property, book value may become an even more imperfect indicator of firm value in the future.

COMBINING SIZE AND VALUATION CRITERIA

The compound annual returns on stocks sorted into 25 quintiles along size and book-to-market ratios from 1958 through 2006 are summarized in Table 12-5.[23]

Historical returns on value stocks have surpassed the returns on growth stocks, and this outperformance is especially true among smaller stocks. The smallest value stocks returned 17.73 percent per year, the highest of any of the 25 quintiles analyzed, while the smallest growth stocks returned only 4.70 percent, the lowest of any quintile. As firms become larger, the difference between the returns on value and growth stocks becomes much smaller. The largest value stocks returned 11.94 percent per year, while the largest growth stocks returned about 9.38 percent.

TABLE 12–5

Returns Ranked by Size and Book-to-Market Ratios, 1958–2012

Entire Period		Size Quintiles				
		Small	2	3	4	Large
Book to Market Quintiles	Value	17.73%	16.39%	16.74%	14.15%	11.94%
	2	16.24%	15.68%	15.18%	14.71%	10.67%
	3	13.56%	14.84%	13.36%	12.92%	10.54%
	4	12.53%	12.17%	13.14%	10.77%	10.21%
	Growth	4.70%	7.88%	8.62%	10.37%	9.38%
Excluding 1975–1983		Size Quintiles				
		Small	2	3	4	Large
Book to Market Quintiles	Value	13.83%	13.04%	13.97%	11.74%	10.71%
	2	12.67%	12.28%	12.72%	13.01%	8.95%
	3	9.66%	12.25%	10.64%	10.64%	9.50%
	4	8.52%	8.81%	10.21%	8.78%	9.00%
	Growth	0.56%	4.55%	6.02%	8.66%	9.01%

When the 1975-to-1983 period is removed, the return to small stocks shrinks, as expected. But it is noteworthy that the *difference* in the returns to small value and growth stocks remains large and virtually unchanged.

The dramatic differences in the cumulative return to smallest quintile growth and value stocks over the period from 1957 through 2012 are shown in Figure 12-5. The sum of $1,000 invested in small growth stocks since December 1997 has accumulated to $12,481 by the end of 2012. In contrast, small value stocks have accumulated to an eye-opening $7.9 million.

Accentuating the difference in the performance of small growth and value stocks is that the risk measured by the beta of the small-cap value stocks is about 1, while that of the small growth stocks is over 1½.

FIGURE 12–5

Returns to Smallest Quintile Growth and Value Stocks 1957–2012

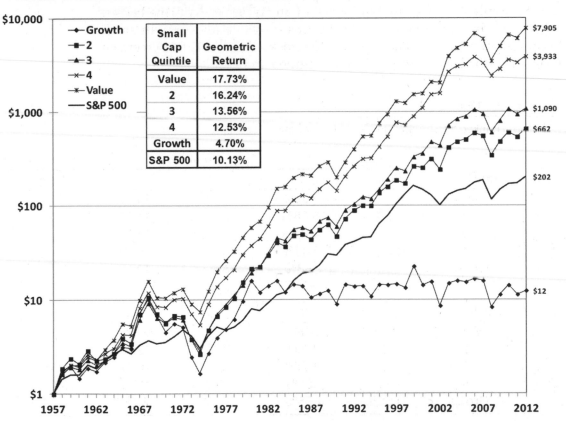

This means that the historical return to small value stocks is more than 7.5 percentage points above the efficient market prediction, while the historical return to small growth stocks has been more than 7 percentage points below its predicted level.

INITIAL PUBLIC OFFERINGS: THE DISAPPOINTING OVERALL RETURNS ON NEW SMALL-CAP GROWTH COMPANIES

Some of the most sought-after small stocks are initial public offerings (IPOs). New companies are launched with enthusiasm that excites investors, who dream that the upstarts will turn into the next Microsofts or Googles. The large demand for IPOs causes most IPOs to surge in price after they are released into the secondary market, offering those investors who were able to buy the stock at the offering prices immediate gains.[24] As a result, the vast majority of these IPOs are classified as growth stocks.

Certainly there have been some big winners among past IPOs. Walmart, which went public in October 1970, turned a $1,000 investment into more than $1,380,000 by the end of 2012. Investors who put $1,000 into Home Depot and Intel when they went public also turned into millionaires—if they held on to their stock. Cisco Systems was another winner. Floated to the public in February 1990, the stock of this networking supplier has delivered an average of 27 percent annual returns to investors through December 2012, although all the gains were made in the first 10 years after the IPO.

But can these big winners compensate for all the losers? To determine whether IPOs are good long-term investments, I examined the buy-and-hold returns of almost 9,000 IPOs issued between 1968 and 2001. I calculated the returns based on whether investors purchased the IPOs either at the end of the first month of trading or at the IPO offer price and held these stocks until December 31, 2003.[25]

There is no question that the losing IPOs far outnumber the winners. Of the 8,606 firms examined, the returns on 6,796 of these firms, or 79 percent, have subsequently underperformed the returns on a representative small stock index, and almost half the firms have underperformed by more than 10 percent per year.

Unfortunately, the huge winners like Cisco and Walmart *cannot compensate* for the thousands of losing IPOs. The *differences* in the returns to a portfolio that buys an equal dollar amount of all the IPOs issued in a given year and a portfolio in which an investor puts an equivalent dollar amount into a Russell 2000 small-cap stock index are featured in

Figure 12-6. Returns are computed from two starting points: (1) from the end of the month when the IPO was first issued and (2) from the usually lower IPO offer price.

The returns on all yearly IPO portfolios issued from 1968 through 2000 were examined to December 31, 2003, to allow for at least three years of subsequent returns to be calculated. The results are clear. From 1968 through 2000, the yearly IPO portfolios underperformed a small-cap stock index in 29 out of 33 years when measured *either* from the last day of trading in the month they were issued *or* from the IPO issue price.

Even in years such as 1971 when the big-winning stocks Southwest Airlines, Intel, and Limited Stores all went public, a portfolio of all the IPOs issued that year trailed the returns on a comparable small-cap stock index when measured through 2003, and the same happened in 1981 when Home Depot went public.

Even in the banner year 1986, when Microsoft, Oracle, Adobe, EMC, and Sun Microsystems all went public and delivered 30+ percent

FIGURE 12–6

Buy-and-Hold Returns of Almost 9,000 IPOs Issued Between 1968 and 2001

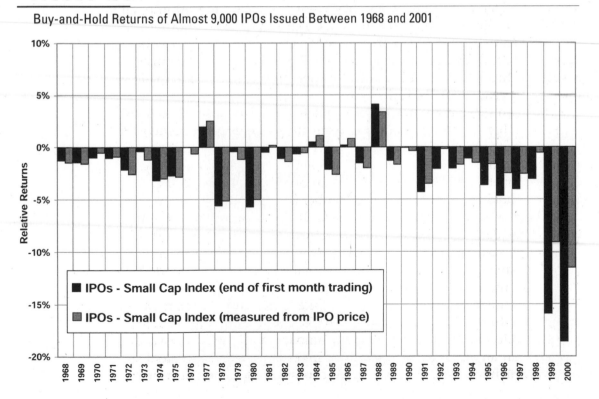

annual returns over the next 16 years, a portfolio of all the IPOs from that year just barely managed to keep up with the small-cap stock index.

The performances of the mostly technology IPOs issued in the late 1990s were disastrous. The yearly IPO portfolios in 1999 and 2000 underperformed the small-cap stock index by 8 and 12 percent per year, respectively, if measured from the IPO price, and 17 and 19 percent per year if measured from the end of the first month of trading.

Even stocks that doubled or more on the opening of trading were very poor long-term investments. Corvis Corporation, which designs products for the management of Internet traffic, went public on July 28, 2000. At the time of the offering, the firm had never sold a dollar's worth of goods and had $72 million in operating losses. Nevertheless, Corvis had a market value of $28.7 billion at the end of the first trading day, a capitalization that would place it in the top 100 most valuable firms in the United States.

It is sobering to contrast Corvis Corporation with Cisco Systems, which went public 10 years earlier. By the time of its IPO in February 1990, Cisco had already been a profitable company, earning healthy profits of $13.9 million on annual sales of $69.7 million. The market value of Cisco's IPO at the end of the first trading day was $287 *million*, exactly one-hundredth of the market value of Corvis Corporation, which at the time had not yet had either sales or profits. Cisco would be classified as a "growth" company in 1990 with a higher-than-average P/E ratio, but Corvis was a "hypergrowth" company.

Corvis Corporation, with an IPO price of $360 (split adjusted) on July 28, 2000, opened trading at $720 and later rose to $1,147 in early August. Subsequently the stock fell to $3.46 in April 2005.

THE NATURE OF GROWTH AND VALUE STOCKS

When choosing "growth" and "value" stocks, investors should keep in mind that these designations are not inherent in the product the firm produces or the industry that the firm is in. The designations depend solely on the market value relative to some fundamental measure of enterprise value, such as earnings or dividends.

Therefore, a firm in the technology sector, which is considered to be an industry with high growth prospects, could actually be classified as a value stock if it is out of favor with investors and sells for a low price relative to fundamentals. Alternatively, a promising auto manufacturer in a mature industry with limited growth potential could be classified a growth stock if its stock is in favor with investors and priced high relative to fundamentals.

In fact, over time many firms and even industries are alternately character-ized as "value" or "growth" as their market price fluctuates.

EXPLANATIONS OF SIZE AND VALUATION EFFECTS

There have been many attempts to explain the size and valuation factors in stock returns. Fama and French had hypothesized that there might be unusual financial stresses in value stocks that only appear during peri-ods of extreme crisis, and that investors demand a premium to hold value stocks in case those circumstances arise. Indeed, value stocks did underperform growth stocks during the Great Depression and the stock market crash of 1929 through 1932. But since then, value stocks have actually done *better* than growth stocks during both bear markets and economic recessions, so it is doubtful this is the answer.[26]

Another possible reason why value stocks outperform growth stocks is that the use of beta to summarize the risk of a stock is too nar-row. Beta is derived from the capital asset pricing theory, a static pricing model that depends on an unchanged set of investment opportunities. In a dynamic economy, real interest rates proxy changes in the opportu-nity set for investors, and stock prices will respond not only to earnings prospects but also to changes in interest rates.

In an article entitled "Bad Beta, Good Beta," John Campbell sepa-rates the beta related to interest rate fluctuations (which he called "good beta") from the beta related to business cycles (which he called "bad beta")[27] based on historical evidence. But recent data are not supportive of this theory, as growth stocks first rose relative to value stocks from 1997 to 2000 when real interest rates were rising, and then the stocks sub-sequently underperformed as real interest rates dropped.

Another theory about why growth stocks have underperformed value stocks is behavioral: investors get overexcited about the growth prospects of firms with rapidly rising earnings and bid them up exces-sively. "Story stocks" such as Intel or Microsoft, which in the past pro-vided fantastic returns, capture the fancy of investors, while those firms providing solid earnings with unexciting growth rates are neglected.[28]

The Noisy Market Hypothesis

A more general theory for the outperformance of value stocks is that stock prices are constantly being impacted by buying and selling that are unrelated to the fundamental value of the firm. These buyers and sellers are called "liquidity" or "noise" traders in the academic literature. Their transactions may be motivated by taxes, fiduciary responsibilities, rebalancing of their portfolio, or other personal reasons. In order to explain the value and size effects we see in the historical data, another assumption needs to be added: that price movements caused by these liquidity traders are not *immediately* reversed by those trading on fundamental information.

This assumption is a deviation from the efficient market hypothesis that claims that at all times the price of a security is the best unbiased estimate of the underlying value of the enterprise. I have called the alternative assumption the "noisy market hypothesis" because the buying and selling by noise or liquidity traders often obscure the fundamental value of the firm.[29]

The noisy market hypothesis can provide an explanation for the size and value effects.[30] A positive liquidity shock raises the price of the stock above its fundamental value and makes that stock more likely to be classified as a "large" or "growth" stock. When this positive shock disappears, these large growth stocks decline in price and thus have lower returns. On the other hand, a negative liquidity shock lowers the price and makes it more likely a stock will belong to the "small" or "value" category, which is likely to be underpriced relative to its fundamentals. When the negative shock disappears, these value stocks have higher returns.

Liquidity Investing

Recently another factor has been found to explain return: the "liquidity" of a stock. Liquidity is a property of an asset that measures the discount that sellers would encounter if they were forced to sell on short notice. Assets with high liquidity are defined to have low discounts, while assets with low liquidity have high discounts. One convenient measure of liquidity is the ratio of the average daily volume of a stock compared with the total number of shares outstanding, often referred to as the *turnover* of the stock. Stocks with high turnover have higher liquidity than stocks with lower turnover.

Recently Roger Ibbotson and others have determined that stocks with low liquidity have significantly higher returns than stocks with high liquidity.[31] Analyzing all New York, Amex, and Nasdaq stocks from 1972 to the present, they determined that stocks with the lowest quartile (25 percent) of turnover have a compound annual return of 14.74 percent per year, almost double the return of stocks with the highest quartile of liquidity. And they determined that this was not just because many of the small stocks have low turnover, and so the liquidity effect is not just mimicking the size effect. In fact, among the smallest quartile of stocks, measured by market value, the impact of liquidity was even more pronounced, as the return on the lowest quartile of these small stocks averaged 15.64 percent per year, against only a 1.11 percent return for those with the highest turnover.[32]

There are several good reasons for the liquidity effect. It has been long recognized that among assets with identical or near identical risk-return profiles, those that are more actively traded sell at a higher price. In the U.S. Treasury market, the "on-the-run" long-term government bonds, which are considered benchmark and most actively traded, command a higher market price than virtually identical bonds with a maturity just a few months' difference. Traders and speculators are willing to pay a premium for assets that they can buy and sell in quantity with low transaction costs. All investors value flexibility—the ability to change their mind or respond to altered circumstances quickly without paying a substantial discount or premium if they wish to sell or buy their asset. Furthermore, many large mutual funds would not be able to purchase large quantities of relatively inactive firms since to do so would require driving up their price to a point where the return is no longer attractive.

The presence of an even stronger liquidity premium among small stocks can be explained since small stocks that are actively traded are subject to speculation, particularly IPOs or those that catch the eye of traders looking for unusual trading activity. After the speculative period ends, these stocks often exhibit poor returns. There is no question that in the post–World War II period, IBM generated more excitement and more trading activity than Standard Oil, although as we showed at the beginning of this chapter, Standard Oil delivered higher returns to investors.

CONCLUSION

Historical research shows that investors can achieve higher long-term returns without taking on increased risk by focusing on the factors relating to the valuation of companies. Dividend yield has been one such factor, and the price/earnings ratio has been another. More recently, liquidity has been identified as another factor. Over time, portfolios of stocks with higher dividend yields, lower P/E ratios, and lower liquidity have outperformed the market more than would be predicted by the efficient market hypothesis.

Nevertheless, investors should be aware that no strategy will outperform the market all the time. Small stocks exhibit periodic surges that have enabled their long-term performance to beat that of large stocks, but most of the time their performance has only matched or fallen behind that of large stocks. Furthermore, value stocks have generally done well in bear markets, although in the last recession, value stocks, because of the high preponderance of financials, underperformed growth stocks. This means that investors must exercise patience if they decide to pursue these return-enhancing strategies.

13

Global Investing

Today let's talk about a growth industry. Because investing world-wide is a growth industry. The great growth industry is international portfolio investing.

—John Templeton, 1984[1]

Chapter 5 showed that the superior long-term returns of stocks were not unique to the United States. Investors in other countries realized returns that were near or even exceeded those in the United States. However, until the late 1980s, foreign markets were almost exclusively the domains of native investors and were considered too remote or risky to be entertained by outsiders.

But no longer. The *globalization* of financial markets is not just a prediction for the future; it is a fact right now. The United States, once the unchallenged giant of capital markets, is today only one of many countries in which investors can accumulate wealth.

At the end of World War II, U.S. stocks composed almost 90 percent of the world's equity capitalization; in 1970, they still made up two-thirds. But today, the U.S. market constitutes less than half of the world's stock values, and that fraction is shrinking. Figure 13-1 shows the percentage of the world equity markets that are headquartered in each country in May 2013.

The developed world's percentage is still high, at over 85.8 percent, but that percentage is declining. As we learned in Chapter 4, the developing world is now producing more than one-half of the world's GDP, a fraction that will expand to two-thirds in the next 20 years. It is certain that the percentage of equity headquartered in the emerging economies will grow rapidly.

F I G U R E   13–1

Distribution of World Equities by Market Value, 2012

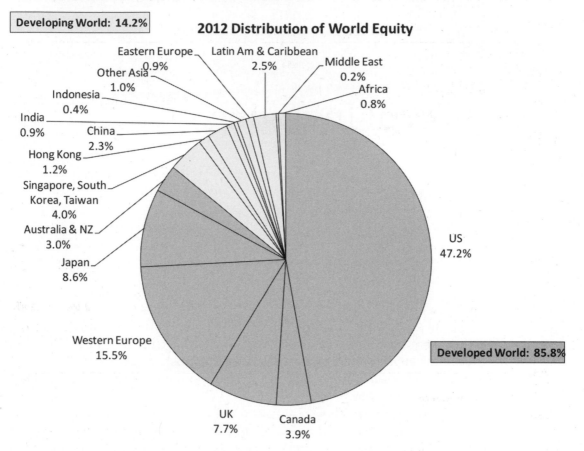

FOREIGN INVESTING AND ECONOMIC GROWTH

The tremendous growth in capital in the emerging economies might prompt some investors to overweight that sector. But the prospect of economic growth is not the reason why one should invest globally. In fact, it will probably surprise readers to learn that there is a negative correlation between economic growth and stock returns, and this finding extends not only to those countries in the developed world but also to those in the developing world.

Figure 13-2A plots the growth of real per capita GDP against dollar returns in the 19 countries that were included in the data used by Dimson, Staunton, and Marsh from 1900 to the present.[2] Australia had

FIGURE 13–2

Dollar Returns and per Capita Real GDP Growth in Developed and Developing Economies

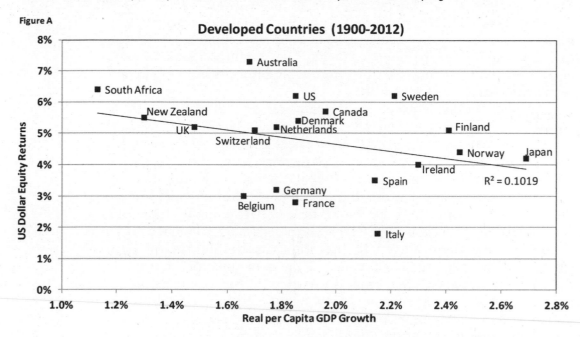

Figure A

Developed Countries (1900-2012)

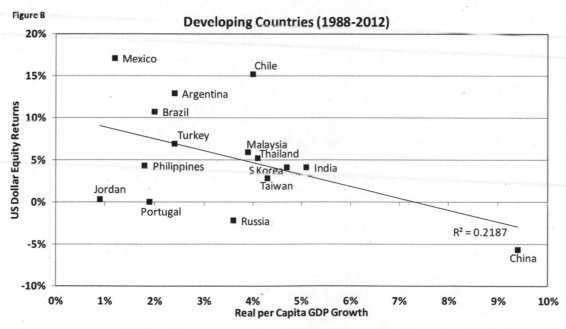

Figure B

Developing Countries (1988-2012)

the fifth-lowest growth rate but had the best returns, and South Africa had the lowest growth rate and the second-best returns. Japan had by far the highest growth rate but below-average stock returns.

As Figure 13-2B shows, the negative correlation between stock returns and growth also extends to the developing countries. The fastest-growing country by far, China, has had the worst returns. Mexico, Brazil, and Argentina are among the slowest-growing countries but have generated excellent returns for investors.

How could this happen? For the same reason that Standard Oil of New Jersey had better returns than IBM even though IBM beat Standard Oil on every measure of growth. Low prices and high dividend yield were among the keys to Standard Oil's superior returns, the same reason why investments in Mexican stocks outpaced those in Chinese stocks.

The conventional wisdom that investors should buy stocks in the fastest-growing countries is wrong for the same reason that buying the fastest-growing firms is wrong. China has indisputably been the world's fastest-growing country over the past three decades, but investors in China realized poor returns because of the overvaluation of Chinese equities. On the other hand, stock prices in Latin America were generally cheap, and the prices remained low relative to fundamental values. Patient investors, buying value instead of hype, won out.

But this result begets the question: If faster growth is not the reason to buy international stocks, what is?

DIVERSIFICATION IN WORLD MARKETS

The reason for investing internationally is to diversify your portfolio and reduce risk. Foreign investing provides diversification in the same way that investing in different sectors of the domestic economy provides diversification. It would be poor investment strategy to pin your hopes on just one stock or one sector of the economy. Similarly it is not a good strategy to buy the stocks only in your own country, especially when developed economies are becoming an ever smaller part of the world's market.

International diversification reduces risk because the stock prices of different countries do not rise and fall in tandem, and this asynchronous movement of returns dampens the volatility of the portfolio. As long as two assets are not perfectly correlated, i.e., their correlation coefficient is less than 1, then combining these assets will lower the risk of your portfolio for a given return or, alternatively, raise the return for a given risk.

International Stock Returns

Table 13-1 displays the historical risk and returns for dollar-based investors in the international markets from 1970 to the present (1988 for emerging market data). Over the entire period, the dollar returns among different regions do not differ greatly.

Investors in U.S. stocks realized a 9.39 percent compound return; those in EAFE (generally non-U.S. developed countries)[3] had a slightly higher 9.74 percent return. Over the period, the correlation between EAFE and U.S. returns was 65 percent, meaning that the risk to dollar investors with an 80 percent U.S. and 20 percent EAFE portfolio would be .175, which is 2 percent below the risk of holding U.S. stocks alone.

Since 1970, Europe realized slightly higher returns than the United States, while Japan realized slightly lower returns. Comprehensive emerging market returns are available from 1988 onward. The emerging market returned 12.73 percent per year over that period, nearly 3 percentage points higher than the return to U.S. stocks, and U.S. stock returns were less correlated with emerging market stock returns than with EAFE returns. It should be noted that since 1988, EAFE returns have trailed U.S. returns, almost entirely because Japan had negative returns from 1988 through 2012.

The Japanese Market Bubble

The Japanese stock market in the last quarter of the twentieth century stands as one of the most remarkable bubbles in world history. In the

TABLE 13-1

Dollar Risks and Returns in International Stocks 1970–2012

| Country | U.S. $ Returns | | Domestic | Exchange | Total | Correlation |
or Region	1970–2012	1988–2012	Risk	Risk	Risk	Coefficient*
World	9.39%	7.23%	17.48%	4.79%	18.17%	87.50%
EAFE	9.74%	5.49%	20.00%	9.62%	22.61%	65.27%
USA	9.63%	9.83%	17.80%	—	17.80%	—
Europe	10.33%	8.83%	20.73%	10.75%	22.13%	76.06%
Japan	9.15%	–0.14%	28.08%	12.52%	33.29%	35.19%
Em Mkts**	—	12.73%	68.77%	17.87%	35.89%	52.37%

*Correlation between U.S. dollar returns and foreign market US dollar returns.

**Data for emerging markets is from 1988 to 2012.

1970s and 1980s, Japanese stock returns averaged more than 10 percentage points per year above U.S. returns and surpassed those from every
other country. The bull market in Japan was so dramatic that by the end
of 1989, for the first time since the early 1900s, the market value of the
American stock market was no longer the world's largest. Japan, a country whose economic base was totally destroyed in World War II and that
had only half the population and 4 percent of the land mass of the
United States, housed the world's biggest stock market.

The superior returns in the Japanese market during the great bull
market attracted billions of dollars of foreign investment. By the end of
the 1980s, valuations on many Japanese stocks reached stratospheric levels. Nippon Telephone and Telegraph, or NTT, the Japanese version of
America's former telephone monopoly AT&T, sported a P/E ratio above
300. This company alone had a market value that dwarfed the aggregate
stock values of all but a handful of countries. Valuations reached and in
some cases exceeded those attained in the great U.S. technology stock
bubble of 2000 and were far above any valuations ever seen in the U.S.
or European markets.

During his travels to Japan in 1987, Leo Melamed, president of the
Chicago Mercantile Exchange, asked his hosts how such remarkably
high valuations could be warranted. "You don't understand," they
responded. "We've moved to an entirely new way of valuing stocks here
in Japan." And that is when, as Martin Mayer reported, Melamed knew
Japanese stocks were doomed.[4] It is when investors cast aside the lessons of history that those lessons come back to haunt them.

When the Nikkei Dow Jones, which had surpassed 39,000 in
December 1989, fell sharply in the following years, the mystique of the
Japanese market was broken. Japanese stocks fell to 7,000 in 2008, less
than 20 percent of their value at the peak of the bull market two decades
earlier.

Many point to the Japanese market as a refutation of the thesis that in
the long run the stock market will always be the superior investment. But
there were glaring warnings of the Japanese bubble. At the peak of the
market, Japanese stocks sold for well over 100 times earnings, more than
3 times the level that our market sold at the top of its biggest bubble that
reached its height in 2000 when technology and Internet stocks peaked. In
contrast, Japanese stocks in 1970 sold at the same earnings multiple that
prevailed in the rest of the world stock markets, and indeed from 1970
onward Japanese stocks have matched the returns in other countries.

The bubble high of the Nasdaq Index in March 2000 was not unlike
that of the Japanese market. Price/earnings ratios in the tech-laden mar-

ket topped 100, and dividend yields fell close to zero. It is not surprising that in 2013, more than a decade after its peak, the Nasdaq Index, just like the Nikkei, is still well below its high.

STOCK RISKS

The risks for dollar investors in foreign stocks are measured by the standard deviation of annual dollar returns. There are two components of risk: fluctuations of stock prices calculated in their local currencies and fluctuations in the exchange rate between the dollar and the local currency. In Table 13.1 these are described as the domestic risk and the exchange risk.

For the non-U.S. developed countries (EAFE), local risk is 20 percent, and exchange risk is almost half that number at 9.62 percent. But the total dollar risk is only 13 percent higher than the local risk, at 22.61 percent. This is because exchange risk often moves in the opposite direction of local risk. Exchange rate risk for the dollar investor is somewhat higher for Japanese stocks than for European stocks.

The interpretation of the dollar risk for the emerging markets requires special care. The raw data show that exchange rate fluctuations actually offset one-half of the domestic risk. But closer examination of the data shows that this result is dominated by the high inflation rates in the earlier data that sent local returns soaring while exchange rates were depreciating rapidly. Since 2000, when most developing countries brought down inflation to lower levels, fluctuations in the exchange rate have actually added, and in some cases added substantially, to the local stock risk.

Should You Hedge Foreign Exchange Risk?

Since foreign exchange risk generally adds to the local risk, it may be desirable for investors in foreign markets to hedge against currency movements. *Currency hedging* means entering into a currency contract or purchasing a security that automatically hedges foreign exchange fluctuations.

But hedging foreign exchange risk is not always the right strategy. The cost of hedging depends on the difference between the interest rate in the foreign country and the dollar interest rate; and if a country's currency is expected to depreciate (typically because of high inflation), the cost of hedging could be quite high.

For example, even though the British pound depreciated from $4.80 to about $1.60 over the past century, the cost of hedging this decline exceeded the depreciation in the pound. Thus the dollar returns to British stocks were higher if investors did not hedge the decline in the pound than if they did.

For investors with long-term horizons, hedging currency risk in foreign stock markets may not be important. In the long run, exchange rate movements are determined primarily by differences in inflation between countries, a phenomenon called *purchasing power parity*. Since equities are claims on real assets, their long-term returns have compensated investors for changes in inflation and thus protected investors from exchange depreciation caused by higher inflation in the foreign countries.

Over shorter periods of time, investors may reduce their dollar risk by hedging exchange risk. Often, bad economic news for a country depresses both its stock market and currency value, and investors can avoid the latter by hedging. Furthermore, if it is the policy of the central bank to lower the currency value in order to stimulate exports and the economy, hedged investors can take advantage of the latter without suffering the losses of the former. For example, investors who took hedged positions in Japanese stocks late in 2012, when Prime Minister Shinzo Abe advocated yen depreciation to stimulate the economy, far outpaced the gains made by those who did not hedge the depreciating yen.

Diversification: Sector or Country?

Although capital markets are becoming more global, there is one aspect of international investing that stands in the way of that trend. International investing today is allocated by the country in which the firm has its headquarters, even if the firm does not sell or even manufacture goods in its headquarters country. To accommodate current practice, in the early 1990s Standard & Poor's announced that no non-U.S.-based companies would be added to its benchmark S&P 500 Index, and in 2002 Standard & Poor's removed the remaining seven foreign-based firms, including such giants as Royal Dutch Petroleum and Unilever, from the index.[5]

Supporters of the headquarters approach argue that government regulations and legal structures of a particular country do matter, even when most of the firm's sales, earnings, and production come from abroad. But these home-country influences will very likely diminish as globalization advances. It is far more logical to pursue an investing strategy by allocating wealth according to the industrial sector in which the firm belongs, wherever its headquarters may be.

Sector investment strategies are popular in the U.S. equity markets but not as popular internationally. But I believe that this will change. In fact, I envision a future of *international incorporations*, where firms choose to be governed by a set of international rules agreed upon among nations and where the headquarters of the company resides will be of very little or no importance. International incorporation standards will be similar to the growing popularity of the accounting standards promulgated by the International Accounting Standards Board over country-based standards. If international incorporation gained prominence, there would be no meaning to "headquartered country," and investment allocations would have to be made on the basis of global sectors or by production and distribution locations. In this future, a U.S.-only portfolio would be very narrow indeed. In that case, a sector approach to international investing may well supplant the country approach in coming years.

Sector Allocation Around the World

Let's take a closer look at the importance of these industrial sectors by region and by country. The 10 Global International Classification (GIC) industrial sectors in five geographic regions (United States, EAFE, Europe, Japan, and the emerging markets)[6] are shown in Table 13-2 by the respective weight of each industrial sector.[7] The 20 largest firms by market value headquartered in and outside the United States are shown in Table 13-3.

Despite the meltdown that followed the financial crisis of 2008, the Financials sector is the largest sector in the world, almost double the size of

TABLE 13–2

Sector Allocation by World Regions, June 2013

	S&P 500	EAFE	Japan	Em Mkts	Europe	Global
Consumer Discretionary	11.8%	11.4%	21.4%	8.2%	9.6%	11.4%
Consumer Staples	10.6%	11.9%	6.6%	9.3%	14.6%	10.6%
Energy	10.6%	7.1%	1.2%	11.6%	9.7%	10.1%
Financials	16.7%	25.2%	20.7%	27.9%	21.4%	21.2%
Healthcare	12.6%	10.4%	6.3%	1.3%	12.8%	10.2%
Industrials	10.1%	12.5%	18.9%	6.4%	11.4%	10.5%
Info Tech	18.0%	4.4%	10.9%	14.6%	2.8%	12.2%
Materials	3.3%	8.3%	6.0%	9.7%	8.4%	6.1%
Telecom	2.8%	5.1%	4.9%	7.6%	5.3%	4.3%
Utilities	3.2%	3.7%	3.0%	3.5%	4.0%	3.3%

TABLE 13-3

Largest U.S. and Foreign Companies, June 2013

Rank	U.S. Companies	Sector	Market Cap ($B)	#	Foreign Companies	Country	Sector	Market Cap ($B)
1	Apple	Info Tech	$415	1	PetroChina	China	Energy	$243
2	Exxon Mobil	Energy	$407	2	I & C Bank of China	China	Financials	$237
3	Microsoft	Info Tech	$298	3	Nestle	Switzerland	Consumer Staples	$218
4	General Electric	Industrials	$247	4	Roche	Switzerland	Healthcare	$213
5	Johnson & Johnson	Healthcare	$239	5	Royal Dutch Shell	Netherlands	Energy	$211
6	Chevron	Energy	$236	6	HSBC Holdings	Britain	Financials	$205
7	Google	Info Tech	$291	7	China Mobile	Hong Kong	Telecom	$204
8	IBM	Info Tech	$229	8	China Constr. Bank	China	Financials	$196
9	Procter & Gamble	Consumer Staples	$213	9	Novartis	Switzerland	Healthcare	$194
10	Berkshire Hathaway	Financials	$284	10	Toyota	Japan	Cons Discr	$194
11	JPMorgan Chase	Financials	$205	11	Samsung	South Korea	Info Tech	$188
12	Pfizer	Healthcare	$200	12	BHP Billiton	Australia	Materials	$160
13	Wells Fargo	Financials	$218	13	Anheuser-Busch	Belgium	Consumer Staples	$152
14	AT&T	Telecom	$191	14	Vodafone	Britain	Telecom	$145
15	Coca-Cola	Consumer Staples	$184	15	AG Bank of China	China	Financials	$143
16	Citigroup	Financials	$157	16	Sanofi	France	Healthcare	$142
17	Philip Morris Int	Consumer Staples	$151	17	BP	Britain	Energy	$136
18	Merck	Healthcare	$146	18	Bank of China	China	Financials	$129
19	Verizon	Telecom	$144	19	GlaxoSmithKline	Britain	Healthcare	$127
20	Bank of America	Financials	$144	20	Total SA	France	Energy	$119

the next-largest sector, Information Technology. In the United States, the Financials sector is the second largest at 16.7 percent of market value, just below that of Technology but well down from the 22 percent weight before the financial crisis. The largest share of the financial market value sector is found in the emerging markets, as four Chinese banks are in the top 20 non-U.S. firms, ranked by market value. Berkshire Hathaway, recently admitted to the S&P 500, is the largest firm in the Financials sector; Berkshire is classified as a financial because of its large stake in insurance companies. In the United States, Buffett's Berkshire is followed by JPMorgan Chase. HSBC Holdings (headquartered in the United Kingdom) and Commonwealth Bank of Australia are the largest EAFE financials.

In the Consumer Discretionary sector, Japan has by far the highest weight of all geographic regions, primarily because of the presence of Toyota Motors, one of the 10 largest non-U.S.-based corporations in the world. In the United States, Walt Disney and Home Depot are the largest firms in this sector, and in EAFE Daimler AG follows Toyota.

Europe has the largest weight in the Consumer Staples sector, with Swiss Nestle and Belgian Anheuser-Busch Inbev both belonging to the top 20 non-U.S. firms by market value. In the United States, Procter & Gamble, Coca-Cola, and Philip Morris International all belong to the top 20 U.S. firms. The Brazilian company AmBev, specializing in soft drinks, is the largest firm in the emerging markets.

In the Energy sector Exxon Mobil is the largest firm by market value in the world. But the Chinese Petrochina is the largest non-U.S. company in terms of market value. Chevron in the United States and Royal Dutch, BP, and Total in Europe all belong to the top 20 non-U.S. firms.

In the Information Technology sector, Apple, which vies with Exxon Mobil for the world's largest firm by market value, is followed by Google, IBM, and South Korean Samsung Electronics, while SAP is the largest European technology firm. In the Health Care sector, Johnson & Johnson is the largest in the world, followed by Roche Holdings and Novartis of Switzerland and U.S. pharmaceutical giants Pfizer and Merck. In the Industrials sector General Electric dominates the list, which is followed by the German Siemens. In the Materials sector, only the Australian BHP Billiton makes the top 20 list, with Monsanto being the highest-valued materials firm in the United States. In Telecom, AT&T and Verizon make the top 20 list in the United States, while China Mobile and the British Vodafone Group make the top 20 non-U.S. firms. Finally, no utility makes the top 20 list of either the U.S. or non-U.S. firms, with Duke Energy being the largest in the United States and the British National Grid being the largest in EAFE.

Private and Public Capital

Exxon Mobil may be the largest company by market value in the world, and it has the largest reserves of oil and gas (25 billion barrels estimated in 2011) of any private company. But if one includes government-owned companies, this U.S. giant falls far from the top of the list. Saudi Arabia's Aramco and Iran's NIOC together have estimated reserves in excess of 600 billion barrels![8] If one were to value these reserves at only $10 a barrel, less than one-tenth the going market price, these two companies are worth in excess of $6 trillion. This is just a fraction of the wealth that is still owned by governments around the world. In many countries, gas, electric, and water facilities are still owned and operated by government, and governments have a large, if not a controlling, interest in many other industries.

Even in such privatized countries as the United States, the federal, state, and local governments own trillions of dollars of wealth in such forms as land, natural resources, roads, dams, schools, and parks. There is strong disagreement about how much of this wealth, if any, should be privatized. But there is good evidence that privatized firms often do experience efficiency gains. Growth of the world's capital stock will come not only from private entrepreneurs but from the privatization of many government-owned assets.

CONCLUSION

The inexorable trend toward integration of the world's economies and markets will certainly continue in this new millennium. No country will be able to dominate every market, and industry leaders are apt to emerge from any place on the globe. The globalization of the world economy means that the strength of management, product lines, and marketing will be far more important factors in achieving success than where the firm is headquartered.

Sticking only to U.S. equities is a risky strategy for investors. No advisor would recommend investing only in those stocks whose name begins with the letters A through F. But sticking only to U.S. equities would be just such a bet since U.S.-based equity will continue to shrink as a share of the world market. Only those investors who have a fully diversified world portfolio will be able to reap the best returns with the lowest risk.

PART III

HOW THE ECONOMIC ENVIRONMENT IMPACTS STOCKS

Gold, Monetary Policy, and Inflation

In the stock market, as with horse racing, money makes the mare go. Monetary conditions exert an enormous influence on stock prices.
—MARTIN ZWEIG, 1990[1]

If Fed Chairman Alan Greenspan were to whisper to me what his monetary policy was going to be over the next two years, it wouldn't change one thing I do.
—WARREN BUFFETT, 1994[2]

On September 20, 1931, the British government announced that England was going off the gold standard. It would no longer exchange gold for deposits at the Bank of England or for British currency, the pound sterling. The government insisted that this action was only "temporary," that it had no intention of forever abolishing its commitment to exchange its money for gold. Nevertheless, it was to mark the beginning of the end of both Britain's and the world's gold standard—a standard that had existed for over 200 years.

Fearing chaos in the currency market, the British government ordered the London Stock Exchange closed. New York Stock Exchange officials decided to keep the U.S. exchange open but also braced for panic selling. The suspension of gold payments by Britain, the second-greatest industrial power, raised fears that other industrial countries might be forced to abandon gold. Central bankers called the suspension "a world financial crisis of unprecedented dimensions."[3] For the first time ever, the New York Stock Exchange banned short selling in an effort to shore up stock share prices.

But much to New York's surprise, stocks rallied sharply after a short sinking spell, and many issues ended the day higher. Clearly, British suspension was not seen as negative for American equities.

Nor was this "unprecedented financial crisis" a problem for the British stock market. When England reopened the exchange on September 23, prices soared. The AP wire gave the following colorful description of the reopening of the exchange:

> Swarms of stock brokers, laughing and cheering like schoolboys, invaded the Stock Exchange today for the resumption of trading after the two-day compulsory close-down—and their buoyancy was reflected in the prices of many securities.[4]

Despite the dire predictions of government officials, shareholders viewed casting off the gold standard as good for the economy and even better for stocks. As a result of the gold suspension, the British government could expand credit by lending reserves to the banking system, and the fall in the value of the British pound would increase the demand for British exports. The stock market gave a ringing endorsement to the actions that shocked conservative world financiers. In fact, September 1931 marked the low point of the British stock market, while the United States and other countries that stayed on the gold standard continued to sink into depression. The lessons from history: liquidity and easy credit feed the stock market, and the ability of the central banks to provide liquidity at will is a critical plus for stock values.

A year and a half later, the United States joined Britain in abandoning the gold standard, and finally every nation eventually went to a fiat, paper money standard. But despite the paper standard's inflationary bias, the world has become comfortable with the new monetary system, and the stock market enjoys the flexibility it accords policy makers.

MONEY AND PRICES

In 1950, President Truman startled the nation in his State of the Union address with a prediction that the typical American family income would reach $12,000 by the year 2000. Considering that median family income was about $3,300 at the time, $12,000 seemed like a princely sum and implied that America was going to make unprecedented economic progress in the next half century. In fact, President Truman's prediction has proved quite modest. The median family income in 2000 was $41,349. However, in 2000 that sum bought less than $6,000 in 1950 prices, a testament to the inflation of the last half century. So instead of the typical family income soaring over 12 times, from $3,300 to $41,349 in roughly half a century, real incomes have only doubled, from $3,300 to $6,000, because of the inflation bite.

Inflation and deflation have characterized history as far back as economists have gathered data. However, since 1955 there has never been a single year in which the U.S. consumer price index has declined.[5] What has changed over the past 60 years that makes inflation the rule rather than the exception? The answer is simple: control of the money supply has shifted from gold to the government. With this shift, the government can always provide enough liquidity so that prices do not decline.

We analyzed the overall price level in the United States and Great Britain over the last 210 years in Chapter 5. There was no overall inflation until World War II and then protracted inflation after the war. Before the Great Depression, inflation occurred only because of war, crop failures, or other crises. But the behavior of prices in the postwar period has been entirely different. The price level has almost never declined: the only question is at what rate prices will rise.

Economists have long known that one variable is paramount in determining the price level: the amount of money in circulation. The robust relation between money and inflation is strongly supported by the evidence. Take a look at Figure 14-1, which displays money and prices in the United States since 1830. The overall trend of the price level has closely tracked that of the money supply normalized for the level of output.

The strong relation between the money supply and consumer prices is a worldwide phenomenon. No sustained inflation is possible without continuous money creation, and every hyperinflation in history has been associated with an explosion of the money supply. There is overwhelming evidence that countries with high monetary growth experience high inflation, while countries with restrained money growth have low inflation.

Why is the quantity of money so closely connected to the price level? Because the price of money, like any good, is determined by supply and demand. The supply of deposits is closely controlled by the central bank. The demand for dollars is derived from the demand of households and firms transacting billions of dollars of goods and services in a complex economy. If the supply of dollars increases more than

FIGURE 14–1

Money and Prices in the United States, 1830–2012

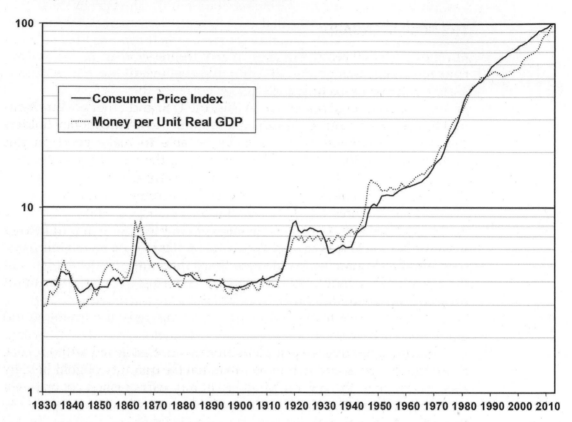

the number of goods produced, this leads to inflation. The classic description of the inflationary process—"too many dollars chasing too few goods"—is as apt today as ever.

One might wonder why the huge monetary expansion of the Federal Reserve (and other central banks) since the monetary crisis has not turned into inflation. Milton Friedman, in *The Monetary History of the United States*, determined that it was the quantity of deposits plus currency, which he defined as M2, that had the closest link with inflation, not the monetary base, which is the sum of reserves and currency. The monetary base in the United States did triple from 2007 to 2013, but almost all the increase went into excess reserves in the banking system that had not been lent out and therefore did not create deposits. To be sure, the Fed must monitor these reserves closely to prevent excess credit creation from turning into inflation. But the low inflation, despite the expansionary policies of the world central banks, has not contradicted the historical link between money and prices.

THE GOLD STANDARD

For the nearly 200 years prior to the Great Depression, most of the industrialized world was on a gold standard. This meant that central banks were obligated to exchange the paper currency they issued for a fixed amount of gold on demand. To do this, the U.S. and other governments had to keep gold reserves in sufficient quantity to assure money holders that the governments would always be able to make good on this exchange. Since the total quantity of gold in the world increased at a slow pace—new gold discoveries were relatively small compared with the world's total gold supply—prices of goods remained stable.

The only times the gold standard was suspended were during crises, such as wars. Great Britain suspended the gold standard during both the Napoleonic Wars and World War I, but in both cases it returned to the gold standard at the original exchange rate. The United States temporarily suspended the gold standard during the Civil War, but it returned to the standard after the war ended.[6]

The adherence to the gold standard is the reason why the world experienced no overall inflation during the nineteenth and early twentieth centuries. But overall price stability was not achieved without cost. Since the money in circulation had to equal the quantity of gold held by the government, the central bank essentially relinquished control over monetary conditions. This meant that the central bank was unable to provide additional money during economic or financial crises. In the 1930s, adherence to the gold standard, which had restrained the government from pursuing inflationary financial policies, turned into a straitjacket from which the government sought to escape.

THE ESTABLISHMENT OF THE FEDERAL RESERVE

Periodic liquidity crises caused by strict adherence to the gold standard prompted Congress in 1913 to pass the Federal Reserve Act that created the Federal Reserve System. The responsibilities of the Fed were to provide an "elastic" currency, which meant that in times of banking crises the Fed would become the lender of last resort. In trying times, the central bank would provide currency to enable depositors to withdraw their deposits without forcing banks to liquidate loans and other assets.

In the long run, money creation by the Fed was still constrained by the gold standard since the government's paper currency, or Federal Reserve notes, promised to pay a fixed amount of gold. But in the short run, the Federal Reserve was free to create money as long as it did not threaten the convertibility of Federal Reserve notes to gold at the exchange rate of $20.67 per ounce that prevailed before the Great Depression. Yet the Fed was never given any guidance by Congress or by the Federal Reserve Act on how to conduct monetary policy and determine the right quantity of money.

THE FALL OF THE GOLD STANDARD

This lack of guidance had disastrous consequences just two decades later. In the wake of the stock crash of 1929, the world economies entered a severe downturn. Falling asset prices and failing businesses made depositors suspicious of banks' assets. When word was received that a few banks were having problems meeting depositors' withdrawals, a run on the banks ensued.

In an astounding display of institutional ineptitude, the Federal Reserve failed to provide extra reserves in order to stem the banking panic and prevent a crash of the financial system, even though the Fed had the explicit power to do so under the Federal Reserve Act. In addition, those depositors who did receive their money sought even greater safety by turning their notes back to the Treasury in exchange for gold, a process that put extreme pressure on the government's gold reserves. The banking panic soon spread from the United States to Great Britain and Continental Europe.

To prevent a steep loss of gold, Great Britain took the first step and abandoned the gold standard on September 20, 1931, suspending the payment of gold for sterling. Eighteen months later, on April 19, 1933, the United States also suspended the gold standard as the Depression and financial crisis worsened.

Investors loved the government's newfound flexibility, and the reaction of the U.S. stock market to gold's overthrow was even more enthusiastic than that in Great Britain. Stocks soared over 9 percent on the day the government left the gold standard and almost 6 percent the next day. This constituted the greatest two-day rally in U.S. stock market history. Investors felt the government could now provide the extra liquidity needed to stabilize commodity prices and stimulate the economy, which they regarded as a boon for stocks. Bonds, however, fell, as investors feared the inflationary consequences of leaving the gold standard. *BusinessWeek*, in a positive editorial on the suspension, asserted:

> With one decisive gesture, [President Roosevelt] throws out of the window all the elaborate hocus-pocus of "defending the dollar." He defies an ancient superstition and takes his stand with the advocates of managed money. . . . The job now is to manage our money effectively, wisely, with self-restraint. It can be done.[7]

POSTDEVALUATION MONETARY POLICY

Ironically, while the right to redeem dollars for gold was denied U.S. citizens, it was soon reinstated for foreign central banks at the devalued price of $35 per ounce. As part of the Bretton Woods agreement, which set up the rules of international exchange rates after the close of World War II, the U.S. government promised to exchange all dollars for gold held by foreign central banks at the fixed rate of $35 per ounce as long as these countries fixed their currency to the dollar.

In the postwar period, as inflation increased and the dollar's worth declined, gold seemed more and more attractive to foreigners. U.S. gold reserves began to dwindle, despite official claims that the United States had no plans to change its gold exchange policy at the fixed price of $35 per ounce. As late as 1965, President Johnson stated unequivocally in the *Economic Report of the President*: "There can be no question of our capacity and determination to maintain the gold value of the dollar at $35.00 per ounce. The full resources of the Nation are pledged to that end."[8]

But this was not so. As the gold reserves dwindled, Congress removed the gold-backing requirement for U.S. currency in 1968. In next year's *Economic Report of the President*, President Johnson declared: "Myths about gold die slowly. But progress can be made—as we have demonstrated. In 1968, the Congress ended the obsolete gold-backing requirement for our currency."[9]

Myths about gold? Obsolete gold-backing requirement? What a turnabout! The government finally admitted that domestic monetary policy would not be subject to the discipline of gold, and the guiding principle of international finance and monetary policy for almost two centuries was summarily dismissed as a relic of incorrect thinking.

Despite the removal of gold backing, the United States continued to redeem gold at $35 an ounce for foreign central banks, although individuals were paying over $40 in the private markets. Seeing that the end of this exchange option was near, foreign central banks accelerated their exchange of dollars for gold. The United States, which held almost $30 billion of gold at the end of World War II, was left with $11 billion by the summer of 1971, and hundreds of millions more were being withdrawn each month.

Something dramatic had to happen. On August 15, 1971, President Nixon, in one of the most extraordinary actions since Roosevelt's 1933 declaration of a Bank Holiday, announced the "New Economic Policy," freezing wages and prices and closing the "gold window" that was enabling foreigners to exchange U.S. currency for gold. The link of gold to money was permanently—and irrevocably—broken.

Although conservatives were shocked at that action, few investors shed a tear for the gold standard. The stock market responded enthusiastically to Nixon's announcement, which was also coupled with wage and price controls and higher tariffs, by jumping almost 4 percent on record volume. But this should not have surprised those who studied history. Suspensions of the gold standard and devaluations of currencies have witnessed some of the most dramatic stock market rallies in history. Investors agreed that gold was a monetary relic.

POSTGOLD MONETARY POLICY

With the dismantling of the gold standard, there was no longer any constraint on monetary expansion, either in the United States or in foreign countries. The first inflationary oil shock from 1973 to 1974 caught most of the industrialized countries off guard, and all suffered significantly higher inflation as governments vainly attempted to offset falling output by expanding the money supply.

Because of the inflationary policies of the Federal Reserve, the U.S. Congress tried to control monetary expansion by passing a congressional resolution in 1975 that obliged the central bank to announce monetary growth targets. Three years later, Congress passed the Humphrey-Hawkins Act, which forced the Fed to testify on monetary policy before Congress twice annually and establish monetary targets. It was the first time since the passage of the Federal Reserve Act that Congress instructed the central bank to take the control of the stock of money. To this day, the financial markets closely watch the Fed chairman's biannual congressional testimony, which takes place in February and July.[10]

Unfortunately, the Fed largely ignored the money targets it set in the 1970s. The surge of inflation in 1979 brought increased pressure on the Federal Reserve to change its policy and seriously control inflation. On Saturday, October 6, 1979, Paul Volcker, who had been appointed in April to succeed G. William Miller as chairman of the board of the Federal Reserve System, announced a radical change in the implementation of monetary policy. No longer would the Federal Reserve set interest rates to guide policy. Instead, it would exercise control over the supply of money without regard to interest rate movements. The market knew that this meant sharply higher interest rates.

The prospect of sharply restricted liquidity was a shock to the financial markets. Although Volcker's Saturday night announcement (later referred to as the "Saturday Night Massacre") did not immediately capture the popular headlines—in contrast to the abundant press coverage devoted to Nixon's 1971 New Economic Policy that froze prices and closed the gold window—it roiled the financial markets. Stocks went into a tailspin, falling almost 8 percent on record volume in the 2½ days following the announcement. Stockholders shuddered at the prospect of sharply higher interest rates that would be necessary to tame inflation.

The tight monetary policy of the Volcker years eventually broke the inflationary cycle. European central banks and the Bank of Japan joined the Fed in calling inflation "public enemy number 1," and they consequently geared their monetary policies toward stable prices. Restricting money growth proved to be the only real answer to controlling inflation.

THE FEDERAL RESERVE AND MONEY CREATION

The process by which the Fed changes the money supply and controls credit conditions is straightforward. When the Fed wants to increase the money supply, it buys a government bond in the *open market*—a market where billions of dollars in bonds are transacted every day. What is unique about the Federal Reserve is that when it buys government bonds in what is called an *open market purchase*, it pays for them by crediting the reserve account of the bank of the customer from whom the Fed bought the bond—thereby creating money. A *reserve account* is a deposit a bank maintains at the Federal Reserve to satisfy reserve requirements and facilitate check clearing.

If the Federal Reserve wants to reduce the money supply, it sells government bonds from its portfolio. The buyer of these bonds instructs his or her bank to pay the seller (the Fed) from the buyer's account. The bank then instructs the Fed to debit the bank's reserve account, and that money disappears from circulation. This is called an *open market sale*. Buying government bonds and selling them are called *open market operations*.

HOW THE FED'S ACTIONS AFFECT INTEREST RATES

We have seen that when the Federal Reserve buys and sells government securities, it influences the amount of reserves in the banking system. There is an active market for these reserves among banks, where billions of dollars are bought and sold each day. This market is called the *federal funds market*, and the interest rate at which these funds are borrowed and lent is called the *federal funds rate*.

Although this market is called the *federal* funds market, the market is not run by the government, nor does it trade government securities. The fed funds market is a private lending market among banks where rates are dictated by supply and demand. However, the Federal Reserve has powerful influence over the federal funds market. If the Fed buys securities, then the supply of reserves is increased, and the interest rate on federal funds goes down because banks then have ample reserves to lend. Conversely, if the Fed sells securities, the supply of reserves is reduced, and the federal funds rate goes up because banks scramble for the remaining supply.

Although federal funds are lent overnight so the funds rate is an overnight rate, the interest rate on federal funds forms the anchor for all other short-term interest rates. These include the prime rate, which is the benchmark rate for most consumer lending; the LIBOR, which is the basis of short-term commercial lending; and rates on short-term Treasury securities. The federal funds rate is the basis of literally trillions of dollars of loans and securities.

Interest rates are an extremely important influence on stock prices because interest rates discount the future cash flows from stocks. Bonds become more attractive when interest rates rise, so investors sell stocks until the returns on stocks again become attractive relative to the returns on bonds. The opposite occurs when interest rates fall.

STOCK PRICES AND CENTRAL BANK POLICY

Given the enormous influence that monetary policy has on stock prices, it is reasonable to expect that following central bank policy could provide investors with superior returns. Indeed, from mid-1950 through the 1980s, that was the case. Stock returns in the 3, 6, and 12 months following a reduction in the federal funds rate were much higher than returns following increases in the funds rate. By reducing stock holdings when the Fed was tightening monetary policy and increasing them when the Fed was loosening monetary policy, investors could achieve superior returns.

But since 1990 the pattern has not been so reliable. Figure 14-2 displays the S&P 500 Index and the fed funds rate from 1990 through 2012. After a long period of easing through the 1990–1991 recession, the Fed raised the fed funds target on February 4, 1994, when the S&P 500 Index was 481. The reaction in the bond and stock market was immediate, as stocks fell 2.5 percent and continued to slide another 7 percent by early April. Bond prices were devastated, as the 10-year Treasury jumped nearly 150 basis points in 1994, suffering its worst losses in years. But after April, stocks stabilized and then rose despite accelerated Fed tightening. By the time the Fed finally lowered rates on July 6, 1995, in response to the weakening economy, the S&P 500 stood at 554, about 15 percent higher than on the day the Fed began to raise rates.

As the economy recovered and inflation threatened once again, the Fed tightened 25 basis points on March 25, 1997; yet stocks continued to

FIGURE 14–2

S&P 500 and Fed Funds Rate, 1990–2013

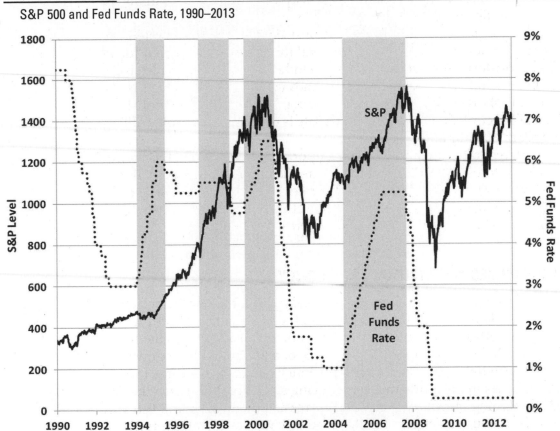

rise. In response to the Asian crisis and chaos in the Treasury market caused by the failure of Long-Term Capital Management in August 1998, the Fed lowered the funds rate on September 29, 1998. But the stock market was 33.0 percent higher than it was 18 months earlier when the Fed first raised rates.

As the U.S. economy sloughed off the Asian crisis, the Fed began tightening again on June 30, 1999, when the S&P Index rose to 1,373. But stocks continued upward, with the S&P 500 hitting its high on March 24, 2000, at 1,527, which was 12 percent higher than the previous June. In all these episodes, investors who had been out of the stock market when the Fed was raising rates would have given up large stock returns.

After the bull market peak in early 2000, the Fed did not start lowering the funds rate until January 3, 2001, after stocks had fallen back to the level they were in June 1999 when the Fed started raising rates. But January 2001 was far too early to get back into the market, as stocks continued to slide until October 2002, when the S&P 500 touched a five-year low of 776.76. By the time the Fed began tightening on June 30, 2004, the S&P 500 was at 1,141. But this was again far too early to get out of stocks, as the bull market continued for more than three years, finally reaching its peak in October 2007 at 1,565, more than 37 percent higher than when the Fed started tightening. As the financial crisis began to impact the economy, the Fed undertook its first easing on September 18, 2007, just three weeks before the peak of the market, clearly not a time to load up on equities.

All told, holding stocks from when the Fed first eased to when it first tightened would have generated a 55 percent cumulative return on the market (excluding dividends) over the period from February 1994 through the end of 2012. The buy-and-hold investors would have achieved a 212 percent return, nearly four times as great.

There is a good reason why stocks are not reacting to Fed policy as they have in the past. Investors have become so geared to watching and anticipating Fed policy that the effect of its tightening and easing is already discounted in the market. If investors expect the Fed to stabilize the economy, this will be built into stock prices long before the Fed even begins to take its stabilizing actions.

STOCKS AS HEDGES AGAINST INFLATION

Although the central bank has the power to moderate (but not eliminate) the business cycle, its policy has the greatest influence on inflation. As noted above, the inflation of the 1970s was due to the overexpansion of the money supply, which was an action the central bank took in the vain hope that it could offset the impact of the OPEC oil supply restrictions. This expansionary monetary policy brought inflation to double-digit levels in most industrialized economies, peaking at 13 percent per year in the United States and exceeding 24 percent in the United Kingdom.

In contrast to the returns of fixed-income assets, the historical evidence is overwhelming that the returns on stocks over long time periods have kept pace with inflation. Since stocks are claims on the earnings of real assets—assets whose value is intrinsically related to the price of the goods and services they produce—one should expect that their long-term returns will not be harmed by inflation. For example, the period since World War II has been the most inflationary period in our history, and yet the real returns on stocks have matched that of the previous 150 years. The ability of an asset such as stocks to maintain its purchasing power during periods of inflation makes equities an *inflation hedge*.

Indeed, stocks were widely praised in the 1950s as hedges against rising consumer prices. As noted in Chapter 11, many investors stayed with stocks at that time, despite seeing the dividend yield on equities fall below the interest rate on long-term bonds. In the 1970s, however, stocks were ravaged by inflation, and it became unfashionable to view equities as an effective hedge against inflation.

What does the evidence say about the effectiveness of stocks as an inflation hedge? The annual compound returns on stocks, bonds, and Treasury bills against inflation over 1-year and 30-year holding periods from 1871 to 2012 are shown in Figure 14-3.

The data indicate that neither stocks nor bonds nor bills are good short-term hedges against inflation. Short-term real returns on these financial assets are highest when the inflation rates are low, and their returns fall as inflation increases. But the real returns on stocks are virtually unaffected by the inflation rate over longer horizons. Bond returns, on the other hand, fall behind the returns on stocks over every holding period.

This was the principal conclusion of Edgar L. Smith's 1924 book, *Common Stocks as Long Term Investments*. Smith showed that stocks outperform bonds in times of falling as well as rising prices, taking the period after the Civil War up to just before the turn of the century as his test case. Smith's results are robust and have held up over the next 90 years of data.

Holding Period Returns and Inflation, 1871–2012

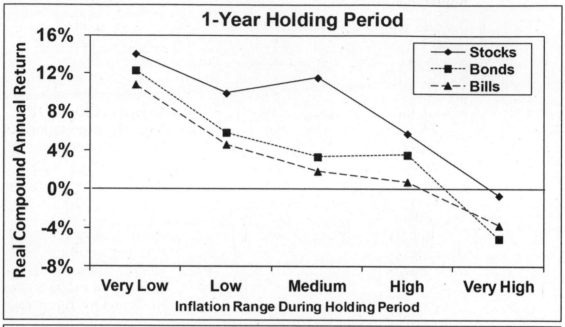

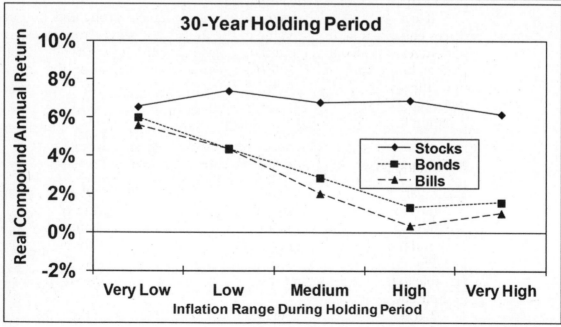

WHY STOCKS FAIL AS A SHORT-TERM INFLATION HEDGE

Higher Interest Rates

If stocks represent real assets, why do they fail as a short-term inflation hedge? A popular explanation is that inflation increases interest rates on bonds, and higher interest rates on bonds depress stock prices. In other words, inflation must send stock prices down sufficiently to increase their dividends or earnings yields to match the higher rates available on bonds. Indeed, this is the rationale of the Fed model described in Chapter 11.

However, this explanation is incorrect. Certainly, expectations of rising prices do increase interest rates. Irving Fisher, the famous early-twentieth-century American economist, noted that lenders seek to protect themselves against inflation by adding the expected inflation to the real interest rate that they demand from borrowers. This proposition has been called the *Fisher equation*, after its discoverer.[11]

But higher inflation also raises the expected future cash flows to stockholders. Stocks are claims on the earnings of real assets, whether these assets are the products of machines, labor, land, or ideas. Inflation raises the costs of inputs and consequently the prices of outputs (and those prices are, in fact, the measure of inflation). Therefore, future cash flows will also rise with the rise in price levels.

It can be shown that when inflation impacts input and output prices equally, the present value of the future cash flows from stocks is not adversely affected by inflation even though interest rates rise. Higher future cash flows will offset higher interest rates so that, over time, the price of stocks—as well as earnings and dividends—will rise at the rate of inflation. In theory the returns from stocks will be an ideal inflation hedge.

Nonneutral Inflation: Supply-Side Effects

The invariance of stock prices to the inflation rate holds when inflation is purely monetary in nature, influencing costs and revenues equally. But there are many circumstances in which earnings cannot keep up with inflation. Stocks declined during the 1970s because the restriction in OPEC oil supplies dramatically increased energy costs. Firms were not able to raise the prices of their output by as much as the soaring cost of their energy inputs.

Earlier in the chapter it was noted that the inflation of the 1970s was the result of bad monetary policy attempting to offset the contractionary effect of OPEC's oil price hikes. Yet one should not minimize the damage done by rising oil prices on U.S. corporate profits. U.S. manufacturers, who for years had thrived on low energy prices, were totally unprepared to deal with surging energy costs. The recession that followed the first OPEC oil squeeze pummeled the stock market. Productivity plummeted, and by the end of 1974 real stock prices, measured by the Dow Jones Industrial Average, had fallen 65 percent from the January 1966 high—the largest decline since the crash of 1929. Pessimism ran so deep that nearly half of all Americans in August 1974 believed the economy was heading toward a depression such as the one the nation had experienced in the 1930s.[12]

Inflation may also lower stock prices when it increases investors' fears that the central bank will take restrictive action by raising short-term real interest rates. Such restrictive policies are often followed by an economic slowdown that also depresses stock prices.

In many economies, inflation, especially in less developed countries, is also closely linked with large government budget deficits and excessive government spending. Inflation therefore often signals that the government is taking too large a role in the economy, which often leads to lower growth, lower corporate profits, and lower stock prices. In short, there are many good economic reasons why stock prices should fall in response to increased inflation.

Taxes on Corporate Earnings

But economic factors are not the only reason stocks are not good short-run hedges against inflation. The U.S. tax code also penalizes investors during inflation. There are two significant areas in which the tax code works to the detriment of shareholders: corporate profits and capital gains.

Earnings are distorted by standard and accepted accounting practices that do not properly take into account the effects of inflation on corporate profits. This distortion shows up primarily in the treatment of depreciation, inventory valuation, and interest costs.

Depreciation of plant, equipment, and other capital investments is based on *historical* costs. These depreciation schedules are not adjusted for any change in the price of capital that might occur during the life of the asset. Inflation increases the cost of the capital, but reported depreciation does not make any adjustment for inflation, depreciation allowances are understated, and taxable earnings are overstated, leaving corporations with higher tax bills.

But depreciation is not the only source of bias in reported earnings. In calculating the cost of goods sold, firms must use the historical cost, with either "first-in–first-out" or "last-in–first-out" methods of inventory accounting. In an inflationary environment, the gap between historical costs and selling prices widens, producing inflationary profits for the firm. These "profits" do not represent an increase in the real earning power of the firm; instead, they represent just that part of the firm's capital—namely, the inventory—that turns over and is realized as a monetary profit. The accounting for inventories differs from the firm's other capital, such as plant and equipment, which are not revalued on an ongoing basis for the purpose of calculating earnings.

The Department of Commerce, the government agency responsible for gathering economic statistics, is well aware of these distortions and has computed both a depreciation adjustment and an inventory valuation adjustment in the national income and product accounts. But the Internal Revenue Service does not recognize any of these adjustments for tax purposes. Firms are required to pay taxes on reported profits, even when these profits are biased upward by inflation. These biases effectively increase the tax rate on capital.

Inflationary Biases in Interest Costs

There is another inflationary distortion to corporate profits that is not reported in government statistics. This distortion is based on the inflationary component of interest costs, and in contrast to depreciation and inventory profits, it leads to a *downward bias* in reported corporate earnings during periods of inflation.

Most firms raise capital by issuing fixed-income assets such as bonds and bank loans. This borrowing leverages the firm's assets, since any profits above and beyond the debt service go to the stockholders. In an inflationary environment, nominal interest costs rise, even if real interest costs remain unchanged. But corporate profits are calculated by deducting *nominal* interest costs, which overstates the real interest costs to the firm. Hence, reported corporate profits are depressed compared with true economic profits.

In fact, the firm is paying back debt with depreciated dollars, so the higher nominal interest expense is exactly offset by the reduction in the real value of the the firm's bonds and loans. But this reduction in the real indebtedness is not reported in any of the earnings reports released by the firm. For highly leveraged firms, this bias could easily outweigh the inventory and depreciation biases. Unfortunately, it is not easy to quantify the leverage bias because it is not easy to separate the share of interest cost due to inflation from that due to real interest rates.

Capital Gains Taxes

In the United States, capital gains taxes are paid on the difference between the cost of an asset and the sale price, with no adjustment made for the impact of inflation on the amount of the real gain. Thus, if asset values rise with inflation, the investor accrues a tax liability that must be paid when the asset is sold, whether or not the investor has realized a real gain. This means that an asset that appreciates by less than the rate of inflation—meaning the investor is worse off in real terms—will still be taxed upon sale.

Chapter 9 showed that the tax code has a dramatic impact on investors' realized after-tax real returns. For even a moderate inflation rate of 3 percent, an investor with a five-year average holding period suffers a 60-basis-point (hundredths of a percentage point) reduction in average after-tax real returns compared with the after-tax returns that he or she would have realized if the rate of inflation had been zero. If the rate of inflation rises to 6 percent, the loss of returns is more than 112 basis points.

The inflation tax has a far more severe effect on realized after-tax real returns when the holding period is short than when it is long. This is because the more frequently an investor buys and sells assets, the more the government can capture the tax on nominal capital gains. Nevertheless, even for long-term investors, the capital gains tax reduces real returns in inflationary times.

CONCLUSION

This chapter documents the role of money in the economy and financial markets. Before World War II, persistent inflation in the United States and other industrialized countries was nonexistent. But when the gold standard was dethroned during the Great Depression, the control of money passed to the central banks. And with the dollar no longer pegged to gold, it was inflation, and not deflation, that proved to be the major problem that central banks sought to control.

The message of this chapter is that stocks are not good hedges against inflation in the short run. However, no financial asset is. In the long run, stocks are extremely good hedges against inflation, while bonds are not. Stocks are also the best financial asset if you fear rapid inflation since many countries with high inflation can still have quite viable, if not booming, stock markets. Fixed-income assets, on the other hand, cannot protect investors from excessive government issuance of money.

Fortunately for investors, central bankers around the world are committed to keeping inflation low, and they have largely succeeded. But if inflation again rears its head, investors will do much better in stocks than in bonds.

Stocks and the Business Cycle

The stock market has predicted nine out of the last five recessions.
— PAUL SAMUELSON, 1966[1]

I'd love to be able to predict markets and anticipate recessions, but since that's impossible, I'm as satisfied to search out profitable companies as Buffett is.

— PETER LYNCH, 1989[2]

A well-respected economist is about to address a large group of financial analysts, investment advisors, and stockbrokers. There is obvious concern in the audience. The stock market has been surging to new all-time highs almost daily, driving down dividend yields to record lows and sending price/earnings ratios skyward. Is this bullishness justified? The audience wants to know if the economy is really going to do well enough to support these high stock prices.

The economist's address is highly optimistic. He predicts that the real gross domestic product of the United States will increase over 4 percent during the next four quarters, a very healthy growth rate. There will be no recession for at least three years, and even if one occurs after that, it will be very brief. Corporate profits, one of the major factors driving

This chapter is an adaptation of my paper "Does It Pay Stock Investors to Forecast the Business Cycle?" in *Journal of Portfolio Management*, vol. 18 (Fall 1991), pp. 27–34. The material benefited significantly from discussions with Professor Paul Samuelson.

stock prices, will increase at double-digit annual rates for at least the next three years. To boot, he predicts that a Republican will easily win the White House in next year's presidential election, a situation obviously comforting to the overwhelmingly conservative audience. The crowd obviously likes what it hears. The audience's anxiety is quieted, and many advisors are ready to recommend that their clients increase their stake in stocks.

The time of this address is the summer of 1987, with the stock market poised to take one of its sharpest falls in history, including the record-breaking 23 percent decline on October 19, 1987. In just a few weeks, most stocks can be bought for about half the price paid at the time of the address. But the biggest irony of all is that the economist is dead right in each and every one of his bullish economic predictions.

The lesson is that the markets and the economy are often out of sync. It is not surprising that many investors dismiss economic forecasts when planning their market strategy. The substance of Paul Samuelson's famous words, cited at the beginning of this chapter, still remains true more than 45 years after they were first uttered.

But do not dismiss the business cycle too quickly when examining your portfolio. The stock market still responds quite powerfully to changes in economic activity. The reaction of the S&P 500 Index to the business cycle from 1871 onward is displayed in Figure 15-1. Stocks frequently begin to decline just before the shaded periods, which indicate recessions, and rally rigorously at signs of an impending economic recovery. If you can predict the business cycle, you can beat the buy-and-hold strategy that has been advocated throughout this book.

But this is no easy task. To make money by predicting the business cycle, one must be able to identify peaks and troughs of economic activity *before* they actually occur, a skill very few if any economists possess. Yet business cycle forecasting is a popular Wall Street endeavor not because it is successful—most of the time it is not—but because the rewards are so large if you can identify the turning point of the business cycle.

WHO CALLS THE BUSINESS CYCLE?

It is surprising to many that the dating of business cycles is not determined by any of the myriad government agencies that collect data on the economy. Instead, the task falls to the National Bureau of Economic Research (the NBER), a private research organization founded in 1920 for the purpose of documenting business cycles and developing a series of national income accounts. In the early years of its existence, the bureau's

FIGURE 15-1

Stock Prices, Earnings, Dividends, and Recessions 1871–2012

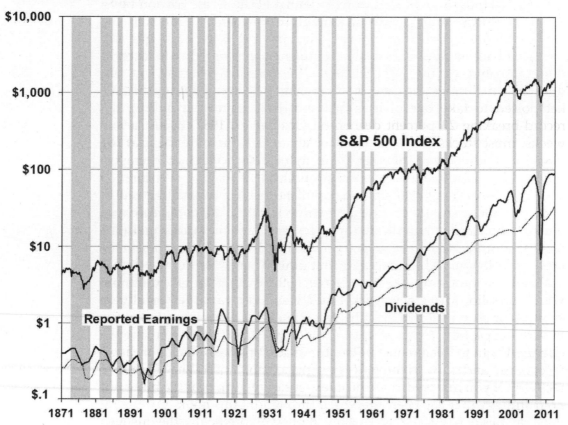

staff compiled comprehensive chronological records of the changes in economic conditions in many of the industrialized economies. In particular, the bureau developed monthly series on business activity for the United States and Great Britain back to 1854.

In a 1946 volume entitled *Measuring Business Cycles*, Wesley C. Mitchell, one of the founders of the bureau, and Arthur Burns, a renowned business cycle expert who later headed the Federal Reserve Board, gave the following definition of a *business cycle*:

> Business cycles are a type of fluctuation found in the aggregate economic activity of nations that organize their work mainly in business enterprises: a cycle consists of expansion occurring at about the same time in many economic activities, followed by similarly general recessions, or contrac-

tions, and revivals that merge into the expansion phase of the next cycle; this sequence of changes is recurrent but not periodic; in duration business cycles vary from more than one year to ten or twelve years and they are not divisible into shorter cycles of similar character.[3]

It is commonly assumed that a recession occurs when real gross domestic product, the most inclusive measure of economic output, declines for two consecutive quarters. But this is not necessarily so. Although this criterion is a reasonable rule of thumb for indicating a recession, there is no single rule or measure used by the NBER. Rather the bureau focuses on four different series to determine the turning points in the economy: employment, industrial production, real personal income, and real manufacturing and trade sales.

The Business Cycle Dating Committee of the National Bureau of Economic Research confirms the business cycle dates. This committee consists of academic economists who are associated with the bureau and who meet to examine economic data whenever conditions warrant. Over the entire period from 1802 through 2012, the United States has experienced 47 recessions, and these recessions have averaged nearly 19 months in length, while expansions have averaged 34 months.[4] This means that, over these 210 years, almost slightly more than one-third of the time the economy has been in a recession. However, since World War II, there have been 11 recessions, averaging 11.1 months in length, while the expansions have averaged 58.4 months. So in the postwar period, the economy has been in a recession less than one-sixth of the time, far less than the prewar average.

The dating of the business cycle is of great importance. The designation that the economy is in a recession or an expansion has political as well as economic implications. For example, when the NBER called the onset of the 1990 recession in July rather than August, it raised quite a few eyebrows in Washington. This was so because the Bush administration had told the public that the Iraqi invasion of Kuwait and the surge in oil prices were responsible for the economic recession. This explanation was undermined when the bureau actually dated the onset of the recession a month earlier. Similarly the 2001 recession began in March when technology spending dropped sharply and well before the 9/11 terrorist attacks.

The Business Cycle Dating Committee is in no rush to call the turning points in the cycle. Never has a call been reversed because of new or revised data that have become available—and the NBER wants to keep it that way. As Robert E. Hall, current chair of the seven-member Business Cycle Dating Committee, indicated, "The NBER has not made an announcement on a business cycle peak or trough until there was almost no doubt that the data would not be revised in light of subse-quent availability of data."[5]

Recent examples of the NBER's dating make the point. The March 1991 trough was not called until 21 months later, in December 1992, and the November bottom of the 2001 recession was not called until July 2003. The peak of the 2002–2007 expansion was not called until December 2008, one year after it began and well after the Lehman crisis had paralyzed financial markets and set stocks tumbling. Clearly, waiting for the bureau to desig-nate business cycles is far too late to be of any use in timing the market.

STOCK RETURNS AROUND BUSINESS CYCLE TURNING POINTS

Almost without exception, the stock market turns down prior to reces-sions and rises before economic recoveries. In fact, out of the 47 reces-sions recorded from 1802 on, 43 of them, or more than 9 out of 10, have been preceded (or accompanied) by declines of 8 percent or more in the total stock returns index. Two exceptions followed World War II: the 1948–1949 recession that immediately followed the war and the 1953 recession, when stocks fell just shy of the 8 percent criterion.

The return behaviors for the 11 post–World War II recessions are sum-marized in Table 15-1. You can see that the stock return index peaked any-

TABLE 15–1

Stock Prices and Business Cycle Peaks, 1948–2012

Recession	Peak of Stock Index (1)	Peak of Business Cycle (2)	Lead Time between Peaks (3)	Decline in Stock Index from (1) to (2)	Maximum 12 Month Decline in Stocks
1948–1949	May 1948	Nov 1948	6	−8.91%	−9.76%
1953–1954	Dec 1952	Jul 1953	7	−4.26%	−9.04%
1957–1958	Jul 1957	Aug 1957	1	−4.86%	−15.32%
1960–1961	Dec 1959	Apr 1960	4	−8.65%	−8.65%
1970	Nov 1968	Dec 1969	13	−12.08%	−29.16%
1973–1975	Dec 1972	Nov 1973	11	−16.29%	−38.80%
1980	Jan 1980	Jan 1980	0	0.00%	−9.55%
1981–1982	Nov 1980	Jul 1981	8	−4.08%	−13.99%
1990–1991	Jul 1990	Jul 1990	0	0.00%	−13.84%
2001	Aug 2000	Mar 2001	7	−22.94%	−26.55%
2007–2009	Oct 2007	Dec 2007	2	−4.87%	−47.50%
		Average	5.4	−7.90%	−20.20%

where from 0 to 13 months before the beginning of a recession. The recessions that began in January 1980 and July 1990 are the only two for which the stock market gave no advance warning of the economic downturn.

As the Samuelson quote at the beginning of this chapter indicates, the stock market is also prone to false alarms, and these have increased in the postwar period. Declines greater than 10 percent in the Dow Jones Industrial Average during the postwar period that were not followed by recessions (the "false alarms") are listed in Table 15-2. The decline of 35.1 percent from August through early December 1987 is the largest decline in the 210-year history of stock returns when the economy did not subsequently fall into a recession.[6]

The trough in the stock return index and the trough in the NBER business cycle are compared in Table 15-3.

The average lead time between the bottom of the market and the bottom of an economic recovery has been 4.6 months, and in 8 of the 11 recessions, the lead time has been in an extremely narrow range of 4 to 6 months. This compares to an average of 5.4 months that the peak in the market precedes the peak in the business cycle. The time between the peak of the market and the peak of the economy also has shown much greater variability that the time between the trough of the market and the trough of the economy.[7]

TABLE 15–2

False Alarms of Recession by Stock Market 1945–2012

Peak of Stock Index	Trough of Stock Index	% Decline
May 29, 1946	May 17, 1947	−23.2%
Dec 13, 1961	Jun 26, 1962	−27.1%
Jan 18, 1966	Sept 29, 1966	−22.3%
Sept 25, 1967	Mar 21, 1968	−12.5%
Apr 28, 1971	Nov 23, 1971	−16.1%
Aug 17,1978	Oct 27, 1978	−12.8%
Nov 29, 1983	Jul 24, 1984	−15.6%
Aug 25, 1987	Dec 4, 1987	−35.1%
Aug 6, 1997	Oct 27, 1997	−13.3%
Jul 17, 1998	Aug 31, 1998	−19.3%
Mar 19, 2002	Oct 9, 2002	−31.5%
Apr 26, 2010	Jul 02, 2010	−13.6%
Apr 29, 2011	Oct 03, 2011	−16.8%

Postwar declines of 10% or more in the Dow Jones Industrial Average when no recession followed within 12 months.

TABLE 15–3

Stock Prices and Business Cycle Troughs, 1948–2012

Recession	Trough of Stock Index (1)	Trough of Business Cycle (2)	Lead Time between Troughs (3)	Rise in Stock Index from (1) to (2)
1948–1949	May 1949	Oct 1949	5	15.59%
1953–1954	Aug 1953	May 1954	9	29.13%
1957–1958	Dec 1957	April 1958	4	10.27%
1960–1961	Oct 1960	Feb 1961	4	21.25%
1970	Jun 1970	Nov 1970	5	21.86%
1973–1975	Sep 1974	Mar 1975	6	35.60%
1980	Mar 1980	Jul 1980	4	22.60%
1981–1982	Jul 1982	Nov 1982	4	33.13%
1990–1991	Oct 1990	Mar 1991	5	25.28%
2001	Sep 2001	Nov 2001	2	9.72%
2007–09	Mar 2009	Jun 2009	3	37.44%
		Average	4.6	23.81%
		Std Dev	1.80	9.51%

It is important to note that by the time the economy has reached the end of the recession, the stock market has risen 23.8 percent on average. Therefore, an investor waiting for tangible evidence that the business cycle has hit bottom has already missed a very substantial rise in the market. And as noted above, the NBER does not announce the dates that recessions end until many months after the economy turns up.

GAINS THROUGH TIMING THE BUSINESS CYCLE

My studies show that if investors could predict *in advance* when recessions will begin and end, they could enjoy superior returns to the returns earned by a buy-and-hold investor.[8] Specifically, if an investor switched from stocks to cash (short-term bonds) four months before the beginning of a recession and back to stocks four months before the end of the recession, he would gain almost 5 percentage points per year on a risk-corrected basis over the buy-and-hold investor. About two-thirds of that gain is the result of predicting the end of the recession, where, as Table 15-3 shows, the stock market hits bottom between four and five months before the end of the economic downturn, and the other third comes from selling stocks four months before the peak. Investors who switch between stocks and bonds just on the months the NBER identifies (well after the fact) as the beginning and end of the recession gain a mere ½ percentage point return over the buy-and-hold investor.

HOW HARD IS IT TO PREDICT THE BUSINESS CYCLE?

If one could predict in advance when recessions will occur, the gains would be substantial. That is perhaps why billions of dollars of resources are spent trying to forecast the business cycle. But the record of predicting business cycle turning points is extremely poor.

Stephen McNees, vice president of the Federal Reserve Bank of Boston, has done extensive research into the accuracy of economic forecasters' predictions. He claims that a major factor in forecast accuracy is the time period over which the forecast was made, and it is precisely at business cycle turning points that the errors were "enormous."[9] Yet, as noted above, it is precisely these business cycle turning points that enable a forecaster to become a successful market timer.

The 1974–1975 recession was particularly tough for economists. Almost every one of the nearly two dozen of the nation's top economists invited to President Ford's anti-inflation conference in Washington in September 1974 was unaware that the U.S. economy was in the midst of its most severe postwar recession to date. McNees, studying the forecasts issued by five prominent forecasters in 1974, found that the median forecast overestimated GNP growth by 6 percentage points and underestimated inflation by 4 percentage points. Early recognition of the 1974 recession was so poor that many economists jumped the gun on the next recession, which didn't strike until 1980—while most economists thought it had begun early in 1979.

From 1976 to 1995, Robert J. Eggert and subsequently Randell Moore documented and summarized the economic forecasts of a noted panel of economic and business experts. These forecasts were compiled and published in a monthly publication entitled *Blue Chip Economic Indicators*.

In July 1979, the *Blue Chip Economic Indicators* report said that a strong majority of forecasters believed that a recession had already started—forecasting negative GNP growth in the second, third, and fourth quarters of 1979. However, the NBER declared that the peak of the business cycle did not occur until January 1980 and that the economy expanded throughout 1979.

Forecasters' ability to predict the severe 1981–1982 recession, when unemployment reached a postwar high of 10.8 percent, was no better. The headline of the July 1981 *Blue Chip Economic Indicators* report read, "Economic Exuberance Envisioned for 1982." Instead, 1982 was a disaster. By November 1981 the forecasters realized that the economy had faltered, and optimism turned to pessimism. Most thought that the economy had entered a recession (which it had done four months earlier), nearly 70 percent thought that it would end by the first quarter of 1982 (which it would not, instead tying the record for the longest postwar recession, ending in November), and 90 percent thought that it would be mild, like the 1971 recession, rather than severe—wrong again!

In April 1985, with the expansion well under way, forecasters were queried about how long the economy would be in an expansion. The average response was for another 20 months, which would put the peak at December 1986, more than 3.5 years before the cycle actually ended. Even the most optimistic forecasters picked spring 1988 as the latest date for the next recession to begin. This question was asked repeatedly throughout 1985 and 1986, and no forecaster imagined that the 1980s expansion would last as long as it did.

Following the stock market crash of October 1987, forecasters reduced their GNP growth estimates of 1988 over 1987 from 2.8 percent to 1.9 percent, the largest drop in the 11-year history of the survey. Instead, economic growth in 1988 was nearly 4 percent, as the economy grew strongly despite the stock market collapse.

As the expansion continued, the belief that a recession was imminent turned into the belief that prosperity was here to stay. The continuing expansion fostered a growing conviction that perhaps the business cycle had been conquered—by either government policy or the "recession-proof" nature of our service-oriented economy. Ed Yardeni, senior economist at Prudential-Bache Securities, wrote a "New Wave Manifesto" in late 1988, concluding that self-repairing, growing economies were likely through the rest of the decade.[10] On the eve of one of the worst worldwide recessions in the postwar era, Leonard Silk, senior economics editor of the *New York Times*, stated in May 1990 in an article entitled "Is There Really a Business Cycle?":

> Most economists foresee no recession in 1990 or 1991, and 1992 will be another presidential year, when the odds tip strongly against recession. Japan, West Germany, and most of the other capitalist countries of Europe and Asia are also on a long upward roll, with no end in sight.[11]

However, by November 1990, *Blue Chip Economic Indicators* reported that the majority of the panel believed the U.S. economy had already slipped, or was about to slip, into a recession. But in November, not only had the economy been in recession for four months, but the stock market had already hit its bottom and was headed upward. Had investors given in to the prevailing pessimism at the time when the recession seemed confirmed, they would have sold after the low was reached and stocks were headed for a strong three-year rally.

The record 10-year expansion of the U.S. economy from March 1991 through March 2001 again spawned talk of "new era economics" and economies without recession.[12] Even in early 2001, the vast majority of forecasters did not see a recession. In fact, in September 2001, just before the terrorist attack, only 13 percent of the economists surveyed by *Blue Chip Economic Indicators* believed the United States was in a recession even though the NBER subsequently indicated that the United States recession had begun six months earlier in March.[13] And by February 2002, less than 20 percent thought the recession had ended in 2001, although the NBER eventually dated November 2001 as the end of the recession.[14] Once again, economists have been unable to call the turning point of the business cycle until well after the date has passed.

Forecasters did no better predicting the Great Recession of 2007–2009. The National Bureau of Economic Research did not actually call the beginning of the recession until December 2008, one year after it began and when the S&P 500 Index had already fallen more than 40 percent. The Federal Reserve did begin easing interest rates in September 2007, three months before the onset of the recession, but the Fed had no concept that a recession was imminent. In the meeting of the Federal Open Market Committee on December 11, 2007, the month the recession began, Fed economist Dave Stockton gave the following summary of the Federal Reserve forecast:

> Obviously we're not forecasting a business cycle peak. So in our forecast, we're not yet saying that we're on the downside of a business cycle. We have a "growth recession" [a slowdown in economic growth] in this forecast and nothing more than that.[15]

CONCLUSION

Stock values are based on corporate earnings, and the business cycle is a prime determinant of these earnings. The gains of being able to predict the turning points of the economic cycle are large, and yet doing so with any precision has eluded economists of all persuasions.

The worst course an investor can take is to follow the prevailing sentiment about economic activity. That will lead investors to buy at high prices when times are good and everyone is optimistic and sell at the low.

The lessons to investors are clear. Beating the stock market by analyzing real economic activity requires a degree of prescience that forecasters do not yet have.

When World Events Impact Financial Markets

I can predict the motion of heavenly bodies, but not the madness of crowds.

—ISAAC NEWTON

As the sun rose over New York City on a beautiful Tuesday morning, September 11, 2001, traders expected a dull day on Wall Street. There were no economic data coming out of Washington, nor any earnings releases scheduled. The previous Friday the markets had fallen on a horrible employment report, but on Monday the markets had bounced back slightly.

The U.S. equity markets had not yet opened, but contracts on the S&P 500 Index futures had been trading all night as usual on the electronic Globex exchange. The futures markets were up, indicating that Wall Street was expecting a firm opening. But then a report came at 8:48 a.m. on what was to be one of the most fateful days in world history: a plane had crashed into the North Tower of the World Trade Center. The pattern of trading over the next 27 minutes, before the market closed, is shown in Figure 16-1.

The news of the plane crash spread quickly, but few imagined what had really happened. Was it a large or small plane? Was it an accident? Or was there something more sinister going on? Although nobody knew the answers yet, immediately the stock index futures market traded down a few points, as it often does when uncertainty increases. Within a

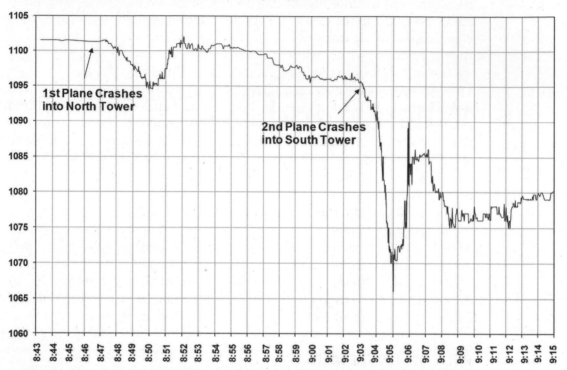

FIGURE 16-1

S&P 500 Futures Market on Tuesday Morning, September 11, 2001

few minutes, however, buyers reappeared, and the index returned to its previous level, as most traders concluded that nothing significant had happened.

Fifteen minutes later, at 9:03, with news cameras focused on the World Trade Center and millions around the world watching, a second plane crashed into the South Tower. The entire world changed in that moment. Americans' worst fears had been realized. This was a terrorist attack. For the first time since World War II, America was under direct attack on its own soil.

By 9:05, two minutes after the second crash, the S&P futures plunged 30 points, about 3 percent, indicating that if the exchanges had been open, nearly $300 billion would have been wiped off U.S. stock values. But then, miraculously, buyers did appear. Despite the enormity of the events unfolding, some traders bet that the market had overreacted to these attacks and decided that this was a good time to buy stocks. The futures firmed and ended the session at 9:15 down about 15 points, gaining back one-half of the earlier loss.

Despite this comeback, the gravity of this attack quickly sank in. All the stock, bond, and commodity exchanges first delayed opening and then canceled trading for the day. In fact, stock exchanges in the United States would remain closed for the remainder of the week, the longest closing since FDR declared a "Bank Holiday" in March 1933 to try to restore America's collapsing banking system.

Foreign stock exchanges, however, remained open. It was 2 p.m. in London and 3 p.m. in Europe when the planes struck. The German DAX index immediately fell more than 9 percent and ended the session around that level. London stocks suffered but not as much. There was a feeling that with the world's financial center, the United States, vulnerable to attack, some business might move to the United Kingdom. The British pound rallied, as did the euro against the dollar. Normally it is the U.S. dollar that gains in international crisis. But this time, with the attack centering on New York, foreign traders were unsure which direction to go.

When the New York Stock Exchange reopened the following Monday, September 17, the Dow Industrials fell 685 points, or 7.13 percent, the seventeenth-largest percentage drop in its history. The Dow continued to fall during the week and closed Friday, September 21, at 8,236—down more than 14 percent from its September 10 close and nearly 30 percent from its all-time high of 11,723 reached on January 14, 2000.

WHAT MOVES THE MARKET?

It was perfectly clear why the markets fell after the terrorist attacks. But it might surprise investors that in the vast majority of cases, major market movements are *not* accompanied by any news of sufficient importance to explain the price change. Since 1885, when the Dow Jones averages were first formulated, there have been 145 days when the Dow Jones Industrial Average has changed by 5 percent or more. Fifteen of these moves took place from September 2008 through March 2009 when the world economy was in the grips of the financial crisis, and another drop occurred on August 8, 2011, when Standard & Poor's downgraded U.S. government debt.

Of all the 145 large changes, only 35 can be identified with a significant world political or economic event, such as wars, political changes, or governmental policy shifts. During and immediately following the financial crisis of 2008, only 4 of the 15 large changes were associated with specific events. Since 1885, less than 1 in 4 major market moves can be clearly linked to a specific world event. A ranking of the 54 largest changes is shown in Table 16-1,[1] and market changes greater than 5 percent that are associated with specific events are shown in Table 16-2.[2]

Monetary policy is the biggest single driver of these massive market outbreaks of euphoria or fear. Out of the five largest moves in the stock market over the past century for which there is a clearly identifiable cause, four have been directly associated with changes in monetary policy. The top news-related changed was the 14.87 percent gain on October 6, 1931, when Hoover proposed a $500 million pool to help banks, and the second largest was the 11.08 percent gain that took place on October 13, 2008, when the Federal Reserve offered unlimited liquidity to foreign central banks to facilitate dollar exchanges.

If you focus in on just the 10 largest daily market moves since 1885, only 2 can be attributed to a specific news event. The record 22.6 percent one-day fall in the stock market on October 19, 1987, is not associated with any one readily identifiable news event. From 1940 until the recent financial crisis, there have been only four days of big moves where the cause is identified: the 7.13 percent drop on September 17, 2001, when the markets reopened after the terrorist attacks; the 7.18 percent drop on

TABLE 16–1

Largest Daily Market Changes, 1888–2012

Rank	Date	Change	Rank	Date	Change	Rank	Date	Change
1	Oct 19, 1987	−22.61%	19	Dec 18, 1899	−8.72%	37	Sep 24, 1931	−7.07%
2	Mar 15, 1933	15.34%	20	Oct 8, 1931	8.70%	38	Jul 20, 1933	−7.07%
3*	Oct 6, 1931	14.87%	21	Aug 12, 1932	−8.40%	39*	Sep 29, 2008	−6.98%
4	Oct 28, 1929	−12.82%	22	Mar 14, 1907	−8.29%	40*	Oct 13, 1989	−6.91%
5	Oct 30, 1929	12.34%	23	Oct 26, 1987	−8.04%	41*	Jul 30, 1914	−6.90%
6	Oct 29, 1929	−11.73%	24	Jun 10, 1932	7.99%	42	Jan 8, 1988	−6.85%
7	Sep 21, 1932	11.36%	25	Oct 15, 2008	−7.87%	43*	Mar 23, 2009	6.84%
8*	Oct 13, 2008	11.08%	26	Jul 21, 1933	−7.84%	44	Oct 14, 1932	6.83%
9	Oct 28, 2008	10.88%	27	Oct 18, 1937	−7.75%	45	Nov 11, 1929	−6.82%
10	Oct 21, 1987	10.15%	28	Dec 1, 2008	−7.70%	46*	May 14, 1940	−6.80%
11	Nov 6, 1929	−9.92%	29	Oct 9, 2008	−7.33%	47	Oct 5, 1931	−6.78%
12	Aug 3, 1932	9.52%	30*	Sep 5, 1939	7.26%	48*	May 21, 1940	−6.78%
13*	Feb 11, 1932	9.47%	31*	Feb 1, 1917	−7.24%	49	Mar 15, 1907	6.70%
14*	Nov 14, 1929	9.36%	32*	Oct 27, 1997	−7.18%	50	Nov 13, 2008	6.67%
15	Dec 18, 1931	9.35%	33	Oct 5, 1932	−7.15%	51*	Jun 20, 1931	6.64%
16	Feb 13, 1932	9.19%	34*	Sep 17, 2001	−7.13%	52	Jul 24, 1933	6.63%
17*	May 6, 1932	9.08%	35	Jun 3, 1931	7.12%	53*	Jul 26, 1934	−6.62%
18*	Apr 19, 1933	9.03%	36	Jan 6, 1932	7.12%	54	Dec 20, 1895	−6.61%

Asterisks are news related.

TABLE 16-2

Largest News-Related Changes in Dow Jones Industrial Average, 1888–2012

Rank	Date	Change	News Headline
3	Oct 6, 1931	14.87%	Hoover urges $500M pool to help banks
8	Oct 13, 2008	11.08%	Fed gives "unlimited liquidity" to foreign central banks
13	Feb 11, 1932	9.47%	Liberalization of Fed discount policy
14	Nov 14, 1929	9.36%	Fed lowers discount rate/tax cut proposed
17	May 6, 1932	9.08%	U.S. steel negotiates 15% wage cut
18	Apr 19, 1933	9.03%	U.S. drops gold standard
30	Sep 5, 1939	7.26%	World War II begins in Europe
31	Feb 1, 1917	−7.24%	Germany announces unrestricted submarine warfare
32	Oct 27, 1997	−7.18%	Attack on Hong Kong dollar
34	Sep 17, 2001	−7.13%	World Trade Center terrorist attack
39	Sep 29, 2008	−6.98%	House voted down $700B bailout package
40	Oct 13, 1989	−6.91%	United Airline buyout collapses
41	Jul 30, 1914	−6.90%	Outbreak of World War I
43	Mar 23, 2009	6.84%	Treasury announces $1T public-private plan to buy bad bank debt
46	May 14, 1940	−6.80%	Germans invade Holland
48	May 21, 1940	−6.78%	Allied reverses in France
51	Jun 20, 1931	6.64%	Hoover advocates foreign debt moratorium
53	Jul 26, 1934	−6.62%	Fighting in Austria; Italy mobilizes
56	Sep 26, 1955	−6.54%	Eisenhower suffers heart attack
60	Jul 24, 2002	6.35%	J.P. Morgan denies involvement with Enron scandal
63	July, 26, 1893	−6.31%	Erie railroad bankrupt
77	Oct 31, 1929	5.82%	Fed lowers discount rate
78	Jun 16, 1930	−5.81%	Hoover to sign tariff bill
79	Apr 20, 1933	5.80%	Continued rally on dropping of gold standard
87	May 2, 1898	5.64%	Dewey defeats Spanish
91	Mar 28, 1898	5.56%	Dispatches of armistice with Spain
93	Aug 8, 2011	−5.55%	Standard and Poor's downgrades U.S. treasury debt
100	Dec 22, 1916	5.47%	Lansing denies U.S. near war
103	Dec 18, 1896	−5.42%	Senate votes for free Cuba
105	Feb 25, 1933	−5.40%	Maryland bank holiday
109	Oct 23, 1933	5.37%	Roosevelt devalues dollar
111	Dec 21, 1916	−5.35%	Sec. of State Lansing implies U.S. near war
120	Apr 9, 1938	5.25%	Congress passes bill taxing U.S. government bond interest
139	Nov 5, 2008	−5.05%	Democrats sweep Congress, presidency
144	Oct 20, 1931	5.03%	ICC raises rail rates
145	Mar 31, 1932	−5.02%	House proposes stock sales tax

October 27, 1997, when foreign exchange speculators attacked the Hong Kong dollar; the 6.91 percent fall on Friday, October 13, 1989, when the leveraged buyout of United Airlines collapsed; and the 6.54 percent drop on September 26, 1955, when President Eisenhower suffered a heart attack.[3]

During the financial crisis of 2008–2009, the other news-related moves (in addition to the Fed liquidity provisions cited above) were the 6.8 percent jump on March 23, 2009, when the Obama administration announced a trillion-dollar public-private partnership to buy "toxic" assets from commercial banks; the 7.0 percent decline on August 29, 2008, when the U.S. House of Representatives rejected the $700 billion TARP, or Troubled Asset Repurchase Program, proposed by Treasury Secretary Paulson and Federal Reserve Chairman Bernanke of the Bush administration; the 5.5 percent loss on August 8 following Standard & Poor's downgrade of U.S. government debt; and the 5.05 percent fall on November 5, following the Democratic sweep of the White House and Congress in the 2008 elections.

War is usually a big market mover. But the market drop on September 17, 2001, following the terrorist attacks was more than twice the 3.5 percent drop that occurred on the day following the attack on Pearl Harbor, and it was more than that of any other one-day decline during a period when the United States was at war.

Even when the day is filled with news events, there can be sharp disagreement over *what* news caused the market change. On November 15, 1991, when the Dow fell more than 120 points, or nearly 4 percent, *Investor's Business Daily* ran an article about the market entitled "Dow Plunges 120 in a Scary Stock Sell-Off: Biotechs, Programs, Expiration and Congress Get the Blame."[4] In contrast, the London-based *Financial Times* published a front-page article written by a New York writer entitled "Wall Street Drops 120 Points on Concern at Russian Moves." What is interesting is that such news, specifically that the Russian government had suspended oil licenses and taken over the gold supplies, was not mentioned even once in the *Investor's Business Daily* article! That one major newspaper can highlight "reasons" that another news outlet does not even report illustrates the difficulty of finding fundamental explanations for the movements of markets.

UNCERTAINTY AND THE MARKET

The stock market hates uncertainty, which is why events that jar investors from their customary framework for analyzing the world can have devastating effects. September 11 serves as the perfect example. Americans were unsure what these terrorist attacks meant for the future. How severe would the drop in air travel—or any travel—be? How big a hit would the approximately $600 billion tourist industry take? Unanswered questions generate anxiety and declining prices.

Uncertainty about the presidency is another downer for stocks. The market almost always declines in reaction to sudden, unexpected changes related to the presidency. As noted previously, President Eisenhower's heart attack on September 26, 1955, caused a 6.54 percent decline in the Dow Industrials, the fifth largest in the postwar period. The drop was a clear sign of Eisenhower's popularity with investors. The assassination of President Kennedy on Friday, November 22, 1963, caused the Dow Industrials to drop 2.9 percent and persuaded the New York Stock Exchange to close two hours early to prevent panic selling. Trading remained suspended the following Monday, November 25, for Kennedy's funeral. Yet the following Tuesday, by which time Lyndon Johnson had taken over the reins of government, the market soared 4.5 percent, representing one of the best days in the postwar period.

When William McKinley was shot on September 14, 1901, the market dropped by more than 4 percent. But stocks regained all their losses on the following trading day. The death of Warren Harding in 1923 caused a milder setback, which was soon erased. Sell-offs such as these often provide good opportunities for investors to buy stocks since the market usually reverses itself quickly following the change in leadership. But there are politicians whom investors never forgive. Stocks rallied over 4 percent in the week following the news of the death of Franklin Roosevelt, never a favorite on Wall Street.

DEMOCRATS AND REPUBLICANS

It is well known that investors generally prefer Republicans to Democrats. Most corporate executives and stock traders are Republicans, and many Republican policies are perceived to be favorable to stocks and capital formation. Democrats are perceived to be less amenable to favorable tax treatment of capital gains and dividends and more in favor of regulation and income redistribution. Yet the stock market has actually done better under Democrats than Republicans.

The performance of the Dow Jones Industrials during every administration since Grover Cleveland was elected in 1888 is shown in Figure 16-2. The greatest bear market in history occurred during Herbert Hoover's Republican administration, while stocks did quite well under

Franklin Roosevelt, despite the fact that the Democrat was frequently reviled in boardrooms and brokerage houses around the country. The immediate reaction of the market—the day before the election to the day after—does indeed conform to the fact that investors like Republicans better than Democrats. Since 1888, the market fell an average of 0.6 percent on the day following a Democratic victory, but it rose by 0.7 percent on the day following a Republican victory. But the market's reaction to the Republicans' success in presidential elections has been muted since World War II. There have been occasions, like Clinton's second-term election victory, when the market soared because the Republicans kept control of Congress, not because Clinton, a Democrat, was reelected.

The returns in the first, second, third, and fourth years of a presidential term are displayed in Table 16-3. The returns in the third year of a presidential term are generally the best. This is striking since the third year includes the disastrous 43.3 percent drop that occurred in 1931, during the third year of Hoover's ill-fated administration and the worst

FIGURE   16–2

Dow Jones Industrial Average and Presidential Terms (Shaded Areas Democratic) 1985–2012

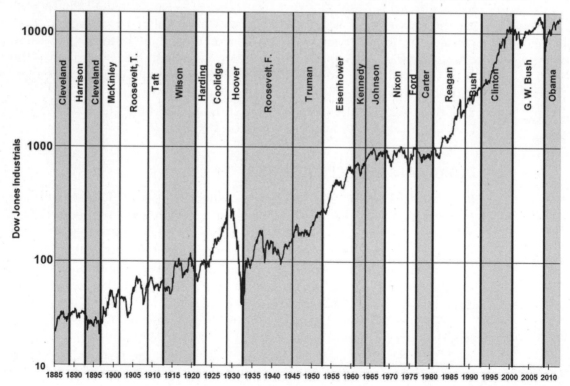

TABLE 16–3

Stock Returns During Presidential Elections and Year in Office 1888–2012

President's Name	Party	Election Date	From: 1 Day Before To: 1 Day After	First Year of Term	Second Year of Term	Third Year of Term	Fourth Year of Term
Harrison	R	11/6/1888	0.4	11.8	−6.6	16.6	13.5
Cleveland	D	11/8/1892	−0.5	−15.3	11.9	11.3	−4.5
McKinley	R	11/3/1896	2.7	18.9	11.0	9.9	−1.3
McKinley	R	11/6/1900	3.3	35.3	0.3	−18.1	28.5
Roosevelt T.	R	11/8/1904	1.3	25.2	2.0	−32.5	39.0
Taft	R	11/3/1908	2.4	16.6	−0.6	0.5	11.7
Wilson	D	11/5/1912	1.8	−13.0	−2.5	24.2	3.7
Wilson	D	11/7/1916	−0.4	−30.9	−5.8	13.5	−19.3
Harding	R	11/2/1920	−0.6	4.0	53.4	−11.1	21.5
Coolidge	R	11/4/1924	1.2	33.3	15.8	36.0	36.5
Hoover	R	11/6/1928	1.2	33.2	−29.6	−32.3	−13.6
Roosevelt F.	D	11/8/1932	−4.5	43.3	−4.13	7.2	43.6
Roosevelt F.	D	11/3/1936	2.3	−26.8	18.6	3.3	−11.8
Roosevelt F.	D	11/5/1940	−2.4	−10.2	−6.1	28.9	12.4
Roosevelt F.	D	11/7/1944	−0.3	30.6	−19.1	−0.5	4.3
Truman	D	11/2/1948	−3.8	7.9	28.8	18.2	8.1
Eisenhower	R	11/4/1952	0.4	3.4	42.3	35.7	11.5
Eisenhower	R	11/6/1956	−0.9	−9.9	25.8	13.5	−3.8
Kennedy	D	11/8/1960	0.8	29.6	−15.8	32.4	18.5
Johnson	D	11/3/1964	−0.2	8.8	−16.0	25.0	6.8
Nixon	R	11/5/1968	0.3	−10.1	−13.1	14.7	12.1
Nixon	R	11/7/1972	−0.1	−4.3	−41.1	24.0	13.2
Carter	D	11/2/1976	−1.0	−9.7	3.6	−2.4	16.2
Reagan	R	11/4/1980	1.7	−12.2	11.6	28.4	−1.4
Reagan	R	11/6/1984	−0.9	14.2	30.1	16.3	−1.6
Bush	R	11/8/1988	−0.4	23.8	−13.9	26.5	6.5
Clinton	D	11/3/1992	−0.9	12.5	0.2	25.4	19.4
Clinton	D	11/5/1996	2.6	35.2	8.6	24.3	4.6
Bush, G.W.	R	11/7/2000*	−1.6	−23.1	−20.9	21.2	6.0
Bush, G.W.	R	11/2/2004	1.1	4.0	14.9	11.0	−37.9
Obama	D	11/4/2008	−1.3	13.7	10.6	1.4	19.0
Obama	D	11/6/2012	−1.5				
Average from 1888 to June 2012	Democratic		−0.6	5.0	0.9	16.1	8.1
	Republican		0.7	9.6	4.8	9.4	8.3
	Overall		0.1	7.7	3.0	13.0	8.4
Average from 1948 to June 2012	Democratic		−0.7	12.3	2.5	15.5	11.6
	Republican		0.0	−1.6	4.0	21.2	0.5
	Overall		−0.3	5.2	3.5	19.7	6.1

*Outcome of race was officially undetermined until December 13, 2000.

1-year performance in more than 120 years. But the third year is not always a charm. The third year of Obama's first term was the worst third year for stocks since Carter's in 1979.

Why the third year of a presidential term stands out is not clear. One would think that the fourth year, when the administration might increase spending or put pressure on the Fed to stimulate the economy for the upcoming election, would be the best year for stocks. But the fourth year, although good, is clearly not the best. Perhaps the market anticipates favorable economic policies in the election year, causing stock prices to rise the year before.

The superior performance under the Democrats in recent years is documented in Table 16-4. This table records the total real and nominal returns in the stock market, as well as the rate of inflation, under Democratic and Republican administrations. Since 1888, the market has fared better in nominal terms under Democrats than under Republicans, but since inflation has been lower when the Republicans have held office, real stock returns have been about the same under each party. But this has not been true over the past 60 years, when the market performed far better under the Democrats whether or not inflation is taken into account. Perhaps this is why the market's reaction to a Democratic presidential victory has not been as negative in recent years as it was in the past.

STOCKS AND WAR

Since 1885, the U.S. economy has been at war or on the sidelines of a world war about one-fifth of the time. The stock market does equally well in nominal returns whether there is war or peace. Inflation, however, has averaged nearly 6 percent during wartime and less than 2 percent during peacetime, so the real returns on stocks during peacetime greatly outstrip those during wars.

While returns are better during peacetime, the stock market has actually been more volatile during peacetime than during war, as measured by the monthly standard deviation of the Dow Industrials. The greatest volatility in U.S. markets occurred in the late 1920s and early 1930s, well before the United States was engaged in World War II, and in 2008 and 2009, during the recent financial crisis. Only during World War I and the short Gulf War did stocks have higher volatility than the historical average.

In theory, war should have a profound negative influence on stock prices. Governments commandeer tremendous resources, while high taxes and huge government borrowings compete with investors' demand

TABLE 16–4

Stock Returns During Presidential Administrations 1888–2012

President's Name	Party	Date	Months in Office	Annualized Nominal Stock Return	Annualized Inflation	Annualized Real Return
Harrison	R	11/88–10/92	48	5.48	−2.73	8.43
Cleveland	D	11/92–10/96	48	−2.88	−3.06	0.19
McKinley	R	11/96–8/01	58	19.42	3.69	15.18
Roosevelt, T.	R	9/01–10/08	86	5.02	1.95	3.01
Taft	R	11/08–10/12	48	9.56	2.59	6.80
Wilson	D	11/12–10/20	96	3.55	9.26	−5.23
Harding	R	11/20–7/23	33	7.43	−5.16	13.28
Coolidge	R	8/23–10/28	63	26.99	0.00	26.99
Hoover	R	11/28–10/32	48	−19.31	−6.23	−13.96
Roosevelt, F.	D	11/32–3/45	149	11.42	2.37	8.83
Truman	D	4/45–10/52	91	13.84	5.49	7.91
Eisenhower	R	11/52–10/60	96	15.09	1.38	13.52
Kennedy	D	11/60–10/63	36	14.3	11.11	13.06
Johnson	D	11/63–10/68	60	10.64	2.76	7.66
Nixon	R	11/68–7/74	69	−1.39	6.02	−6.99
Ford	R	8/74–10/76	27	16.56	7.31	8.62
Carter	D	11/76–10/80	48	11.66	10.01	1.50
Reagan	R	11/80–10/88	96	14.64	4.46	9.75
Bush	R	11/88–10/92	48	14.05	4.22	9.44
Clinton	D	11/92–10/00	96	18.74	2.59	15.74
Bush, G.W.	R	11/00–10/08	96	−2.75	2.77	−5.38
Obama	D	11/08–12/12	50	12.10	1.41	10.54
Average from 1888 to Dec 2012	Democrat		674	10.80	3.86	6.80
	Republican		816	8.47	1.90	6.45
	Overall		100%	9.53	2.78	6.61
Average from 1952 to Dec 2012	Democrat		290	14.20	3.47	10.48
	Republican		432	8.37	3.80	4.45
	Overall		100%	10.71	3.67	6.87

for stocks. Whole industries are nationalized to further the war effort. Moreover, if losing the war is deemed a possibility, stocks could well decline as the victors impose sanctions on the vanquished. However, the economies of Germany and Japan were quickly restored to health following World War II, and stocks subsequently boomed.

Markets During the World Wars

The market was far more volatile during World War I than during World War II. The market rose nearly 100 percent during the early stages of World War I, then fell 40 percent when the United States became involved in the hostilities, and finally rallied when the Great War ended. In contrast, during the six years of World War II, the market never deviated more than 32 percent from its prewar level.

The outbreak of World War I precipitated a panic, as European investors scrambled to get out of stocks and into gold and cash. After Austria-Hungary declared war on Serbia on July 28, 1914, all the major European stock exchanges closed. The European panic spread to New York, and the Dow Jones Industrials closed down nearly 7 percent on Thursday, July 30, the most drastic decline since the 8.3 percent drop during the Panic of 1907. Minutes before the opening of the New York Stock Exchange on Friday, the exchange voted to close for an indefinite period.

The market did not reopen until December. Never before had the New York Stock Exchange been closed for such an extended period, nor has it since. Emergency trades were permitted, but only by approval of a special committee and only at prices at or above the last trade before the exchange closed. Even then, the trading prohibition was observed in the breach, as illegal trades were made outside the exchange (on the curb) at prices that continued to decline through October. Unofficially, by autumn, prices were said to be 15 to 20 percent below the July closing.

It is ironic that the only extended period during which the New York Stock Exchange was closed occurred when the United States was not yet at war or in any degree of financial or economic distress. In fact, when the exchange was closed, traders realized that the United States would be a strong economic beneficiary of the European conflict. Once investors realized that America was going to make the munitions and provide raw materials to the belligerents, public interest in stocks soared.

By the time the exchange reopened on December 12, prices were rising rapidly. The Dow Industrials finished the historic Saturday session about 5 percent higher than the closing prices the previous July. The rally continued, and 1915 records the best single-year increase in the history of the Dow Industrials, as stocks rose a record 82 percent. Stocks continued to rise in 1916 and hit their peak in November, with prices more than twice the level they were when the war had started more than two years earlier. But then stocks settled back about 10 percent when the United States formally entered the war on April 16, 1917, and fell another 10 percent through November 1918, when the Armistice was signed.

The message of the great boom of 1915 was not lost on traders a generation later. When World War II erupted, investors took their cue from what happened at the beginning of the previous world war. When Great Britain declared war on Germany on September 3, 1939, the rise was so explosive that the Tokyo Stock Exchange was forced to close early. When the market opened in New York, a buying panic erupted. The Dow Industrials gained over 7 percent, and even the European stock exchanges were firm when trading reopened.

The enthusiasm that followed the onset of World War II quickly faded. President Roosevelt was determined not to let corporations earn easy profits as they had in World War I. These profits had been a source of public criticism, as Americans felt that the war costs were not being borne equally as its young men died overseas while corporations earned record income. An excess profits tax enacted by Congress during World War II removed the wartime premium that investors had expected from the conflict.

The day before the Japanese attacked Pearl Harbor, the Dow was down 25 percent from its 1939 high and still less than one-third its 1929 peak. Stocks fell 3.5 percent on the day following Pearl Harbor and continued to fall until they hit a low on April 28, 1942, when the United States suffered losses in the early months of the war in the Pacific.

But when the tide of war turned toward the Allies, the market began to climb. By the time Germany signed its unconditional surrender on May 7, 1945, the Dow Industrials were 20 percent above the prewar level. The detonation of the atomic bomb over Hiroshima, a pivotal event in the history of warfare, caused stocks to surge 1.7 percent as investors recognized that the end of the war was near. But World War II did not prove as profitable for investors as World War I, as the Dow was up only 30 percent during the six years from the German invasion of Poland to V-J Day.

Post-1945 Conflicts

The Korean War took investors by surprise. When North Korea invaded its southern neighbor on June 25, 1950, the Dow fell 4.65 percent, greater than the day following Pearl Harbor. But the market reaction to the growing conflict was contained, and stocks never fell more than 12 percent below their prewar level.

The Vietnam War was the longest and one of the least popular of all U.S. wars. The starting point for U.S. involvement in the conflict can be placed at August 2, 1964, when two American destroyers were reportedly attacked in the Gulf of Tonkin.

A year and a half after the Gulf of Tonkin incident, the Dow reached an all-time high of 995, more than 18 percent higher than before the Tonkin attack. But it fell nearly 30 percent in the following months after the Fed tightened credit to curb inflation. By the time American troop strength reached its peak in early 1968, the market had recovered. Two years later, when Nixon sent troops into Cambodia and interest rates were soaring and a recession was looming, the market fell again, down nearly 25 percent from its prewar point.

The peace pact between the North Vietnamese and the Americans was signed in Paris on January 27, 1973. But the gains made by investors over the eight years of war were quite small, as the market was held back by rising inflation and interest rates as well as other problems not directly related to the Vietnam War.

If the war in Vietnam was one of the longest American wars, the 1991 Gulf War against Iraq in the Middle East was the shortest. The trigger occurred on August 2, 1990, when Iraq invaded Kuwait, sending oil prices skyward and sparking a U.S. military buildup in Saudi Arabia. The rise in oil prices combined with an already slowing U.S. economy to drive the United States deeper into a recession. The stock market fell precipitously, and on October 11, the Dow slumped over 18 percent from its prewar levels.

The United States began its offensive action on January 17, 1991. It was the first major war fought in a world where markets for oil, gold, and U.S. government bonds were traded around the clock in Tokyo, Singapore, London, and New York. The markets judged the victors in a matter of hours. Bonds sold off in Tokyo for a few minutes following the news of the U.S. bombing of Baghdad, but the stunning reports of the United States and its allies' successes sent bonds and Japanese stocks straight upward in the next few minutes. Oil traded in the Far East collapsed in price, as Brent crude fell from $29 a barrel before hostilities to $20.

On the following day, stock prices soared around the world. The Dow jumped 115 points, or 4.4 percent, and there were large gains throughout Europe and Asia. By the time the United States deployed ground troops to invade Kuwait, the market had known for two months that victory was at hand. The war ended on February 28, and by the first week in March, the Dow was more than 18 percent higher than when the war started.

As noted at the outset of this chapter, the war on terrorism began with the terrorists' attacks on New York and the Pentagon on September

11, 2001. The Dow Industrials were down 16 percent from their close of 9,606 on September 10 to an intraday low of 8,062 reached on Friday, September 21. But the market rebounded sharply by the next week, and it had recovered to 9,120 by the time the United States began offensive action against the Taliban in Afghanistan on October 7.

Because of aggressive easing policies by the Federal Reserve and the successful early execution of the Afghanistan War, the Dow surpassed its September 10 level on November 13 and continued rising to year-end. From its intraday low of 8,062 on September 21 to its intraday high of 10,184 on December 28, the Dow rose an astounding 26.3 percent in three months.

The market continued its rise to 10,673 on March 19, 2002, but the bear market, which had begun two years earlier, was far from over. A sluggish economy, combined with the accounting scandals of Enron, WorldCom, and others, sent stocks into another dive that didn't end until October 10, 2002, when the Dow hit an intraday low of 7,197. From the intraday high of 11,750 reached on January 14, 2000, through the low of October 10, 2002, the Dow Industrials fell nearly 39 percent, a decline far less than the S&P 500 Index that was bloated by overpriced technology stocks.

The market subsequently rallied to over 9,000, but anxiety about a second U.S. operation in Iraq sent stocks back down to 7,524 five months later on March 11, 2003, just days before the invasion. But as it responded 12 years earlier when the Gulf War started, the market rallied on news of the invasion and continued to rise despite the growing insurgency in Iraq that made the war particularly unpopular.

Notwithstanding the Republican defeat in Congress in November 2006, stocks hit new all-time highs in the summer of 2007, more than recovering all the ground that had been lost during the 2000-to-2002 bear market. From the end of March 2003, the first month of the Iraq invasion, through June 2007, the annual return on the market was an extremely strong 17.5 percent per year until all these gains were derailed by the financial crisis.

CONCLUSION

When investigating the causes of major market movements, it is sobering to realize that less than one in four can be linked to a news event of major political or economic import. This confirms the unpredictability of the market and the difficulty in forecasting market moves. Those who sold in panic at the outbreak of World War I missed out on 1915, the best year ever in the stock market. But those who bought at the onset of World War II, believing there would be a replay of the World War I gains, were sorely disappointed because of the government's determination to cap wartime profits. World events may shock the market in the short run, but thankfully they have proved unable to dent the long-term returns that have become characteristic of stocks over the long run.

Stocks, Bonds, and the Flow of Economic Data

The thing that most affects the stock market is everything.
—JAMES PALYSTED WOOD, 1966

It's 8:28 a.m. eastern daylight time, Friday, July 5, 1996. Normally a trading day wedged between a major U.S. holiday and a weekend is slow, with little volume or price movement. But not today. Traders around the world are anxiously glued to their terminals, eyes riveted on the scrolling news that displays thousands of headlines daily. All week, stock, bond, and currency traders have anticipated this day. It is just two minutes before the most important announcement each month—the U.S. employment statistics. The Dow has been trading within a few points of its all-time high, reached at the end of May. But interest rates have been rising, giving traders cause for concern. The seconds tick down. At 8:30 sharp, the headlines scroll across the screen:

> PAYROLL UP 239,000, UNEMPLOYMENT AT SIX-YEAR LOW OF 5.3 PERCENT, WAGES UP 9 CENTS AN HOUR, BIGGEST INCREASE IN 30 YEARS.

President Clinton hailed the economic news, claiming, "We have the most solid American economy in a generation; wages for American workers are finally on the rise again."

But the financial markets were stunned. Long-term bond prices immediately collapsed as traders expected the Fed to tighten, and interest rates rose by nearly a quarter point. Although the stock market would not open for an hour, the S&P 500 Index futures, which represent claims on this benchmark index and are described in detail in the next chapter, fell from about 2 percent. European stock markets, which had been open for hours, sold off immediately. The benchmark DAX index in Germany, CAC in France, and FT-SE in Britain instantly fell almost 2 percent. Within seconds, world equity markets lost $200 billion, and world bond markets fell at least as much.

This episode demonstrates that what Main Street interprets as good news is often bad news on Wall Street. This is because it is more than mere profits that move stocks; interest rates, inflation, and the future direction of the Federal Reserve's monetary policy also have a major impact.

ECONOMIC DATA AND THE MARKET

News moves markets. The timing of much news is unpredictable—like war, political developments, and natural disasters. In contrast, news based on data about the economy comes at preannounced times that are set a year or more in advance. In the United States, there are hundreds of scheduled releases of economic data each year—mostly by government agencies, but increasingly by private firms. Virtually all the announcements deal with the economy, particularly economic growth and inflation, and all have the potential to move the market significantly.

Economic data not only frame the way traders view the economy but also impact traders' expectations of how the central bank will implement its monetary policy. Stronger economic growth or higher inflation increases the probability that the central bank will either tighten or stop easing monetary policy. All these data influence traders' expectations about the future course of interest rates, the economy, and ultimately stock prices.

PRINCIPLES OF MARKET REACTION

Markets do not directly respond to what is announced; rather, they respond to the *difference* between what the traders expect to happen and what *actually* happens. Whether the news is good or bad for the economy is of no importance. If the market expects that 200,000 jobs were lost last month but the report shows that only 100,000 jobs were lost, this will be considered "stronger-than-expected" economic news by the financial markets—having about the same effect on markets as a gain of 200,000 jobs would when the market expected a gain of only 100,000.

The reason why markets react only to the difference between expectations and what actually occurs is that the prices of securities already incorporate all the information that is expected. If a firm is expected to report bad earnings, the market has already priced this gloomy information into the stock price. If the earnings report is not as bad as anticipated, the price will rise on the announcement. The same principle applies to the reaction of bond and foreign exchange prices to economic data.

Therefore, to understand why the market moves the way it does, you must identify the *market expectation* for the data released. The market expectation, often referred to as the *consensus estimate*, is gathered by news and research organizations. They poll economists, professional forecasters, traders, and other market participants for their predictions for an upcoming government or private release. The results of their surveys are sent to the financial press and are widely reported online and in many other news outlets.[1]

INFORMATION CONTENT OF DATA RELEASES

The economic data are analyzed for their implications for future economic growth, inflation, and central bank policy. The following principle summarizes the reaction of the bond markets to the release of data relating to economic growth:

> Stronger-than-expected economic growth causes both long- and short-term interest rates to rise. Weaker-than-expected economic growth causes interest rates to fall.

Faster-than-expected economic growth raises interest rates for several reasons. First, stronger economic activity makes consumers feel more confident and more willing to borrow against future income, increasing loan demand. Faster economic growth also motivates firms to expand production. As a result, both firms and consumers will likely increase their demand for credit and push interest rates higher.

A second reason why interest rates rise in tandem with a stronger-than-expected economic report is that such growth might be inflationary, especially if it is near the end of an economic expansion. Economic growth associated with increases in productivity, which often occur in the early and middle stages of a business expansion, is rarely inflationary.

Going back to the example above, inflationary fears were the principal reason why interest rates soared when the Labor Department released its report on July 5, 1996. Traders feared that the large increase in wages caused by the tight labor markets and falling unemployment would cause inflation, a nemesis to both the bond and the stock markets.

Reports on economic growth also have significant implications for the actions of central banks. The threat of inflation from an overly strong economy will make it likely that the central bank will tighten credit. If the aggregate demand is expanding too rapidly relative to the supply of goods and services, the monetary authority can raise interest rates to prevent the economy from overheating.

Of course, in the case of a weaker-than-expected employment report, the bond market will rise as interest rates decline in response to weaker credit demand and lower inflationary pressures. Recall that the price of bonds moves in the opposite direction of interest rates.

An important principle is that the market reacts more strongly after several similar reports move in the same direction. For example, if an inflation report is higher than expected, then the following month the market will react even more strongly to another higher-than-expected reading. The reason for this is that there is a lot of noise in individual reports, and a single month's observation may be reversed in subsequent data. But if the subsequent data confirm the original report, then it is more likely that a new trend has been established, and the market will move accordingly.

ECONOMIC GROWTH AND STOCK PRICES

It surprises the general public and even the financial press when a strong economic report sends the stock market lower. But stronger-than-expected economic growth has two important implications for the stock market, and each tugs in the opposite direction. A strong economy increases future corporate earnings, which is bullish for stocks. But it also raises interest rates, which raises the discount rate at which these future profits are discounted. Similarly, a weak economic report may lower expected earnings; but if interest rates decline, stock prices could possibly move up because of the decline in the rate at which these profits are discounted. It is a struggle, in asset pricing terms, between the numerator, which contains future cash flows, and the denominator, which discounts those cash flows.

Which effect is stronger—the change in the interest rate or the change in corporate profits— often depends on where the economy is in the business cycle. Recent analysis shows that in a recession, a stronger-than-expected economic report increases stock prices since the implications for corporate profits are more important than the change in interest rates at this stage in the business cycle.[2] Inversely, a weaker-than-expected report depresses stock prices. During economic expansions, and particularly toward the end of an expansion, the interest rate effect is usually stronger since inflation is a greater threat.

Many stock traders look at the movements in the bond market to guide their trading. This is particularly true of portfolio managers who actively apportion their portfolio between stocks and bonds on the basis of changes in interest rates and expected stock returns. When interest rates fall after a weak economic report, these investors are immediately ready to increase the proportion of stocks that they hold, since the relative returns on stocks or bonds have, at that moment, turned in favor of stocks. On the other hand, investors who recognize that the weak employment report means lower future earnings may sell stocks. The stock market often gyrates throughout the day as investors digest the implications of the data for earnings and interest rates.

THE EMPLOYMENT REPORT

The *employment report*, compiled by the Bureau of Labor Statistics (BLS), is the single most important data report released by the government each month. To measure employment, the BLS does two entirely different surveys, one that measures employment and the other that measures unemployment. The *payroll survey* counts the total number of *jobs* that companies have on their payrolls, while the household survey counts the number of people who have and are looking for jobs. The *payroll survey*, sometimes called the *establishment survey*, collects payroll data from nearly 400,000 business establishments and government workers, covering nearly 50 million workers, about 40 percent of the total workforce. It is this survey that most forecasters use to judge the future course of the economy. Of the greatest importance to traders is the change in the *nonfarm payroll* (the number of farm workers is excluded since it is very volatile and not associated with cyclical economic trends).

The *unemployment rate* is determined from an entirely different survey than the payroll survey. It is the unemployment rate, however, that often gets the top billing in the evening news. The unemployment rate is calculated from a "household survey" in which data from about 60,000 households are accumulated. It asks, among other questions, whether anyone in the household has "actively" sought work over the past four weeks. Those who answer yes are classified as unemployed. The resulting number of unemployed people is divided by the number of people in the total labor force, which yields the unemployment rate. The labor force in the United States, defined as those employed plus those unemployed, constitutes about two-thirds of the adult population. This ratio had risen steadily in the 1980s and 1990s as more women have successfully sought work, but it has fallen recently.

The BLS statistics can be very tricky to interpret. Because the payroll and household data are based on totally different surveys, it is not unusual for payroll employment to go up at the same time that the unemployment rate rises and vice versa. One reason is because the payroll survey counts jobs, while the household survey counts people. So workers with two jobs are counted only once in the household survey but twice in the payroll survey. Furthermore, self-employed individuals are not counted in the payroll survey but are counted in the household survey. Finally, increases in the number seeking work in the early stage of an economic recovery may increase the unemployment rate due to the influx of job seekers into an improved labor market.

For these reasons, many economists and forecasters downplay the importance of the unemployment rate in forecasting the business cycle. But this does not diminish the political impact of this number. The unemployment rate is an easily understood figure that represents the fraction of the workforce looking for but not finding work. Much of the public looks more to this statistic than any other to judge the health of the economy. Furthermore, Fed Chairman Ben Bernanke made the unemployment rate a threshold for when the Federal Reserve would begin to raise interest rates following the financial crisis and Great Recession. As a result, the unemployment rate is now considered very important by traders and market watchers.

Since 2005, the Automatic Data Processing (ADP) Corporation has released its own payroll data, called *The ADP National Employment Report*, two days before the BLS labor report. The ADP report is a measure of nonfarm private employment, based on approximately one-half of ADP's 500,000 U.S. business clients and approximately 23 million employees. Because ADP processes the paychecks for one out of every six private-sector employees in the United States every pay period across a broad range of industries, firm sizes, and geographies, ADP's numbers provide a good clue for the upcoming labor data.

THE CYCLE OF ANNOUNCEMENTS

The employment report is just one of several dozen economic announcements that come out every month. The usual release dates for the vari-

FIGURE 17-1

Typical Monthly Economic Data Calendar

Monday	Tuesday	Wednesday	Thursday	Friday
1 10:00 Purchasing Mgrs. Index** (PMI)	**2** Vehicle Sales*	**3** 8:15 ADP Employment Est.** 10:00 Service PMI**	**4** 8:30 Jobless Claims** Trade Report*	**5** 8:30 Employment Report****
8	**9**	**10**	**11** 8:30 Jobless Claims**	**12** 8:30 PPI**** 9:55 U of Mich Cons Conf
15 8:30 NY Fed* Retail Sales***	**16** 8:30 CPI*** 9:15 Ind Prod* 10:00 NAHB Index**	**17** 8:30 Housing Starts*** Building Permits***	**18** 8:30 Jobless Claims** 10:00 Philly Fed*	**19**
22 10:00 Existing Home Sales**	**23** 8:30 Durable Goods Orders**	**24** 10:00 New Home Sales*	**25** 8:30 Jobless Claims** Durable Goods**	**26**
29	**30** 8:30 Quarterly GDP*** 9:00 Case-Shiller Home Prices* 10:00 Conf Board Cons Conf*	**31** 8:30 Empl Cost Index* Income, Spending, PCE Defl*** 9:45 Chicago PMI*		

Stars Rank Importance to Market (** = most important)**

ous data reports in a typical month are displayed in Figure 17-1. The number of asterisks represents the importance of the report to the financial market.

ADP's payroll report is the culmination of important data on economic growth that come out around the turn of the month. On the first business day of each month, a survey by the Institute for Supply Management (ISM, formerly the National Association of Purchasing Managers) called the *purchasing managers index* (PMI) is released.

The institute's report surveys 250 purchasing agents of manufacturing companies and inquires about whether orders, production, employment, or other indicators are rising or falling, and it forms an index from these data. A reading of 50 means that half the managers report rising activity and half report falling activity. A reading of 52 or 53 is the sign of a normally expanding economy. A reading of 60 represents a strong economy in which three-fifths of the managers report growth. A reading below 50 represents a contracting manufacturing sector, and a reading below 40 is almost always a sign of recession. Two days later, on the third business day of the month, the ISM publishes a similar index for the service sector of the economy.

There are other releases of timely data reports on manufacturing activity. The Chicago Purchasing Managers report comes out on the last business day of the month, the day before the national PMI report. The Chicago area is well diversified in manufacturing, so about two-thirds of the time the Chicago index will move in the same direction as the national index. Since 1968, the Philadelphia Fed Manufacturing Report has been published on the third Thursday of every month, which had made it the first manufacturing report to be published each month. But in recent years, the New York Fed, not to be outdone by its southern neighbor, has published the Empire State report on New York manufacturing a few days earlier. And since 2008, Markit Group Limited, a London-based financial information service corporation, has published Purchasing Managers' Reports for many international countries (including the United States), which comes out before the ISM report.

Also of importance are the consumer sentiment indicators: one from the University of Michigan and another from the Conference Board, a business trade association. These surveys query consumers about their current financial situation and their expectations of the future. The Conference Board survey, released on the last Tuesday of the month, is considered a good early indicator of consumer spending. For many years, the University of Michigan monthly index was not published until after the Conference Board release, but pressure for early data reports has persuaded the university to release a preliminary report before the Conference Board.

INFLATION REPORTS

Although the employment report forms the capstone of the news about economic growth, the market knows that the Federal Reserve is equally if not more interested in the inflation data. That's because inflation is the primary variable that the central bank can control in the long run. Some of the earliest signals of inflationary pressures arrive with the midmonth inflation statistics.

The first monthly inflation release is the *producer price index* (PPI), which was known before 1978 as the "wholesale price index." The PPI, first published in 1902, is one of the oldest continuous series of statistical data published by the government.

The PPI measures the prices received by producers for goods sold at the wholesale level, the stage before the goods are resold to the public.

About one-quarter of the PPI comes from the price of capital goods sold to manufacturers, and about 15 percent of the PPI is energy related. There are no services in the producer price index. At the same time the PPI is announced, indexes for the prices of intermediate and crude goods (often called "pipeline inflation") are released, both of which track inflation at earlier stages of production.

The second monthly inflation announcement, which follows the PPI by a day or so, is the all-important *consumer price index* (CPI). The CPI does cover the prices of services as well as goods. Services, which include rent, housing, transportation, and medical services, now make up over half the weight of the CPI.

The consumer price index is considered the benchmark measure of inflation. When price-level comparisons are made, on both a historical and an international basis, the consumer price index is almost always the chosen index. The CPI is also the price index to which so many private and public contracts, as well as social security and government tax brackets, are linked.

The financial market probably gives a bit more weight to the consumer price index than to the producer price index because of the CPI's widespread use in indexing and political importance. But many economists regard the producer price index as more sensitive to early price trends, as inflation often shows up at the wholesale level before it shows up at the retail level.

Core Inflation

Of importance to the market is not only the overall inflation rate but inflation that excludes the volatile food and energy sectors. Since weather has a great influence on food prices, a rise or fall in the price of food over a month does not have much meaning for the overall inflationary trend. Similarly, the fluctuations of oil and natural gas prices are due to weather conditions, temporary supply disruptions, and speculative trading that do not necessarily persist into future months. To obtain an index of inflation that measures the more persistent and long-term trends of inflation, the government also computes the core consumer and producer price indexes, which measure inflation excluding food and energy.

The core rate of inflation is more important to the central banks in the overall index, which includes food and energy, because it better identifies the underlying trend of prices. Forecasters are usually able to predict the core rate of inflation better than the overall rate since the latter is influenced by the volatile food and energy sectors. An error of three-tenths of a percentage point in the consensus forecast for the month-to-month rate of inflation might not be that serious, but such an error would be considered quite large for the core rate of inflation and would significantly affect the financial markets.

The index the Federal Reserve has used as its prime inflation indicator is the *personal consumption expenditure* (PCE) *deflator*, which is a price index calculated for the consumption component of the GDP accounts. The PCE deflator differs from the consumer price index in that the PCE deflator uses a more up-to-date weighting scheme and includes the cost of the employer-paid as well as the employee-paid medical insurance. The PCE deflator generally runs about ¼ to ½ percentage point below the CPI and is the index that the Fed refers to in its 2 percent inflation target.

Employment Costs

Other important releases bearing on inflation relate to labor costs. The monthly employment report issued by the BLS contains data on the hourly wage rate and sheds light on cost pressures arising in the labor market. Since labor costs average nearly two-thirds of a firm's production costs, increases in the hourly wage not matched by increases in productivity will increase labor costs and threaten to cause inflation. Every calendar quarter, the government also releases the employment cost index. This index includes benefit costs as well as wages, and it is considered the most comprehensive report of labor costs.

IMPACT ON FINANCIAL MARKETS

The following summarizes the impact of inflation on the financial markets:

A lower-than-expected inflation report lowers interest rates and boosts bond and stock prices. Inflation worse than expected raises interest rates and depresses stock and bond prices.

That inflation is bad for bonds should come as no surprise. Bonds are fixed-income investments whose cash flows are not adjusted for inflation. Bondholders demand higher interest rates to protect their purchasing power when inflation increases.

Worse-than-expected inflation is also bad for the stock market. As noted in Chapter 14, stocks have proved to be poor hedges against inflation in the short run. Stock investors know that worsening inflation increases the effective tax rate on both corporate earnings and capital gains and induces the central bank to tighten credit, raising real interest rates.

CENTRAL BANK POLICY

Central bank policy is of primary importance to financial markets. Martin Zweig, a noted money manager, described the relationship this way:

> In the stock market, as with horse racing, money makes the mare go. Monetary conditions exert an enormous influence on stock prices. Indeed, the monetary climate—primarily the trend in interest rates and Federal Reserve policy—is the dominant factor in determining the stock market's major direction.[3]

Chapter 16 showed that four of the top five largest one-day rallies in Wall Street history were involved with monetary policy. Lowering short-term interest rates and providing more credit to the banking system are actions that are almost always extremely welcome by stock investors. When the central bank eases credit, it lowers the rate at which stock future cash flows are discounted and stimulates demand, which increases future earnings.

The Federal Reserve holds eight scheduled meetings of the Federal Open Market Committee per year, and after each one a statement is released. The last meeting of each quarter, when the Fed holds a news conference, is of particular importance. Fed testimony to Congress, particularly the semiannual testimony to the House and Senate in February and July, is very significant. But the chairman can drop hints about a change in the direction of policy at any time, so any speech has the capability of moving markets.

Chapter 14 indicated that from the 1950s through the 1980s, tightening by the Fed was associated with poor returns over the next year, whereas easing boosted the market. Because changes in the Fed's monetary authority are now anticipated far in advance, changes in the rate have not been as reliable in recent years. But surprise intermeeting moves by the central bank are as powerful as ever. The unexpected ½-point cut in the funds rate from 6.5 to 6 percent that took place on January 3, 2001, sent the S&P 500 Index up 5 percent and the tech-heavy Nasdaq up an all-time record 14.2 percent. And when Fed Chairman Ben Bernanke announced that the Fed was planning to phase out its quantitative easing on June 19, 2013, the stock and bond markets suffered their largest loss in almost two years.

The only case in which stocks will react poorly to central bank easing is if the monetary authority eases excessively, so that the market fears an increase in inflation. But if the central bank eases excessively, an investor would prefer to be in stocks than bonds, because fixed-income assets are hurt more than stocks by unexpected inflation.

CONCLUSION

The reactions of financial markets to the release of economic data are not random but instead can be predicted by economic analysis. Strong economic growth invariably raises interest rates, but it has an ambiguous effect on stock prices, especially in the late states of an economic expansion as higher interest rates battle against stronger corporate profits. Higher inflation is bad for both the stock and bond markets. Central bank easing is very positive for stocks and has historically sparked some of the strongest stock rallies.

This chapter emphasizes the short-run reaction of financial markets to economic data. Although it is fascinating to observe and understand the market's reaction, investing on the basis of these data releases is a tricky game that is best left to speculators who can stomach the short-term volatility. Most investors will do well to watch from the sidelines and stick to an investment strategy for the long run.

PART IV

STOCK
FLUCTUATIONS IN
THE SHORT RUN

18

Exchange-Traded Funds, Stock Index Futures, and Options

When I was a kid—a runner for Merrill Lynch at 25 dollars a week— I'd heard an old timer say, "The greatest thing to trade would be stock futures—but you can't do that, it's gambling."

—LEO MELAMED, 1988[1]

Warren Buffett thinks that stock futures and options ought to be out- lawed, and I agree with him.

—PETER LYNCH, 1989[2]

If someone were to ask what security traded on a stock exchange had the largest dollar volume in the United States in 2012, what would you guess? Apple, Google, Exxon-Mobil? The surprising answer is a security that was not in existence before 1993 and does not even represent a com- pany. The security with the highest dollar volume is *spiders*, the nickname given to the S&P 500 Depository Receipts (SPDRs), an exchange-traded fund that represents the value of the S&P 500 Index. In 2012, over 50 bil- lion shares were traded, representing a value of over $7 trillion.

EXCHANGE-TRADED FUNDS

Exchange-traded funds (ETFs) are the most innovative and successful new financial instruments since stock index futures contracts debuted two decades earlier. ETFs are shares issued by an investment company that represent an underlying portfolio. They are traded throughout the day on an exchange where the prices are determined by supply and demand. Most ETFs issued in the 1990s tracked only well-known stock indexes, but more recently they have been tracking new customized indexes and even actively managed portfolios.

The growth of exchange-traded funds has been explosive. Figure 18-1 shows the growth of mutual fund assets and ETFs since 1995.[3] At the end of 2012, ETF assets totaled over $1.3 trillion, and although only 10 percent of the $134 trillion in standard mutual funds, ETFs have grown thirteenfold since 2002.

FIGURE 18–1

Growth of Mutual Fund and ETF Assets 1995–2012

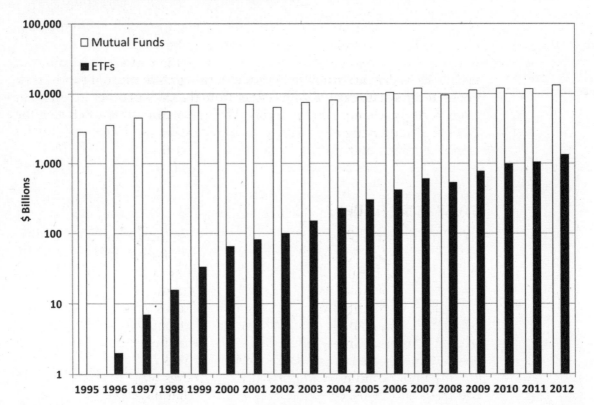

Spiders were the first and most successful ETF, launched in 1993. But spiders were soon joined by others, with nicknames like *cubes*, a corruption of the QQQ ticker symbol given to the Nasdaq-100 Index, and *diamonds*, with the ticker symbol DIA, which represents the Dow Jones Industrial Average.

These ETFs track their respective indexes extremely closely. That's because designated institutions, market makers, and large investors, called *authorized participants*, can buy the underlying shares of the stocks in the index and deliver them to the issuer in exchange for units of ETFs and deliver units of ETFs in exchange for the underlying shares. The minimum size for such an exchange, called a *creation unit*, is usually 50,000 shares. For example, an authorized participant who delivers 50,000 shares of spiders to State Street Bank & Trust will receive a prorated number of shares of each member of the S&P 500 Index. These authorized participants keep the prices of the ETFs extremely close to the value of the index. For the active ETFs, such as spiders and cubes, the bid-asked spread is as low as 1 cent.

There are several advantages of ETFs over mutual funds. ETFs, unlike mutual funds, can be bought or sold at any time during the day. Second, an investor can sell ETFs short, hoping to make a profit by buying them back at a lower price. This proves to be a very convenient way of hedging portfolio gains if an investor fears the market may fall. And finally, ETFs are extremely tax efficient since, unlike mutual funds, they generate almost no capital gains either from the sales of other investors or from portfolio changes to the index. This is because swaps between the ETFs and underlying shares are considered *exchanges in kind* and are not taxable events. Later in this chapter we will list the advantages and disadvantages of ETFs compared with alternative forms of index investing.

STOCK INDEX FUTURES

ETFs are really the outgrowth of one of the most important trading innovations of the last 50 years—the development of stock index futures in the early 1980s. Despite the enormous popularity of these new exchange-traded funds, the total dollar volume in ETFs is still dwarfed by the dollar volume represented by trading in index futures, most of which began trading in Chicago but are now traded on electronic exchanges. Shifts in overall market sentiment often impact the index futures market first and then are transmitted to stocks traded in New York.

To understand how important index futures were to stock prices in the 1980s and 1990s, one need only look at what happened on April 13,

1992. It began as an ordinary trading day, but at about 11:45 in the morning, the two big Chicago futures exchanges, the Board of Trade and the Mercantile Exchange, were closed when a massive leak from the Chicago River coursed through the tunnels under the financial district and triggered extensive power outages. The intraday movement of the Dow Industrials and the S&P futures is shown in Figure 18-2. As soon as the Chicago futures trading was halted, the volatility of the stock market declined significantly.

It almost looks as if the New York Stock Exchange went "brain dead" when there was no lead from Chicago. The volume in New York dropped by more than 25 percent on the day the Chicago futures market was closed; and some dealers claimed that if the futures exchange remained inoperative, it would cause liquidity problems and difficulty in executing some trades in New York.[4] Michael Metz, a market strategist at Oppenheimer & Co., declared: "It's been absolutely delightful; it seems so sedate. It reminds me of the halcyon days on Wall Street before the program traders took hold."[5]

Who are these *program traders* that investors hear so much about, and what do they do? The floor of the New York Stock Exchange has always been alive with a constant din of people scurrying about delivering orders and making deals. But in the mid-1980s, just a few years after index futures were introduced, the background noise was punctuated every so often by the rat-tat-tat of dozens of automated machines printing hundreds of buy or sell tickets. These orders were almost always from stock index futures *arbitrageurs*—that is, program traders who rely on differences between the prices of stock index futures traded in Chicago and the prices of the component stocks traded in New York.

The noise signaled that the futures market was moving quickly in Chicago and that stock prices would soon change accordingly in New York. It was an eerie warning, something akin to the buzz of locusts in biblical times, portending decimated crops and famine. And famine it might be, for during the 1980s and early 1990s some of the most vicious declines in stock prices have been preceded by computers tapping out orders emanating from the futures markets.

In those days, most of the changes in the overall level of stocks did not originate on Wall Street but on Wacker Drive at the Chicago Mercantile Exchange. *Specialists* on the New York Stock Exchange, those dealers assigned to make and supervise markets in specific stocks, kept their eyes glued on the futures markets to find out where stocks would be heading. These dealers learned from experience not to stand in the way of index futures when they are moving quickly. If they did, they

FIGURE 18–2

When Stock Index Futures Closed Down, April 13, 1992

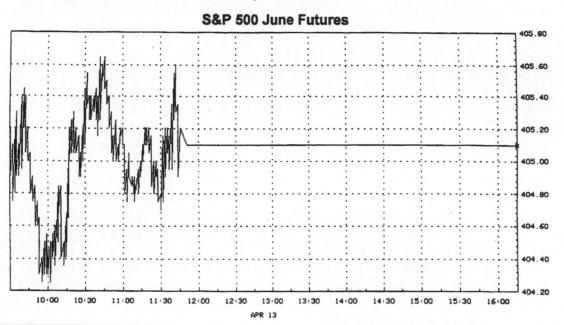

S&P 500 June Futures

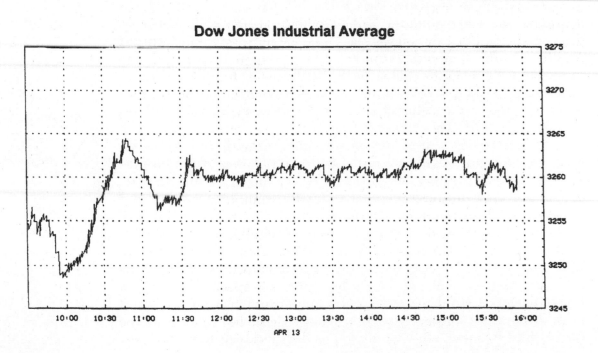

Dow Jones Industrial Average

might get caught in an avalanche of trading such as the one that buried several specialists on October 19, 1987, that fateful day when the Dow crashed nearly 23 percent.

BASICS OF THE FUTURES MARKETS

Most investors regard index futures and exchange-traded funds as esoteric securities that have little to do with the market in which stocks are bought and sold. Many investors do very well trading stocks without any knowledge of these new instruments. But no one can comprehend the short-run market movements without an understanding of stock index futures and ETFs.

Futures trading goes back hundreds of years. The term *futures* was derived from the promise to buy or deliver a commodity at some future date at some specified price. Futures trading first flourished in agricultural crops, where farmers wanted to have a guaranteed price for the crops they would harvest at a later date. Markets developed where buyers and sellers who wanted to avoid uncertainty could come to an agreement on the price for future delivery. The commitments to honor these agreements, called *futures contracts*, were freely transferable, and markets developed where they were actively traded.

Stock index futures were launched in February 1982 by the Kansas City Board of Trade using the Value Line Index of about 1,700 stocks. Two months later, at the Mercantile Exchange in Chicago, the world's most successful stock index future, based on the S&P 500 Index, was introduced. By 1984, the value of the contracts traded on this index future surpassed the dollar volume on the New York Stock Exchange for all stocks. Today, the value of stocks represented by S&P 500 futures trading exceeds $100 billion *per day*.

All stock index futures are constructed similarly. In the case of the seller, the S&P Index future is a promise to deliver a fixed multiple of the value of the S&P 500 Index at some date in the future, called a *settlement date*. In the case of the buyer, the S&P Index future is a promise to receive a fixed multiple of the S&P 500 Index's value. The multiple for the S&P Index future is 250, so if the S&P 500 Index is 1,700, the value of one contract is $425,000. In 1998, a *miniversion* of the contract (called an *e-mini*), with a multiple of 50 times the index, was offered, and it trades on the electronic markets. The dollar volume of these minis now far exceeds that of the larger-sized contracts.

There are four evenly spaced settlement dates each year. They fall on the third Friday of March, June, September, and December. Each settlement date corresponds to a contract. If you buy a futures contract, you are entitled to receive (if *positive*) or obligated to pay (if *negative*) 250 times the difference between the value of the S&P 500 Index on the settlement date and the price at which you purchased the contract.

For example, if you buy one September S&P futures contract at 1,700, and on that third Friday of September the S&P 500 Index is at 1,410, you have made 10 points, which translates into $2,500 profit ($250 times 10 points). Of course, if the index has fallen to 1,690 on the settlement date, you will lose $2,500. For every point the S&P 500 Index goes up or down, you make or lose $250 per contract.

On the other hand, the returns to the seller of an S&P 500 futures contract are the mirror image of the returns to the buyer. The seller makes money when the index falls. In the previous example, the seller of the S&P 500 futures contract at 1,700 will lose $2,500 if the index at settlement date rises to 1,710, while he would make the same amount if the index fell to 1,690.

One source of the popularity of stock index futures is their unique settlement procedure. If you bought a standard futures contract, you would be entitled at settlement to receive, or if you sold it, to deliver, a specified quantity of the good for which you have contracted. Many apocryphal stories abound about how traders, forgetting to close out their contract, find bushels of wheat, corn, or frozen pork bellies dumped on their lawn on settlement day.

If commodity delivery rules applied to the S&P 500 Index futures contracts, delivery would require a specified number of shares for each of the 500 firms in the index. Surely this would be extraordinarily cumbersome and costly. To avoid this problem, the designers of the stock index futures contract specified that settlement be made in cash, computed simply by taking the difference between the contract price at the time of the trade and the value of the index on the settlement date. No delivery of stock takes place. If a trader does not close a contract before settlement, his or her account would just be debited or credited on settlement date.

The creation of cash-settled futures contracts was no easy matter. In most states, particularly Illinois where the large futures exchanges are located, settling a futures contract in cash was considered a wager—and wagering, except in some special circumstances, was illegal. In 1974, however, the Commodity Futures Trading Commission, a federal agency, was established by Congress to regulate all futures trading. Since futures trading was now governed by this new federal agency and since there was no federal prohibition against wagering, the prohibitory state laws were superseded.

INDEX ARBITRAGE

The prices of commodities (or financial assets) in the futures market do not stand apart from the prices of the underlying commodity. If the value of a futures contract rises sufficiently above the price of the commodity that can be purchased for immediate delivery in the open market, often called the *cash* or *spot market*, traders can buy the commodity, store it, and then deliver it at a profit against the higher-priced futures contract on the settlement date. If the price of a futures contract falls too far below its current spot price, owners of the commodity can sell it today, buy the futures contract, and take delivery of the commodity later at a lower price—in essence, earning a return on goods that would be in storage anyway.

Such a process of buying and selling commodities against their futures contracts is one type of arbitrage. Arbitrage involves traders called arbitrageurs who take advantage of temporary discrepancies in the prices of identical or nearly identical goods or assets. Arbitrage is very common in both the stock index futures market and the ETF market. If the price of futures contracts sufficiently exceeds that of the underlying S&P 500 Index, it pays for arbitrageurs to buy the underlying stocks and sell the futures contracts. If the futures price falls sufficiently below that of the index, arbitrageurs will sell the underlying stocks and buy the futures. On the settlement date, the futures price must equal the underlying index by the terms of the contract, so the difference between the futures price and the index—called a *premium* if it is positive and a *discount* if it is negative—is an opportunity for profit.

Arbitrage in the ETF market is similar, except here an arbitrageur must buy or sell all the stocks in the index and simultaneously make an offsetting transaction in the ETF in the open market. An arbitrageur in the ETF makes a profit when the prices of the stocks that she buys to create the ETF are less than the funds that she receives by selling the ETF. Alternatively, if the prices she receives from selling the stocks in the index exceed the cost of buying the ETF, the arbitrageur will buy the ETF, exchange it into its component stocks, and sell them in the open market.

Index arbitrage has become a finely tuned art. The prices of stock index futures and ETFs usually stay within very narrow bands of the index value based on the price of the underlying shares. When the buying or selling of stock index futures or ETFs drives the price outside this band, arbitrageurs step in, and a flood of orders to buy or sell are immediately transmitted to the exchanges that trade the underlying stocks in the index. These simultaneously placed orders are called *programmed trading*, and they consist of either *buy programs* or *sell programs*. When market commentators talk about "sell programs hitting the market," they mean that index arbitrageurs are selling stock and buying futures or ETFs that have fallen to a discount.

PREDICTING THE NEW YORK OPEN WITH GLOBEX TRADING

Although trading in index futures closes at 4:15 p.m. eastern time, 15 minutes after the close of the New York stock exchanges, trading reopens in index futures at 4:30 p.m. in an electronic market called *Globex*. Globex has no centralized floor, and traders post their bids and offers on computer screens where all interested parties have instant access. Trading in Globex proceeds all night until 9:15 the next morning, 15 minutes before the start of stock trading in New York.

Index futures trading can be active just after the close of regular trading on the NYSE and Nasdaq. Trading is especially popular in the weeks following the end of a quarter, when many firms release their earnings reports and give guidance about future earnings and revenues. Unless there is breaking news, trading is usually slow during the night hours, although activity can pick up if there is dramatic movement on the Tokyo or European stock exchanges. Trading again becomes very active around 8:30 a.m., when many of the government economic data, such as the employment report and the consumer price index, are announced.

Market watchers can use the Globex futures in the S&P, the Nasdaq, and the Dow to predict how the market will open in New York. The *fair market value* of these index futures is calculated based on the arbitrage conditions between the future and current prices of stocks.

The fair market value for the futures contract is determined on the basis of the current index value when markets are open and on the previous closing level when markets are closed. Because of the continuous stream of news, the futures price overnight will usually be either above or below the fair market value computed at the close. If, for instance, China reports better-than-expected data or the European markets are up, then the U.S. stock futures prices will often trade above fair market value computed on the basis of previous closing prices. The amount by which the futures contracts trade above or below their fair market value will be the best estimate of where stocks will trade when the exchanges open in New York. Many financial news channels post the overnight prices of the S&P 500, Dow, and Nasdaq futures to inform viewers of the likely opening of the market.

The formula to calculate the fair market value of the futures contracts depends on two variables: the dividend yield on stocks and the interest rate. If an investor puts a sum of money today in risk-free bonds, that sum will earn interest at the ongoing interest rate. If instead the investor buys a portfolio of stocks and simultaneously sells a one-year futures contract that guarantees the price of those stocks one year from now, the investor will earn the dividend yield on stocks and be guaranteed a return on his stocks that is the difference between the futures price and the current price.

Since both these investments deliver a guaranteed, riskless sum, they must earn the same rate of return. Whether the futures price trades above or below the current (or spot) value of the index depends on the difference between the short-term interest rate and the dividend yield. Before the financial crisis, when interest rates almost always exceeded the dividend yield, the future price of stocks was above the spot price. Since the financial crisis, as short-term rates have hovered near zero, the futures price of stock indexes is below the spot price.

DOUBLE AND TRIPLE WITCHING

Index futures play some strange games with stock prices on the days when futures contracts expire. Recall that index arbitrage works through the simultaneous buying or selling of stocks against futures contracts. On the day that contracts expire, arbitrageurs unwind their stock positions at precisely the same time that the futures contracts expire.

As noted earlier, index futures contracts expire on the third Friday of the last month of each quarter: in March, June, September, and December. Index options and options on individual stocks, which are described later in the chapter, settle on the third Friday of every month. Hence four times a year, all three types of contracts expire at once. This expiration has, in the past, often produced violent price movements in the market, and it has consequently been termed a *triple witching hour*. The third Friday of a month when there are no futures contract settlements is called a *double witching*, and it displays less volatility than triple witching.

There is no mystery why the market is volatile during double or triple witching dates. On these days, the specialists on the New York Stock Exchange and the market makers on the Nasdaq are instructed to buy or sell large blocks of stock on the close, whatever the price, because institutional investors are closing out their arbitrage positions. If there is a huge imbalance of buy orders, prices will soar; if sell orders predominate, prices will plunge. These swings, however, do not matter to arbitrageurs, since the profit on the future position will offset losses on the stock position and vice versa.

In 1988, the New York Stock Exchange persuaded the Chicago Mercantile Exchange to change its procedures and stop futures trading at the close of Thursday's trading and settle the contracts at Friday opening prices rather than at Friday closing prices. This change gave specialists more time to seek out balancing bids and offers, and it has greatly moderated the movements in stock prices on triple witching dates.

MARGIN AND LEVERAGE

One of the reasons for the popularity of futures contracts is that the cash needed to enter into the trade is a very small part of the value of the contract. Unlike stocks, there is no money that transfers between the buyer and seller when a futures contract is bought or sold. A small amount of good-faith collateral, or *margin*, is required by the broker from both the buyer and seller to ensure that both parties will honor the contract at settlement. For the S&P 500 Index, the current initial margin is about 5 percent of the value of the contract. This margin can be kept in Treasury bills with interest accruing to the investor, so trading a futures contract involves neither a transfer of cash nor a loss of interest income.

The *leverage*, or the amount of stock that you control relative to the amount of margin you have to put down with a futures contract, is enormous. For every dollar of cash (or Treasury bills) that you put in margin against an S&P futures contract, you command about $20 of stock value. And for *day trading*, when you close your positions by the end of the day, the margin requirements are significantly less. These low margins contrast with the 50 percent margin requirement for the purchase of individual stocks or ETFs that has prevailed since 1974.

This ability to control $20 or more of stock with $1 of cash is reminiscent of the rampant speculation that existed in the 1920s before the establishment of minimum stock margin requirements. In the 1920s, individual stocks were frequently purchased with a 10 percent margin. It was popular to speculate with such borrowed money, because as long as the market was rising, few investors lost money. But if the market dropped precipitously, margin buyers often found that not only did they lose their equity, but they were also indebted to the brokerage firm. Buying futures contracts with low margins can result in similar repercussions today. The tendency of low margins to fuel market volatility is discussed in the next chapter.

TAX ADVANTAGES OF ETFS AND FUTURES

The use of ETFs or index futures greatly increases an investor's flexibility to manage portfolios. Suppose an investor has built up gains in individual stocks but is now getting nervous about the market. Selling one's individual stocks may trigger a large tax liability.

But by using ETFs (or futures), a good solution is available. The investor sells enough ETFs to cover the value of the portfolio that he seeks to hedge and continues to hold his individual stocks. If the market declines, the investor profits on his ETF position, offsetting the losses of the stock portfolio. If the market instead goes up, contrary to expectation, the loss on ETFs will be offset by the gains on the individual stock holdings. This is called *hedging stock market risk*. Since the investor never sells his individual stocks, he triggers no tax liability from these positions.

Another advantage of ETFs is that they can yield a profit from a decline in the market even if one does not own any stock. Selling ETFs substitutes for *shorting stock*, or selling stock you do not own in anticipation that the price will fall and you can buy it back at a lower price. Using ETFs to bet on a falling market is much more convenient than shorting a portfolio of stocks since regulations prohibit individual stocks from being shorted if their price has declined by more than 10 percent.[6]

WHERE TO PUT YOUR INDEXED INVESTMENTS: ETFS, FUTURES, OR INDEX MUTUAL FUNDS?

With the development of index futures and ETFs, investors have three major choices to match the performance of one of many stock indexes: exchange-traded funds, index futures, and index mutual funds, which are described in detail in Chapter 23. The important characteristics of each type of investment are given in Table 18-1.

As far as trading flexibility, ETFs and index futures far outshine mutual funds. ETFs and index futures can be bought or sold any time during the trading day and after hours on the Globex and other exchanges. In contrast, mutual funds can be bought or sold only at the market close, and the investor's order must often be in several hours earlier. ETFs and index futures can also be shorted to hedge one's portfolio or speculate on a market decline, which mutual funds cannot. And ETFs can be margined like any stock (with current Fed regulations at 50 percent), while index futures possess the highest degree of leverage, as investors can control stocks worth 20 or more times the margin deposit.

TABLE 18–1

Comparison of Indexed Investments

	ETFs	Index Futures	Indexed Mutual Funds
Continuous trading	Yes	Yes	No
Can be sold short	Yes	Yes	No
Leverage	Can borrow 50%	Can borrow over 90%	None
Expense ratio	Extremely low	None	Very low
Trading costs	Stock	Futures commission	None
Dividend reinvestment	No	No	Yes
Tax efficiency	Extremely good	Poor	Very good

The trading flexibility of ETFs or futures can be either a bane or a boon to investors. It is easy to overreact to the continuous stream of optimistic and pessimistic news, causing an investor to sell near the low or buy near the high. Furthermore, the ability to short stocks (except for hedging) or to leverage might tempt investors to play their short-term hunches on the market. This is a very dangerous game. For most investors, restricting the frequency of trades and reducing leverage will be beneficial to their total returns.

On the cost side, all these vehicles are very efficient. Index mutual funds are available at an annual cost of 15 basis points or less a year, and most ETFs are even cheaper. But both ETFs and futures must be bought through a brokerage account, and this involves paying both a commission and a bid-asked spread, although these are quite low for actively traded ETFs. On the other hand, most index funds are *no-load funds*, meaning there is no commission when the fund is bought or sold. Furthermore, although index futures involve no annual costs, these contracts must be rolled over into new contracts at least once a year, entailing additional commissions.

It is on the tax side that ETFs really shine. Because of the structure of ETFs, these funds generate very few if any capital gains. Index mutual funds are also very tax efficient, but they do throw off capital gains. This means funds must sell individual shares from their portfolio if investors redeem their shares or if stocks are removed from the index. Although capital gains have been small for most index funds, they are larger than ETFs.[7] Futures are not tax efficient since any gains or losses must be realized at the end of the year whether the contracts are sold or not.

Of course, these tax differences between ETFs and index mutual funds do not matter if an investor holds these funds in a tax-sheltered account, such as an individual retirement account (IRA) or a Keogh plan (futures are not allowed in these accounts). However, if these funds are held in taxable accounts, the after-tax return on ETFs is apt to be higher than it would be for even the most efficient index fund.

The bottom line is that unless you like to speculate and leverage your cash, you will want to avoid index futures. However, if you want to speculate on the direction of the market, I recommend *index options*, which are described below and which limit an investor's loss.

Whether to hold ETFs or low-cost index mutual funds is a very close decision. If you like to trade in and out of the market frequently, ETFs are for you. If you like to invest in the market on a monthly basis or automatically reinvest your dividends, then no-load index funds may be the better instrument. However, automatic reinvestment of dividends is now widespread for stocks and ETFs if you request that option to your brokerage firm. This development further tips the scale in favor of ETFs over index mutual funds.

INDEX OPTIONS

Although ETFs and index futures are very important to investment professionals and institutions, the options market has caught the fancy of many investors. And this is not surprising. The beauty of an option is embedded in its very name: you have the option, but not the obligation, to buy or sell stocks or indexes at a given price by a given time. For the option buyer, this option, in contrast to the futures, automatically limits your maximum liability to the amount you invested.

There are two major types of options: puts and calls. *Calls* give you the right to buy a stock (or stocks) at a fixed price within a given period of time. *Puts* give you the right to sell a stock. Puts and calls have existed on individual stocks for decades, but they were not bought and sold through an organized trading system until the establishment of the Chicago Board Options Exchange (CBOE) in 1974.

What attracts investors to puts and calls is that liability is strictly limited. If the market moves against options buyers, they can forfeit the purchase price, forgoing the option to buy or sell. This contrasts sharply with futures contracts, with which, if the market goes against buyers, losses can mount quickly. In a volatile market, futures can be extremely risky, and it could be impossible for investors to exit a contract without substantial losses.

In 1978, the CBOE began trading options on the popular stock indexes, such as the S&P 500 Index.[8] The CBOE options trade in multiples of $100 per point of index value—cheaper than the $250-per-point multiple on the popular S&P 500 Index futures.

An index allows investors to buy the stock index at a set price within a given period of time. Assume that the S&P 500 Index is now selling for 1,700, but you believe that the market is going to rise. Let us assume you can purchase a call option at 1,750 for three months for 30 points, or $3,000. The purchase price of the option is called the *premium*, and the price at which the option has value when it expires—in this case 1,750—is called the *strike price*. At any time within the next three months you can, if you choose, exercise your option and receive $100 for every point that the S&P 500 Index is above 1,750.

You need not exercise your option to make a profit. There is an extremely active market for options, and you can always sell them before expiration to other investors. In this example, the S&P 500 Index will have to rise above 1,780 for you to show a profit if you hold until the expiration, since you paid $3,000 for the option. But the beauty of options is that, if you guessed wrong and the market falls, the most you can lose is the $3,000 premium you paid.

An index put works exactly the same way as a call, but in this case the buyer makes money if the market goes down. Assume you buy a put on the S&P 500 Index at 1,650, paying a $3,000 premium. Every point the S&P 500 Index is below 1,650 at expiration will recoup $100 of your initial premium. If the index falls to 1,620 by expiration, you have broken even. Every point below 1,620 gives you a profit on your option.

The price that you pay for an index option is determined by the market and depends on many factors, including interest rates and dividend yields. But the most important factor is the expected volatility of the market itself. Clearly, the more volatile the market, the more expensive it is to buy either puts or calls. In a dull market, it is unlikely that the market will move sufficiently high (in the case of a call) or low (in the case of a put) to give options buyers a profit. If this low volatility is expected to continue, the prices of options will be low. In contrast, in volatile markets, the premiums on puts and calls are bid up as traders consider it more likely that the options will have value by the time of their expiration.[9]

The price of options depends on the judgments of traders about the likelihood that the market will move sufficiently to make the rights to buy or sell stock at a fixed price valuable. But the theory of options pricing was given a big boost in the 1970s when two academic economists, Fischer Black and Myron Scholes, developed the first mathematical formula to price options. The *Black-Scholes formula* was an instant success. It gave traders a benchmark for valuation where previously they used only their intuition. The formula was programmed on traders' handheld calculators and PCs around the world. Although there are conditions when the formula must be modified, empirical research has shown that the Black-Scholes formula closely approximates the price of traded options. Myron Scholes won the Nobel Prize in Economics in 1997 for his discovery.[10]

Buying Index Options

Options are actually more basic instruments than futures or ETFs. You can replicate any future or ETF with options, but the reverse is not true. Options offer the investor far more strategies than futures. Such strategies can range from the very speculative to the extremely conservative.

Suppose you want to be protected against a decline in the market. You can buy an index put, which increases in value as the market declines. Of course, you have to pay a premium for this option, very much like an insurance premium. If the market does not decline, you have forfeited your premium. But if it does decline, the increase in the value of your put has cushioned, if not completely offset, the decline in your stock portfolio.

Another advantage of puts is that you can buy just the amount of protection that you like. If you want to protect yourself against only a total collapse in the market, you can buy a put that is way *out-of-the-money*, in other words, a put whose strike price is far below that of the current level of the index. This option pays off only if the market declines precipitously. In addition, you can also buy puts with a strike price above the current market, so the option retains some value even if the market does not decline. Of course, these *in-the-money* puts are far more expensive.

There are many recorded examples of fantastic gains in puts and calls. But for every option that gains so spectacularly in value, there are thousands of options that expire worthless. Some market professionals estimate that 85 percent of individual investors who play the options market lose money. Not only do options buyers have to be right about the direction of the market, but also their timing must be nearly perfect, and their selection of the strike price must be appropriate.

Selling Index Options

Of course, for anyone who buys an option, someone must sell—or write—an options contract. The sellers, or writers, of call options believe that the market will not rise sufficiently to make a profit for options buyers. Sellers of call options usually make money when they sell options since the vast majority of options expire worthless. But should the market move sharply against the options sellers, their losses could be enormous.

For that reason, most sellers of call options are investors who already own stock. This strategy, called *buy and write*, is popular with many investors since it is seen as a win-win proposition. If stocks go down, they collect a premium from buyers of the call, and so the investors are better off than if they had not written the option. If stocks do nothing, they also collect the premium on the call, and they are still better off. If stocks go up, call writers still gain more on the stocks they own than they lose on the call they wrote, so they are still ahead. Of course, if stocks go up strongly, they miss some of the rally since they have promised to deliver stock at a fixed price. In that case, call writers certainly would have been better off if they had not sold the call. But they still make more money than if they had not owned the stocks at all.

The buyers of put options are insuring their stock against price declines. But who are the sellers of these options? They are primarily those who are willing to buy the stock, but only if the price declines. A seller of a put collects a premium, but she receives the stock only if it falls sufficiently to go below the strike price. Since put sellers are not as common as call sellers, premiums on puts that are out-of-the-money are frequently quite high.

THE IMPORTANCE OF INDEXED PRODUCTS

The development of stock index futures and options in the 1980s was a major development for investors and money managers. Heavily capitalized firms, such as those represented in the Dow Jones Industrial Average, have always attracted money because of their outstanding liquidity. But with stock index futures, investors were able to buy the whole market, as represented by the popular indexes.

Ten years later, exchange-traded funds gave investors still another way to diversify across all markets at low cost. These ETFs had the familiarity of stocks but, like index futures, much higher liquidity and superior tax efficiency. Today when investors want to take a position in the market, it is most easily done with stock index futures or exchange-traded funds. Index options give investors the ability to insure the value of their portfolio at the lowest possible price and save on transaction costs and taxes.

Despite the opposition of such notable investors as Warren Buffett and Peter Lynch, there is no hard evidence that these index products have increased volatility or harmed investors. In fact, it is my belief that these index products have increased the liquidity of the world's stock markets, enabled better diversification, and led to higher stock prices than would have prevailed without them.

Market Volatility

The word crisis *in Chinese is composed of two characters: the first, the symbol of danger, . . . the second, of opportunity.*

Does the past portend the future? The Dow Jones Industrial Average from 1922 through 1932 and from 1980 through 1990 is shown in Figure 19-1A and B. There is an uncanny similarity between these two bull markets. In October 1987, the editors of the *Wall Street Journal*, looking at the stock chart up to that time, felt the similarity was so portentous that they printed a similar graph in their paper that hit the streets on Monday morning, October 19, 1987. Little did they know that that day would witness the greatest one-day drop in U.S. stock market history, far exceeding the great crash of October 29, 1929. Ominously, the market continued to trade very much like 1929 for the remainder of the year. Many forecasters, citing the similarities between the two periods, were certain that disaster loomed and advised their clients to sell.

But the similarity between the 1929 and the 1987 episodes stopped at year's end. The stock market recovered from its October 1987 crash, and by August 1989, it hit new high ground. In contrast, two years after the October 1929 crash, the Dow, in the throes of the greatest bear market in U.S. history, had lost more than two-thirds of its value and was about to lose two-thirds more.

What was different? Why did the eerie similarities between these two events diverge so dramatically? The simple answer is that in 1987 the central bank had the power to control the ultimate source of liquidity in the economy—the supply of money. And in contrast to 1929, it did

F I G U R E   19–1

1929 and 1987 Stock Crashes

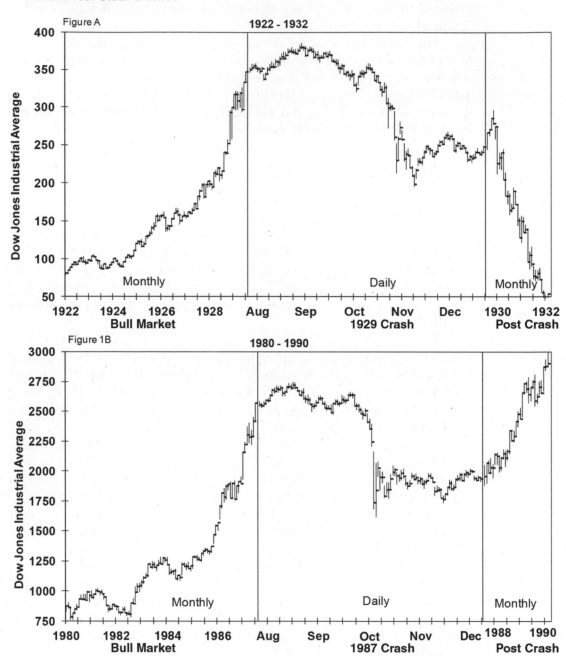

not hesitate to use it. Heeding the painful lessons of its mistakes in the early 1930s, the Fed temporarily flooded the economy with money and pledged to stand by all bank deposits to ensure that all aspects of the financial system would function properly.

The public was assured. There were no runs on banks, no contraction of the money supply, and no deflation in commodity and asset values. Indeed, the economy itself expanded despite the market collapse. The October 1987 stock market crash taught investors an important lesson—the world was indeed different from 1929, and a sharp sell-off can be an opportunity for profit, not a time to panic

THE STOCK MARKET CRASH OF OCTOBER 1987

The stock crash of Monday, October 19, 1987, was one of the most dramatic financial events of the postwar era. The 508-point, or 22.6 percent, decline in the Dow Jones Industrials from 2,247 to 1,739 was by far the largest point drop up to that time and the largest one-day percentage drop in all history. Volume on the New York Stock Exchange soared to a record, exceeding 600 million shares on both Monday and Tuesday, and for that fateful week the number of shares traded exceeded the volume for all of 1966.

The crash on Wall Street reverberated around the world. Tokyo, which two years later was going to enter its own massive bear market, fell the least, but it still experienced a record one-day drop of 15.6 percent. Stocks in New Zealand fell nearly 40 percent, and the Hong Kong market closed because collapsing prices brought massive defaults in the stock index futures market. In the United States alone, stock values on that infamous day dropped about $500 billion, and the total worldwide decline in stock values exceeded $1 trillion. A similar percentage decline in today's market would wipe out $10 trillion worldwide, a sum greater than the gross domestic product of every country but the United States.[1]

The stock market decline began in earnest the week prior to "Black Monday," as October 19 came to be called. At 8:30 a.m. on the preceding Wednesday, the Department of Commerce reported that the United States suffered a $15.7 billion merchandise trade deficit, which at that time was one of the largest in U.S. history and far in excess of market expectations. The reaction in the financial markets was immediate. Yields on long government bonds rose to over 10 percent for the first time since November 1985, and the dollar declined sharply. The Dow Industrials fell 95 points, or 4 percent, on Wednesday, a record point drop at that time.

The situation continued to worsen on Thursday and Friday as the Dow fell 166 points, or 7 percent, to 2,246. Late Friday afternoon, about 15 minutes prior to close, heavy selling hit the stock index futures markets in Chicago. The indexes had fallen below crucial support levels, which led to the barrage of selling in Chicago by those wanting to get out of stocks at almost any price.

The December S&P 500 futures contract fell to an unprecedented 3 percent below the spot index. The development of such a wide discount meant that money managers were willing to sell large orders at a significant concession in order to sell fast, rather than risk that their sell orders for individual stocks might sit in New York, unexecuted. At the close of trading on Friday, the stock market had experienced its worst week in nearly five decades.

Before New York opened the following Monday, there were ominous portents from the world markets. Overnight in Tokyo, the Nikkei average fell 2½ percent, and there were sharp declines in Sydney and Hong Kong. In London, prices had fallen by 10 percent as many money managers were trying to sell U.S. stocks trading there before the anticipated decline hit New York.

Trading on the New York Stock Exchange on Black Monday was chaotic. No Dow Jones Industrial stock traded near the 9:30 opening bell, and only 7 Dow stocks traded before 9:45. By 10:30 that morning, 11 Dow stocks still had not opened. "Portfolio insurers," described later in this chapter, heavily sold stock index futures, trying to insulate their clients' exposure to the plunging market. By late afternoon, the S&P 500 Index futures were selling at a 25-point, or 12 percent, discount to the spot market, a spread that was previously considered inconceivable. By the late afternoon, huge sell orders transmitted by program sellers cascaded onto the New York Exchange through the computerized system. The Dow Industrials collapsed almost 300 points in the final hour of trading, bringing the toll for the day to a record 508 points, or 22.6 percent.

Although October 19 is remembered in history as the day of the great stock crash, it was actually the next day—"Terrible Tuesday," as it has become known—that the market almost failed. After opening up over 10 percent from Monday's low, the market began to plunge by midmorning, and shortly after noon it fell below its Monday close. The S&P 500 Index futures market collapsed to 181—an incredible 40 points, or 22 percent, under the reported index value. If index arbitrage had been possible, the futures prices would have dictated a Dow at 1,450. Stock prices in the world's largest market, on this calculation, were off nearly 50 percent from their high of 2,722 set just seven weeks earlier.

It was at this time that near meltdown hit the market. The NYSE did not close, but trading was halted in almost 200 stocks. For the first time, trading was also halted in the S&P 500 Index futures in Chicago.

The only futures market of any size that remained open was the Major Market Index that traded on the Chicago Board of Trade and represented blue chip stocks similar to the Dow Industrials. These blue chips were selling at such deep discounts to the prices in New York that values proved irresistible to some investors. And since it was the only market that remained open, these brave buyers stepped in, and futures shot up an equivalent of 120 Dow points, or almost 10 percent, in a matter of minutes. When traders and the exchange specialists saw the buying come back into the blue chips, prices rallied in New York, and the worst of the market panic passed. A subsequent investigative report by the *Wall Street Journal* indicated that this futures market was a key to reversing the catastrophic market collapse.[2]

THE CAUSES OF THE OCTOBER 1987 CRASH

There was no single precipitating event—such as a declaration of war, a terrorist act, an assassination, or a bankruptcy—that caused Black Monday. However, worrying trends had threatened the rising stock market for some time: sharply higher long-term rates caused by a falling dollar and the rapid development of a new strategy, called *portfolio insurance*, that was designed to insulate portfolios from a decline in the overall market. The latter was born from the explosive growth of stock index futures markets detailed in the previous chapter, markets that did not even exist six years earlier.

Exchange Rate Policies

The roots of the surge in interest rates that preceded the October 1987 stock market crash are found in the futile attempts by the United States and other G7 countries (Japan, the United Kingdom, Germany, France, Italy, and Canada) to prevent the dollar from falling in the international exchange markets.

The dollar had bounded to unprecedented levels in the middle of the 1980s on the heels of huge Japanese and European purchases of dollar securities and a strong U.S. economy. Foreign investors were attracted to high dollar interest rates, in part driven by record U.S. budget deficits but also by a strengthening of the U.S. economy and the capital-friendly presidency of Ronald Reagan. By February 1985, the dollar became massively overvalued, and U.S. exports became very uncompetitive, severely worsening the U.S. trade deficit. The dollar then reversed course and began a steep decline.

Central bankers initially cheered the fall of the overpriced dollar, but they grew concerned when the dollar continued to decline and the U.S. trade deficit, instead of improving, worsened. Finance ministers met in February 1987 in Paris with the goal of supporting the dollar. They worried that if the dollar became too cheap, their own exports to the United States, which had grown substantially when the dollar was high, would suffer.

The Federal Reserve reluctantly participated in the dollar stabilization program, whose success depended on either an improvement in the U.S. trade position or, absent that, a commitment by the Federal Reserve to raise interest rates to support the dollar.

But the trade deficit did not improve; in fact, it worsened after the initiation of the exchange stabilization policies. Traders, nervous about the deteriorating U.S. trade balance, demanded ever higher interest rates to hold U.S. assets. Leo Melamed, chairman of the Chicago Mercantile Exchange, was blunt when asked about the origins of Black Monday: "What caused the crash was all that f— around with the currencies of the world."[3]

The stock market initially ignored rising interest rates. The U.S. market, like most equity markets around the world, was booming. The Dow Jones Industrials, which started 1987 at 1,933, reached an all-time high of 2,725 on August 22—250 percent above the August 1982 low reached five years earlier. All world markets participated. Over the same five-year period, the British stock market was up 164 percent; the Swiss, 209 percent; German, 217 percent; Japanese, 288 percent; and Italian, 421 percent.

But rising bond rates, coupled with higher stock prices, spelled trouble for the equity markets. The long-term government bond rate, which began the year at 7 percent, topped 9 percent in September and continued to rise. As stocks rose, the dividend and earnings yield fell, and the gap between the real yield on bonds and the earnings and dividend yields on stocks reached a postwar high. By the morning of October 19, the long-term bond yield had reached 10.47 percent despite the fact that inflation was well under control. The record gap between the yields on stocks and the real yields on bonds set the stage for the stock market crash.

The Futures Market

The S&P 500 futures market also clearly contributed to the market crash. Since the introduction of the stock index futures market, a new trading technique, called portfolio insurance, had been introduced into portfolio management.

Portfolio insurance was, in concept, not much different from an oft-used technique called a *stop-loss order*. If an investor buys a stock and wants to protect herself from a loss (or if it has gone up, protect her profit), it is possible to place a sell order below the current price that will be triggered when and if the price falls to or below this specified level.

But stop-loss orders are not guarantees that you can get out of the market. If the stock falls below your specified price, your stop-loss order becomes a *market order* to be executed at the *next best* price. If the stock *gaps*, or declines dramatically, your order could be executed far below your hoped-for price. This means a panic might develop if many investors place stop-loss orders around the same price. A price decline could trigger a flood of sell orders, overwhelming the market.

Portfolio insurers, who sold the stock index futures against large portfolios to protect them against market decline, felt they were immune to such problems. It seemed extremely unlikely that the S&P 500 Index futures would ever decline dramatically in price and that the whole U.S. capital market, the world's largest, could fail to find buyers. This is one reason why the stock market continued to rise in the face of sharply higher long-term rates.

But the entire market did gap on October 19, 1987. During the week of October 12, the market declined by 10 percent, and a large number of sell orders flooded the markets. So many traders and money managers using portfolio insurance strategies tried to sell index futures to protect their clients' profits that the futures market collapsed. There were absolutely no buyers, and liquidity vanished.

What the overwhelming majority of stock traders once thought inconceivable became a reality. Since the prices of index futures were so far below the prices of the stocks selling in New York, investors halted their buying of shares in New York altogether. The world's largest market failed to attract any buyers.

Portfolio insurance withered rapidly after the crash. It was not an insurance scheme at all, because the continuity and liquidity of the market could not be assured. There was, however, an alternative form of portfolio protection: index options. With the introduction of these options markets in the 1980s, investors could explicitly purchase insurance against market declines by buying puts on a market index. Options buyers never needed to worry about suffering price gaps or being able to get out of their position since the price of the insurance was specified at the time of purchase.

Certainly there were factors other than portfolio insurance contributing to Black Monday. But portfolio insurance and its ancestor, the stop-loss order, abetted the fall. All these schemes are rooted in the basic trading philosophy of letting profits ride and cutting losses short. Whether implemented with stop-loss orders, index futures, or just a mental note to get out of a stock once it declines by a certain amount, this philosophy can set the stage for dramatic market moves.

CIRCUIT BREAKERS

As a result of the crash, the Chicago Mercantile Exchange, where the S&P 500 Index futures traded, and the New York Stock Exchange implemented rules that restricted or halted trading when certain price limits were triggered. To prevent destabilizing speculation when the Dow Jones Industrial Average changes by at least 2 percent, the New York Stock Exchange's Rule 80a placed "trading curbs" on index arbitrage between the futures market and the New York Stock Exchange.[4]

But of greater importance were measures that sharply restricted or stopped trading on both the futures market and the New York Stock Exchange when market moves are very large. From 1988 through early 2013, new rules dictated that trading must be halted 1 hour, 2 hours, and the rest of the trading day if the Dow Industrials fell by 10 percent, 20 percent, and 30 percent, respectively. In April 2013 the SEC altered the circuit breaker rules to provide for a 15-minute break when the S&P 500 fell by 7 percent and another when the market fell 13 percent. Trading would be halted for the entire day if the market fell by 20 percent. Futures trading must stop when the New York Stock Exchange is closed.[5]

The rationale behind these circuit breakers is that halting trading gives investors time to reassess the situation and formulate their strategy based on rapidly changing prices. This time-out could bring buyers into the market and help market makers maintain liquidity.

The argument against halts is that they increase volatility by discouraging short-term traders from buying when prices fall sharply since they might be prevented from unwinding their position if trading is subsequently halted. This could lead to an acceleration of price declines toward the price limits, thereby increasing short-term volatility, as occurred when prices fell to these limits on October 27, 1997.[6]

FLASH CRASH—MAY 6, 2010

Monday October 19, 1987, and the following Tuesday stand as the most volatile days in U.S. stock market history. But investors were equally unnerved by the market collapse on May 6, 2010, an event that became known as the "flash crash." Just after 2:30 p.m. eastern time, the Dow Industrials collapsed by more than 600 points or about 6 percent in a matter of minutes and recovered just as quickly. There was no economic or financial news that could account for the decline. Furthermore, thousands of individual stocks traded at prices that were more than 60 percent below (and a few far above) the prices they sold at just a few minutes earlier; some shares in well-known stocks traded as low as a penny a share.

Stock prices had been under pressure all day because of the European debt crisis. At 2:42 p.m., with no significant news forthcoming and the Dow Industrials down by more than 300 points, stocks hit an "air pocket." The benchmark index fell more than 600 points in just 5 minutes, hitting a low at 2:47 p.m., 999 points, or nearly 10 percent, below the previous day's close. In 5 minutes, over \$800 billion was erased from U.S. equity values. In the next 30 minutes the market rallied by 700 points before closing the day at 10,520, down 348 points. Figure 19-2 traces the market minute by minute through the day, a pattern of price volatility that eerily resembles the October 1987 stock market crash depicted in Figure 19-1A but taking place over a much shorter period of time.

After almost 5 months of investigations, the U.S. Securities and Exchange Commission and Commodity Futures Trading Commission issued a joint report[7] blaming an unusually large, \$4 billion sale of S&P 500 futures by a large mutual fund that began at 2:41 p.m. and lasted 3 minutes, sending the market down quickly by another 3 percent.[8] Many of these sales were initially absorbed by *high-frequency traders* (HFTs), who are directed by computer programs to buy and sell securities rapidly to gauge market depth and predict future prices. But as the market continued to fall, many HFTs began to sell into a very thin and unstable market, precipitating further price declines.[9] At 2:45:28 p.m., trading on the e-mini was halted for five seconds when the Chicago Mercantile Exchange circuit breaker was triggered, and during that short pause buyers appeared and prices recovered quickly.

The fall in the broad-based market averages was unnerving enough, but what caught the eye of many traders were the extraordinary low prices that some blue chips fell to just after the S&P futures contracts hit their low. Procter & Gamble recorded a trade of \$39.37, more than 50 percent below its opening price of \$86, and the consulting firm Accenture,

F I G U R E   19–2

"Flash Crash," May 6, 2010

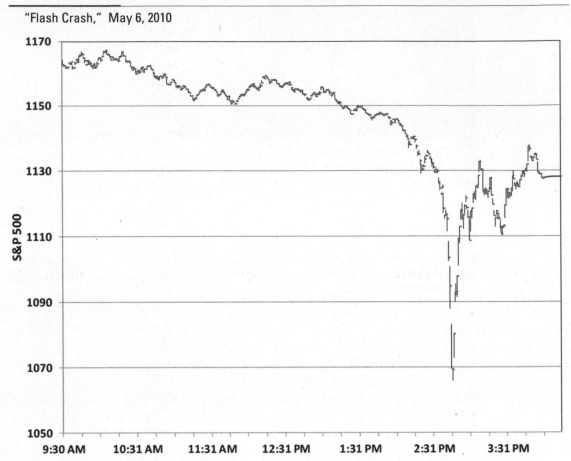

also a member of the S&P 500, which had traded at $38 at 2:47, fell to *one penny* a share just two minutes later! Accenture was not alone. There were eight other stocks in the broad-based S&P 1500 Index that traded at one cent per share.[10] All told, there were 20,000 trades in 300 securities that were 60 percent or more away from the price they traded at just minutes earlier. After the close, the NYSE, in consultation with the Financial Industry Regulatory Authority (FINRA), "broke," or canceled, all trades that were 60 percent or more above or below their previous price.

It is very likely that these extreme prices would not have been realized if specialists, those exchange representatives who maintained markets in assigned stocks before the advent of computerized trading, still controlled the flow of buy and sell orders. These specialists would have stepped in to buy these stocks at prices well above the absurdly low price they traded at. But most modern computerized trading systems were programmed to react very differently than the specialists would have. When prices begin to fall steeply, the programs are instructed to withdraw from the market. This is because large moves in individual stocks are almost always associated with company-specific news that computerized traders do not have access to. These computers are programmed to profit from the normal ebb and flow of trading activity that clearly was absent that day.

When stock prices tumbled, a system of trading pauses that had been instituted by the New York Stock Exchange, termed *liquidity replenishment points*, kicked in. But instead of providing liquidity, the pause sent some sell orders to other markets where dealers maintained *stub quotes*. Stub quotes are "placeholders," i.e., quotes far from the market price (usually at a penny bid, $100,000 asked), and are not meant to be traded against. But with no other orders on the books, these stub quotes were executed for many stocks.

In response to the flash crash, the SEC staff worked with the exchanges and FINRA to promptly implement a circuit breaker pilot program for trading in individual securities that would apply across all markets. These new rules pause trading in a security for five minutes if that security has experienced a 10 percent price change over the preceding five minutes. On June 10, 2010, the SEC approved the application of the circuit breakers to stocks included in the S&P 500 Index, and on September 10, the SEC approved an expansion of the program to securities included in the Russell 1000 Index and certain ETFs. In April 2013, the SEC changed the 10 percent price change trigger to a "limit-up and limit-down" rule that was tailored to the volatility of the individual security. For stocks trading over $3 a share (except leveraged ETFs), the limit remains at 10 percent, except for the first and last 15 minutes of trading, when the limit is expanded to 20 percent.[11]

The flash crash, coming just a year after the deepest bear market in 75 years, eroded the public's trust in a fair and orderly market for equities. Many cited the SEC indictment of high-frequency traders as evidence that the market is rigged against the small investor. But high-frequency trading declined after the flash crash, and a number of researchers questioned whether the trading played a significant role in that day's decline. New rules established by the SEC have virtually eliminated the kind of "errant" and extreme trades that took place during the flash crash.

But from a broader perspective, individual investors should not fear short-term market volatility. Should you not want to shop in a store where every so often it announces "10 percent to 20 percent off the price of all items for the next 30 minutes?" Short-run volatility has always been part of the stock market, and the flash crash had no lasting effect on the recovery from the 2007–2009 bear market.

THE NATURE OF MARKET VOLATILITY

Although most investors express a strong distaste for market fluctuations, volatility must be accepted to reap the superior returns offered by stocks. Accepting risk is required for above-average returns: investors cannot make any more than the risk-free rate unless there is some possibility that they can make less.

While the volatility of the stock market deters many investors, it fascinates others. The ability to monitor a position on a minute-by-minute basis fulfills the need of many to quickly validate their judgment. For many the stock market is truly the world's largest casino.

Yet this ability to know exactly how much one is worth at any given moment can also provoke anxiety. Many investors do not like the instantaneous verdict of the financial market. Some retreat into investments such as real estate, for which daily quotations are not available. Others believe that not knowing the current price somehow makes an investment less risky. As Keynes stated 75 years ago about the investing attitudes of the endowment committee at Cambridge University:

> Some Bursars will buy without a tremor unquoted and unmarketable investments in real estate which, if they had a selling quotation for immediate cash available at each audit, would turn their hair grey. The fact that you do not know how much its ready money quotation fluctuates does not, as is commonly supposed, make an investment a safe one.[12]

HISTORICAL TRENDS OF STOCK VOLATILITY

The annual variability of the U.S. stock, measured by the standard deviation of the monthly returns, from 1834 to 2012 is plotted in Figure 19-3. It is striking that there is so little overall trend in the volatility of the market.

The period of greatest volatility was during the Great Depression, and the year of highest volatility was 1932. The annualized volatility of 1932 was 63.7 percent, nearly 20 times higher than 1993, which is the least volatile year on record with a standard deviation of 3.36. The volatility of

FIGURE 19–3

Volatility of Stock Market 1834–2012 Measured as Standard Deviation of Monthly Returns

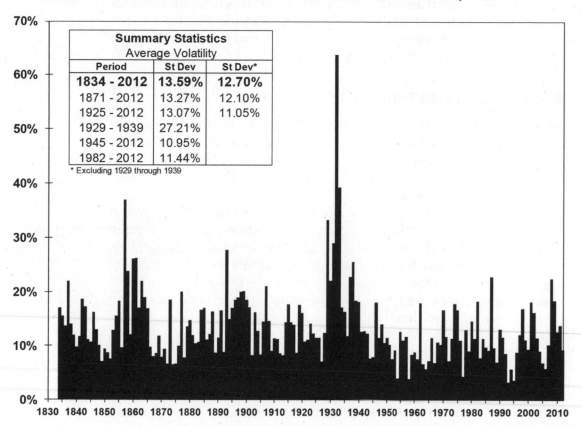

Summary Statistics		
Average Volatility		
Period	St Dev	St Dev*
1834 - 2012	**13.59%**	**12.70%**
1871 - 2012	13.27%	12.10%
1925 - 2012	13.07%	11.05%
1929 - 1939	27.21%	
1945 - 2012	10.95%	
1982 - 2012	11.44%	

* Excluding 1929 through 1939

1987 was the highest since the Great Depression, just edging out 2008, the year of the financial crisis. Excluding the 1929-to-1939 period, volatility has averaged about 12 percent and has remained remarkably stable at between 13 and 14 percent over the past 180 years.

Figure 19-4A displays the average daily percentage change in the Dow Jones Industrial Average for each year from 1896 to the present. The average daily change over the past 117 years is 0.74 percent. Except for the 1930s, there was a downtrend in volatility from 1896 to 1960 and a subsequent uptrend. Some of the uptrend is due to the faster response of markets to economic developments; information that used to take hours if not days to be fully reflected in market averages is now processed in minutes if not seconds. Some of the downward trend in the Dow volatility in the early twentieth century is due to the increase in the

FIGURE 19-4

Daily Volatility of Dow-Jones Industrial Average 1896–2012

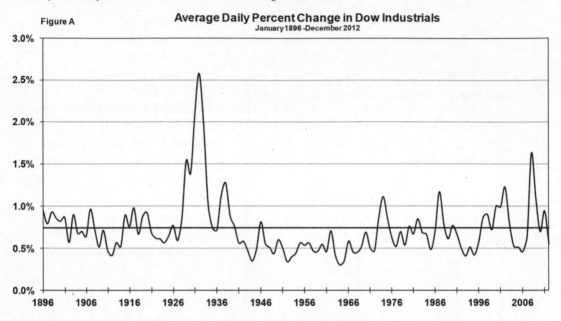

Figure A

Average Daily Percent Change in Dow Industrials
January 1896 -December 2012

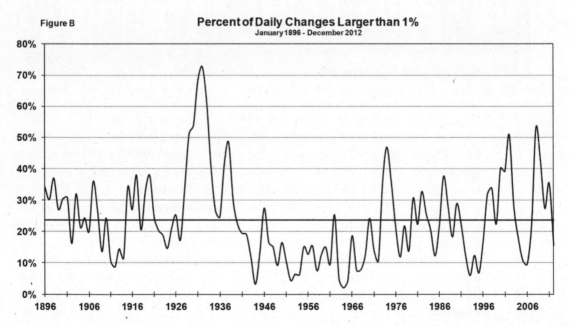

Figure B

Percent of Daily Changes Larger than 1%
January 1896 - December 2012

number of stocks in the Dow Industrials from 12 to 20 and then to 30 in 1928. The daily volatility during the crisis year 2008 at 1.63 percent was the highest since the Great Depression.

The percentage of trading days when the Dow Industrials changed by more than 1 percent is shown in Figure 19-4B. It has averaged 24 percent over the period, or about once per week. But it has ranged from as low as 1.2 percent in 1964 to a high of 67.6 percent in 1932, when the Dow changed by more than 1 percent in more than two out of every three trading days. The financial crisis generated the highest volatility, and the deepest recession, since the Great Depression of the 1930s.

Most of the periods of high volatility occur during bear markets. The standard deviation of daily returns is more than 25 percent higher in recessions than in expansions. There are two reasons why volatility increases in a recession. First, recessions, being the exception rather than the rule, are marked by greater economic uncertainty than expansions. The second is that if earnings fall, then the burden of fixed costs causes greater volatility of profits. This leads to increased volatility in stock prices.

If earnings turn into losses, then the equity value of the firms is like an out-of-the-money call option that pays off only if the firm eventually earns enough profits to cover its costs. Otherwise, it is worthless. It is not a puzzle why stock volatility was the greatest during the Great Depression when, with aggregate profits negative, the equity market was trading like an out-of-the-money call.

THE VOLATILITY INDEX

Measuring *historical* volatility is a simple matter, but it is far more important to measure the volatility that investors *expect* in the market. This is because expected volatility is a signal of the level of anxiety in the market, and periods of high anxiety have often marked turning points for stocks.

By examining the prices of put and call options on the major stock market indexes, one can determine the volatility that is built into the market, which is called the *implied volatility*.[13] In 1993, the Chicago Board Options Exchange introduced the *CBOE Volatility Index*, also called the *VIX Index* or the *VIX* (first mentioned in Chapter 3), based on actual index options prices on the S&P 500 Index, and it calculated this index back to the mid-1980s.[14] A weekly plot of the VIX from 1986 appears in Figure 19-5.

In the short run, there is a strong negative correlation between the VIX and the *level* of the market. When the market is falling, investors are

FIGURE 19–5

The Volatility Index (VIX) 1986–2012

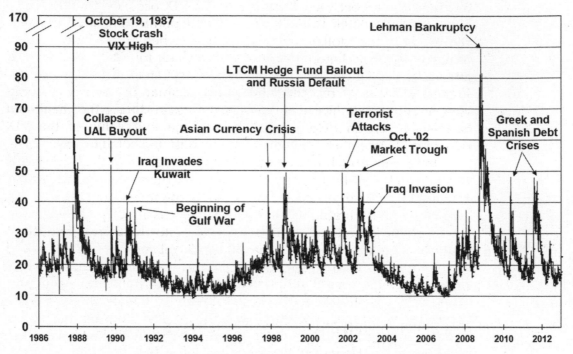

willing to pay more for downside protection, and they purchase puts, causing the VIX to rise. When the market is rising, the VIX typically falls as investors gain confidence and are less anxious to insure their portfolio against a loss.

This correlation may seem puzzling since one might expect investors to seek more protection when the market is high rather than low. One explanation of the behavior of the VIX is that historical volatility is higher in bear markets than bull markets, so falling markets cause the VIX to rise. But a more persuasive argument is that changes in investor confidence change investors' willingness to hedge through buying puts. As put prices are driven up, arbitrageurs who sell will sell stocks to hedge their position, sending stock prices down. The reverse occurs when investors feel more confident of stock returns.

It is easy to see in Figure 19-5 that the peaks in the VIX corresponded to periods of extreme uncertainty and sharply lower stock prices. The VIX peaked at 172 on the Tuesday following the October 19, 1987, stock market crash, far eclipsing any other high.

In the early and mid-1990s, the VIX sank to between 10 and 20. But with the onset of the Asian crises in 1997, the VIX moved up to a 20-to-30 range. Spikes between 40 and 50 in the VIX occurred on three occasions: in October 1987 when the Dow fell 550 points during the attack on the Hong Kong dollar, in August 1998 when Long-Term Capital Management was liquidated, and in the week following the terrorist attacks of September 11, 2001. After the 1987 stock market crash, the highest VIX was 90, reached shortly after Lehman Brothers went bankrupt in September 2008. The VIX peaked again during the Greek and Spanish sovereign debt crises. The all-time low value of the VIX occurred in December 1993 when the volatility index fell to 8.89.

In recent years, buying when the VIX is high and selling when it is low has proved to be a profitable strategy for the short term. But so has buying during market spills and selling during market peaks. The real question is how high is high and how low is low. For instance, an investor might have been tempted to buy into the market on Friday, October 16, 1987, when the VIX reached 40. Yet such a purchase would have proved disastrous given the record one-day collapse that followed on Monday.

THE DISTRIBUTION OF LARGE DAILY CHANGES

Chapter 16 noted that there were 145 days from 1885 through 2012 when the Dow Jones Industrials changed by 5 percent or more: 68 up and 77 down. Seventy-nine of these days, or nearly two-thirds of the total, occurred from 1929 through 1933. The most volatile year by far in terms of daily changes was 1932, which contained 35 days when the Dow moved by at least 5 percent. The longest period of time between two successive changes of at least 5 percent was the 17-year period that preceded the October 19, 1987, stock crash.

The calendar properties of large daily changes are displayed in Figure 19-6. Most of the large changes have occurred on Monday, while Tuesday has experienced by far the least (excluding Saturday). Monday has the largest number of down days, and Wednesday has by far the highest number of up days.

Thirty-six of the large changes occurred in October, which has witnessed more than twice the number of large moves as any other month. October's reputation as a volatile month is fully justified. Not only has October witnessed nearly one-quarter of all big moves, but it has also seen the two greatest stock crashes in history, in October 1929 and October 1987. It is interesting to note that nearly two-thirds of the large

FIGURE   19–6

Distribution of Dow-Industrial Changes Over 5 Percent, 1885–2012

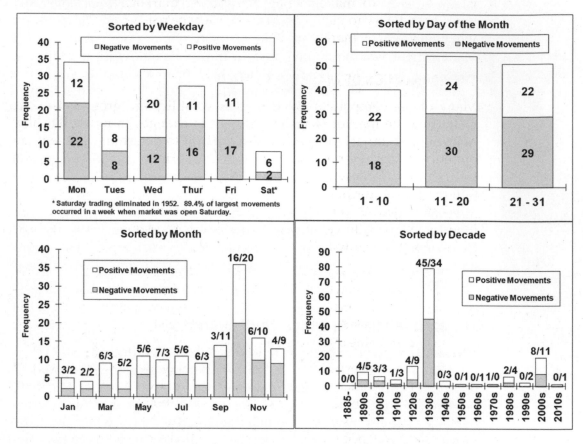

declines have occurred in the last four months of the year. Chapter 21 examines other seasonal properties of stock returns.

One of the most surprising bits of information about large market moves relates to the period of the greatest stock market collapse. From September 3, 1929, through July 8, 1932, the Dow Jones Industrials fell nearly 89 percent. During that period, there were 37 episodes when the Dow changed by 5 percent or more. Surprisingly, 21 of those episodes were increases! Many of these sharp rallies were the result of short covering, which occurred as speculators who thought the market was on a one-way street rushed to sell stock they did not own and were then forced to buy it back, or cover their positions, once the market rallied.

It is not uncommon for markets that appear to be trending in one direction to experience occasional sharp moves in the other direction. In a bull market, the expression "up the staircase, down the elevator" is an apt description of market behavior. Ordinary investors must beware: it is not as easy to make money in trending markets as it looks, and investors who try to play these markets must be ready to bail out quickly when they see the market change direction.

THE ECONOMICS OF MARKET VOLATILITY

Many of the complaints about market volatility are grounded in the belief that the market reacts excessively to changes in news. But how news should impact the market is so difficult to determine that few can quantify the proper impact of an event on the price of a stock. As a result, traders often "follow the crowd" and try to predict how other traders will react when news happens.

Over half a century ago, Keynes illustrated the problem of investors who try to value stock by economic fundamentals as opposed to following the crowd:

> Investment based on genuine long-term expectation is so difficult today as to be scarcely practicable. He who attempts it must surely lead much more laborious days and run greater risk than he who tries to guess better than the crowd how the crowd will behave; and, given equal intelligence, he may make more disastrous mistakes.[15]

In 1981, Robert Shiller of Yale University devised a method of determining whether stock investors tended to overreact to changes in dividends and interest rates, the fundamental building blocks of stock values.[16] From the examination of historical data, he calculated what the value of the S&P 500 Index should have been given the subsequent realization of dividends and interest rates. We know what this value is because, as shown in Chapter 10, stock prices are the present discounted value of future cash flows.

What he found was that stock prices were far too variable to be explained merely by the subsequent behavior of dividends and interest rates. Stock prices appeared to overreact to changes in dividends, failing to take into account that most of the changes in dividend payouts were only temporary.[17] For example, investors priced stocks in a recession as if they expected dividends to go much lower, completely contrary to historical experience.

The word *cycle* in *business cycle* implies that ups in economic activity will be followed by downs and vice versa. Since earnings and profits tend to follow the business cycle, they too should behave in a cyclical manner, returning to some average value over time. Under these circumstances, a temporary drop in dividends (or earnings) during a recession should have a very minor effect on the price of a stock, which discounts dividends into the infinite future.

When stocks are collapsing, worst-case scenarios loom large in investors' minds. On May 6, 1932, after stocks had plummeted 85 percent from their 1929 high, Dean Witter issued the following memo to its clients:

> There are only two premises which are tenable as to the future. Either we are going to have chaos or else recovery. The former theory is foolish. If chaos ensues nothing will maintain value; neither bonds nor stocks nor bank deposits nor gold will remain valuable. Real estate will be a worthless asset because titles will be insecure. No policy can be based upon this impossible contingency. Policy must therefore be predicated upon the theory of recovery. The present is not the first depression; it may be the worst, but just as surely as conditions have righted themselves in the past and have gradually readjusted to normal, so this will again occur. The only uncertainty is when it will occur. . . . I wish to say emphatically that in a few years present prices will appear as ridiculously low as 1929 values appear fantastically high.[18]

Two months later the stock market hit its all-time low and rallied strongly. In retrospect, these words reflected great wisdom and sound judgment about the temporary dislocations of stock prices. Yet at the time they were uttered, investors were so disenchanted with stocks and so filled with doom and gloom that the message fell on deaf ears. Chapter 22 discusses why investors often overreact to short-term events and fail to take the long view of the market.

THE SIGNIFICANCE OF MARKET VOLATILITY

Despite the drama of the October 1987 market collapse, there was amazingly little lasting effect on the world economy or even the financial markets. Because the 1987 episode did not augur either a further collapse in stock prices or a decline in economic activity, it will never attain the notoriety of the crash of 1929. Yet its lesson is perhaps more important. Economic safeguards, such as prompt Federal Reserve action to provide liquidity to the economy and assure the proper functioning of the financial markets, can prevent an economic debacle of the kind that beset our economy during the Great Depression.

This does not mean that the markets are exempt from violent fluctuations. Since the future will always be uncertain, psychology and sentiment often dominate economic fundamentals. As Keynes perceptively stated more than 70 years ago in *The General Theory*, "The outstanding fact is the extreme precariousness of the basis of knowledge on which our estimates of prospective yield have to be made."[19] Precarious estimates are subject to sudden change, so prices in free markets will be volatile. But history has shown that investors who are willing to step into the market when others are running to the exits reap the benefits of market volatility.

Technical Analysis and Investing with the Trend

Many skeptics, it is true, are inclined to dismiss the whole procedure [chart reading] as akin to astrology or necromancy; but the sheer weight of its importance in Wall Street requires that its pretensions be examined with some degree of care.
—BENJAMIN GRAHAM AND DAVID DODD, 1934[1]

THE NATURE OF TECHNICAL ANALYSIS

Flags, pennants, saucers, and *head-and-shoulders formations. Stochastics, moving-average convergence-divergence indicators,* and *candlesticks.* Such is the arcane language of the technical analyst, an investor who forecasts future returns by the use of past price trends. Few areas of investment analysis have attracted more critics; yet no other area has a core of such dedicated, ardent supporters. Technical analysis, often dismissed by academic economists as being as useful as astrology, is being given a new look, and some of the recent evidence is surprisingly positive.

Technical analysts, or *chartists* as they are sometimes called, stand in sharp contrast to *fundamental analysts,* who use such variables as dividends, earnings, and book values to forecast stock returns. Chartists ignore these fundamental variables, maintaining that information important to predicting future price movements can be gleaned by analyzing past price patterns. Some of these patterns are the result of shifts in market psychology that tend to repeat themselves, whereas others are caused by informed investors who have special knowledge of the prospects of the firm. If these patterns are read properly, chartists maintain, investors can use them to outperform the market and share in the gains of those who are more knowledgeable about a stock's prospects.

CHARLES DOW, TECHNICAL ANALYST

The first well-publicized technical analyst was Charles Dow, the creator of the Dow Jones Industrial Average. But Charles Dow did not analyze only charts. In conjunction with his interest in market movements, Dow founded the *Wall Street Journal* and published his strategy in editorials in the early 1900s. Dow's successor, William Hamilton, extended Dow's technical approach and published the *Stock Market Barometer* in 1922. Ten years later, Charles Rhea formalized Dow's concepts in a book entitled *Dow Theory*.

Charles Dow likened the ebb and flow of stock prices to waves in an ocean. He claimed that there was a *primary wave*, which, like the tide, determined the overall trend. Upon this trend were superimposed secondary waves and minor ripples. He also claimed you could identify which trend the market was in by analyzing a chart of the Dow Jones Industrial Average, the volume in the market, and the Dow Jones Rail (now called the Transportation) Average.

Those who follow the Dow's theory acknowledge that the strategy would have gotten an investor out of the stock market before the October 1929 stock crash. Martin J. Pring, a noted technical analyst, argues that, starting in 1897, investors who purchased stock in the Dow Jones Industrial Average and followed each Dow theory buy-and-sell signal would have seen an original investment of $100 reach $116,508 by January 1990, as opposed to $5,682 with a buy-and-hold strategy (these calculations exclude reinvested dividends).[2] But confirming profits that come from trading based on the Dow theory is difficult because the buy-and-sell signals are purely subjective and cannot be determined by precise numerical rules.

THE RANDOMNESS OF STOCK PRICES

Although the Dow theory might not be as popular as it once was, technical analysis is still alive and well. The idea that you can identify the major trends in the market, riding bull markets while avoiding bear markets, is still the fundamental goal of technical analysts.

Yet most economists still attack the fundamental tenet of the chartists—that stock prices follow predictable patterns. To these academic researchers, the movements of prices in the market more closely conform to a pattern called a *random walk* than to special formations that forecast future returns.

The first economist to come to this conclusion was Frederick MacCauley, an economist in the early part of the twentieth century. His comments at a 1925 dinner meeting of the American Statistical Association on the topic of "forecasting security prices" were reported in the association's official journal:

> MacCauley observed that there was a striking similarity between the fluctuations of the stock market and those of a chance curve which may be obtained by throwing dice. Everyone will admit that the course of such a purely chance curve cannot be predicted. If the stock market can be forecast from a graph of its movements, it must be because of its difference from the chance curve.[3]

More than 30 years later, Harry Roberts, a professor at the University of Chicago, simulated movements in the market by plotting price changes that resulted from completely random events, such as flips of a coin. These simulations looked like the charts of actual stock prices, forming shapes and following trends that are considered by chartists to be significant predictors of future returns. But since the next period's price change was, by construction, a completely random event, such patterns could not logically have any predictive content. This early research supported the belief that the apparent patterns in past stock prices were the result of completely random movements.

But does the randomness of stock prices make economic sense? Factors influencing supply and demand do not occur randomly and are often quite predictable from one period to the next. Shouldn't these predictable factors make stock prices move in nonrandom patterns?

In 1965, Professor Paul Samuelson of MIT showed that the randomness in security prices did not contradict the laws of supply and demand.[4] In fact, such randomness was a result of a free and efficient market in which investors had already incorporated all the known factors influencing the price of the stock. This is the crux of the *efficient market hypothesis*.

If the market is efficient, prices will change only when new, unanticipated information is released to the market. Since unanticipated information is as likely to be better than expected as it is to be worse than expected, the resulting movement in stock prices is random. Price charts will therefore look like a random walk and cannot be predicted.[5]

SIMULATIONS OF RANDOM STOCK PRICES

If stock prices are indeed random, their movements should not be distinguishable from simulations generated randomly by a computer. Figure 20-1 extends the experiment conceived by Professor Roberts 60 years ago. Instead of generating only closing prices, I programmed the computer to generate intraday prices, creating the popular high-low-close bar graphs that are found in most newspapers and chart publications.

There are eight charts in Figure 20-1. Four have been generated by a random-number generator. In these charts, there is absolutely no way to predict the future from the past, because future movements are designed to be totally independent from the past. The other four charts were chosen from actual data of the Dow Jones Industrial Average. Before reading further, try to determine which four are actual historical prices and which are computer generated.

Such a task is quite difficult. In fact, most of the top brokers at a leading Wall Street firm found it impossible to tell the difference between the real and counterfeit data. Two-thirds of brokers did correctly identify Figure 20-1D, which depicts the period around the October 19, 1987, stock crash. For the remaining seven charts, the brokers showed no ability to distinguish actual from computer-generated data. The true historical prices are represented by charts B, D, E, and H, while the computer-generated data are charts A, C, F, and G.[6]

TRENDING MARKETS AND PRICE REVERSALS

Despite the fact that many "trends" are in fact the result of the totally random movement of stock prices, many traders will not invest against a trend that they believe they have identified. Two of the most well-known sayings of market timers are "Make the trend your friend" and "Trust the thrust."

Martin Zweig, a well-known market timer who used fundamental and technical variables to forecast market trends, forcefully stated: "I can't overemphasize the importance of staying with the trend of the market, being in gear with the tape, and not fighting the major movements. Fighting the tape is an open invitation to disaster."[7]

When a trend appears established, technical analysts draw channels consisting of parallel upper and lower bounds within which the

FIGURE 20–1

Real and Simulated Stock Indexes

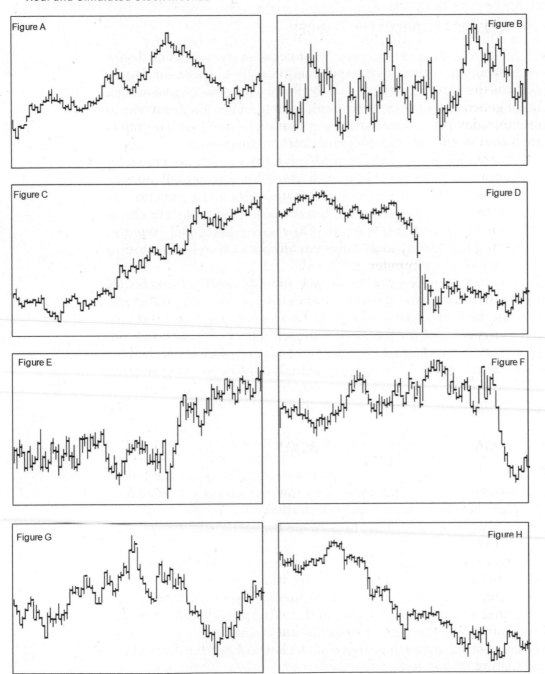

market has traded. The lower bound of a channel is frequently called a *support level* and the upper bound a *resistance level*. When the market breaks the bounds of the channel, a large market move often follows.

The very fact that many traders believe in the importance of trends can induce behavior that makes trend following so popular. While the trend is intact, traders sell when prices reach the upper end of the channel and buy when they reach the lower end, attempting to take advantage of the apparent fluctuations of stock prices within the channel. If the trendline is broken, many of these traders will reverse their positions: buying if the market penetrates the top of the trendline or selling if it falls through the bottom. This behavior often accelerates the movement of stock prices and reinforces the importance of the trend.

Options trading by trend followers also reinforces the behavior of market timers. When the market is trading within a channel, traders will sell put and call options at strike prices that represent the lower and upper bounds of the channel. As long as the market remains within the channel, these speculators collect premiums as the options expire worthless.

If the market penetrates the trading range, options sellers are exposed to great risks. Recall that sellers of options (as long as they do not own the underlying stock) face a huge potential liability, a liability that can be many times the premium that they collected upon sale of the option. When such unlimited losses loom, these options writers "run for cover," or buy back their options, accelerating the movement of prices.

MOVING AVERAGES

Successful technical trading requires not only identifying the trend but, more important, identifying when the trend is about to reverse. A popular tool for determining when the trend might change examines the relationship between the current price and a moving average of past price movements, a technique that goes back to at least the 1930s.[8]

A *moving average* is simply the arithmetic average of a given number of past closing prices of a stock or index. For each new trading day, the oldest price is dropped and the most recent price is added to compute the average.

Moving averages are far less volatile than daily prices. When prices are rising, the moving average is below the market price and, technical analysts claim, forms a support level for stock prices. When prices are falling, the moving average is above current prices and forms a resistance level. Analysts claim that a moving average allows investors to identify the basic market trend without being distracted by the day-to-day volatility of the market. When prices penetrate the moving average, this indicates that powerful underlying forces are signaling a reversal of the basic trend.

The most popular moving average uses prices for the past 200 trading days, and it is therefore called the *200-day moving average*. It is frequently plotted in newspapers and investment letters as a key determinant of investment trends. One of the early supporters of this strategy was William Gordon, who indicated that, over the period from 1897 to 1967, buying stocks when the Dow broke above the moving average produced nearly seven times the return as buying when the Dow broke below the average.[9] Robert Colby and Thomas Meyers claim that for the United States the best time period for a moving average of weekly data is 45 weeks, just slightly longer than the 200-day moving average.[10]

Testing the Dow Jones Moving-Average Strategy

In order to test the 200-day moving-average strategy, I examined the daily record of the Dow Jones Industrial Average from 1885 to the present. In contrast to the previous studies on moving-average strategies, the holding-period returns include the reinvestment of dividends when the strategy calls for investing in the market and calls for investing in short-term interest-bearing securities when one is not. Annualized returns are examined over the entire period as well as the subperiods.

I adopted the following criteria to determine the buy-sell strategy: Whenever the Dow Jones Industrial Average closed by *at least* 1 percent above its 200-day moving average (not including the current day), stocks were purchased at the current day's closing prices; and whenever the Dow Industrials closed by *at least* 1 percent below its 200-day moving average, stocks were sold at the closing prices. When sold, the portfolio was invested in Treasury bills.

There are two noteworthy aspects of this strategy. The 1 percent band around the 200-day moving average is used in order to reduce the number of times an investor would have to move in and out of the market. The smaller the band, the greater the number of buys and sells.[11] A very small band would cause traders to be "whipsawed," a term used to describe the alternate buying and then selling of stocks in an attempt to beat the market. Whipsawing dramatically lowers investor returns because of the large increase in transaction costs.

The second aspect of this strategy assumes that an investor buys or sells stocks at the closing price rather than during the trading day. Only in recent years has the exact intraday level of the popular averages been computed. Using historical data, it is impossible to determine times when the market average penetrated the 200-day moving average during the day. By specifying that the average must close above or below the average of the two hundred preceding closes, I present a theory that could have been implemented in practice through the whole time period.[12]

Back-Testing the 200-Day Moving Average

Figure 20-2 displays the daily and 200-day moving averages of the Dow Jones Industrial Average during two select periods: from 1924 to 1936 and 2001 to 2012. The time periods when investors are out of the stock market (and in short-term bonds) are shaded; otherwise, investors are fully invested in stocks.

The returns from the 200-day moving-average strategy and a buy-and-hold strategy over the whole period are summarized in Table 20-1. From January 1886 through December 2012, the 9.73 percent annual return from the timing strategy beat the annual return on the holding strategy of 9.39 percent. As noted earlier, the timing strategy had its biggest success avoiding the 1929-to-1932 crash. If that period is excluded,

T A B L E   20–1

Annualized Returns of Timing and Holding Strategies, 1886–2012

Period	Holding Strategy		Timing Strategy				% in Market	# of Switches
	Return	Risk	No Trans Costs		Net Trans Costs			
			Return	Risk	Return	Risk		
1886–2012	9.39%	21.4%	9.73%	16.5%	8.11%	17.2%	62.4%	376
Subperiods								
1886–1925	9.08%	23.7%	9.77%	17.7%	8.10%	18.0%	56.6%	122
1926–1945	6.25%	31.0%	11.13%	21.8%	9.47%	22.7%	62.2%	60
1946–2012	10.53%	16.2%	9.28%	14.1%	7.71%	15.0%	66.5%	194
1990–2012	9.57%	15.7%	4.92%	15.6%	2.66%	16.8%	70.1%	100
2001–2012	4.07%	16.4%	1.33%	12.3%	−1.09%	13.2%	60.5%	58
Excl. 1929–1932 Crash								
1886–2012	10.60%	20.1%	9.92%	16.3%	8.38%	16.9%	63.6%	358
1926–1945	13.94%	24.5%	12.38%	20.3%	11.21%	20.8%	70.8%	42

FIGURE 20–2

Dow-Jones Industrials and the 200-Day Moving-Average Strategy

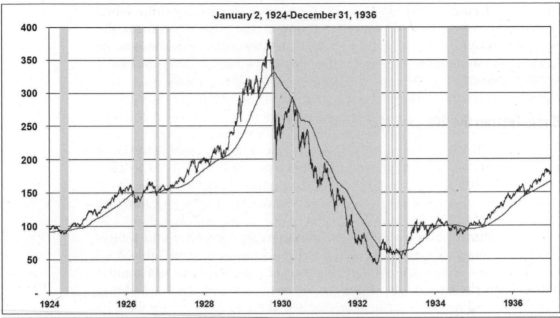

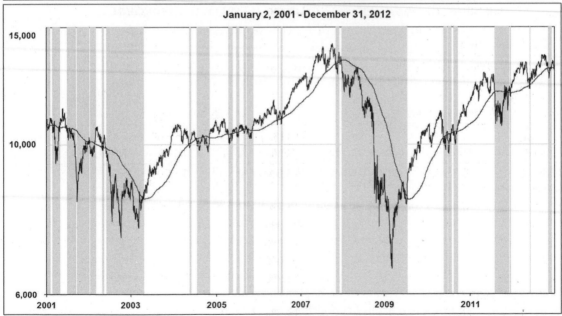

Shaded areas are out of the market.

the returns of the timing strategy are 68 basis points per year behind the holding strategy, although the timing strategy has lower risk.

Moreover, if the transaction costs of implementing the timing strategy are included in the calculations, the excess returns over the whole period, including the 1929-to-1932 Great Crash, more than vanish. Transaction costs include brokerage costs and bid-asked spreads, as well as the capital gains tax incurred when stocks are sold, and are assumed to be on average half a percent when buying or selling the market. This number probably underestimates such costs, especially in the earlier years, but likely overstates these costs in more recent years.

Looks are deceiving. When examining the returns from 2001 onward in Figure 20-2, it appears as if the returns from the timing strategy would swamp the buy-and-hold strategy, but that is not the case. The buy-and-hold strategy from 2001 to 2012 beats the timing strategy by more than 2 percentage points per year even before transaction costs are factored in. This is because the poor returns from the timing strategy occur when markets are not in a strong uptrend or downtrend and the market crosses the 200-day moving average many times, incurring large costs.

Although the returns from the timing strategy often fall behind that of a buy-and-hold investor, the major gain from the timing strategy is that the timing investor is out of stocks before the bottom of every major bear market. Since the market timer is in the market less than two-thirds of the time, the standard deviation of returns is reduced by about one-quarter over the returns of a buy-and-hold investor. This means that on an annual risk-adjusted basis, the return on the 200-day moving-average strategy is still impressive, even when transaction costs are included.

Avoiding Major Bear Markets

I noted that over the 126-year history of the Dow Jones Industrial Average, the 200-day moving-average strategy had its greatest triumph during the boom and crash of the 1920s and early 1930s. Using the criteria outlined above, investors would have bought stocks on June 27, 1924, when the Dow was at 95.33 and, with only two minor interruptions, ridden the bull market to the top at 381.17 on September 3, 1929. Investors would have exited the market on October 19, 1929, at 323.87, just 10 days before the Great Crash. Except for a brief period in 1930, the strategy would have kept investors out of stocks through the worst bear market in history. They would have finally reentered the market on August 6, 1932, when the Dow was 66.56, just 25 points higher than its absolute low.

Investors following the 200-day moving-average strategy would also have avoided the October 19, 1987, crash, selling out at the close of the previous Friday, October 16. However, in contrast to the 1929 crash, stocks did not continue downward. Although the market fell 23 percent on October 19, investors would not have reentered the market until the following June when the Dow was only about 5 percent below the exit level of October 16. Nonetheless, following the 200-day moving-average strategy would have avoided October 19 and 20, traumatic days for many investors who held stocks.

Moreover, investors using the 200-day moving average did avoid most of the terrible 2007–2009 bear market, as timing investors exited stocks on January 2, 2008, when the Dow Industrials was at 13,044, about 8 percent below its October 2007 peak, and did not reenter the market until July 15, 2009, when the Dow was 8,616, about 40 percent lower. But in 2010, 2011, and 2012, these investors were whipsawed, switching in and out of stocks 20 times, which caused about 20 percentage points to be clipped from the investors' returns before transaction costs.

Distribution of Gains and Losses

The 200-day moving-average strategy does avoid large losses, but it suffers many small declines. Figure 20-3 shows the distribution of yearly gains and losses (after transaction costs) of the timing and the holding strategy for the Dow Industrials for every year from 1886 through 2012. The timing strategist participates in most bull markets and avoids bear markets, but the losses suffered when the market fluctuates with little trend are significant.

The distribution of gains and losses is quite similar to that of a buy-and-hold investor who has purchased index puts to cushion market declines. As noted in Chapter 18, purchasing index puts is equivalent to buying an insurance policy on the market. If no losses are realized, the cost of the puts drains returns. Similarly, the timing strategy involves a large number of small losses that come from moving in and out of the market. That is why the modal annual return for the timing strategy is from zero to minus 5 percent, while the modal return for a buy-and-hold investor is plus 5 to 10 percent. The most negative yearly return from the timing strategy occurred in 2000, when investors had to execute 16 switches and suffered a negative return that exceeded 33 percent, far below the negative 5 percent return realized by the buy-and-hold investor.

FIGURE 20–3

Distribution of Annual Gains and Losses: Dow Industrials: Timing Versus Buy-and-Hold Strategy

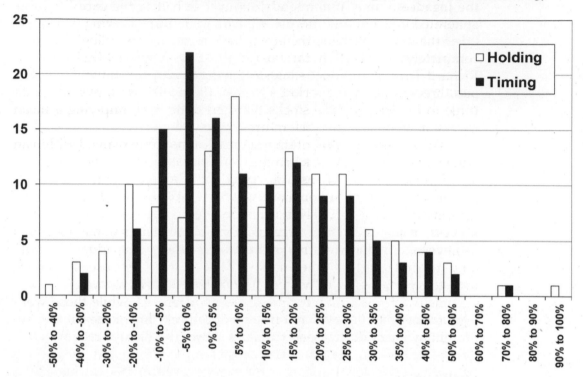

MOMENTUM INVESTING

Technical analysis can also be used to buy individual stocks. Academic economists call this *momentum investing*, and it has received increasing attention. Momentum strategies, unlike fundamental strategies, rely purely on past returns, regardless of earnings, dividends, or other valuation criteria. Momentum investors buy stocks that have recently risen in price and sell stocks that have recently fallen, expecting that the stock price will, for a time, continue to move in the same direction.

While this may seem at odds with the old maxim of "buy low, sell high," there is substantial research to support this "buy-high, sell-higher" strategy. In 1993, Narasimhan Jegadeesh and Sheridan Titman found that stocks with the highest 10 percent returns over the past six months outperformed stocks with the lowest 10 percent returns by about 1 percent per month over the next six months.[13, 14] Other technical strategies, such as buying stocks priced near their 52-week high, have also been shown to be successful.[15]

It should be emphasized that these momentum strategies work only in the short term and should not be part of a long-term strategy. In the Jegadeesh and Titman study, more than half of the excess returns generated in the first 12 months were lost over the following two years. Over the longer periods, the advantage of buying "winning" stocks is completely eliminated. In fact, an earlier study by Werner De Bondt and Richard Thaler found that stocks that performed poorly over the previous three- to five-year period significantly *outperformed*, over the next three to five years, those stocks that had done well, implying a mean reversion of longer-run stock returns.[16]

The success of momentum investing cannot be explained within an efficient market framework. It appears that investors initially underreact to information, which causes the stock price to continue to respond to the news over time rather than adjusting instantaneously to the new information. Unfortunately momentum investing does not guarantee success: recent evidence suggests that while professional investors achieve excess returns with a momentum strategy, individual investors tend to underperform the market. This may be because individual investors often focus on the very best performing stocks, which tend to become overpriced quickly and suffer poor returns, while those well-performing stocks that do not make it to the very top of the list and are bought by professionals tend to have the best momentum returns.[17]

CONCLUSION

Proponents claim that technical analysis can identify the major trends of the market and determine when those trends might reverse. Yet there is considerable debate about whether such trends exist or whether they are just runs of good and bad returns that are the result of random price movements.

Burton Malkiel has been quite clear in his denunciation of technical analysis. In his bestselling work *A Random Walk Down Wall Street*, he proclaims:

> Technical rules have been tested exhaustively by using stock price data on both major exchanges, going back as far as the beginning of the 20th century. The results reveal conclusively that past movements in stock prices cannot be used to foretell future movements. The stock market has no memory. The central proposition of charting is absolutely false, and investors who follow its precepts will accomplish nothing but increasing substantially the brokerage charges they pay.[18]

Yet this contention, once supported nearly unanimously by academic economists, is cracking. Recent econometric research has shown that such simple trading rules as 200-day moving averages or short-term price momentum can be used to improve returns.[19]

Despite the ongoing academic debate, technical analysis has a huge number of adherents on Wall Street and among many savvy investors. The analysis in this chapter gives a cautious nod to these strategies, as long as transaction costs are not high. But as I have noted throughout this book, actions by investors to take advantage of the past may change returns in the future. As Benjamin Graham stated so well more than 70 years ago:

> A moment's thought will show that there can be no such thing as a scientific prediction of economic events under human control. The very "dependability" of such a prediction will cause human actions which will invalidate it. Hence thoughtful chartists admit that continued success is dependent upon keeping the successful method known to only a few people.[20]

A final word: Technical analysis requires the full-time attention of the investor. On October 16, 1987, the Dow fell below its 200-day moving average at the very end of trading on the Friday before the crash. But if you failed to sell your stocks that afternoon, you would have been swept downward by the 22 percent nightmare of Black Monday.

21

Calendar Anomalies

October. This is one of the peculiarly dangerous months to speculate in stocks. The others are July, January, September, April, November, May, March, June, December, August, and February.

—MARK TWAIN

The dictionary defines *anomaly* as something inconsistent with what is naturally expected. And what is more unnatural than to expect to beat the market by predicting stock prices based solely on the day or week or month of the year? Yet it appears that you can. Research has revealed that there are predictable times during which the stock market, and certain groups of stocks in particular, do particularly well.

The analysis in the first edition of *Stocks for the Long Run*, published in 1994, was based on long data series analyzed through the early 1990s. The calendar anomalies reported in that edition invited investors to outperform the market by adopting strategies to these unusual calendar events. However, as more investors learn of and act on these anomalies, the prices of stocks may adjust so that much, if not all, of the anomaly is eliminated. That certainly would be the prediction of the efficient market hypothesis.

In this edition of *Stocks for the Long Run*, I also look at the evidence since 1994 to determine whether the anomaly survived or not. The results are surprising. Some anomalies have weakened and even reversed, while others remain as strong as they have always been. Here is a rundown.

SEASONAL ANOMALIES

The most important historical calendar anomaly is that small-capitalization stocks have far outperformed larger stocks in January. This effect is so strong that without January's return, small stocks would have a *lower* return than large stocks since 1925.[1]

This outperformance of small stocks in January has been dubbed the *January effect*. It was discovered in the early 1980s by Donald Keim,[2] based on research he did as a graduate student at the University of Chicago. It was the first significant finding that flew in the face of the efficient market hypothesis that claimed there was no predictable pattern to stock prices.

The January effect might be the granddaddy of all calendar anomalies, but it is not the only one. Stocks generally do much better in the first half of the month than the second half, do well before holidays, and plunge in the month of September. Furthermore, they do exceptionally well between Christmas and New Year's Day; and until very recently, they have soared on the last trading day of December, which is actually the day that launches the January effect.

THE JANUARY EFFECT

Of all the calendar-related anomalies, the January effect has been the most publicized. From 1925 through 2012, the average arithmetic return on the S&P 500 Index in the month of January was 1.00 percent, while the average returns on the small stocks came to 5.36 percent. The 4.36-percentage-point excess return of small stocks in January far exceeds the difference in annual returns between large and small stocks. In other words, from February through December, the average returns on small stocks have fallen short of the returns on large stocks. On the basis of history, the only advantageous time to hold small stocks is the month of January.

To see how important the January effect is, examine Figure 21-1. It shows the total returns index on large and small stocks and on small stocks if the January return on small stocks is replaced with that of the S&P 500 Index in January. A single dollar invested in small stocks in 1926 would grow to $11,480 by the end of 2012, while the same dollar would grow to only $3,063 in large stocks. Yet if the small stocks' return in January is eliminated, the total return to small stocks accumulates to only $469, less than one-sixth of the cumulative return on large stocks.

Figure 21-1 also shows that if the large January small stock returns persist in the future, it could lead to some astounding investment

FIGURE 21–1

Small and Large Stocks, With and Without the January Effect, 1926–2012

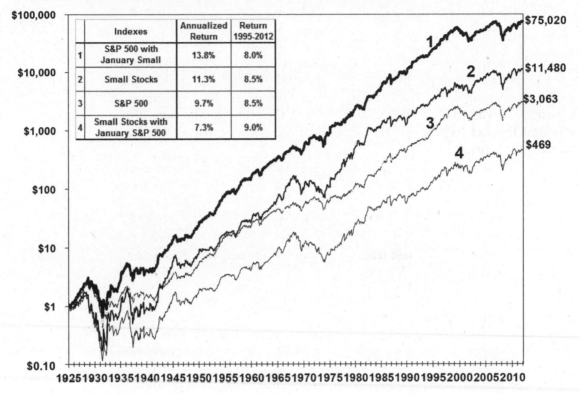

	Indexes	Annualized Return	Return 1995-2012
1	S&P 500 with January Small	13.8%	8.0%
2	Small Stocks	11.3%	8.5%
3	S&P 500	9.7%	8.5%
4	Small Stocks with January S&P 500	7.3%	9.0%

results. By buying small stocks at the end of December and transferring them back to the S&P 500 Index at the end of January, a $1 investment in this strategy at the end of 1925 would have grown to $75,020 by the end of 2012, a striking 13.8 percent annual rate of return.

There have been only 20 years since 1925 when large stocks have outperformed small stocks in January. Furthermore, when small stocks underperform large stocks, it is usually not by much: the worst underperformance was 5.1 percent in January 1929. In contrast, since 1925, returns on small stocks have exceeded returns on large stocks in January by at least 5 percent for 28 years, by at least 10 percent for 13 years, and by over 20 percent for 2 years.

The January effect also prevailed during the most powerful bear market in our history. From August 1929 through the summer of 1932, when small stocks lost over 90 percent of their value, small stocks posted consecutive January monthly returns of plus 13 percent, 21 percent, and

10 percent in 1930, 1931, and 1932, respectively. It is testimony to the power of the January effect that investors could have increased their wealth by 50 percent during the greatest stock crash in history by buying small stocks at the end of December in those three years and selling them at the end of the following January, putting their money in cash for the rest of the year!

A fascinating feature of the January effect is that you do not have to wait the entire month to see the big returns from small stocks roll in. Most of the buying in small stocks begins on the last trading day of December (often in the late afternoon), as some investors pick up the bargain stocks that are dumped by others on New Year's Eve. Strong gains in small stocks continue on the first trading day of January and with declining force through the first week of trading. On the basis of research published in 1989, on the first trading day of January alone, small stocks earned nearly 4 percentage points more than large stocks.[3] By the middle of the month, the January effect is largely exhausted.

When any anomaly such as the January effect is found, it is important to examine its international reach. When researchers turned to foreign markets, they found that the January effect was not just a U.S. phenomenon. In Japan, the world's second-largest capital market, the excess returns on small stocks in January came to 7.2 percent per year, more than in the United States.[4] As you shall see later in the chapter, January is the best month for both large and small stocks in many other countries of the world.[5]

How could such a phenomenon go unnoticed for so long by investors, portfolio managers, and financial economists? Because in the United States, the returns in January are nothing special for large stocks that form the bulk of those indexes that are analyzed. That's not to say that January is not a good month for large stocks, as large stocks do quite well in January, particularly in foreign markets. But in the United States, January is by no means the best month for stocks of large firms.

Causes of the January Effect

Why have investors favored small stocks in January? No one knows for sure, but there are several hypotheses. In contrast to institutions, individual investors hold a disproportionate amount of small stocks, and they are more sensitive to the tax consequences of their trading. Small stocks, especially those that have declined in the preceding 11 months, are subject to tax-motivated selling in December. This selling depresses the price of individual issues. In January after the selling ends, these stocks bounce back in price.

There is some evidence to support this explanation. Stocks that have fallen throughout the year fall even more in December and then often rise dramatically in January. Furthermore, there is some evidence that before the introduction of the U.S. income tax in 1913, there was no January effect. And in Australia, where the tax year runs from July 1 through June 30, there are abnormally large returns to small stocks in July.

If taxes are a factor, however, they cannot be the only one, for the January effect holds in countries that do not have a capital gains tax. Japan did not tax capital gains for individual investors until 1989, but the January effect existed prior to that date. Furthermore, capital gains were not taxed in Canada before 1972, and yet there was a January effect in that country as well. Finally, stocks that have risen throughout the previous year and should not be subject to tax-loss selling still rise in January, although not by as much as stocks that have fallen the previous year.

There are other potential explanations for the January effect. Workers often receive extra income, such as from bonuses and other forms of compensation, at year-end. These individuals often invest their cash in stocks in the first week of January. Data show that there is a sharp increase in the ratio of public buy orders to public sell orders around the turn of the year. Since the public holds a large fraction of small stocks, this could be an important clue to understanding the January effect.[6]

Although all these explanations appear quite reasonable, none jibes with what is called an "efficient capital market." If money managers know that small stocks will surge in January, these stocks should be bought well before New Year's Day to capture these spectacular returns. That would cause the price of small stocks to rise in December, which would prompt other managers to buy them in November, and so on. In the process of acting on the January effect, the price of stocks would be smoothed out over the year, and the phenomenon would disappear.

The January Effect Weakened in Recent Years

Perhaps all the publicity about the January effect has motivated investors and traders to take advantage of this calendar anomaly, since the effect has largely disappeared since 1994. From 1995 through January 2012, the average January return on the Russell 2000 Index of small stocks has been 1.36 percent, only slightly more than the 0.70 percent return on the S&P 500 Index. Furthermore, the return on the Russell

2000 on the last trading day of December and the first trading day of January, which had previously been so high, has been no higher than that of the S&P 500 Index, and both have been approximately zero. Finally, the excess return on small stocks during the first seven trading days in January, which had been so large before 1995, has also vanished.

LARGE STOCK MONTHLY RETURNS

Other seasonal patterns are associated with stock returns besides the January effect. The monthly returns on the Dow Industrials and S&P 500 Index are displayed in Figure 21-2. November and December have been good months, and according to recent data, they continue to be. But January's return, formerly one of the best, has faltered in recent years. April has also been an excellent month, but except for July, the rest of the summer through early fall has returns well below normal. The expression "Sell in May and go away" certainly has some empirical justification. Since World War II, there has been no evidence of the "summer rally" that used to be much trumpeted by brokers and investment advisors in the 1950s and 1960s.

These monthly patterns of returns have a worldwide reach. January historically has been an excellent month in foreign countries. The January returns for the 20 countries covered by the Morgan Stanley Capital Market Index, shown in Figure 21-3, have all exceeded the average return.

In every country, January returns are greater than average, and on average the January return more than doubles the return for the other 11 months. But January has lost its magic abroad, as it has in the United States. Since 1994, January returns have actually been negative and have fallen short of the yearly average in 14 countries, including the United States.

THE SEPTEMBER EFFECT

While July has good returns, watch out for the rest of the summer, especially September. September is by far the worst month of the year, and in the United States, it is the only month to have a negative return including reinvested dividends. September is followed closely by October, which, as Chapter 19 indicated already, has a disproportionate percentage of crashes.

Figure 21-4 tracks the Dow Jones Industrial Averages from 1885 through 2012, both including and excluding the month of September. An

FIGURE 21–2

Monthly Returns on Dow Jones Industrials and S&P 500

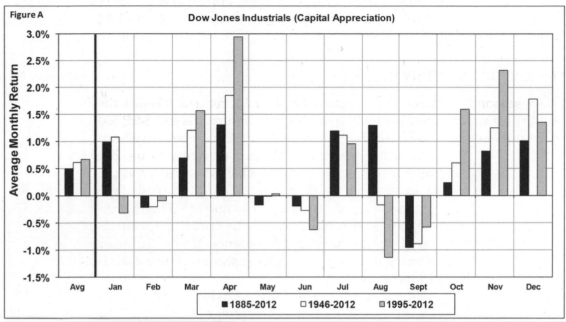

Figure A — Dow Jones Industrials (Capital Appreciation)

■1885-2012   □1946-2012   ▨1995-2012

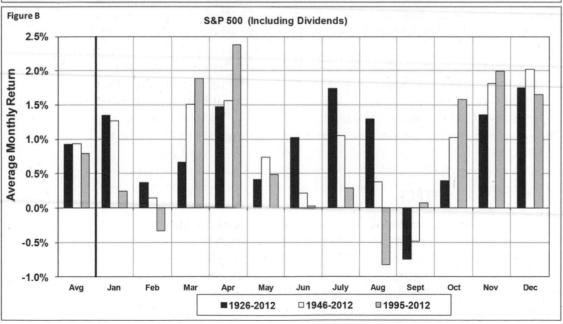

Figure B — S&P 500 (Including Dividends)

■1926-2012   □1946-2012   ▨1995-2012

FIGURE 21–3

International January and September Effects, 1970–2012

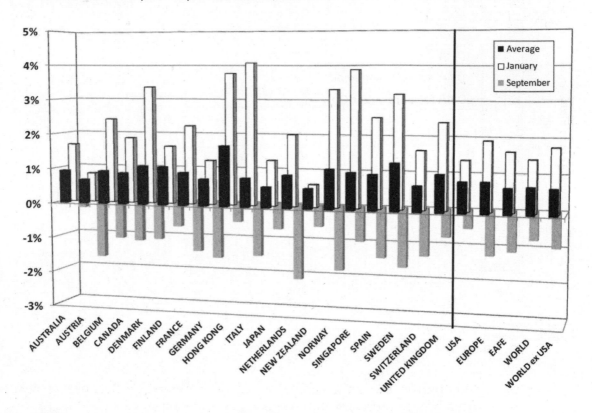

investment of $1 in the Dow Jones Average in 1885 would be worth $511 by the end of 2012 (dividends excluded). In contrast, $1 invested in the Dow only in the month of September would be worth only 23 cents! On the other hand, if you put your money in the stock market every month *except* September, your dollar would have been worth $2,201 at the end of 2012.

The poor returns in September also prevail in the rest of the world. It is amazing that September is the only month of the year that has negative returns in a value-weighted index. That means that in September investors would do better holding zero-interest currency than putting their assets in the stock market. September has had negative returns in *all* 20 of the countries covered by the Morgan Stanley developed market indexes, as well as the major world indexes, including the EAFE Index and the Morgan Stanley all-world index.

In contrast to the January effect, which has largely disappeared in recent data, the September effect is still running full steam ahead,

FIGURE 21–4

The September Effect: Dow-Jones Industrial Average, 1885–2012

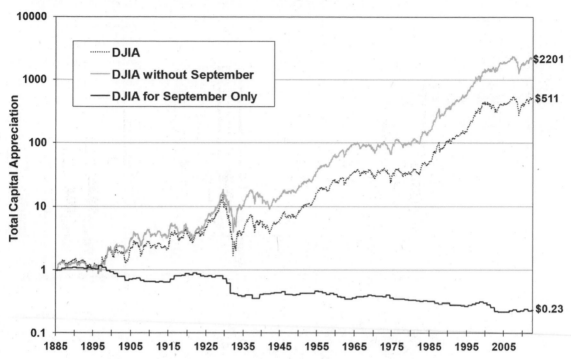

although in the United States much of the market's decline has now been brought forward into August since the first edition of *Stocks for the Long Run* was published. In fact, since 1995, September returns, measured by the S&P 500 index, have become slightly positive in the United States, but September returns have remained negative in 17 of the other 19 developed countries.

We can only speculate on why returns are so poor in September. Maybe the poor returns are related to the approach of winter and the depressing effect of rapidly shortening daylight. Psychologists stress that sunlight is an essential ingredient to well-being: recent research has confirmed that the New York Stock Exchange does significantly worse on cloudy days than it does on sunny days.[7] But this explanation falters "down under," as September is also a poor month in Australia and New Zealand, where the month marks the beginning of spring and longer days.[8]

Perhaps the poor returns in September are the result of investors' liquidating stocks (or holding off buying more stocks) to pay for their summer vacations. As discussed below, until recently Monday was by far the worst-performing day of the week. For many, September is the monthly version of Monday, the time you face work after a period of leisure. But even the September effect may in the future succumb to the efficient market. As noted above, investors in the United States are beginning to sell stocks earlier, dropping August to the worst-performing month since 1995.

OTHER SEASONAL RETURNS

Although psychologists say that many silently suffer depression around Christmas and New Year's, stock investors believe 'tis the season to be jolly. Table 21-1 displays the daily price returns, as measured by the Dow Jones Industrial Average, for various times in the year and in the month.

TABLE 21-1

Dow-Jones Industrial Average Daily Price Returns 1885–2012

	1885–2012	1885–1925	1926–1945	1946–1989	1946–2012	1995–2012
Overall Averages						
Whole month	0.0233%	0.0192%	0.0147%	0.0273%	0.0293%	0.0342%
First half of month	0.0402%	0.0203%	0.0621%	0.0500%	0.0465%	0.0365%
Second half of month	0.0062%	0.0182%	–0.0316%	0.0040%	0.0112%	0.0316%
Last day of month	0.0926%	0.0875%	0.1633%	0.1460%	0.0746%	–0.0923%
Days of the Week						
Monday	–0.0902%	–0.0874%	–0.2106%	–0.1313%	–0.0558%	0.0741%
Tuesday	0.0415%	0.0375%	0.0473%	0.0307%	0.0422%	0.0870%
Wednesday	0.0566%	0.0280%	0.0814%	0.0909%	0.0665%	0.0092%
Thursday	0.0246%	0.0012%	0.0627%	0.0398%	0.0274%	0.0091%
Friday	0.0630%	0.0994%	0.0064%	0.0942%	0.0577%	–0.0063%
With Sat	0.0539%	0.0858%	–0.0169%	0.0747%	NA	NA
Without Sat	0.0714%	0.3827%	0.3485%	0.0961%	0.0566%	–0.0063%
Saturday	0.0578%	0.0348%	0.0964%	0.0962%	NA	NA
Holiday Returns						
Day before holiday						
July 4th	0.2989%	0.2118%	0.8168%	0.2746%	0.1976%	0.1598%
Christmas	0.3544%	0.4523%	0.3634%	0.3110%	0.2918%	0.2582%
New Year's	0.2964%	0.5964%	0.3931%	0.2446%	0.0840%	–0.2394%
Holiday avg	0.3165%	0.4201%	0.5244%	0.2767%	0.1911%	0.0595%
Christmas week	0.2247%	0.3242%	0.2875%	0.1661%	0.1331%	0.0425%

Over the past 127 years, daily price returns, between Christmas and New Year's, have averaged nearly 10 times the average return.

Even more striking is the difference between stock returns in the first and second half of the month.[9] Over the entire 127-year period studied, the percentage change in the Dow Jones Industrial Average during the first half of the month—which includes the last trading day of the previous month up to and including the fourteenth day of the current month—is almost seven times the gain that occurs during the second half.[10] The average percentage changes in the Dow Jones Industrial Average over every calendar day of the month are shown in Figure 21-5.

Over the whole period it is striking how the average percentage gain on the last trading day of the month (and the thirtieth calendar day, when that is not the last trading day) and the first six calendar days is

FIGURE   21–5

Daily Price Returns on the Dow Industrial Average, 1885–2012

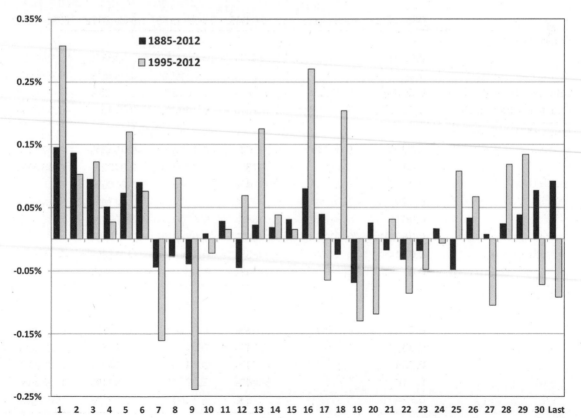

more than equal to the entire return for the month! The net change in the Dow Industrials is negative for all the other days.

But this pattern has changed somewhat in recent years. Although the gains on the first six days of the month have actually become greater, the change on the last day of the month has turned sharply negative, while the first day of the month is even more positive.

The strong gains at the beginning of the month are likely related to the inflow of funds into the equity market from workers who automatically have part of their pay invested directly into the market on the first day of the month. One notices another gain on the sixteenth of the month, where workers who are paid twice per month put funds into stocks. Yet since 1995, the return in the first half of the month now only slightly exceeds that of the second half.

DAY-OF-THE-WEEK EFFECTS

Many people hate Mondays. After two days of relaxing and doing pretty much what you like, having to face work on Monday is a drag. And stock investors apparently feel the same way. Monday has been by far the worst day of the week for the market. Over the past 127 years, the returns on Monday have been decisively negative—so negative that if Monday returns were instead like Tuesday through Friday, the historical real return on the stocks would exceed 13 percent per year, nearly double the historical average!

Although investors hate Mondays, they have relished Fridays. Friday has been the best day of the week, yielding price returns about three times the daily average. Even when markets were open on Saturday (every month before 1946 and nonsummer months before 1953), Friday price returns were the best.

But these daily patterns have changed dramatically in recent years. Since 1995, Monday has gone from the worst to second best, just trailing Tuesday. And Friday has not only gone from the best to the worst day but has actually recorded negative average returns. One reason for this change is that many stock traders like to hedge their equity positions over the weekend and sell their long positions at or near Friday's close. Friday's negative returns might also be caused by traders who, having learned that Monday is usually a bad day, sell on Friday. Traders then reestablish their stock positions on Monday, causing returns on those days to increase. Whatever the reasons, the change demonstrates that well-publicized anomalies are often arbitraged out of the market.

Another calendar anomaly is that stocks do very well before major holidays, as shown in Table 21-1. Price returns before the Fourth of July, Christmas, and New Year's Eve are, on average, almost 14 times the average daily price return. But some of these anomalies, like the day-of-the-week effect, have changed in recent years. Although stock returns on the day before July Fourth and Christmas have remained strong, returns on the last day of the trading year have switched from a strongly positive 0.30 percent to a decisively negative 0.24 percent since 1994. The negative returns on the last trading day in recent years are probably caused by a large number of "sell-on-close" orders that are automatically executed to offset positions in stock index futures, ETFs, and other customized hedge instruments. The downward movement of stock prices generally occurs in the last 30 minutes of trading. Of course, it is possible that once this pattern becomes widely known, it too will disappear.

Finally, there appears to be a diurnal pattern of stock returns. Evidence has shown that there is usually a sinking spell in the morning, especially on Monday. During lunch the market firms, then pauses or declines in the midafternoon before rising strongly in the last half hour of trading. This often leads the market to close at the highest levels of the day.

WHAT'S AN INVESTOR TO DO?

These anomalies are an extremely tempting guide to formulating an investing strategy. But these calendar-related returns do not always occur, and as investors become more aware of them, some have moderated while others have disappeared altogether. The famous January effect has been mostly absent over the past two decades. Still other anomalies have completely reversed, such as the returns of stocks on the last trading day of the year and the returns on Mondays and Fridays. But some, such as the large returns early in the month and the poor returns in September, remain.

Trying to take advantage of these anomalies requires the buying and selling of stock, which incurs transaction costs and (unless you are trading within tax-sheltered funds) may realize capital gains taxes. Nevertheless, investors who have already decided to buy or sell, but have some latitude in choosing the timing of such a transaction, might wish to take these calendar anomalies into account before making their trades.

Behavioral Finance and the Psychology of Investing

The rational man — like the Loch Ness monster — is sighted often, but photographed rarely.

—DAVID DREMAN, 1998[1]

The market is most dangerous when it looks best; it is most inviting when it looks worst.

—FRANK J. WILLIAMS, 1930[2]

This book is filled with data, figures, and charts that support an internationally diversified, long-term strategy for stock investors. Yet advice is much easier to take in theory than to put in practice. The finance profession is increasingly aware that psychological factors can thwart rational analysis and prevent investors from achieving the best results. The study of these psychological factors has burgeoned into the field of *behavioral finance*.

This chapter is written as a narrative to make it easier to understand the basic research and issues of behavioral finance. Dave is an investor who falls into psychological traps that prevent him from being effective. You may notice similarities between his behavior and your own. If so, the advice given in this chapter should help you become a more successful investor. Dave first talks to his wife, Jennifer, and then to an investment counselor who understands behavioral finance. The narrative begins in the fall of 1999, several months prior to the peak in the technology and Internet bubble that dominated markets at the turn of the century.

THE TECHNOLOGY BUBBLE, 1999 TO 2001

TIME: OCTOBER 1999

Dave: Jen, I've made some important investment decisions. Our portfolio contains nothing but these "old fogy" stocks like Philip Morris, Procter & Gamble, and Exxon. These stocks just aren't doing anything right now. My friends Bob and Paul at work have been making a fortune in Internet stocks. I talked with my broker, Allan, about the prospects of these stocks. He said the experts think the Internet is the wave of the future. I'm selling some of our stocks that just aren't moving, and then I'm getting into the Internet stocks like AOL, Yahoo!, and Inktomi.

Jennifer: I've heard that those stocks are very speculative. Are you sure you know what you're doing?

Dave: Allan says that we are entering a "New Economy," spurred by a communications revolution that is going to completely change the way we do business. Those stocks that we owned are Old Economy stocks. They had their day, but we should be investing for the future. I know these Internet stocks are volatile, and I'll watch them very carefully so we won't lose money. Trust me. I think we're finally on the right track.

TIME: MARCH 2000

Dave: Jen, have you seen our latest financial statements? We're up 60 percent since October. The Nasdaq crossed 5,000, and no one I've heard believes it will stop there. The excitement about the market is spreading, and it has become the topic of conversation around the office.

Jen: You seem to be trading in and out of stocks a lot more than you did before. I can't follow what we own!

Dave: Information is hitting the market faster and faster. I have to continually adjust my portfolio. Commissions are now so cheap that it pays to trade on any news affecting stocks. Trust me—look how well we're doing.

TIME: JULY 2000

Jen: Dave, I've looked at our broker's statement. We don't hold those Internet stocks any more. Now we own (she reads from the statement)

Cisco, EMC, Oracle, Sun Microsystems, Nortel Networks, JDS Uniphase. I don't know what any of these companies do. Do you?

Dave: When the Internet stocks crashed in April, I sold out right before we lost all our gains. Unfortunately, we didn't make much on those stocks, but we didn't lose either.

I know we're on the right track now. Those Internet companies weren't making any money. All the new firms we now own form the backbone of the Internet, and all are profitable. Allan told me an important principle: Do you know who made the most money in the California gold rush of the 1850s? Not the gold miners. Some of the early diggers found gold, but most found nothing. The real winners from the gold rush were those who sold supplies to the miners—pickaxes, boots, pans, and hiking gear. The lesson is very clear; most of the Internet companies are going to fail, but those supplying the backbone of the Internet—those supplying the routers, software, and fiber-optic cables—will be the big winners.

Jen: But I think I heard some economist say those companies are way overpriced now; they're selling for hundreds of times earnings.

Dave: Yes, but look at their growth over the last five years—no one has ever seen this before. The economy is changing, and many of the traditional yardsticks of valuation don't apply. Trust me; I'll monitor these stocks. I got us out of those Internet stocks in time, didn't I?

Time: November 2000

Dave (*to himself*): What should I do? The last few months have been dreadful. I'm down about 20 percent. Just over two months ago, Nortel was over 80. Now it is around 40. Sun Microsystems was 65, and now it is around 40. These prices are so cheap. I think I'll use some of my remaining cash to buy more shares at these lower prices. Then my stocks don't have to go up as much for me to get even.

Time: August 2001

Jen: Dave, I've just looked at our brokerage statement. We've been devastated! Almost three-quarters of our retirement money is gone. I thought you were going to monitor our investments closely. Our portfolio shows nothing but huge losses.

Dave: I know; I feel terrible. All the experts said these stocks would rebound, but they kept going down.

Jen: This has happened before. I don't understand why you do so badly. For years you watch the market closely, study all these financial reports, and seem to be very well informed. Yet you still make the wrong decisions. You buy near the highs and sell near the lows. You hold on to losers while selling your winners. You . . .

Dave: I know, I know. My stock investments always go wrong. I think I'm giving up on stocks and sticking with bonds.

Jen: Listen, Dave. I have talked to a few other people about your investing troubles, and I want you to go see an investment counselor. Investment counselors use behavioral psychology to help investors understand why they do poorly. An investment counselor will help you correct this behavior. Dave, I made you an appointment already. Please go see him.

BEHAVIORAL FINANCE

TIME: NEXT WEEK

Dave was skeptical. He thought that understanding stocks required knowledge of economics, accounting, and mathematics. Dave never heard the word *psychology* used in any of those subjects. Yet he knew he needed help, and it couldn't hurt to check it out.

Investment Counselor (IC): I have read your profile and talked to your wife extensively. You are very typical of the investor that we counsel here. I adhere to a new branch of economics called *behavioral finance*. Many of the ideas my profession explores are based on psychological concepts that have rarely before been applied to the stock market and portfolio management.

Let me give you some background. Until recently, finance was dominated by theories that assumed investors maximized their expected utility, or well-being, and always acted rationally. This was an extension of the rational theory of consumer choice under certainty applied to uncertain outcomes.

In the 1970s two psychologists, Daniel Kahneman and Amos Tversky, noted that many individuals did not behave as this theory predicted. Kahneman and Tversky developed a new model—called prospect theory—of how individuals actually behave and make decisions when faced with uncertainty.[3] Their model established them as the pioneers of behavioral finance, and their research has been making much headway in the finance profession.

Fads, Social Dynamics, and Stock Bubbles

IC: Let us first discuss your decision to get into the Internet stocks. Think back to October 1999. Do you remember why you decided to buy those stocks?

Dave: Yes. My stocks were simply not going anywhere. My friends at work were investing in the Internet and making a lot of money. There was so much excitement about these stocks; everyone claimed that the Internet was a communications revolution that would change business forever.

IC: When everyone is excited about the market, you should be extremely cautious. Stock prices are not based just on economic values but on psychological factors that influence the market. Yale economist Robert Shiller, one of the leaders of the behavioral finance movement, has emphasized that fads and social dynamics play a large role in the determination of asset prices.[4] Shiller showed that stock prices have been far too volatile to be explained by fluctuations in economic factors, such as dividends or earnings.[5] He has hypothesized that much of the extra volatility can be explained by fads and fashions that have a large impact on investor decisions.

Dave: I did have my doubts about these Internet stocks, but everyone else seemed so sure they were winners.

IC: Note how others influenced your decision against your better judgment. Psychologists have long known how hard it is to remain separate from a crowd. This was confirmed by a social psychologist named Solomon Asch. He conducted a famous experiment where subjects were presented with four lines and asked to pick the two that were the same length. The right answer was obvious, but when confederates of Dr. Asch presented conflicting views, the subjects often gave the incorrect answer.[6]

Follow-up experiments confirmed that it was not social pressure that led the subjects to act against their own best judgment but their disbelief that a large group of people could be wrong.[7]

Dave: Exactly. So many people were hyping these stocks that I felt there had to be something there. If I didn't buy the Internet stocks, I thought that I was missing out.

IC: I know. The Internet/technology bubble is a perfect example of social pressures influencing stock prices. The conversations around the office, the newspaper headlines, and the analysts' predictions—they all fed the craze to invest in these stocks. Psychologists call this penchant to follow the crowd the *herding instinct*—the tendency of individuals to adapt their thinking to the prevailing opinion.

The Internet bubble has many precedents. In 1852, Charles Mackay wrote the classic *Extraordinary Delusions and the Madness of Crowds*, which chronicled a number of financial bubbles during which speculators were driven into a frenzy by the upward movement of prices: the South Sea bubble in England and the Mississippi bubble in France around 1720 and the tulip mania in Holland a century earlier.[8] Let me read you my favorite passage from the book. See if you can relate to this:

> We find that whole communities suddenly fix their minds upon one subject, and go mad in its pursuit; that millions of people become simultaneously impressed with one delusion and run after it. . . . Sober nations have all at once become desperate gamblers, and risked most of their existence upon the turn of a piece of paper. . . . Men, it has been well said, think in herds. . . . They go mad in herds, while they only recover their senses slowly and one by one.

Dave (*shaking his head*): This happens again and again through history. Even though others were pointing to those very same excesses last year, I was convinced that "this time is different."

IC: As were many others. The propensity of investors to follow the crowd is a permanent fixture of financial history. There are many times when the "crowd" is right,[9] but often following the crowd can lead you astray.

Dave, have you ever been in a new town and found yourself choosing between two restaurants? One perfectly rational way of deciding, if they are close in distance, is to see which restaurant is busier since there's a good chance that at least some of those patrons have tried both restaurants and have chosen to eat at the better one. But when you eat at the busier restaurant, you are increasing the chance that the next diner, using the same reasoning, will also eat there, and so on. Eventually, everybody will be eating at that one restaurant even though the other one could be much better.

Economists call this decision-making process an *information cascade*, and they believe that it happens often in financial markets.[10] For example, when one company bids for another, often other suitors will join in. When an IPO gets a strong following, other investors join in. Individuals have a feeling that "someone knows something" and that they shouldn't miss out. Sometimes that's right, but very often that is wrong.

Excessive Trading, Overconfidence, and the Representative Bias

IC: Dave, let me shift the subject. From examining your trading records, I see that you were an extremely active trader.

Dave: I had to be. Information was constantly bombarding the market; I felt I had to reposition my portfolio constantly to reflect the new information.

IC: Let me tell you something. Trading does nothing but cause extra anxiety and lower returns. A couple of economists published an article in 2000 called "Trading Is Hazardous to Your Wealth." (And, I may add, to your health also.) Examining the records of tens of thousands of traders, they showed that the returns of the heaviest traders were 7.1 percent below the returns of those who traded infrequently.[11]

Dave: You're right. I think trading has hurt my returns. I thought that I was one step ahead of the other guy, but I guess I wasn't.

IC: It is extraordinarily difficult to be a successful trader. Even bright people who devote their entire energies to trading stocks rarely make superior returns. The problem is that most people are simply *overconfident* in their own abilities. To put it another way, the average individual—whether a student, a trader, a driver, or anything else—believes he or she is better than average, which of course is statistically impossible.[12]

Dave: What causes this overconfidence?

IC: Overconfidence comes from several sources. First, there is what we call a *self-attribution bias* that causes one to take credit for a favorable turn of events when credit is not due.[13]

Dave: Does this ever ring true! I remember in March 2000 bragging to my wife about how smart I was to have bought those Internet stocks. And was I wrong!

IC: Your early success fed your overconfidence.[14] You and your friends attributed your stock gains to skillful investing, even though those outcomes were frequently the result of chance.

Another source of overconfidence comes from the tendency to see too many parallels between events that seem the same.[15] This is called the *representative bias*. This bias actually arises because of the human learning process. When we see something that looks familiar, we form a representative heuristic to help us learn. But the parallels we see are often not valid, and our conclusions are misguided.

Dave: The investment newsletters I get say that every time such-and-such event has occurred in the past, the market has moved in a certain direction, implying that it is bound to do so again. But when I try to use that advice, it never works.

IC: Conventional finance economists have been warning for years about finding patterns in the data when, in fact, there are none. Searching past data for patterns is called "data mining," and it is easier than ever to do, with computing power becoming so cheap.[16] Throw in a load of variables to explain stock price movements, and you are sure to find some spectacular fits—like over the past 100 years stocks have risen on every third Thursday of the month when the moon is full!

The representative bias has been responsible for some spectacularly wrong moves in the stock market, even when the situations seem remarkably similar. When World War I broke out in July 1914, officials at the New York Stock Exchange thought it was such a calamity, that the exchange closed down for five months. Wrong! The United States became the arms merchant for Europe; business boomed, and 1915 was one of the single best years in stock market history.

When Germany invaded Poland in September 1939, investors looked at the behavior of the market when World War I broke out. Noting the fantastic returns, they bought stocks like mad and sent the market up by more than 7 percent on the next day's trading! But this was wrong again. FDR was determined not to let the corporations prosper from World War II as they had from World War I. After a few more up days, the stock market headed into a severe bear market, and it wasn't until nearly six years later that the market returned to its September 1939 level. Clearly, the representative bias was the culprit for this error, and the two events weren't as similar as people thought.

Psychologically, human beings are not designed to accept all the randomness that is out there.[17] It is very discomforting to learn that most movements in the market are random and do not have any identifiable cause or reason. Individuals possess a deep psychological need to know why something happens. That is where the reporters and "experts" come in. They are more than happy to fill the holes in our knowledge with explanations that are wrong more often than not.

Dave: I can relate personally to this bias. I remember that before I bought the technology stocks in July 2000, my broker compared these companies to the suppliers providing the gear for the gold rushers of the 1850s. It seemed like an insightful comparison at the time, but in fact the situations were very different. It is interesting that my broker, who is supposed to be the expert, is subject to the same overconfidence that I am.

IC: There is actually evidence that experts are even more subject to over-confidence than the nonexperts. The so-called experts have been trained to analyze the world in a particular way, and they sell their advice based on finding supporting—not contradictory—evidence.[18]

Recall the failure of analysts in 2000 to change their earnings fore-casts for the technology sector despite the news that suggested that something was seriously wrong with their view of the whole industry. After being fed an upbeat outlook by corporations for many years, ana-lysts had no idea how to interpret the downbeat news, so most just ignored it.

The propensity to shut out bad news was even more pronounced among analysts in the Internet sector. Many were so convinced that these stocks were the wave of the future that, despite the flood of ghastly news, many downgraded these stocks only *after* they had fallen 80 or 90 percent!

Confronting news that does not correspond to one's worldview cre-ates what is called *cognitive dissonance*. Cognitive dissonance is the dis-comfort we encounter when we address evidence that conflicts with our view or suggests that our abilities or actions are not as a good as we thought. We all display a natural tendency to minimize this discomfort, which makes it difficult for us to recognize our overconfidence.

Prospect Theory, Loss Aversion, and the Decision to Hold on to Losing Trades

Dave: I see. Can we talk about individual stocks? Why do I end up hold-ing so many losers in my portfolio?

IC: Remember I said before that Kahneman and Tversky had kicked off behavioral finance with prospect theory? A key concept in their theory was that individuals form a reference point from which they judge their performance. Kahneman and Tversky found that from that reference point individuals are much more upset about losing a given amount of money than about gaining the same amount. The researchers called this behavior *loss aversion*, and they suggested that the decision to hold or sell an investment will be dramatically influenced by whether your stock has gone up or down—in other words, whether you have had a gain or loss.

Dave: One step at a time. What is this "reference point" you talk about?

IC: Let me ask you a question. When you buy a stock, how do you track its performance?

Dave: I calculate how much the stock has gone up or down since I bought it.

IC: Exactly. Often the reference point is the purchase price that investors pay for the stock. Investors become fixated on this reference point to the exclusion of any other information. Richard Thaler from the University of Chicago, who has done seminal work in investor behavior, refers to this as *mental accounting* or *narrow framing*.[19]

When you buy a stock, you open a mental account, with the purchase price as the reference point. Similarly, when you buy a group of stocks together, either you will think of the stocks individually, or you may aggregate the accounts together.[20] Whether your stocks are showing a gain or loss will influence your decision to hold or sell the stock. Moreover, in accounts with multiple losses, you are likely to aggregate individual losses together because thinking about one big loss is an easier pill for you to swallow than thinking of many smaller losses. Avoiding the realization of losses becomes the primary goal of many investors.

Dave: You're right. The thought of realizing those losses on my technology stocks petrified me.

IC: That is a completely natural reaction. Your pride is one of the main reasons why you avoided selling at a loss. Every investment involves an emotional as well as financial commitment that makes it hard to evaluate objectively. You felt good that you sold out of your Internet stocks with a small gain, but the networking stocks you subsequently bought never showed a gain. Even as prospects dimmed, you not only hung on to those stocks but bought more, hoping against hope that they would recover.

Prospect theory predicts that many investors will do as you did—increase your position, and consequently your risk, in an attempt to get even.[21] Interestingly, researchers have found that individuals do sell mutual funds that have lost money, and chase those that record gains. But behavioral finance also has a good explanation for that. With funds, investors can always blame the fund manager for picking bad stocks, which you can't do if you make your own decisions about which stock to buy.[22]

Dave: I never bought any mutual funds, so I only had myself to blame for my losses. I thought that buying more shares when the price sank would increase my chances of recouping my losses when the price went back up.

IC: You and millions of other investors. In 1982, Leroy Gross wrote a manual for stockbrokers in which he called this phenomenon the "get-even-itis disease."[23] He claimed get-even-itis has probably caused more destruction to portfolios than any other mistake.

It is hard for us to admit we've made a bad investment, and it is even harder for us to admit that mistake to others. But to be a successful investor, you have no choice but to do so. Decisions on your portfolio must be made on a forward-looking basis. What has happened in the past cannot be changed. It is a "sunk cost," as economists say. When prospects don't look good, sell the stock whether or not you have a loss.

Dave: I thought the stocks were cheap when I bought more shares. Many were down 50 percent or more from their highs.

IC: Cheap relative to what? Cheap relative to their past price or their future prospects? You thought that a price of 40 for a stock that had been 80 made the stock cheap; what you never considered is the possibility that 40 was still too high. This demonstrates another one of Kahneman and Tversky's behavioral findings: *anchoring*, or the tendency of people facing complex decisions to use an "anchor" or a suggested number to form their judgment.[24] Figuring out the "correct" stock price is such a complex task that it is natural to use the recently remembered stock price as an anchor and then judge the current price a bargain.

Dave: If I follow your advice and sell my losers whenever prospects are dim, I'm going to register a lot more losses on my trades.

IC: Good! Most investors do exactly the opposite, to their detriment. Research has shown that investors sell stocks for a gain 50 percent more frequently than they sell stocks for a loss.[25] This means that stocks that are above their purchase price are 50 percent more likely to be sold than stocks that show a loss. Traders do this even though it is a bad strategy from a trading standpoint and a tax standpoint.

Let me tell you of one short-term trader I successfully counseled. He showed me that 80 percent of his trades made money, but he was down overall since he had lost so much money on his losing trades that they drowned out his winners.

After I counseled him, he became a successful trader. Now he says that only one-third of his trades make money, but overall he's way ahead. When things don't work out as he planned, he gets rid of losing trades quickly while holding on to his winners. There is an old adage on Wall Street that sums up successful trading: "Cut your losers short and let your winners ride."

Rules for Avoiding Behavioral Traps

Dave: I don't feel secure enough to trade again soon. I just want to learn the right long-term strategy. How can I get over these behavioral traps and be a successful long-term investor?

IC: Dave, I'm glad you are not trading, since trading is right for only a very small fraction of my clients.

To be a successful long-term investor, you must set up rules and incentives to keep your investments on track—this is called *precommitment*.[26] Set an asset allocation rule and then stick to it. If you have enough knowledge, you can do this yourself, or else you can do it with an investment advisor. Don't try to second-guess your rule. Remember that the basic factors generating returns change far less than we think as we watch the day-to-day ups and downs of the market. A disciplined investment strategy is almost always a winning strategy.

If you wish, you don't have to eliminate your trading altogether. If you do buy stocks for a short-term trade, establish an absolute selling point to minimize your losses. You don't want to let your losses mount, rationalizing that the stock will eventually come back. Also, don't tell your friends about your trades. Living up to their expectations will make you even more reluctant to take a loss and admit that you were wrong.

Dave: I have to admit that I often enjoyed trading.

IC: If you really enjoy trading, set up a small trading account that is completely separate from the rest of your portfolio. All brokerage costs and all taxes must be paid from this account. Consider that the money you put into this trading account may be completely lost, because it very well may be. And you should never consider exceeding the rigid limit you place on how much money you put into that account.

If that doesn't work, or if you feel nervous about the market or have a compulsion to trade, call me; I can help. And according to news reports, there are some reformed traders who are establishing Traders' Anonymous programs designed to help people who cannot resist the temptations of trading too frequently.[27] Maybe you should look into those programs.

Myopic Loss Aversion, Portfolio Monitoring, and the Equity Risk Premium

Dave: Because of how badly I was doing in the market, I even considered giving up on stocks and sticking with bonds, although I know that in the long run that is a very bad idea. How often do you suggest that I monitor my stock portfolio?

IC: Important question. If you buy stocks, it is very likely that the value will drop below the price you paid, if but for a short time after your purchase. We have already spoken about how loss aversion makes this decline very disturbing. However, since the long-term trend in stocks is upward, if you wait a period of time before checking your portfolio, the probability that you will see a loss decreases.

Two economists, Shlomo Bernartzi and Richard Thaler, tested whether the "monitoring interval" affected the choice between stocks and bonds.[28] They conducted a "learning experiment" in which they allowed individuals to see the returns on two unidentified asset classes. One group was shown the yearly returns on stocks and bonds, and other groups were shown the same returns, but instead of annually, the returns were aggregated over periods of 5, 10, and 20 years. The groups were then asked to pick an allocation between stocks and bonds.

The group that saw yearly returns invested a much smaller fraction in stocks than the groups that saw returns aggregated into longer intervals. This was because the short-term volatility of stocks dissuaded people from choosing that asset class, even though over longer periods it was clearly a better choice.

This tendency to base decisions on the short-term fluctuations in the market has been referred to as *myopic loss aversion*. Since over longer periods, the probability of stocks showing a loss is much smaller, investors influenced by loss aversion would be more likely to hold stocks if they monitored their performance less frequently.

Dave: That's so true. When I look at stocks in the very short run, they seem so risky that I wonder why anyone holds them. But over the long run, the superior performance of equities is so overwhelming, I wonder why anyone doesn't hold stocks!

IC: Exactly. Bernartzi and Thaler claim that myopic loss aversion is the key to solving the *equity premium puzzle*.[29] For years, economists have been trying to figure out why stocks have returned so much more than fixed-income investments. Studies show that over periods of 20 years or more, a diversified portfolio of equities not only offers higher after-inflation returns but is actually safer than government bonds. But because investors concentrate on an investment horizon that is too short, stocks seem very risky, and investors must be enticed to hold stocks with a fat premium. If investors evaluated their portfolio less frequently, the equity premium might fall dramatically.

Bernartzi and Thaler have shown that the high equity premium is consistent with myopic loss aversion and yearly monitoring of returns. But they also showed that if investors had evaluated their portfolio allocation only once every 10 years, the equity premium needed to be only 2 percent to entice investors into stocks. With an evaluation period of 20 years, the premium fell to only 1.4 percent, and it would have been close to 1 percent if the evaluation period were 30 years. Stock prices would have had to rise dramatically to reduce the premium to these low levels.

Dave: Are you saying that perhaps I should not look at my stocks too frequently?

IC: You can look at them all you want, but don't alter your long-term strategy. Remember to set up rules and incentives. Commit to a long-run portfolio allocation, and do not alter it unless there is significant evidence that a certain sector is becoming greatly overpriced relative to its fundamentals, as the technology stocks did at the top of the bubble.

Contrarian Investing and Investor Sentiment: Strategies to Enhance Portfolio Returns

Dave: Is there a way for an investor to take advantage of others' behavioral weakness and earn superior returns from them?

IC: Standing apart from the crowd might be quite profitable. An investor who takes a different view is said to be a *contrarian*, one who dissents from the prevailing opinion. Contrarian strategy was first put forth by Humphrey B. Neill in a pamphlet called "It Pays to Be Contrary," first circulated in 1951 and later turned into a book entitled *The Art of Contrary Thinking*. In it Neill declared: "When everyone thinks alike, everyone is likely to be wrong."[30]

Some contrarian approaches are based on psychologically driven indicators such as investor "sentiment." The underlying idea is that most investors are unduly optimistic when stock prices are high and unduly pessimistic when they are low.

This is not a new concept either. The great investor Benjamin Graham stated almost 80 years ago, "[T]he psychology of the speculator militates strongly against his success. For by relation of cause and effect, he is most optimistic when prices are high and most despondent when they are at bottom."[31]

Dave: But how do I know when the market is too pessimistic and too optimistic? Is that not subjective?

IC: Not entirely. Investors Intelligence, a firm based in New Rochelle, New York, publishes one of the long-standing indicators of investment sentiment. Over the past 50 years, the company has evaluated scores of market newsletters, determining whether each letter is bullish, bearish, or neutral about the future direction of stocks.

From Investors Intelligence data, I computed an index of investor sentiment by finding the ratio of bullish newsletters to bullish plus bearish newsletters (omitting the neutral category). I then measured the returns on stocks subsequent to these sentiment readings.

The investor sentiment indicator since January 1986 is plotted in Figure 22-1. The crash of October 1987 was accompanied by investor pessimism. For the next few years, whenever the market went down, as it did in May and December 1988 and February 1990, investors feared another crash, and sentiment dropped sharply. Bullish sentiment also fell below 50 percent during the Iraqi invasion of Kuwait, the bond market collapse of 1994, the Asian crisis of October 1997, the LTCM bailout of the late summer of 1998, the terrorist attacks of September 2001, and

FIGURE 22–1

Investor Intelligence Sentiment Indicator 1986–2012

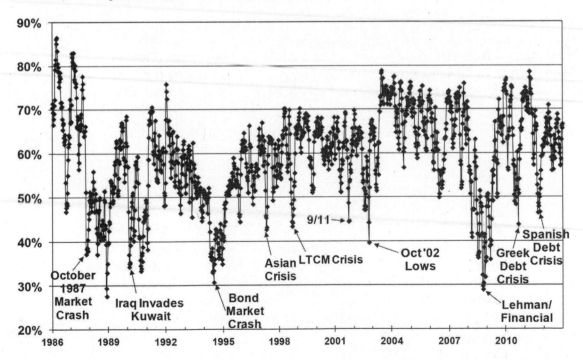

the market bottom of October 2002. Sentiment also plunged at the bottom of the great bear market that followed the financial crisis of 2008, and it also dipped during the Greek and Spanish sovereign debt crises These have all been excellent times to invest.

It is of note that the VIX, the measure of implied market volatility computed from options prices, spikes upward at virtually the same time investor sentiment plunges.[32] Anxiety in the market, which can be measured from the premiums on put options, is strongly negatively correlated with investor sentiment.

Out-of-Favor Stocks and the Dow 10 Strategy

Dave: Can you use contrarian strategy to pick individual stocks?

IC: Yes. Contrarians believe that the swings of optimism and pessimism infect individual stocks as well as the overall markets. Therefore, buying out-of-favor stocks can be a winning strategy.

Werner De Bondt and Richard Thaler examined portfolios of both past stock winners and losers to see if investors became overly optimistic or pessimistic about future returns from studying the returns of the recent past.[33] Portfolios of winning and losing stocks were analyzed over five-year intervals. Portfolios that had been winners in the past five years subsequently lagged the market by 10 percent, while the subsequent returns on the loser portfolio beat the market by 30 percent.

One of the explanations for why this strategy works relates to the representativeness heuristic we talked about before. People extrapolate recent trends in stock prices too far into the future. Although there is some evidence that short-term momentum is positive in stock returns, over the longer term many stocks that have done poorly outperform, and stocks that have done well underperform. Another strategy based on out-of-favor stocks is called the *Dogs of the Dow* or the *Dow 10 strategy*.[34]

Dave: There has been so much to absorb from today's session. It seems like I fell into almost all of these behavioral traps. The comforting news is that I'm not alone and that your counseling has helped other investors.

IC: Not only have they been helped, but they have also prospered. For many people, success in investing requires a much deeper knowledge of themselves than does success in their jobs or even in their personal relationships. There is much truth to an old Wall Street adage, "The stock market is a very expensive place to find out who you are."

PART V

BUILDING WEALTH
THROUGH STOCKS

Fund Performance, Indexing, and Beating the Market

I have little confidence even in the ability of analysts, let alone untrained investors, to select common stocks that will give better than average results. Consequently, I feel that the standard portfolio should be to duplicate, more or less, the DJIA.

—Benjamin Graham, 1934[1]

How can institutional investors hope to outperform the market . . . when, in effect, they are the market?

—Charles D. Ellis, 1975[2]

There is an old story on Wall Street. Two managers of large equity funds go camping in a national park. After setting up camp, the first manager mentions to the other that he overheard the park ranger warning that black bears had been seen around this campsite. The second manager smiles and says, "I'm not worried; I'm a pretty fast runner." The first manager shakes his head and says, "You can't outrun black bears; they've been known to sprint over 25 miles an hour to capture their prey!" The second manager responds, "Of course I know that I can't outrun the bear. The only thing that's important is that I can outrun you!"

In the competitive world of money management, performance is measured not by absolute returns but the returns relative to some benchmark. For stocks these benchmarks include the S&P 500 Index, the Wilshire 5000, global stock indexes, or the latest "style" indexes popular on Wall Street. But there is a crucially important difference about investing compared with virtually any other competitive activity: Most of us have no chance of being as good as the group of individuals who practice for hours to hone their skills. But anyone can be as good as the *average* investor in the stock market with no practice at all.

The reason for this surprising statement is based on a very simple fact: the sum of all investors' holdings must be equal to the market, and the performance of the market must, by definition, be the *average* dollar-weighted performance of each and every investor. Therefore, for each investor's dollar that outperforms the market, there must be another investor's dollar that underperforms the market. By just matching the performance of the overall market, you are guaranteed to do no worse than average.

But how do you match the performance of the whole market? Until 1975, this goal would have been virtually impossible for all but the most affluent investors. Who can hold shares in each of the thousands of firms listed on U.S. exchanges?

However, since the mid-1970s, index mutual funds and then exchange-traded funds have been developed to match the performance of these broad stock indexes. Over the last several decades, the average investor could match the performance of a wide variety of market indexes with very low costs and a very modest investment. And over the last several years, new indexes have been developed, based on the research discussed in Chapter 12, that may allow investors to outperform the averages.

THE PERFORMANCE OF EQUITY MUTUAL FUNDS

Many claim that striving for average market performance is not the best strategy. If there are enough poorly informed traders who consistently underperform the market, then it might be possible for informed investors or professionals who study stocks to outperform the market.

Unfortunately, the past record of the vast majority of such actively managed funds does not support this contention. There are two ways to measure long-term fund returns. One is to compute the returns of all funds that have survived over the period examined. But the long-term returns on these funds suffer from *survivorship bias* that overestimates the returns available to investors. This survivorship bias exists because poorly performing funds are often terminated, leaving only the more successful ones with superior track records to be included in the data. The second, and more accurate, method is to compute, year by year, the average performance of all equity mutual funds that were available to investors in that year.

Both of these computations are shown in Table 23-1. From January 1971 through December 2012, the average U.S. equity mutual fund returned 9.23 percent annually, 1 percentage point behind the Wilshire 5000 and 0.88 percentage point behind the S&P 500 Index.

Indeed, the survivor funds returned 0.25 percent more per year than the Wilshire 5000, but there were only 86 such funds out of thousands. And all these fund returns exclude sales and redemption fees that would reduce their net returns to investors even more.[3]

The underperformance of mutual funds does not happen every year. Actively managed equity funds did, on average, outperform the Wilshire 5000 and the S&P 500 Indexes during the period from 1975 through 1983 when small stocks returned a spectacular 35.32 percent per year. Equity mutual funds generally do well when small stocks outperform large stocks, as many money managers seek to boost performance by buying smaller-sized firms. But since 1983, when the small stocks surge ended, the performance of the average mutual fund has been worse than over the whole period. Even survivor funds have underperformed the Wilshire 5000 Index over the last three decades.

TABLE   23–1

Equity Mutual Funds and Benchmark Returns, 1971–2012

	All Funds	"Survivor" Funds	Wilshire 5000	S&P 500	Small Stocks	All Funds Minus Wilshire 5000	"Survivor" Funds Minus Wilshire 5000
1971–2012	9.23% (17.67%)	10.48% (17.27%)	10.23% (18.18%)	10.11% (17.74%)	11.85% (21.93%)	0.99%	0.25%
1975–1983	18.83% (12.92%)	20.28% (13.06%)	17.94% (14.98%)	15.84% (15.59%)	35.32% (14.35%)	0.89%	2.34%
1984–2012	8.92% (17.05%)	9.72% (16.56%)	10.19% (17.63%)	10.44% (17.44%)	8.54% (18.93%)	–1.27%	–0.47%

Std. deviation in parentheses

The percentage of general equity funds that has outperformed the Wilshire 5000 and the S&P 500 Index each year from 1972 to 2012 is displayed in Figure 23-1.

During this 40-year period, there were only 12 years when a majority of mutual funds beat the Wilshire 5000. All but two of these years occurred during a period when small stocks outperformed large stocks. In the last 25 years, there have been only 6 years when more than one-half of equity mutual funds outperformed the broad market.

The underperformance of mutual funds did not begin in the 1970s. In 1970, Becker Securities Corporation startled Wall Street by compiling the track record of managers of corporate pension funds. Becker showed that the median performance of these managers lagged behind the S&P 500 by 1 percentage point and that only one-quarter of them were able to outperform the market.[4] This study followed on the heels of academic

FIGURE 23–1

Percentage of Equity Funds that Outperform Market Indexes, 1972–2012

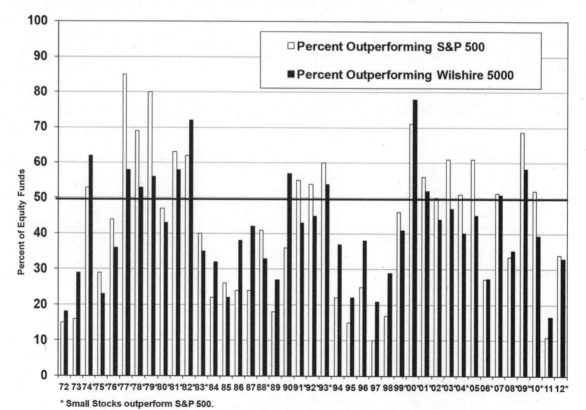

* Small Stocks outperform S&P 500.

articles, particularly those by William Sharpe and Michael Jensen, that also confirmed the underperformance of equity mutual funds.

Figure 23-2 displays the distribution of the difference between the returns of 86 mutual funds that have survived since January 1972 and the Wilshire 5000.

Only 38, or less than one-half, of the 86 funds that have survived over the past 35 years have been able to outperform the Wilshire 5000. Only 22 have been able to outperform the market by more than 1 percent per year, while only 7 have bettered the market by at least 2 percent. On the other hand, over half of the surviving funds underperformed the market, and almost half of those underperformed by more than 1 percent per year. And as noted above for Table 23-1, the actual returns on many of these funds are worse since these returns exclude sales and redemption fees.

Despite the generally poor performance of equity mutual funds, there are some winners as shown in Table 23-2. The best-performing mutual fund over the entire period is the Sequoia Fund, run by the investment firm of Ruane, Cunniff, & Goldfarb, which gave investors a

F I G U R E   23–2

Performance of Surviving Mutual Funds Relative to the Wilshire 5000, 1972–2012

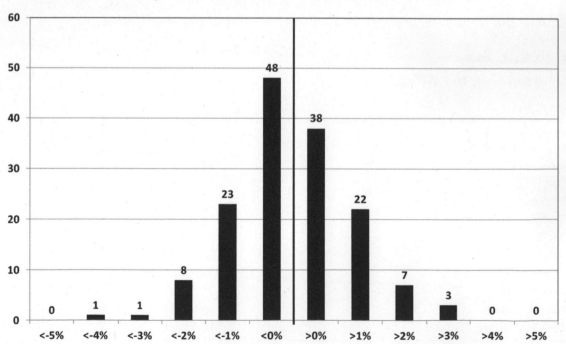

14.2% annual return from 1972 through 2012, beating the Wilshire 5000 Return by 4 percentage points per year. The fund closely follows Warren Buffett's philosophy and has a large portion of its holdings in Berkshire Hathaway. In second place is Mutual Shares Z Fund, run by Franklin Templeton, with a return of 13.7 percent per year. Fidelity's Magellan Fund occupies third place by posting a 13.6 percent annual return from 1971 through December 2012, followed by the Columbia Acorn Fund (previously known as the Liberty Acorn Fund), run by Charles McQuaid and Robert Mohn, posting a 12.9% return.

Despite these sparkling returns, chance may have played a large role in these outperformers. The probability that a fund would beat the Wilshire 5000 by 4 percentage points or more over this period by chance alone is 1 in 12. That means out of the 86 funds examined, one would expect 7 to have done this well, but only one did.

Yet luck could not explain Magellan's performance from 1977 through 1990. During that period, the legendary stock picker Peter Lynch ran the Magellan Fund and outperformed the market by an incredible 13 percent per year. Magellan took somewhat greater risks in achieving this return,[5] but the probability that Magellan would outperform the Wilshire 5000 by this margin over that 14-year period by luck alone is only 1 in 500,000!

An even longer record of outperformance belongs to Warren Buffett, the legendary investor in Berkshire Hathaway, a small textile

TABLE 23–2

Top Performing Mutual Funds 1972–2012

Mutual Fund	Annual Return
Sequoia Fund	14.2%
Mutual Shares Z	13.7%
Fidelity Magellan Fund	13.6%
Columbia Acorn Fund	12.9%
T Rowe Price Small Cap	12.9%
Fidelity Contrafund	12.4%
Davis NY Venture A	12.4%
Invesco Comstock A	12.3%
Fidelity Adv Diversified O	12.2%
Janus Fund D	12.1%
Wilshire 5000	**10.2%**
S&P 500 Index	**10.1%**

firm that he purchased in 1965. Berkshire was not part of the universe examined above since it is a "closed-end" fund, which contains both traded and nontraded assets. Buffett's annualized return from 1972 through 2012 is 20.1 percent per year, more than 10 percentage points per year in excess of the S&P 500. The probability that this return was achieved purely by chance is less than one in a billion.

In 1984, in honor of the fiftieth anniversary of the publication of Graham and Dodd's *Security Analysis*, Buffett delivered a speech at Columbia University entitled the "The Superinvestors of Graham-and-Doddsville," which detailed nine money managers who have greatly outperformed the market by using the value-oriented approach advocated by Graham and Dodd.[6] Buffett's claim is supported by the data presented in Chapter 12 that show the outperformance of value-tilted strategies.

FINDING SKILLED MONEY MANAGERS

It is easy to determine that Warren Buffett's and Peter Lynch's performances were due to their skill in picking stocks. But for more mortal portfolio managers, it is extremely difficult to determine with any degree of confidence whether the superior returns of money managers are due to skill or luck. Table 23-3 computes the probability that managers with better-than-average stock-picking ability will outperform the market.[7]

The results are surprising. Even if money managers choose stocks that have an expected return of 1 percent per year better than the market, there is only a 62.7 percent probability that they will exceed the average market return after 10 years and only a 71.2 percent probability that they will exceed the average market return after 30 years. If managers pick

T A B L E   23–3

Probability of Outperforming Market Given Historical Risks and Returns from 1972–2012

Expected Excess Return	Holding Period (Years)						
	1	2	3	5	10	20	30
1%	54.1%	55.7%	57.0%	59.0%	62.7%	67.6%	71.2%
2%	58.1%	61.3%	63.8%	67.5%	74.0%	81.9%	86.7%
3%	61.9%	66.6%	70.1%	75.2%	83.2%	91.3%	95.2%
4%	65.7%	71.6%	75.8%	81.7%	89.9%	96.4%	98.6%
5%	69.2%	76.1%	80.8%	86.9%	94.4%	98.8%	99.7%

stocks that will outperform the market by 2 percent per year, there is still only a 74.0 percent chance that they will outperform the market after 10 years. This means there is a 1-in-4 chance that they will still fall short of the average market performance. The length of time needed to be reasonably certain that superior managers will outperform the market will most surely outlive their trial period for determining their real worth.

Detecting a bad manager is an equally difficult task. In fact, a money manager would have to underperform the market by 4 percent a year for almost 15 years before you could be statistically certain (defined to mean being less than 1 chance in 20 of being wrong) that the manager is actually poor and not just having bad luck. By that time, your assets would have fallen to half of what you would have had by indexing to the market.

Even extreme cases are hard to identify. Surely you would think that a manager who picks stocks that are expected to outperform the market by an average of 5 percent per year, a feat achieved by no surviving mutual fund since 1970, would quickly stand out. But that is not necessarily so. After one year there is only a 7-in-10 chance that such a manager will outperform the market. And the probability rises to only 76.8 percent that the manager will outperform the market after two years.

Assume you gave a young, undiscovered Peter Lynch—someone who over the long run will outperform the market with a 5 percent per year edge—an ultimatum: that he will be fired if he does not at least match the market after two years. Table 23-3 shows that the probability he will beat the market over two years is only 76.1 percent. This means there is almost a 1-in-4 chance that he will still underperform the market and you will fire Lynch, judging him incapable of picking winning stocks!

Persistence of Superior Returns

Do some money managers have "hot hands," meaning that if they outperformed the averages in the past, they are likely to do it again in the future? The conclusions of numerous studies are not clear-cut. There is some evidence that funds that outperform in one year are more likely to outperform the next.[8] This short-run persistence is probably because managers follow a particular "style" of investing, and styles often stay in favor over several years.

But over longer periods, the ability of fund managers to continue to outperform the market finds less support. Edward Elton, Martin Gruber, and Christopher Blake claim that outperformance persists over three-year periods,[9] but Burton Malkiel, Jack Bogle, and others disagree.[10, 11] In any case, performance can change suddenly and unpredictably. Perhaps Magellan's underperformance after Peter Lynch left the fund did not surprise some investors. But Bill Miller's hot hand with Legg Mason's Value Trust, which recorded a record 15 consecutive years of beating the S&P 500 Index, suddenly and unexpectedly turned cold in 2006 and 2007.

REASONS FOR UNDERPERFORMANCE OF MANAGED MONEY

The generally poor performance of funds relative to the market is not because the fund managers are picking losing stocks. Their performance lags the benchmarks largely because funds impose fees and trading costs that are often as high as 2 percent or more per year. First, in seeking superior returns, a manager buys and sells stocks, which involves paying brokerage commissions and also paying the bid-asked spread, or the difference between the buying and the selling price of shares. Second, investors pay management fees (and possibly sales, or "load," fees) to the organizations and individuals that sell these funds. Finally, managers are often competing with other managers with equal or superior skills at choosing stocks. As noted earlier, it is a mathematical impossibility for everyone to do better than the market—for every dollar that outperforms the average, some other investor's dollar must underperform the average.

A LITTLE LEARNING IS A DANGEROUS THING

It is interesting that an investor who has some knowledge of the principles of equity valuations often performs worse than someone with no knowledge who decides to index his portfolio. For example, take the novice—an investor who is just learning about stock valuation. This is the investor to whom most of the books entitled *How to Beat the Market* are sold. A novice might note that the stock has just reported very good earnings but its price is not rising as much as he believes is justified by this good news, and so he buys the stock.

Yet informed investors know that special circumstances caused the earnings to increase and that these circumstances will not likely be repeated in the future. Informed investors are therefore more than happy to sell the stock to novices, realizing that the rise in the price of the stock is not justified. Informed investors make a return on their special knowledge. They make their return from novices who believe they have found a bargain. Uninformed indexed investors, who do not even know what the earnings of the company are, often do better than the investor who is just beginning to learn about equities.

The saying "a little learning is a dangerous thing" proves itself to be quite apt in financial markets. Many seeming anomalies or discrepancies in the prices of stocks (or most other financial assets, for that matter) are due to the trading of informed investors with special information that is not easily processed by others. When a stock looks too cheap or too dear, the easy explanation—that emotional or ignorant traders have incorrectly priced the stock—is usually wrong. Most often there is a good reason why stocks are priced as they are. This is why beginners who buy individual stocks on the basis of their own research often do quite badly.

PROFITING FROM INFORMED TRADING

As novices become more informed, they will no doubt find some stocks that are genuinely undervalued or overvalued. Trading these stocks will begin to offset their transaction costs and their poorly informed, losing trades. At some point, a trader might become well enough informed to overcome the transaction costs and match, or perhaps exceed the market return. The key word here is *might*, because the number of investors who have consistently been able to outperform the market is small indeed. And for individuals who do not devote much time to analyzing stocks, the possibility of consistently outperforming the averages is remote.

Yet the apparent simplicity of picking winners and avoiding losers lures many investors into active trading. We learned in Chapter 22 that there is an inherent tendency of individuals to view themselves and their performance as above average. The investment game draws some of the best minds in the world. Many investors are wrongly convinced that they are smarter than the next guy who is playing the same investing game. But even being just as smart as the next investor is not good enough. Being average at the game of finding market winners will result in underperforming the market as transaction costs diminish returns.

In 1975, Charles D. Ellis, a managing partner at Greenwood Associates, wrote an influential article called "The Loser's Game." In it he showed that, with transaction costs taken into account, average money managers must outperform the market by margins that are not possible, given that they themselves are the major market players. Ellis concludes: "Contrary to their oft articulated goal of outperforming the market averages, investment managers are not beating the market; the market is beating them."[12]

HOW COSTS AFFECT RETURNS

Trading and managerial costs of 2 or 3 percent a year might seem small compared with the year-to-year volatility of the market and, as well, might seem small to investors who are gunning for 20 or 30 percent annual returns. But such costs are extremely detrimental to long-term wealth accumulation. Investing $1,000 at a compound return of 11 percent per year, near the average nominal return on stocks since World War II, will accumulate $23,000 over 30 years. A 1 percent annual fee will reduce the final accumulation by almost a third. With a 3 percent annual fee, the accumulation amounts to just over $10,000, less than half the market return. Every extra percentage point of annual costs requires investors aged 25 to retire 2 years later than they would have in the absence of such costs.

THE INCREASED POPULARITY OF PASSIVE INVESTING

Many investors have realized that the poor performance of actively managed funds relative to benchmark indexes strongly implies that they would do very well to just *equal* the market return of one of the broad-based indexes. Thus, the 1990s witnessed an enormous increase in *passive investing*, the placement of funds whose sole purpose was to match the performance of an index.

The oldest and most popular of the index funds is the Vanguard 500 Index Fund.[13] The fund, started by visionary John Bogle, raised only $11.4 million when it debuted in 1976, and few thought the concept would survive. But slowly and surely, indexing gathered momentum, and the fund's assets reached $17 billion at the end of 1995.

In the latter stages of the 1990s bull market, the popularity of indexing soared. By March 2000, when the S&P 500 Index reached its all-time high, the fund claimed the title of the world's largest equity fund, with assets over $100 billion. Indexing became so popular that in the first six months of 1999 nearly 70 percent of the money that was invested went into index funds.[14] By 2013, all Vanguard 500 Index funds had attracted over $275 billion in assets, and Vanguard's Total Stock Market Funds, which include smaller stocks, attracted $250 billion.

One of the attractions of index funds is their extremely low cost. The total annual cost in the Vanguard 500 Index Fund is only 0.15 percent of market value (and as low as 2 basis points for large institutional investors). Because of proprietary trading techniques and interest income from loaning securities, Vanguard S&P 500 Index funds for individual investors have fallen only 9 basis points behind the index over the last 10 years, and its S&P 500 Index fund for institutional investors has actually outperformed the benchmark index.[15]

THE PITFALLS OF CAPITALIZATION-WEIGHTED INDEXING

Despite the past success of index funds, their popularity, especially those funds linked to the S&P 500 Index, may cause problems for index investors in the future. The reason is simple. If a firm's mere entry into the S&P 500 causes the price of its stock to rise, due to the anticipated buying by index funds, index funds will hold a number of overpriced stocks that will depress future returns.

An extreme example of overpricing occurred when Yahoo!, the well-known Internet firm, was added to the S&P 500 Index in December 1999. Standard & Poor's announced after the close of trading on November 30 that Yahoo! would be added to the index on December 8. The next morning, Yahoo! opened at $115—up almost $9 per share from its close the day before—and continued upward to close at $174 a share on December 7, when index funds had to buy the shares in order to match the index. In just 5 trading days between the announcement of Yahoo!'s inclusion in the index until it formally became a member, the stock surged 64 percent. Volume during those 5 days averaged 37 million shares, more than three times the average on the previous 30 days. On December 7, when index funds had to own the stock, volume hit 132 million shares, representing $22 billion of Yahoo! stock traded.

This story is repeated with most stocks added to the index, although the average size of the gain is considerably less than Yahoo!'s. Standard & Poor's published a study in September 2000 that had determined how adding a stock to an S&P index influenced the price. This study noted that from the announcement date to the effective date of admission in the S&P 500 Index, shares rose by an average of 8.49 percent.[16] During the next 10 days following their entrance, these stocks fell by an average of 3.23 percent, or about one-third of the preentry gain. Yet one year after the announcement, these postentry losses were wiped out, and the average gain of new entrants was 8.98 percent. All these percentages were corrected for movements in the overall market. A later study has shown that although the preentry gain has fallen in recent years, the price of stocks admitted to the S&P 500 still has jumped over 4 percent in response to the announcement.[17]

FUNDAMENTALLY WEIGHTED VERSUS CAPITALIZATION-WEIGHTED INDEXATION

Despite the overpricing of new entrants into the S&P 500 Index, virtually all indexes that have a significant investment following, such as those created by Standard & Poor's, the Russell Investment Group, or Wilshire Associates, are *capitalization weighted*. That means that each firm in the index is weighted by the *market value*, or the current price times the number of shares outstanding. More recently, most of these indexes adjust the quantity of shares by excluding *insider holdings*, which consist of large positions held by insiders and governments from the total shares outstanding. Government holdings can be especially large in the emerging economies. The number of shares after this adjustment is called *float-adjusted shares*, where *float* refers to the number of shares that are readily available to buy.[18]

To be sure, capitalization-weighted indexes have some very good properties. First, as noted earlier in the chapter, these indexes represent the *average* dollar-weighted performance of all investors, so that for anyone who does better than the index, someone else must do worse. Furthermore, these portfolios, under the assumptions of an efficient market, give investors the "best" trade-off between risk and return. This means that for any given risk level, these capitalization-weighted portfolios give the highest returns; and for any given return, these portfolios give the lowest risk. This property is called *mean-variance efficiency*.

But the assumptions under which these desirable properties prevail are very stringent. Capitalization-weighted portfolios are optimal only if the market is *efficient* in the sense that the price of each stock is at all points in time an unbiased estimate of the true underlying value of the enterprise. This does not mean that the price of each stock is always right; but it does mean that there is no easily obtainable information that allows investors to make a better estimate of its true value. Under efficient markets, if a stock goes from $20 to $25 a share, the best estimate of the change in the underlying value of the enterprise is also 25 percent, and there are *no* factors unrelated to fundamental value that could change the stock price.

But as we learned in Chapter 12, there are many reasons why stock prices change that do not reflect changes in the underlying value of the firm. Transactions made for liquidity, fiduciary, or tax reasons can impact stock prices, as well as speculators acting on unfounded or exaggerated information. When stock price movements can be caused by factors unrelated to fundamental changes in firm value, market prices are "noisy" and are no longer unbiased estimates of true value. As noted earlier in the book, I call this way of looking at the market the noisy market hypothesis, and I find it an attractive alternative to the efficient market hypothesis that has dominated the finance profession over the last 40 years.

If the noisy market hypothesis is a better representation of how markets work, the capitalization-weighted indexes are no longer the best portfolios for investors. A better index is a *fundamentally weighted* index, in which each stock is weighted by some measure of a firm's fundamental financial data, such as dividends, earnings, cash flows, and book value, instead of the market capitalization of its stock.[19]

Fundamentally weighted indexes work in the following manner. Assume earnings are chosen as the measure of firm value. If E represents the total dollar earnings of the stocks chosen for the index, and E_j is the earnings from a particular firm j, then the weight given to firm j in the fundamental index is E_j/E, its share of total earnings rather than its share of the market value as is done in capitalization-weighted indexes.

In a capitalization-weighted index, stocks are never sold no matter what price they reach. This is because if markets are efficient, the price represents the fundamental value of the firm, and no purchase or sale is warranted.

However, in a fundamentally weighted index, if a stock price rises but the fundamental, such as earnings, does not, then shares are sold until the value of the stock in the index is brought down to the original levels. The opposite happens when a stock falls for reasons not related to fundamentals—in this case shares are purchased at the lower price to bring the stock's value back to the original levels. Making these sales or purchases is called *rebalancing* the fundamentally weighted portfolio, and it usually takes place once per year.

One of the advantages of fundamentally weighted portfolios is that they avoid "bubbles," those meteoric increases in the prices of stocks that are not accompanied by increases in dividends, earnings, or other objective metrics of firm values. This was certainly the case in 1999 and early 2000 when the technology and Internet stocks jumped to extraordinary valuations based on the hope that their profits would eventually justify their price. Any fundamentally weighted portfolio would have sold these stocks as their prices rose, while capitalization-weighted indexes continued to hold them because the efficient market hypothesis assumes that all price increases are justified.

Note that fundamental indexation does not identify which stocks are overvalued or undervalued. It is a "passive" index, and the purchases and sales of individual stocks are made according to a predetermined formula. Certainly some overpriced stocks will be bought and some underpriced stocks sold. But it can be shown that if prices are determined by the noisy market hypothesis, then, on average, a portfolio that buys stocks that go down more than fundamentals and sells stocks that go up more than fundamentals will boost returns over a capitalization-weighted index and reduce risk.[20]

THE HISTORY OF FUNDAMENTALLY WEIGHTED INDEXATION

The motivation for fundamentally weighted indexation began in the international markets. In the 1980s, when Japan's stock market was in a bubble, many investors with internationally diversified portfolios were seeking a consistent way to reduce the weight of Japanese stocks. At that time Morgan Stanley Capital International (MSCI) formulated an international index that weighted each country by GDP rather than market capitalization and fortunately reduced the allocation to Japanese stocks.[21]

In 1987 Robert Jones of Goldman Sachs's quantitative asset management group developed and managed a U.S. stock index in which the weights of each firm in the index were corporate profits. Jones referred to his strategy as "economic investing" because the proportion of each firm in the index was related to its economic importance rather its market capitalization.[22] Later David Morris, founder and CEO of Global Wealth Allocation, devised a strategy that combined several fundamental factors into one "wealth" variable.

In 2003, Paul Wood and Richard Evans published research on a fundamentally based approach that evaluated a profit-weighted index of the 100 largest companies.[23] In early 2005, Robert D. Arnott of Research Affiliates, along with Jason Hsu and Philip Moore, published a paper in the *Financial Analysts Journal* entitled "Fundamental Indexation" that exposed the flaws of capitalization-weighted indexes and laid the case for fundamentally based strategies.[24] In December 2005, the first fundamentally weighted ETF was launched by Powershares (FTSE RAFI US1000) to track an index constructed by Research Affiliates based on sales, cash flows, book values, and dividends. Six months later, WisdomTree Investments launched 20 ETFs based on dividends and followed up in 2007 with six more based on earnings.

The historical evidence to support fundamentally weighted indexation is impressive. From 1964 through 2012, the compound annual return on a dividend-weighted index based on virtually all U.S. stocks was 10.84 percent per year, 117 basis points above a similar capitalization-weighted portfolio based on the same stocks, while the volatility and beta of the dividend-weighted portfolio were less than the capitalization-weighted portfolio. This return outperformance with lower volatility was reported across size sectors and internationally. Specifically, from 1996 through 2012, a dividend-weighted MSCI EAFE Index outperformed an EAFE Index by nearly 3½ percentage points per year.

The long-term outperformance of fundamentally weighted indexes principally relies on their emphasis of value-based strategies. Stocks with higher-than-average dividend yields or lower-than-average P/E ratios receive greater weights in fundamentally weighted indexes than capitalization-weighted indexes. But fundamentally weighted indexes are better diversified than portfolios of only value stocks, and historically they have had better risk-returns trade-offs. In short, fundamentally weighted indexes have very attractive characteristics that challenge the supremacy of capitalization-weighted indexes for long-term investors.

CONCLUSION

The past performance of actively managed equity funds is not encouraging. The fees that most funds charge do not provide investors with superior returns and can be a significant drag on wealth accumulation. Furthermore, a good money manager is extremely difficult to identify, for luck plays a role in all successful investment outcomes.

When costs are taken into account, a large percentage of actively managed equity funds significantly lag the benchmark indexes, and most investors would be better off in capitalization-weighted or fundamentally weighted index funds.

Structuring a Portfolio for Long-Term Growth

[The] long run is a misleading guide to current affairs. In the long run we are all dead. Economists set themselves too easy, too useless a task if in tempestuous seasons they can only tell us when the storm is long past, the ocean will be flat.

—JOHN MAYNARD KEYNES, 1924[1]

My favorite holding period is forever.

—WARREN BUFFETT, 1994[2]

No one can argue with Keynes's statement that in the long run we are all dead. But a vision of the long run must serve as a guide for action today. Those who keep their focus and perspective during trying times are far more likely to emerge as successful investors. Knowing that the sea will be flat after the storm passes is not useless, as Keynes asserted, but enormously comforting.

PRACTICAL ASPECTS OF INVESTING

To be a successful long-term investor is easy in principle but difficult in practice. It is easy in principle because the strategy of buying and holding a diversified portfolio of stocks, forgoing any forecasting ability, is available to all investors, no matter what their intelligence, judgment, or financial status. Yet it is difficult in practice, because we are all vulnerable to emotional forces that can lead us astray. Tales of those who have quickly achieved great wealth in the market tempt us to play a game very different from what we had intended.

Selective memory also pushes us in the wrong direction. Those who follow the market closely often exclaim: "I knew that stock (or the market) was going up! If I had only acted on my judgment, I would have made a mint!" But hindsight plays tricks on our minds. We forget the doubts we had when we made the decision not to buy. Hindsight can distort our past experiences and affect our judgment, encouraging us to play hunches and try to outsmart other investors, who in turn are playing the same game.

For most investors, going down this path leads to disastrous results. We take far too many risks, our transactions costs are high, and we find ourselves giving in to the emotions of the moment—pessimism when the market is down and optimism when the market is high. This leads to frustration as our misguided actions result in substantially lower returns than we could have achieved by just staying in the market.

GUIDES TO SUCCESSFUL INVESTING

Achieving good returns in stocks requires keeping a long-term focus and a disciplined investment strategy. The principles enumerated below are taken from the research described in this book and enable both new and seasoned investors to better achieve their investing goals.

1. Keep your expectations in line with history. Historically stocks have returned between 6 and 7 percent after inflation over the last two centuries and have sold at an average P/E ratio of about 15.

A 6.5 percent annual real return, which includes reinvested dividends, will nearly double the purchasing power of your stock portfolio every decade. If inflation stays within the 2 to 3 percent range, nominal stock returns will be 9 percent per year, which doubles the money value of your stock portfolio every eight years.

Despite this excellent long-run record, stock returns are not independent of their valuation. A 6 to 7 percent real return is consistent with a market that trades at about 15 times estimated earnings.

But there is no reason why a 15 P/E ratio will always be the "right" ratio for stock prices. Chapter 12 maintains that there may be reasons, such as lower transaction costs and lower returns on bonds, why the stock market may rise to a higher P/E ratio in the future.

2. Stock returns are much more stable in the long run than in the short run. Over time stocks, in contrast to bonds, compensate investors for higher inflation. Therefore, as your investment horizon becomes longer, put a larger fraction of your assets in equities.

The percentage of your portfolio that you should hold in equities depends on individual circumstances. But based on historical data, an investor with a long-term horizon should keep an overwhelming portion of his or her financial assets in equities. Chapter 6 showed that over holding periods of 20 years or longer, stocks have both a higher return and lower after-inflation risk than bonds.

The only long-term risk-free assets are Treasury inflation-protected securities. In recent years the real yield on these bonds has ranged between minus 1 percent and plus 1 percent, which is considerably below the historical returns on stocks. The difference between the returns on stocks and the returns on bonds is called the equity premium, and historically it has favored stocks in all countries where data are available.

3. Invest the largest percentage of your stock portfolio in low-cost stock index funds.

Chapter 23 showed that the broad-based indexes, such as the Wilshire 5000 and the S&P 500 Index, have outperformed nearly two out of three mutual funds since 1971. By matching the market year after year, an indexed investor is likely to be near the top of the pack when the long-term returns are tallied.

There are many exchange-traded and indexed mutual funds that closely track the major stock market indexes. Investors in capitalization-weighted index funds should insist on a total annual expense ratio under 0.15 percent.

4. Invest at least one-third of your equity portfolio in international stocks, currently defined as those not headquartered in the United States. Stocks in high-growth countries often become overpriced and yield poor returns for investors.

Today the United States has only about one-half of the world's equity capital, and that fraction is declining rapidly. Owning foreign stocks is a must in today's global economy. In the future, the geographic location of the firm's headquarters will lose its importance as an investment factor. What, where, and to whom a firm sells its products will dominate a new classification system.

Despite the increase in the short-term correlation between country returns, the case for international investing is persuasive. In all countries studied, the return on stocks has handily beaten that on bonds and fixed-income assets over the last century. Do not overweight high-growth countries whose valuation ratio exceeds 20 times earnings. The data presented in Chapter 13 show that investors often overpay for such growth.

5. Historically, value stocks—those with lower P/E ratios and higher dividend yields—have superior returns and lower risk than growth stocks. Tilt your portfolio toward value by buying passive indexed portfolios of value stocks or, fundamentally weighted index funds.

Chapter 12 demonstrated that stocks with low P/E ratios and high dividend yields have outperformed the market over the past 50 years and have done so with lower risk. One reason for this outperformance is that prices of stocks are often influenced by factors not related to their true value, such as liquidity and tax-motivated transactions, rumor-based speculation, and buying and selling by momentum traders. In these circumstances, stocks priced low relative to their fundamentals will likely offer investors a better risk-return profile.

Investors can take advantage of this mispricing by buying low-cost passively managed portfolios of value stocks or fundamentally weighted indexes that weight each stock by its share of dividends or earnings rather than by its market value. Historically, fundamentally weighted indexes have had higher returns and lower risks than capital-ization-weighted indexes.

6. Finally, establish firm rules to keep your portfolio on track, especially if you find yourself giving in to the emotion of the moment. If you are particularly anxious about the market, sit down and reread the first chapter of this book.

Swings in investor emotion often send stock prices above and below their fundamental values. The temptations to buy when everyone is bullish and sell when everyone is bearish are hard to resist. Since it is so difficult to stand apart from this market sentiment, most investors who trade frequently have poor returns. Chapter 22 shows how behavioral finance helps investors understand and avoid common psychological pitfalls that cause poor market performance. Chapters 1 and 5 keep investors focused on the big picture about risk and return.

IMPLEMENTING THE PLAN AND THE ROLE
OF AN INVESTMENT ADVISOR

I wrote *Stocks for the Long Run* to spell out what returns could be expected on stocks and bonds and to analyze the major factors influencing those returns. Many investors will consider this book a "do-it-yourself guide" to choosing stocks and structuring a portfolio. But knowing the right investments is not the same as implementing the right investment strategy. As Peter Bernstein so aptly indicated in the Foreword, there are many pitfalls on the path to successful investing that prevent investors from achieving their intended goals.

The first pitfall is trading frequently in an attempt to "beat the market." Many investors are not satisfied earning a 9 percent annual return on stocks when they know there are always stocks that will double or triple in price over the next 12 months. Finding such gems is extremely gratifying, and many dream of buying the next corporate giant in its infancy. But the evidence is overwhelming that investors seeking these winners suffer poor returns as transaction costs and bad timing sink returns.

Investors who have been burned by picking individual stocks often turn to mutual funds in their search for higher returns. But choosing a mutual fund poses similar obstacles. "Hot managers" with superior past performance replace "hot stocks" as the new strategy to beat the market. As a result, many investors end up playing the same game as they had with individual stocks and also suffer below-average returns.

Those who finally abandon trying to pick the best funds are tempted to pursue an even more difficult strategy. They attempt to beat the market by timing market cycles. Surprisingly, it is often the best-informed investors who fall into this trap. With the abundance of financial news, information, and commentary at our beck and call, it is extraordinarily difficult to stay aloof from market opinion. As a result, one's impulse is to capitulate to fear when the market is plunging or to greed when stocks are soaring.

Many try to resist this impulse. The intellect may say "Stay the course!" but this is not easy to do when one hears so many others—including well-respected "experts"—advising investors to beat a hasty retreat. It is easier to follow what everyone else is doing rather than act independently. And as John Maynard Keynes aptly stated in *The General Theory*, "Worldly wisdom teaches that it is better for reputation to fail conventionally than to succeed unconventionally."[3] Failing by following the advice of "experts" is far easier than failing by rejecting the investment consensus and standing apart from the crowd.

What does all this mean to the reader of this book? Proper investment strategy is as much of a psychological as an intellectual challenge. As with other challenges in life, it is often best to seek professional help to structure and maintain a well-diversified portfolio. If you should decide to seek help, be sure to select a professional investment advisor who agrees with the basic principles of diversification and long-term investing that I have espoused in these chapters. It is within the grasp of all to avoid investing pitfalls and reap the generous rewards that are available in equities.

CONCLUDING COMMENT

The stock market is exciting. Its daily movements dominate the financial press and mark the flows of billions of dollars of investment capital. But stock markets are far more than the quintessential symbol of capitalism. Stock markets are now found in virtually every country in the world, and they are the driving forces behind the allocation of the world's capital and the fundamental engines of economic growth. The main thesis of this book, that stocks represent the best way to accumulate wealth in the long run, remains as true today as it was when I published the first edition of *Stocks for the Long Run* in 1994.

NOTES

Chapter 1

1. Benjamin Graham and David Dodd, *Security Analysis*, New York: McGraw-Hill, 1934, p. 11.
2. Roger Lowenstein, "A Common Market: The Public's Zeal to Invest," *Wall Street Journal*, September 9, 1996, p. A11.
3. Comment on a CNBC show in March 2009, at the bottom of the 2008–2009 bear market.
4. Irving Fisher, *The Stock Market Crash and After*, New York: Macmillan, 1930, p. xi.
5. "The Crazy Things People Say to Rationalize Stock Prices," *Forbes*, April 27, 1992, p. 150.
6. Raskob catered to investors who wanted to get rich quickly by devising an alternative scheme by which investors borrowed $300, adding $200 of personal capital, to invest $500 in stocks. Although in 1929 this was certainly not as good as putting money gradually into the market, even this plan beat investment in Treasury bills after 20 years.
7. Irving Fisher, *How to Invest When Prices Are Rising*, Scranton, PA: G. Lynn Sumner & Co., 1912.
8. Edgar L. Smith, *Common Stocks as Long-Term Investments*, New York: Macmillan, 1925, p. v.
9. Ibid., p. 81.
10. "Ordinary Shares as Investments," *The Economist*, June 6, 1925, p. 1141.
11. John Maynard Keynes, "An American Study of Shares Versus Bonds as Permanent Investments," *The Nation & The Athenaeum*, May 2, 1925, p. 157.
12. Edgar Lawrence Smith, "Market Value of Industrial Equities," *Review of Economic Statistics*, vol. 9 (January 1927), pp. 37–40, and "Tests Applied to an Index of the Price Level for Industrial Stocks," *Journal of the American Statistical Association*, Supplement, March 1931, pp. 127–135.
13. Siegfried Stern, *Fourteen Years of European Investments, 1914–1928*, London: Bankers' Publishing Co., 1929.
14. Chelcie C. Bosland, *The Common Stock Theory of Investment, Its Development and Significance*, New York: Ronald Press, 1937.
15. From the Foreword by Irving Fisher in Kenneth S. Van Strum, *Investing in Purchasing Power*, New York: Barron's, 1925, p. vii. Van Strum was a writer for *Barron's* weekly and confirmed Smith's research.
16. Robert Loring Allen, *Irving Fisher: A Biography*, Cambridge: Blackwell, 1993, p. 206.
17. *Commercial and Financial Chronicle*, September 7, 1929.
18. "Fisher Sees Stocks Permanently High," *New York Times*, October 16, 1929, p. 2.
19. Lawrence Chamberlain and William W. Hay, *Investment and Speculations*, New York: Henry Holt & Co., 1931, p. 55, emphasis his.
20. Benjamin Graham and David Dodd, *Security Analysis*, 2nd ed., New York: McGraw-Hill, 1940, p. 357.

21. He estimated the undervaluation at approximately 25 percent of "intrinsic value." Alfred Cowles III and Associates, *Common Stock Indexes 1871–1937*, Bloomington, IN: Principia Press, 1938, p. 50.

22. Wilford J. Eiteman and Frank P. Smith, *Common Stock Values and Yields*, Ann Arbor: University of Michigan Press, 1962, p. 40.

23. "Rates of Return on Investment in Common Stocks," *Journal of Business*, vol. 37 (January 1964), pp. 1–21.

24. Ibid., p. 20.

25. *Journal of Business*, vol. 49 (January 1976), pp. 11–43.

26. *Stocks, Bonds, Bills, and Inflation Yearbooks, 1983–1997*, Chicago: Ibbotson and Associates.

27. William Baldwin, "The Crazy Things People Say to Rationalize Stock Prices," *Forbes*, April 27, 1992, pp. 140–150.

28. Three months later, in December 1995, Shulman capitulated to the bullish side, claiming his longtime emphasis on dividend yields was incorrect.

29. Roger Lowenstein, "A Common Market: The Public's Zeal to Invest," *Wall Street Journal*, September 9, 1996, p. A1.

30. Floyd Norris, "In the Market We Trust," *New York Times*, January 12, 1997.

31. Henry Kaufman, "Today's Financial Euphoria Can't Last," *Wall Street Journal*, November 25, 1996, p. A18.

32. Robert Shiller and John Campbell, "Valuation Ratios and the Long-Run Stock Market Outlook," *Journal of Portfolio Management*, vol. 24 (Winter 1997). The Shiller model is discussed in more detail in Chapter 11.

33. *Newsweek*, April 27, 1998. Cover stories about the stock market in major newsweeklies have often been poorly timed. *BusinessWeek*'s cover article "The Death of Equities" on August 13, 1979, occurred 14 years after the market had peaked and 3 years before the beginning of the greatest bull market in stocks.

34. I immediately rebutted their arguments in the *Wall Street Journal* (see the Jonathan Clements interview of me in "Throwing Cold Water on Dow 36,000 View," *Wall Street Journal*, September 21, 1999), stating that their analysis was faulty and that stocks must have real returns exceeding those on U.S. Treasury inflation-protected bonds, whose yield had reached 4 percent at that time.

35. "Big Cap Tech Stocks Are a Sucker's Bet," *Wall Street Journal*, March 14, 2000, p. A8.

36. Paul Sloan, "The Craze Collapses," *U.S. News & World Report Online*, November 30, 2000.

37. The word *hedge* means "to offset," as someone making an investment in a foreign market may want to hedge, or offset, adverse currency movements with a transaction in the forward market. Hedge funds often, but not always, took positions that were contrary to the stock market.

38. Jeremy Grantham, "A Global Bubble Warns Against the Stampede to Diversify," *Financial Times*, April 24, 2007, p. 38.

39. In fact, just days before the Lehman bankruptcy, the REIT Index was only 25 percent below its record level that it reached in July 2007. In contrast, homebuilder stocks peaked in July 2005 and were already down more than 60 percent by the time the Lehman crisis broke.

40. See "At Lehman, How a Real-Estate Start's Reversal of Fortune Contributed to Collapse," *Wall Street Journal*, October 1, 2008.

Chapter 2

1. As early as June, Natixis, a French investment bank, had cut off all activity with Lehman, and in early September, it was reported by *The Financial Crisis Inquiry Report* that JPMorgan, Citigroup, and Bank of America all demanded more collateral from Lehman with the threat that they might "cut Lehman off if they don't receive it."

2. Risk spreads, such as the TED spread (Treasuries over Eurodollars), the LIBOR-OIS spread (LIBOR over Fed funds), commercial paper over Treasuries, and others jumped dramatically. By Wednesday the Bloomberg Financial Conditions Index of Risk had deteriorated to four to five standard deviations below normal levels based on the past 16 years of data. (See Michael G. Rosenberg, "Financial Conditions Watch," *Bloomberg*, September 18, 2008.)

3. On Monday, September 15, the Primary Fund valued Lehman's commercial paper at 80 cents on the dollar. On Tuesday it posted on its website, "The value of the debt securities issued by Lehman Brothers Holdings, Inc (face value $785 million) and held by the Primary Fund has been valued at zero effective as of 4:00 p.m. New York time today. As a result, the NAV of the Primary Fund, effective as of 4:00 p.m. is $0.97 per share."

4. I recalled lecturing my students in the 1980s, when Treasury bill rates were 16 percent, that investors were thrilled to get yields as high as 10 basis points in the 1930s. Students shook their heads in disbelief, and we all laughed about this curious piece of history that we thought could never happen again.

5. The standard deviation of quarterly changes in nominal GDP fell from 5.73 percent from 1947 to 1983 to 2.91 percent from 1983 to 2009.

6. The Jerome Levy Economics Institute of Bard College, Working Paper No. 74, May 1992; see also Robert Pollin, "The Relevance of Hyman Minsky," *Challenge*, March/April 1997.

7. Subprime mortgages were not solely the creation of Wall Street firms. Politicians who wanted to give millions of Americans their first chance to realize the "American Dream" of home ownership encouraged the government-sponsored lenders Fannie Mae and Freddie Mac to issue these loans to those who would not ordinarily qualify for conventional mortgages.

8. Since mortgages are denominated in dollars, it is the nominal, not the real, index that is of interest to bond buyers.

9. It is true that there were substantial declines in nominal house prices during the Great Depression and that the real estate price index declined 25.9 percent between 1928 and 1932. But that was entirely due to a deflation in the general price index, as the CPI fell almost exactly the same percentage. Since the Federal Reserve had committed to avoid deflation and could do so through the power of money creation, it would be quite reasonable to assume that researchers would ignore those data.

10. "Absence of Fear," CFA Society of Chicago Speech, June 28, 2007, reported by Robert Rodriguez, CEO of First Pacific, http://www.fpafunds.com/docs/special-commentaries/absence_of_fear.pdf?sfvrsn=2.

11. Deutsche Bank Trustee Reports, http://csmoney.cnn.com/2007/10/15/markets/junk_mortgages.fortune/index.htm?postversion=2007101609.

12. Noelle Knox, "43% of first time home buyers put no money down," *USA Today*, January 18, 2006, p. 1A.

13. Charles Himmelberg, Chris Mayer, and Todd Sinai, "Assessing High House Prices, Bubbles, Fundamentals and Misperceptions," *Journal of Economic Perspectives*, vol. 19, no. 4 (Fall 2005), pp. 67–92. They also wrote an article, "Bubble Trouble? Not Likely," which appeared on the editorial page of the *Wall Street Journal* (September 19, 2005) at the peak of housing prices.

14. According to Home Mortgage Disclosure Act data, the national share of purchase loans for second homes—defined as "other than owner-occupied as a principal dwelling"—increased from 8.6 to 14.2 percent from 2000 to 2004. That represents an annual average growth rate of 16 percent during that time period. The actual number of purchase loans doubled, increasing from 405,000 to 881,200. See Keunwon Chung, *Second-Home Boom*, at http://www.realtor.org/resorts/resorts/reisecond homeresearch. Chung is a statistical economist at the National Association of Realtors

15. Robert Shiller, *Irrational Exuberance*, 2nd ed., Princeton, NJ: Princeton University Press, 2005, Chap. 2. Also see *Forbes* columnist Gary Shilling, e.g., "End of the Bubble Bailouts," *Forbes*, August 29, 2006.

16. Dean Baker, "The Menace of an Unchecked Housing Bubble," *Economists' Voice*, vol. 3, no. 4 (2006), article 1; "The Run-Up in Home Prices: Is It Real or Is It Another Bubble?," *CEPR*, August 2002; and "The Housing Bubble and the Financial Crisis," *Real-World Economics Review*, no. 46, March 20, 2008.

17. Others who warned about the economic crisis were Gary Shilling ("End of the Bubble Bailouts," *Forbes*, August 29, 2006), an economic consultant and *Forbes* columnist, and George Magnus ("What This Minsky Moment Means," *FT*, August 22, 2007), senior economic advisor to UBS.

18. Many who questioned the sustainability of the price rise noted that when increases in demand bring about a rise in the price of real estate, the consequent increase in supply dampens and reverses price increases. Only factors that are fixed in supply, such as scarce land, will experience a sustained increase in prices if demand permanently rises. Since land costs for residential real estate are only about 20 percent of the total price of a home, land prices would have to rise fivefold in order for the price of a home to double in value.

19. This was just published three months shy of his untimely death at age 68.

20. Testimony of Dr. Alan Greenspan before the Committee of Government Oversight and Reform, October 23, 2008, p. 2.

21. Some blame Greenspan's naïve belief in the market and the efficient market hypothesis (EMH) for his silence. But if Greenspan always thought market prices were right, he would have never made his "irrational exuberance" speech in December 1996. Furthermore EMH does not say that prices are "always right"; in fact, they are most always wrong based on all future information that becomes available. The EMH does imply, because of the interaction of informed traders, that market prices are not "obviously" wrong in a way that makes it easy for the average investor to profit. As noted above, there was widespread disagreement, even among experts, about whether there was a paradigm shift in the housing market that justified higher prices.

22. John G. Taylor, professor at Stanford and author of *Getting off Track: How Government Actions and Invention Caused, Prolonged, and Worsened the Financial Crisis*, blamed Greenspan's Fed for keeping interest rates too low too long. Other who blamed the Fed for causing the housing crisis included Gerald O'Driscoll, Jr., of the Cato

Institute, David Malpass, president of Encima Global, and Representative Ron Paul of Texas, a steadfast critic of the Fed.

23. BBC news sourcing Federal Reserve, Bank of England, and SIFMA, news.bbc.co.uk /2/hi/business/7073131.stm.

24. These funds carried fancy names such as High-Grade Structured Credit Strategies Enhanced Leverage Fund.

25. Bear Stearns and Citibank tried to insulate themselves by issuing funds and special investment vehicles that were off-balance-sheet items. As defaults mounted, investors complained that they were not fully apprised of the risks of these securities, and the firms' legal counsel recommended that they take back many of these mortgages onto their own balance sheets.

26. When federal government debt is not explicitly backed by the central bank, it is no longer assumed "riskless," as was illustrated in the Eurozone crisis of 2011–2012.

27. The new facility was called the Asset-Backed Commercial Paper Money Market Mutual Fund Liquidity Facility.

28. Non-interest-bearing accounts (demand deposits) were used by business to process wage and other payments. Their security was deemed of paramount importance by the Fed in order to keep the payments systems functioning.

29. In 1996 the ratio of the FDIC's trust fund to deposits, called the designated deposit ratio, was set at 1.25 percent, but by September 2008 it fell below 1.0 percent.

30. Bernanke earned his doctorate eight years after I received mine in the same specialty from the Department of Economics. Although the economics department at MIT. was known to have a "Keynesian" orientation, monetarist thought and, in particular, monetary history were well covered.

31. Reported on November 8, 2002. Chapter 14 gives a more extensive description of monetary policy.

32. 12 USC 343. As added by act of July 21, 1932 (47 Stat. 715); and amended by acts of Aug. 23, 1935 (49 Stat. 714) and Dec. 19, 1991 (105 Stat. 2386).

33. See Chapter 8 in Henry M. Paulson, Jr., *On the Brink*, New York: Hachette Book Group, 2010.

34. See Peter Chapman, *The Last of the Imperious Rich: Lehman Brothers 1844–2008*, New York: Penguin Group, 2010, pp. 262–263.

35. Bernanke, a Republican, did not relish bailing out these financial firms. At a town hall meeting in Kansas City in July 2009, he stated, "I was not going to be the Federal Reserve Chairman who presided over the second Great Depression. I had to hold my nose . . . I'm as disgusted as you are [when I had to bail out these financial companies]." Reported by the Associated Press, Monday, July 27, 2009, "Bernanke Had to 'Hold My Nose' over Bailouts."

36. Allan Meltzer, "What Happened to the 'Depression'?" *Wall Street Journal*, August 31, 2009.

Chapter 3

1. The decline would be greater if quarterly data were available. Quarterly GDP was not available until 1946.

2. Joseph Swanson and Samuel Williamson, "Estimates of National Product and Income for the United States Economy, 1919–1941," *Explorations in Economic History*, vol. 10, no. 1 (1972); and Enrique Martínez-García and Janet Koech, "A Historical

Look at the Labor Market During Recessions," Federal Reserve Bank of Dallas, *Economic Letter*, vol. 5, no. 1 (January 2010).

3. That decline occurred between July 2008 and December 2008 as oil prices plummeted.

4. This is calculated from the 27 percent price-level decline (1/.73) noted above.

5. There were other factors moderating the fall in GDP during the Great Contraction that were absent during the Great Depression: the existence of FDIC deposit insurance; generous unemployment compensation; the automatic reduction of tax revenues as income and asset prices fell, which cushioned the decline in disposable income; and the expansion of federal government spending.

6. From Table A-1, in Milton Friedman and Anna Schwartz, *A Monetary History of the United States, 1867–1960*, Princeton, NJ: Princeton University Press, 1963.

7. In real terms, the 1974 and 2008 stock market declines were almost identical due to the far greater inflation that occurred in the 1973–1974 episode.

8. On the morning of October 20, the VIX (computed using slightly different index options) hit almost 170. Since then, the VIX reached 50 in 1997 during the Asian monetary crisis, in 1998 when Long-Term Capital Management collapsed, in 2001 immediately following the 9/11 terrorist strikes, and at the bottom of the previous bear market in 2002. See Chapter 19 for more details.

9. See Chapters 16 and 19 for a more detailed analysis of market volatility and the events that caused it.

10. In dollar terms, all markets fell by at least 50 percent. Italy, Finland, Belgium, Russia, Greece, and Austria fell by at least 70 percent, and Ireland fell by more than 80 percent. After rallying from their March 2009 lows, a number of European markets fell to new lows during the euro crisis, including Italy, Portugal, Spain, and Greece. The Athens Stock Exchange Index fell 92.7 percent from its high in September 1999 to June 2012.

11. The JPMorgan Index of emerging market currencies fell about 19 percent relative to the dollar from October 2007 through March 2009. On average, in local currencies, emerging markets fell about 53 percent, approximately the same as developed markets.

12. General Growth Properties, containing some of the highest-quality malls in the United States, fell from over $20 a share when Lehman went under to less than 20 cents as creditors demanded repayment of loans extended.

13. The more speculative Morgan Stanley Dot Com Index fell 96 percent from January 2000 through March 2002.

14. By September 2012, two and one-half years after the bear market bottom, these stocks were still down 89 percent, 95 percent, and 98 percent, respectively, from their highs.

15. Banks that largely avoided the financial crisis, such as Wells Fargo, which had lost up to 80 percent of its equity value at the bottom of the bear market, and JPMorgan, which has lost over 70%, both rebounded to new highs in 2013.

16. Because of the decline in the price level in the Great Depression, the decline in *real* earnings was even less severe in the 1930s. See Chapter 10 for more discussion.

17. See Chapter 11 for a more complete explanation.

18. According to the Case-Shiller indexes, real estate prices peaked in May 2006 and had already fallen about 8 percent by the time that the stock market peaked in October 2007. Residential real estate prices peaked in May 2006.

19. MIT Center for Real Estate prices, all commercial index.
20. Atif Mian and Amir Sufi, "Household Leverage and the Recession of 2007–09," *IMF Economic Review*, vol. 58, no. 1 (2010), pp. 74–117.
21. Even though Federal Reserve notes (currency) offer investors a zero return, investors considered a small negative return a small price to pay for holding millions of dollars in a convenient and safe monetary instrument.
22. Despite this quote, King denied that he had any knowledge that the rate was manipulated during the financial crisis.
23. Barclays claimed that the U.K. Financial Services Authority approved its low submission rates in order to prop up faith in the financial system during the financial crisis.
24. This is based on an arithmetic average of 19 commodities, with petroleum productions given a weight of one-third.
25. According to the law firm Davis Polk & Wardwell LLP in its "Summary of the Dodd-Frank Wall Street Reform and Consumer Protection Act, Enacted into Law on July 21, 2010."
26. The Dodd-Frank Act also prohibits the use of other funds, such as the Stabilization Fund, which was used to guarantee $50 billion for money market mutual funds shortly after Lehman filed for bankruptcy.
27. According to a Treasury report issued in January 2013, as of December 31, 2012, the Treasury had received over $405 billion in total cash back on TARP investments, equaling nearly 97 percent of the $418 billion disbursed under the program.

Chapter 4

1. Pew Research Center, "The Impact of Long-Term Unemployment," July 26, 2010.
2. This comes from the National Center for Health Statistics: *National Vital Statistics Reports*, www.cd.gov/nchs. Nonwhite life expectancies have lagged that of whites, but the difference is narrowing and is now about 4 years.
3. James Vaupel, "Setting the Stage: A Generation of Centenarians?," *Washington Quarterly*, vol. 23, no. 3 (2000), pp. 197–200.
4. "Forever Young," *Economist*, page 15, March 27, 2004.
5. Pauline Givord and Jean-Yves Fournier, "Decreasing Participation Rates for Old and Young People in France," Institute of Economics and Statistics, 2001.
6. Of course, individuals could retire earlier than this if they curtail their consumption sufficiently during their retirement period. The retirement period noted above is derived assuming that retirees consume at a rate of 80 percent of their level before retirement.
7. See Robert D Arnott and Denis B Chaves, "Demographic Changes, Financial Markets, and the Economy," *Financial Analysts Journal*, vol. 68, no. 1 (January/ February 2012), p. 23; and Zheng Liu and Mark M. Spiegel, "Boomer Retirement: Headwinds for U.S. Equity Markets?," *Federal Reserve of San Francisco Economic Letter*, August 22, 2011. The first popular work that described the impact of demographics on stock prices was written by Harry Dent, *The Great Boom Ahead*, in 1989. His dire predictions based on individual-country demographics are revealed in *The Great Depression Ahead*, published in 2009.
8. Homi Khara, "The Emerging Middle Class in Developing Countries," Working Paper No. 285, OECD Development Centre.

9. Charles Tansey, "Expanding U.S. Sales Overseas with Export Financing," *Trade and Industry Development*, February 29, 2012, http://www.tradeandindustrydev.com /Industry/Manufacturing/expanding-us-sales-overseas-export-financing-6169.

10. In the United States, productivity is defined as output per hour worked, although in Europe it is often defined as output per worker.

11. Productivity growth was slightly higher immediately following World War II, but since 1960, productivity growth in the United States has shown no significant downward trend.

12. Robert Gordon, "Is U.S. Economic Growth Over? Faltering Innovation Confronts Six Headwinds," NBER #18315, August 2012. For a rejoinder, see the response by John Cochrane of the University of Chicago in his blog at http://johnhcochrane .blogspot.com/2012/08/gordon-on-growth.html.

13. Tyler Cowen, *The Great Stagnation: How America Ate All the Low-Hanging Fruit of Modern History, Got Sick, and Will (Eventually) Feel Better*, New York: Dutton Adult, 2011.

14. These are not the dates when these items were discovered but when they became operational or widespread in the general population in the United States and most other advanced economies.

15. As quoted in *The Economist*, January 12, 2013, p. 21.

16. El-Erian wrote "The New Normal," which appeared in May 2009 monthly *PIMCO Newsletter*, and Bill Gross followed up a month later with "Staying Rich in the New Normal," where he specified the growth parameters in the new normal.

17. Jeremy Grantham of GMO and Christopher Brightman of Research Affiliates.

18. Michael Rothschild, *Bionomics*, New York: Henry Holt, 1990.

19. Charles I. Jones, "Sources of U.S. Economic Growth in a World of Ideas," *American Economic Review*, vol. 92, no. 1 (March 2002), p. 234; and Charles I. Jones and Paul M. Romer, "The New Kaldor Facts: Ideas, Institutions, Population, and Human Capital, *American Economic Journal: Macroeconomics*, vol. 2 (January 2010), pp. 224–245.

20. For another optimistic take, see Martin Neil Baily, James M. Manyika, and Shalabh Gupta, "U.S. Productivity Growth: An Optimistic Perspective," *International Productivity Monitor*, Spring 2013, pp. 3–12.

21. Ben Bernanke, Graduation Address, Bard College at Simon's Rock, MA, May 18, 2013.

Chapter 5

1. G. William Schwert, "Indexes of United States Stock Prices from 1802 to 1897," *Journal of Business*, vol. 63 (July 1990), pp. 399–426.

2. See Walter Werner and Steven Smith, *Wall Street*, New York: Columbia University Press, 1991, for a description of some early dividend yields. See also earlier work by William Goetzmann and Phillipe Jorion, "A Longer Look at Dividend Yields," *Journal of Business*, vol. 68, no. 4 (1995), pp. 483–508, and William Goetzmann, "Patterns in Three Centuries of Stock Market Prices," *Journal of Business*, vol. 66, no. 2 (1993), pp. 249–270. A brief description of the early stock market is found in Appendix 1 at the end of this chapter.

3. William Goetzmann and Roger G. Ibbotson, "A New Historical Database for NYSE 1815–1925: Performance and Predictability," reprinted in *The Equity Risk Premium*, New York: Oxford University Press, 2006, pp. 73–106.

4. Goetzmann and Ibbotson formed two stock return series, one assuming that those stocks for which they could not find dividends had zero dividends (their "low-dividend-yield" estimate) and another that assumes those stocks for which they could not find dividends had the same average dividend yield as those for which they did have dividends (their "high-dividend-yield" estimate). The midpoint of their high and low estimate is 6.52 percent, slightly higher than the 6.4 percent that I had originally assumed.

5. Robert Shiller, *Market Volatility*, Cambridge, MA: MIT Press, 1989.

6. *Ibbotson Stocks, Bonds, Bills, and Inflation (SBBI) Classic Yearbook*, published annually by Morningstar, Chicago.

7. Blodget, an early-nineteenth-century economist, estimated the wealth of the United States at that time to be nearly $2.5 billion, so that $1.33 million would be only about one-half of 1 percent of the total wealth; from S. Blodget, Jr., *Economica, A Statistical Manual for the United States of America*, 1806 ed., p. 68.

8. See Jeremy Siegel, "The Real Rate of Interest from 1800–1990: A Study of the U.S. and the U.K.," *Journal of Monetary Economics*, vol. 29 (1992), pp. 227–252, for a detailed description of the process by which a historical yield series was constructed.

9. This is explored in more detail in Chapter 14.

10. Ironically, despite the inflationary bias of a paper money system, well-preserved paper money from the early nineteenth century is worth many times its face value on the collectors' market, far surpassing gold bullion as a long-term investment. An old mattress found containing nineteenth-century paper money is a better find for an antiquarian than an equivalent sum hoarded in gold bars!

11. This long-run real return on U.S. stock was dubbed "Siegel's constant" by Andrew Smithers and Stephen Wright, *Valuing Wall Street: Protecting Wealth in Turbulent Markets*, New York: McGraw-Hill, 2000.

12. Bill Gross, "The Death of the Cult of Equities," *PIMCO Newsletter*, August 2012.

13. GDP growth is consistent with investors consuming about one-half the annual 6.6 percent long-term real return from stocks.

14. TIPS yields briefly shot up to 3 percent as the fears of another Great Depression sent investors scurrying to buy nonlinked bonds that would protect them against deflation.

15. For a rigorous analysis of the equity premium, see Jeremy Siegel and Richard Thaler, "The Equity Premium Puzzle," *Journal of Economic Perspectives*, vol. 11, no. 1 (Winter 1997), pp. 191–200; and more recently, "Perspectives on the Equity Risk Premium," *Financial Analysts Journal*, vol. 61, no. 1 (November/December 2005), pp. 61–73, reprinted in Rodney N. Sullivan, *Bold Thinking on Investment Management*, CFA Institute, 2005, pp. 202–217.

16. See Stephen J. Brown, William N. Goetzmann, and Stephen A. Ross, "Survival," *Journal of Finance*, vol. 50 (1995), pp. 853–873.

17. Elroy Dimson, Paul Marsh, and Michael Staunton, *Triumph of the Optimists: 101 Years of Global Investment Returns*, Princeton, NJ: Princeton University Press, 2002.

18. Dimson, Marsh, and Staunton, *Triumph of the Optimists*. The researchers added three countries to their list since publication.

19. In fact, *Triumph of the Optimists* may have actually *understated* long-term international stock returns. The U.S. stock markets and other world markets for which we have data did very well in the 30 years prior to 1900, when the *Triumph* study begins. U.S. stock returns measured from 1871 significantly outperform those returns taken from 1900. Data from the United Kingdom show similar returns.

20. Until recently, the oldest continuously operating firm was Dexter Corp., founded in 1767, a Connecticut maker of special materials that was purchased in September 2000 by Invitrogen Corp., which in 2008 merged with Applied Biosystems to form Life Technologies Inc. The second oldest was Bowne & Co. (1775), which specializes in printing. RR Donnelley acquired Bowne in 2010. The oldest banks with active markets for their shares are the First National Bank of Pennsylvania, founded in 1782 (now owned by Wells Fargo), and the Bank of New York Corp. (now BNY-Mellon), founded in 1784.

21. Werner and Smith, *Wall Street*, p. 82.

22. Two other canals, the Chesapeake and Delaware and the Schuylkill, were both joint-stock companies, and both had sold over $1 million in stock by 1825. I owe this observation to Stephen Skye, president of the Neversink Valley Museum of History and Innovation.

Chapter 6

1. Irving Fisher, et al., *How to Invest When Prices Are Rising*, Scranton, PA: G. Lynn Sumner & Co., 1912, p. 6.

2. R. Arnott, "Bonds, Why Bother?," *Journal of Indexes*, May/June 2009.

3. Chapter 22 on behavioral economics analyzes how investors' aversion to taking losses, no matter how small, affects portfolio performance.

4. This would mean that bond *yields* and stock prices move in the same direction.

5. This section, which contains some advanced material, can be skipped without loss of continuity.

6. For an excellent review of this literature, see Luis M. Viceira and John Y. Campbell, *Strategic Asset Allocation: Portfolio Choice for Long-Term Investors*, New York: Oxford University Press, 2002. Also see Nicholas Barberis, "Investing for the Long Run When Returns Are Predictable," *Journal of Finance*, vol. 55 (2000), pp. 225–264. Paul Samuelson has shown that mean reversion will increase equity holdings if investors have a risk-aversion coefficient greater than unity, which most researchers find is the case. See Paul Samuelson, "Long-Run Risk Tolerance When Equity Returns Are Mean Regressing: Pseudoparadoxes and Vindications of 'Businessmen's Risk,'" in W. C. Brainard, W. D. Nordhaus, and H. W. Watts, eds., *Money, Macroeconomics, and Public Policy*, Cambridge, MA: MIT Press, 1991, pp. 181–200. See also Zvi Bodie, Robert Merton, and William Samuelson, "Labor Supply Flexibility and Portfolio Choice in a Lifecycle Model," *Journal of Economic Dynamics and Control*, vol. 16, no. 3 (July–October 1992), pp. 427–450. Bodie, Merton, and Samuelson have shown that equity holdings can vary with age because stock returns can be correlated with labor income.

Chapter 7

1. Chicago Gas Company, an original member of the 12 Dow stocks, became Peoples Energy, Inc., and was a member of the Dow Utilities Average until May 1997.

2. The procedure for computing the Dow Jones averages when a new (or split) stock is substituted is as follows: the component stock prices are added up before and after the change, and a new divisor is determined that yields the same average as before

the change. Because of stock splits, the divisor generally moves downward over time, but the divisor could increase if higher-priced stocks are substituted for a lower-priced ones, as occurred in September 2013.

3. A price-weighted index has the property that when a component stock splits, the split stock has a reduced impact on the average, and all the other stocks have a slightly increased impact. Before 1914, the divisor was left unchanged when a stock split, and the stock price was multiplied by the split ratio when computing the index. This led to rising stocks having greater weight in the average, something akin to value-weighted stock indexes today.

4. This return is probably an underestimate, since the average yield on Dow stocks tends to be higher than the overall market.

5. For a related situation in which a long-standing benchmark was broken because of inflation, see the first section in Chapter 11, "An Evil Omen Returns."

6. In 2004 Standard & Poor's went to a "float-adjusted" weighting of shares that excluded shares held by insiders, other corporations, and governments. This reduced the weights of such large corporations as Walmart in the S&P 500 Index, where many shares are owned by the Walton family.

7. The 2013 criteria for admission include (1) the market capitalization must be at least $4 billion, (2) the U.S. portion of fixed assets and revenues must be the largest of all the assets and revenues (need not exceed 50 percent), (3) there must be four consecutive quarters of positive earnings as reported (GAAP earnings), and (4) the corporate governance structure must be consistent with U.S. practice.

8. There is admittedly some double counting of volume in the Nasdaq dealer system because the dealer buys the security rather than acts as an auctioneer. See Anne M. Anderson and Edward A. Dyl, "Trading Volume: NASDAQ and the NYSE," *Financial Analysts Journal*, vol. 63, no. 3 (May/June 2007), p. 79.

9. Closely related to the CRSP indexes is the Dow Jones Wilshire 5000 Index, which was founded in 1974 and contains approximately 5,000 firms.

10. The original Value Line Index of 1,700 stocks, which was based on a geometric average of the changes in the individual stocks, was biased downward. This eventually led Value Line to abandon the geometric average in favor of the arithmetic one, which could be replicated.

Chapter 8

1. Criteria for listing and other information are found on Standard & Poor's website.

2. In 1997 the SIC codes were expanded to include firms in Canada and Mexico, and the revised list was renamed the North American Industrial Classification System (NAICS).

3. Fannie Mae and Freddie Mac were removed from the index when the two firms went into receivership in July 2008.

4. The calculations in Table 8-3 include the return from all the spin-offs and distributions, while those in Table 8-2 assume all stock distributions are sold and reinvested in the surviving company.

5. The firm retained its ticker symbol MO, or "Big Mo," as traders affectionately call Philip Morris.

6. If the firm remains private, the returns are assumed to accumulate at the same level as that of the S&P 500 Index.

7. This is an estimate based on detailed research that showed an 89-basis-point out-performance from the index origin to the end of 2006. Since that time, the financial companies, almost all of which were added since 1957, have greatly underperformed the market.

Chapter 9

1. Letter to M. Leroy, 1789.
2. *McCulloch v. Maryland*, 1819.
3. Excerpts from "The Templeton Touch" by William Proctor, quoted in Charles D. Ellis, ed., *Classics*, Homewood, IL: Dow Jones-Irwin, 1989, p. 738.
4. Figure 9-2 assumes a total real return of 7 percent (real appreciation of 5 percent, a dividend yield of 2 percent) and tax rates of 23.8 percent on capital gains and dividend income. If inflation is 3 percent, the total before-tax return on stocks will be 10 percent in nominal terms. The increase in the maximum capital gains tax from 15 percent to 23.8 percent has nearly doubled the inflation tax on capital gains.
5. For married couples filing in 2013, the marginal capital gains tax (including the Medicare tax) is 0 up to $72,500, 15 percent up to $250,000, 18.8 percent up to $450,000, and 23.8 percent over $450,000.

Chapter 10

1. Robert Arnott, "Dividends and the Three Dwarfs," *Financial Analysts Journal*, vol. 59, no. 2 (March/April 2003), p. 4.
2. Real per share earnings have increased at about one-half the rate of real GDP, while NIPA corporate profits grow at the same rate as GDP.
3. After-tax corporate profits are taken from Table 1.12, line 45, of NIPA. "National" income (as opposed to "domestic income") includes the return from U.S. capital earnings in foreign markets.
4. Myron J. Gordon, *The Investment, Financing, and Valuation of the Corporation*, Homewood, IL: Irwin, 1962.
5. This also assumes that there is no differential tax on capital gains and dividends. See Chapter 9 for more discussion of this issue.
6. Firms that pay no dividends, such as Warren Buffett's Berkshire Hathaway, have value because their assets, which earn cash returns, can be liquidated and disbursed to shareholders in the future.
7. John Burr Williams, *The Theory of Investment Value*, Cambridge, MA: Harvard University Press, 1938, p. 30.
8. Although earnings filed with the IRS may differ from these.
9. I am indebted to David Bianco, chief U.S. equity strategist from Deutsche Bank, for much of this information.
10. These standards are no long called SFAS. All rules are now organized in one "accounting standard codification" (ASC), and FASB now issues an "accounting standard update," or ASU.
11. See Dan Givoly and Carla Hayn, "Rising Conservatism: Implications for Financial Analysis," *Financial Analysts Journal*, vol. 58, no. 1 (January–February 2002), pp. 56–74.

12. International Financial Reporting Standards (IFRS) allow the write-ups of asset values in some situations.

13. These differences in the two series prompted the BEA to put out a brief entitled "Comparing NIPA Profits with the S&P 500 Profits" written by Andrew W. Hodge in *Survey of Current Business*, vol. 91 (March 2011). The BEA defines *corporate profits* as the income earned from the current production by U.S. corporations based on "adjusting, supplementing, and integrating financial based and tax-based source data." Hodges indicates that Table 1.12, line 45, provides the most comparable data to the S&P 500 earnings.

14. This undercapitalization takes place both in accounting and in the GDP accounts. See Leonard Nakamura, "Investing in Intangibles: Is a Trillion Dollars Missing from GDP?," *Business Review*, Federal Reserve Bank of Philadelphia, Fourth Quarter 2001, pp. 27–37. In 2013 the BEA began to count research and development as investment in the GDP accounts.

15. These issues are also discussed in Chapter 14.

16. Wall Street analysts forecast operating earnings knowing which items those firms have traditionally included or excluded from their reports. GAAP earnings are rarely forecast since it is difficult to predict when firms will take special charges for restructuring or report onetime items such as capital gains.

17. The 65 percent number is often taken as the benchmark to analyze how good the quarter was for earnings in general.

Chapter 11

1. Graham and Dodd, "The Theory of Common-Stock Investment," *Security Analysis*, New York: McGraw-Hill, 1940, 2nd ed., p. 343.

2. *Business Week*, August 9, 1958, p. 81.

3. "In the Markets," *Business Week*, September 13, 1958, p. 91.

4. Molodovsky, "The Many Aspects of Yields," *Financial Analysts Journal*, vol. 18, no. 2 (March–April 1962), pp. 49–62.

5. See, Siegel, Jeremy J., "The S&P Gets Its Earnings Wrong," *The Wall Street Journal*," February 25, 2009, p. A13.

6. If all earnings were paid as dividends, the dividend yield would equal the earnings yield. The earnings yield may differ from the commonly cited ROE, or return on equity, which usually measures the ratio of profits to the *book* value of equity rather than its market value.

7. In 2013 Robert Shiller was awarded the Nobel Prize in Economics in part because of his work on stock market volatility and behavioral finance.

8. J. Y. Campbell and R. J. Shiller, "Valuation Ratios and the Long-Run Stock Market Outlook," *Journal of Portfolio Management*, Winter 1998, pp. 11–26. Their earlier paper was Campbell and Shiller, "Stock Prices, Earnings and Expected Dividends," *Journal of Finance*, vol. 43, no. 3 (July 1988), pp. 661-676. Robert Shiller posted a paper, "Price Earnings Ratios as Forecasters of Returns: The Stock Market Outlook in 1996," on his website on July 21, 1996, which served as the basis for his presentation to the Federal Reserve.

9. The CAPE model is able to explain just under one-third of the variation in future 10-year real stock returns, a high value for stock forecasting equations.

10. In Figure 11-3, the 10-year forward real stock returns are set at 6.54 percent (the long-run average) from January 2013 onward. The Shiller CAPE model predicts a 10-year average real return of 4.16 percent from 2013 to 2023. If that prediction is substituted for the next 10 years, the forecast and actual returns would converge at the end of 2012.

11. In that July 1996 paper, Shiller forecast that the real S&P 500 would decline by 38.07 percent over the next 10 years. Although the S&P 500 appreciated by 41 percent after inflation over that period and real stock returns were 5.6 percent, the CAPE ratios warnings became more accurate as the bull market progressed. In fact from March 1999, the real S&P 500 Index fell by more than 50 percent, vindicating Shiller's bearishness.

12. Other sources include an increase in the trend rate of growth of earnings and the "aggregation bias" that results because a few firms account for much of the losses in a recession. See Jeremy J. Siegel, "The CAPE Ratio: A New Look," working paper, May 2013.

13. NIPA profits have been deflated by the identical divisor used from S&P 500 earnings during the period 1967–2012 and extended back to 1928.

14. Joel Lander, Athanasios Orphanides, and Martha Douvogiannis, "Earnings Forecasts and the Predictability of Stock Returns: Evidence from Trading the S&P," Federal Reserve, January 1997. Reprinted in the *Journal of Portfolio Management*, vol. 23 (Summer 1997), pp. 24–35. It refers to an earlier version that was presented in October 1996.

15. James Tobin, "A General Equilibrium Approach to Monetary Theory," *Journal of Money, Credit, and Banking*, vol. 1 (February 1969), pp. 15–29.

16. Andrew Smithers and Stephen Wright, *Valuing Wall Street: Protecting Wealth in Turbulent Markets*, New York: McGraw-Hill, 2000.

17. Much of this material has come from exhaustive studies by David Bianco of Deutsche Bank on the S&P 500 margin. See Bianco, "S&P 500 Margins: Facts and Fiction," *DB Markets Research*, May 17, 2013, and Bianco, *Monthly US Strategy Update*, January 24, 2013, p. 26.

18. Charles M. Jones, "A Century of Stock Market Liquidity and Trading Costs," working paper, May 23, 2002.

19. John B. Carlson and Eduard A. Pelz, "Investor Expectations and Fundamentals: Disappointment Ahead?," Federal Reserve Bank of Cleveland, *Economic Commentary*, May 1, 2000.

20. Rajnish Mehra and Edward C. Prescott, "The Equity Premium: A Puzzle," *Journal of Monetary Economics*, vol. 15 (March 1985), pp. 145–162.

21. Mehra and Prescott used the Cowles Foundation data going back to 1872. In their research, they did not even mention the mean reversion characteristics of stock returns that would have shrunk the equity premium even more.

22. See Jeremy Siegel, "Perspectives on the Equity Risk Premium," *Financial Analysts Journal*, vol. 61, no. 1 (November/December 2005), pp. 61–73. Reprinted in Rodney N. Sullivan, ed., *Bold Thinking on Investment Management, The FAJ 60th Anniversary Anthology*, Charlottesville, VA: CFA Institute, 2005, pp. 202–217.

23. Chelcie C. Bosland, *The Common Stock Theory of Investment*, New York: Ronald Press, 1937, p. 132.

Chapter 12

1. Graham and Dodd, "Price Earnings Ratios for Common Stocks," *Security Analysis*, 2nd ed., New York: McGraw-Hill, 1940, p. 530.

2. Greek letters are used to designate the coefficients of regression equations. Beta, the second coefficient, is calculated from the correlation of an individual stock's (or portfolio's) return with a capitalization-weighted market portfolio. The first coefficient, alpha, is the average historical return on the stock or portfolio above or below the return on the market.

3. See William Sharpe, "Capital Asset Prices: A Theory of Market Equilibrium Under Conditions of Risk," *Journal of Finance*, vol. 19, no. 3 (September 1964), p. 442, and John Lintner, "The Valuation of Risk Assets and the Selection of Risky Investment in Stock Portfolios and Capital Budgets," *Review of Economics and Statistics*, vol. 47, no. 1 (1965), pp. 221–245.

4. From 1980 the beta of Exxon-Mobil was 0.60 versus 0.93 for IBM.

5. Eugene Fama and Ken French, "The Cross Section of Expected Stock Returns," *Journal of Finance*, vol. 47 (1992), pp. 427–466.

6. Eugene Fama and Ken French, "The CAPM Is Wanted, Dead or Alive," *Journal of Finance*, vol. 51, no. 5 (December 1996), pp. 1947–1958.

7. Benjamin Graham and David Dodd, *Security Analysis*, New York: McGraw Hill, 1934.

8. Rolf Banz, "The Relationship Between Return and Market Value of Common Stock," *Journal of Financial Economics*, vol. 9 (1981), pp. 3–18.

9. These data are adapted from *Stocks, Bonds, Bills, and Inflation (SBBI) 2007 Yearbook*, Chicago: Morningstar Publications, Chap. 7.

10. The small-cap stock index is the bottom-quintile (20 percent) size of the NYSE stocks until 1981, then it is the performance of the Dimensional Fund Advisors Small Company Fund from 1982 through 2000, and then it is the Russell 2000 Index from 2001 onward.

11. Graham and Dodd, *Security Analysis*, 2nd ed., 1940, p. 381.

12. See Robert Litzenberger and Krishna Ramaswamy, "The Effects of Personal Taxes and Dividends on Capital Asset Prices: Theory and Empirical Evidence," *Journal of Financial Economics*, 1979, pp. 163–195.

13. James P. O'Shaughnessy, *What Works on Wall Street*, 3rd ed., New York: McGraw-Hill, 2003.

14. John R. Dorfman, "Study of Industrial Averages Finds Stocks with High Dividends Are Big Winners," *Wall Street Journal*, August 11, 1988, p. C2.

15. Interestingly, an equal investment in the 30 Dow Jones Industrial stocks beats the performance of the S&P 500 Index from 1957 through 2012 by 80 basis points even though the Dow's beta is less than 1. The managing editor of the *Wall Street Journal* has the primary responsibility for the selection of the Dow stocks. As noted in Chapter 7, the companies in the S&P 500 Index are chosen primarily on the basis of market value, assuming that the firm is profitable.

16. S. F. Nicholson, "Price-Earnings Ratios," *Financial Analysts Journal*, July/August 1960, pp. 43–50; and Sanjoy Basu, "Investment Performance of Common Stocks in Relation to Their Price-Earnings Ratio: A Test of the Efficient Market Hypothesis," *Journal of Finance*, vol. 32 (June 1977), pp. 663–682.

17. Graham and Dodd, *Security Analysis*, 1934, p. 453. Emphasis theirs.

18. Yet even Graham and Dodd must have felt a need to be flexible on the issue of what constituted an "excessive" P/E ratio. In their second edition, published in 1940, the same sentence appears with the number 20 substituted for 16 as the upper limit of a reasonable P/E ratio! (Graham and Dodd, *Security Analysis*, 2nd ed., 1940, p. 533.)

19. Firms with zero or negative earnings were put into the high-P/E-ratio quintile. Returns were calculated from February 1 to February 1 so that investors could use actual instead of projected earnings for the fourth quarter.

20. Dennis Stattman, "Book Values and Expected Stock Returns," unpublished MBA honors paper, University of Chicago; and Fama and French, "The Cross Section of Expected Stock Returns."

21. Graham and Dodd, *Security Analysis*, 1934, pp. 493–494.

22. Unpublished work estimating the alpha from quintile selection of value strategies from 1987 through 2006 using the data on the Fama-French website, http:// mba.tuck.dartmouth.edu/pages/ faculty/ken.french/data_library.html.

23. These data come from the Fama-French website cited in the preceding note.

24. Obtaining IPOs at the offering prices, especially ones that are in great demand, is very difficult, as investment banks and brokerage firms ration these shares to their best customers.

25. About one-third of these firms survived in their current corporate form through December 31, 2003. If they did not, I substituted the return on the Ibbotson small-cap stock index (see note 9).

26. John Y. Campbell (with Jens Hilscher and Jan Szilagyi), "In Search of Distress Risk," revision of National Bureau of Economic Research Working Paper No. 12362, Cambridge, MA, March 2007.

27. John Y. Campbell and Tuomo Vuolteenaho, "Bad Beta, Good Beta," *American Economic Review*, vol. 94, no. 5 (December 2004), pp. 1249–1275.

28. Behavioral finance is the topic of Chapter 22.

29. See Jeremy Siegel, "The Noisy Market Hypothesis," *Wall Street Journal*, June 14, 2006.

30. September 2006. Robert D. Arnott, Jason C. Hsu, Jun Liu, and Harry Markowitz, "Can Noise Create Size and Value Effects?" (October 24, 2011), AFA 2008 New Orleans Meetings Paper, available at SSRN, http://ssrn.com/abstract=936272 or http://dx.doi.org/10.2139/ssrn.936272.

31. Roger G Ibbotson, Zhiwu Chen, Daniel Y. J. Kim, and Wendy Y. Hu, "Liquidity as an Investment Style," forthcoming, *Financial Analysts Journal*.

32. For more information, see Chapter 9, "Liquidity Investing," in *SBBI, 2013 Classic Handbook*.

Chapter 13

1. From a transcript of an address delivered to the Annual Conference of the Financial Analysts Federation, May 2, 1984.

2. See the section on worldwide equity and bond returns in Chapter 5.

3. EAFE stands for Europe, Australasia, and the Far East, and as of June 2013 it contained Australia, Austria, Belgium, Denmark, Finland, France, Germany, Hong Kong, Ireland, Israel, Italy, Japan, Netherlands, New Zealand, Norway, Portugal, Singapore, Spain, Sweden, Switzerland, and the United Kingdom. The list excludes Canada. Greece was demoted to an emerging nation in June 2013.

4. Martin Mayer, *Markets*, New York: Norton, 1988, p. 60.

5. The other five were the Canadian companies Nortel Networks, Alcan, Barrick Gold, Placer Dome, and Inco.

6. The United States is represented by the S&P 500 Index, and the non-U.S. developed regions are represented by the EAFE Index (described in note 3), Europe (iShares

S&P Europe 350, symbol IEU), and the emerging markets (iShares MSCI Emerging Markets Index, symbol EEM).

7. All these firms are ranked by the market value of the equity and do not include any debt. Rankings by total assets would thus differ from what is shown on the following tables.

8. *Economist*, "Supermajordammerung," August 3, 2013, p. 22.

Chapter 14

1. Martin Zweig, *Winning on Wall Street*, updated ed., New York: Warner Books, 1990, p. 43.

2. Linda Grant, "Striking Out at Wall Street," *U.S. News & World Report*, June 30, 1994, p. 59.

3. "World Crisis Seen by Vienna Bankers," *New York Times*, September 21, 1931, p. 2.

4. "British Stocks Rise, Pound Goes Lower," *New York Times*, September 24, 1931, p. 2.

5. The year-over-year inflation declined to minus 2.1 percent in July 2008 on the heels of the collapse in oil prices, but for the full calendar year there was no deflation during the recession that followed the financial crisis.

6. When the government issued non-gold-backed money during the Civil War, the notes were called "greenbacks" because the only "backing" was the green ink printed on the notes. Yet just 20 years afterward, the government redeemed every one of those notes in gold, completely reversing the inflation of the Civil War period.

7. "We Start," *BusinessWeek*, April 26, 1933, p. 32.

8. *Economic Report of the President*, Washington, D.C.: Government Printing Office, 1965, p. 7.

9. *Economic Report of the President*, Washington, D.C.: Government Printing Office, 1969, p. 16.

10. In 2000, Congress allowed the Humphrey-Hawkins Act to lapse, but legislation still required the Federal Reserve chairman to report biannually to Congress.

11. See Irving Fisher, *The Rate of Interest*, New York: Macmillan, 1907. The exact Fisher equation for the nominal rate of interest is the sum of the real rate plus the expected rate of inflation plus the cross product of the real rate and the expected rate of inflation. If inflation is not too high, this last term can often be ignored.

12. Gallup poll taken August 2–5, 1974.

Chapter 15

1. "Science and Stocks," *Newsweek*, September 19, 1966, p. 92.

2. Peter Lynch, *One Up on Wall Street*, New York: Penguin Books, 1989, p. 14.

3. Wesley C. Mitchell and Arthur Burns, "Measuring Business Cycles," *NBER Reporter*, 1946, p. 3.

4. The data from 1802 through 1854 are taken from Wesley C. Mitchell, *Business Cycles: The Problem and Its Setting*, Studies in Business Cycles No. 1, Cambridge, MA: National Bureau of Economic Research, 1927, p. 444. The data on U.S. recessions are taken from the NBER's website (http://www.nber.org), which lists business cycles from 1854 onward.

5. Robert Hall, "Economic Fluctuations," *NBER Reporter*, Summer 1991, p. 1.

6. Chapter 19 will discuss the 1987 stock crash and explain why it did not lead to an economic downturn.

7. There are two ways to treat the 2000-to-2002 bear market. The first interpretation is that there was one bear market that peaked on a total return basis on September 1, 2000, and bottomed on October 9, 2002, for a loss of 47.4 percent. The second is that there were two bear markets: one bear market with a drop of 35.7 percent from September 1, 2000, through September 21, 2001, just 10 days after the 9/11 terrorist attacks, then a subsequent rally of 22.1 percent to March 19, 2002; and finally another bear market of 33.0 percent, ending in October.

8. See "Does It Pay Stock Investors to Forecast the Business Cycle?" *Journal of Portfolio Management*, vol. 18 (Fall 1991), pp. 27–34

9. Stephen K. McNees, "How Large Are Economic Forecast Errors?," *New England Economic Review*, July/August 1992, p. 33.

10. "New Wave Economist," *Los Angeles Times*, March 18, 1990, Business Section, p. 22.

11. Leonard Silk, "Is There Really a Business Cycle?," *New York Times*, May 22, 1992, p. D2.

12. See Steven Weber, "The End of the Business Cycle?," *Foreign Affairs*, July/August 1997.

13. *Blue Chip Economic Indicators*, September 10, 2001, p. 14.

14. *Blue Chip Economic Indicators*, February 10, 2002, p. 16.

15. Transcript of Federal Open Market Committee meeting on December 11, 2007, p. 35.

Chapter 16

1. Table 16-1 excludes the 15.34 percent change from March 3 to March 15, 1933, to account for the U.S. Bank Holiday.

2. This expands the research originally published in David M. Cutler, James M. Poterba, and Lawrence H. Summers, "What Moves Stock Prices," *Journal of Portfolio Management*, Spring 1989, pp. 4–12.

3. The decline in October 1989, although often attributed to the collapse of the leveraged buyout, can be questioned since the market was already down substantially on very little news before the collapse was announced.

4. Virginia Munger Kahn, *Investor's Business Daily*, November 16, 1991, p. 1.

Chapter 17

1. Usually both the median and range of estimates are reported. The consensus estimate does vary a bit from service to service, but the estimates are usually quite close.

2. John H. Boyd, Jian Hu, and Ravi Jagannathan, "The Stock Market's Reaction to Unemployment News: 'Why Bad News Is Usually Good for Stocks,'" EFA 2003 Annual Conference, December 2002, Paper No. 699.

3. Martin Zweig, *Winning on Wall Street*, New York: Warner Books, 1986, p. 43.

Chapter 18

1. Leo Melamed is the founder of the International Money Market, the home of the world's most successful stock index futures market. Quoted in Martin Mayer, *Markets*, New York: Norton, 1988, p. 111.

2. Peter Lynch, *One Up on Wall Street*, New York: Penguin, 1989, p. 280.
3. *2013 Investment Company Fact Book*, Investment Company Institute, p. 9.
4. Robert Steiner, "Industrials Gain 14.53 in Trading Muted by Futures Halt in Chicago," *Wall Street Journal*, April 14, 1992, p. C2.
5. "Flood in Chicago Waters Down Trading on Wall Street," *Wall Street Journal*, April 14, 1992, p. C1. Today the proliferation of electronic trading has made it impossible for an incident such as the one that crippled the Chicago exchange 20 years ago to happen again.
6. The SEC eliminated the "uptick rule" (shorting prohibited unless the last change was an uptick) in 2007, but in February 2010 the SEC reinstated the rule to apply when the price declines by 10 percent or more.
7. From 1997 through 2012, there was no capital gain distribution from spiders (S&P 500 ETFs), while the Vanguard 500 Index Fund has had several (although none since 2000).
8. In fact, the largest 100 stocks of the S&P 500 Index, called the *S&P 100*, compose the most popularly traded index options. Options based on the S&P 500 Index are more widely used by institutional investors.
9. Chapter 19 will discuss the VIX, a valuable index of option volatility.
10. The original article was published in 1973: Fischer Black and Myron Scholes, "The Pricing of Options and Corporate Liabilities," *Journal of Political Economy*, vol. 81, no. 3, pp. 637–654. Fischer Black was deceased when the Nobel Prize was awarded in 1997. Myron Scholes shared the Nobel Prize with William Sharpe and Bob Merton, the latter contributing to the discovery of the formula.

Chapter 19

1. This is based on a $55 trillion worldwide total stock value at the end of 2012.
2. James Stewart and Daniel Hertzberg, "How the Stock Market Almost Disintegrated a Day After the Crash," *Wall Street Journal*, November 20, 1987, p. 1.
3. Martin Mayer, *Markets*, New York: Norton, 1988, p. 62.
4. The New York Stock Exchange Index replaced the Dow Jones Industrials to compute the 2 percent rule.
5. Before 1998, the New York Stock Exchange suspended trading for one-half hour when the Dow fell by 350 points and closed the exchange when the Dow fell by 550 points. Both of these halts were triggered on October 27, 1997, when the Dow Industrials fell by 554 points in response to the Asian currency crisis. Because of intense criticism of these closings, the NYSE sharply widened the limits to keep trading open. The new trading limits for closing the exchange have never yet been breached.
6. When the markets reopened after the 350-point limit was reached, traders were so anxious to exit that the 550-point limit was reached in a matter of minutes. See also note 5.
7. SEC and CFTC, *Findings Regarding the Market Events of May 6, 2010*, September 30, 2010.
8. These were sold through the e-mini market, valued at about $50,000 per contract.
9. These explanations were immediately challenged by the Chicago Monetary Exchange, which claimed that the large sell order represented less than 5 percent of the total volume in the S&P futures market during the 3½ minutes that preceded the

market bottom at 1:45:28. The CME response can be found on its website at http://cmegroup.mediaroom.com/index.php?s=43&item=3068.

10. Tom Lauricella and Peter McKay, "Dow Takes a Harrowing 1010.14 Point Trip," *Wall Street Journal*, May 7, 2010.
11. For leveraged securities or securities trading under $3, the limits are higher.
12. Charles D. Ellis, ed., "Memo for the Estates Committee, King's College, Cambridge, May 8, 1938," *Classics*, Homewood, IL: Dow Jones-Irwin, 1989, p. 79.
13. This is done by solving for the volatility using the Black-Scholes options pricing formula. See Chapter 18.
14. Until 2003, the VIX was based on the S&P 100 (the largest 100 stocks in the S&P 500 Index).
15. John Maynard Keynes, *The General Theory of Employment, Interest, and Money*, First Harbinger Edition, New York: Harcourt, Brace & World, 1965, p. 157. (This book was originally published in 1936 by Macmillan & Co.)
16. Robert Shiller, *Market Volatility*, Cambridge, MA: MIT Press, 1989. The seminal article that spawned the excess volatility literature was "Do Stock Prices Move Too Much to Be Justified by Subsequent Changes in Dividends?," *American Economic Review*, vol. 71 (1981), pp. 421–435
17. Robert Shiller was awarded the 2013 Nobel Prize in Economics in part for this research on market volatility.
18. Memorandum from Dean Witter, May 6, 1932.
19. Keynes, *The General Theory*, p. 149.

Chapter 20

1. Benjamin Graham and David Dodd, *Security Analysis*, New York: McGraw-Hill, 1934, p. 618.
2. Martin Pring, *Technical Analysis Explained*, 3rd ed., New York: McGraw-Hill, 1991, p. 31. Also see David Glickstein and Rolf Wubbels, "Dow Theory Is Alive and Well!," *Journal of Portfolio Management*, April 1983, pp. 28–32.
3. *Journal of the American Statistical Association*, vol. 20 (June 1925), p. 248. Comments made at the Aldine Club in New York on April 17, 1925.
4. Paul Samuelson, "Proof That Properly Anticipated Prices Fluctuate Randomly," *Industrial Management Review*, vol. 6 (1965), p. 49.
5. More generally, the sum of the product of each possible price change times the probability of its occurrence is zero. This is called a *martingale*, of which a random walk (50 percent probability up, 50 percent probability down) is a special case.
6. Figure 20-1B covers February 15 to July 1, 1991; Figure 20-1E covers January 15 to June 1, 1992; and Figure 20-1H covers June 15 to November 1, 1990.
7. Martin Zweig, *Winning on Wall Street*, New York: Warner Books, 1990, p. 121.
8. See William Brock, Josef Lakonishok, and Blake LeBaron, "Simple Technical Trading Rules and the Stochastic Properties of Stock Returns," *Journal of Finance*, vol. 47, no. 5 (December 1992), pp. 1731–1764. The first definitive analysis of moving averages comes from a book by H. M. Gartley, *Profits in the Stock Market*, New York: H. M. Gartley, 1930.
9. William Gordon, *The Stock Market Indicators*, Palisades, NJ: Investors Press, 1968.
10. Robert W. Colby and Thomas A. Meyers, *The Encyclopedia of Technical Market Indicators*, Homewood, IL: Dow Jones-Irwin, 1988.

11. In fact, if stock prices are random walks, the number of buy and sell is inversely proportional to the size of the band.

12. Historically, the daily high and low levels of stock averages were calculated on the basis of the highest or lowest price each stock reached at any time during the day. This is called the *theoretical high* or *low*. The *actual high* is the highest level reached at any given time by the stocks in the average.

13. Narasimhan Jegadeesh and Sheridan Titman, "Returns to Buying Winners and Selling Losers: Implications for Stock Market Efficiency," *Journal of Finance*, vol. 48, no. 1 (March 1993), pp. 65–91.

14. Moskowitz and Grinblatt have found that much of the success of these strategies is due to the price momentum in industries rather than of individual stocks. See Tobias Moskowitz and Mark Grinblatt, "Do Industries Explain Momentum?," *Journal of Finance*, vol. 54, no. 4 (August 1999), pp. 1249–1290.

15. Thomas J. George and Chuan-Yang Hwang, "The 52-Week High and Momentum Investing," *Journal of Finance*, vol. 59, no. 5 (October 2004), pp. 2145–2176.

16. Werner F. M. De Bondt and Richard Thaler, "Does the Stock Market Overreact?," *Journal of Finance*, vol. 40, no. 3 (July 1985), pp. 793–805.

17. Glenn N. Pettengill, Susan M. Edwards, and Dennis E. Schmitt, "Is Momentum Investing a Viable Strategy for Individual Investors?," *Financial Services Review*, vol. 15, no. 3 (2006), pp. 181–197.

18. Burton Malkiel, *A Random Walk Down Wall Street*, New York: Norton, 1990, p. 133.

19. See William Brock, Josef Lakonishok, and Blake LeBaron, "Simple Technical Trading Rules and the Stochastic Properties of Stock Returns," *Journal of Finance*, vol. 47, no. 5 (December 1992), pp. 1731–1764, and Andrew Lo, Harry Mamaysky, and Jiang Wang, "Foundations of Technical Analysis: Computational Algorithms, Statistical Inference, and Empirical Implementation," *Journal of Finance*, vol. 55 (2000), pp 1705–1765.

20. Benjamin Graham and David Dodd, *Security Analysis*, 2nd ed., New York: McGraw-Hill, 1940, pp. 715–716.

Chapter 21

1. This includes the dramatic 1975-to-1983 period during which small stocks returned over 30 percent per year.

2. Donald Keim, "Size-Related Anomalies and Stock Return Seasonality: Further Empirical Evidence," *Journal of Financial Economics*, vol. 12 (1983), pp. 13–32.

3. Robert Haugen and Josef Lakonishok, *The Incredible January Effect*, Homewood, IL: Dow Jones-Irwin, 1989, p. 47.

4. See Gabriel Hawawini and Donald Keim, "On the Predictability of Common Stock Returns: World-Wide Evidence," in Robert A. Yarrow, Vojislav Macsimovic, and William T. Ziemba, eds., *Handbooks in Operations Research and Management Science*, vol. 9, North Holland, 1995, Chap. 17, pp. 497–544.

5. For an excellent summary of all this evidence, see Gabriel Hawawini and Donald Keim, "The Cross Section of Common Stock Returns: A Review of the Evidence and Some New Findings," in Donald B. Keim and William T. Ziemba, eds., *Security Market Imperfections in Worldwide Equity Markets*, Cambridge: Cambridge University Press, 2000.

6. Jay Ritter, "The Buying and Selling Behavior of Individual Investors at the End of the Year," *Journal of Finance*, vol. 43 (1988), pp. 701–717.

7. Edward M. Saunders, Jr., "Stock Prices and Wall Street Weather," *American Economic Review*, vol. 83 (December 1993), pp. 1337–1345.

8. Of course, many investors in the Australian and New Zealand market live north of the equator.

9. R. A. Ariel, "A Monthly Effect in Stock Returns," *Journal of Financial Economics*, vol. 18 (1987), pp. 161–174.

10. The difference in the returns to the Dow stocks between the first and second halves of the month is accentuated by the inclusion of dividends. Currently, about two-thirds of the Dow Industrial stocks pay dividends in the first half of the month, which means that the difference between the first- and second-half returns is greater than reported here.

Chapter 22

1. David Dreman, *Contrarian Investment Strategies: The Next Generation*, New York: Simon & Schuster, 1998.

2. Frank J. Williams, *If You Must Speculate, Learn the Rules*, Burlington, VT: Freiser Press, 1930.

3. Daniel Kahneman and Amos Tversky, "Prospect Theory: An Analysis of Decision Under Risk," *Econometrica*, vol. 47, no. 2 (March 1979).

4. Robert Shiller, "Stock Prices and Social Dynamics," *Brookings Papers on Economic Activity*, Washington, DC: Brookings Institution, 1984.

5. Robert Shiller, "Do Stock Prices Move Too Much to Be Justified by Subsequent Movements in Dividends?" *American Economic Review*, vol. 71, no. 3 (1981), pp. 421–436. See Chapter 19 for further discussion.

6. Solomon Asch, *Social Psychology*, Englewood Cliffs, NJ: Prentice Hall, 1952.

7. Morton Deutsch and Harold B. Gerard, "A Study of Normative and Informational Social Influences upon Individual Judgment," *Journal of Abnormal and Social Psychology*, vol. 51 (1955), pp. 629–636.

8. Charles Mackay, *Memoirs of Extraordinary Popular Delusions and the Madness of Crowds*, London: Bentley, 1841.

9. See James Surowiecki, *The Wisdom of Crowds*, New York: Anchor Books, 2005.

10. Robert Shiller, "Conversation, Information, and Herd Behavior," *American Economic Review*, vol. 85, no. 2 (1995), pp. 181–185; S. D. Bikhchandani, David Hirshleifer, and Ivo Welch, "A Theory of Fashion, Social Custom and Cultural Change," *Journal of Political Economy*, vol. 81 (1992), pp. 637–654; and Abhijit V. Banerjee, "A Simple Model of Herd Behavior," *Quarterly Journal of Economics*, vol. 107, no. 3 (1992), pp. 797–817.

11. Brad Barber and Terrance Odean, "Trading Is Hazardous to Your Wealth: The Common Stock Investment Performance of Individual Investors," *Journal of Finance*, vol. 55 (2000), pp. 773–806.

12. B. Fischhoff, P. Slovic, and S. Lichtenstein, "Knowing with Uncertainty: The Appropriateness of Extreme Confidence," *Journal of Experimental Psychology: Human Perception and Performance*, vol. 3 (1977), pp. 552–564.

13. A. H. Hastorf, D. J. Schneider, and J. Polefka, *Person Perception*, Reading, MA: Addison-Wesley, 1970. This is also called the *Fundamental Attribution Error*.

14. For reference to a model that incorporates success as a source of overconfidence, see Simon Gervais and Terrance Odean, "Learning to Be Overconfident," *Review of Financial Studies*, vol. 14, no. 1 (2001), pp. 1–27.

15. For references to models that incorporate the representative heuristic as a source of overconfidence, see either N. Barberis, A. Shleifer, and R. Vishny, "A Model of Investor Sentiment," National Bureau of Economic Research (NBER) Working Paper No. 5926, NBER, Cambridge, MA, 1997, or Kent Daniel, David Hirshleifer, and Avandihar Subrahmanyam, "Investor Psychology and Security Market Under- and Overreactions," *Journal of Finance*, vol. 53, no. 6 (1998), pp. 1839–1886.

16. For a reference to data mining, see Andrew Lo and Craig MacKinlay, "Data-Snooping Biases in Tests of Financial Asset Pricing Models," *Review of Financial Studies*, vol. 3, no. 3 (Fall 1999), pp. 431–467.

17. See Nassim Taleb, *Fooled by Randomness: The Hidden Role of Chance in Life and the Markets*, 2005.

18. Dreman, *Contrarian Investment Strategies*.

19. Richard Thaler, "Mental Accounting and Consumer Choice," *Marketing Science*, vol. 4, no. 3 (Summer 1985), pp. 199–214 and Nicholas Barberis, Ming Huang and Richard H. Thaler, "Individual Preferences, Monetary Gambles, and Stock Market Participation: A Case for Narrow Framing," The American Economic Review, vol. 96, no. 4 (Sep., 2006), pp. 1069-1090.

20. Richard H. Thaler, "Mental Accounting Matters," *Journal of Behavioral Decision Making*, vol. 12 (1999), pp. 183–206.

21. Hersh Shefrin and Meir Statman, "The Disposition to Sell Winners Too Early and Ride Losers Too Long: Theory and Evidence," *Journal of Finance*, vol. 40, no. 3 (1985), pp. 777–792.

22. See Tom Chang, David Solomon, and Mark Westerfield, "Looking for Someone to Blame: Delegation, Cognitive Dissonance, and the Disposition Effect," May 2013.

23. Leroy Gross, *The Art of Selling Intangibles*, New York: New York Institute of Finance, 1982.

24. Amos Tversky and Daniel Kahneman, "Judgment Under Uncertainty: Heuristics and Biases," *Science*, vol. 185 (1974), pp. 1124–1131.

25. Terrance Odean, "Are Investors Reluctant to Realize Their Losses?" *Journal of Finance*, vol. 53, no. 5 (October 1998), p. 1786.

26. Hersh Shefrin and Richard Thaler, "An Economic Theory of Self-Control," *Journal of Political Economy*, vol. 89, no. 21 (1981), pp. 392–406.

27. See Paul Sloan, "Can't Stop Checking Your Stock Quotes," *U.S. News & World Report*, July 10, 2000.

28. Shlomo Bernartzi and Richard Thaler, "Myopic Loss Aversion and the Equity Premium Puzzle," *Quarterly Journal of Economics*, 1995, pp. 73–91.

29. See Chapter 5 for a further description of the equity premium puzzle.

30. Humphrey B. Neill, *The Art of Contrary Thinking*, Caldwell, ID: Caxton Printers, 1954, p. 1.

31. Benjamin Graham and David Dodd, *Security Analysis*, New York: McGraw-Hill, 1934, p. 12.

32. A discussion of the VIX is found in Chapter 19.

33. Werner F. M. De Bondt and Richard H. Thaler, "Does the Stock Market Overreact?" *Journal of Finance*, vol. 49, no. 3 (1985), pp. 793–805.

34. This strategy is discussed in great detail in Chapter 12.

Chapter 23

1. Benjamin Graham and Seymour Chatman, ed., *Benjamin Graham: The Memoirs of the Dean of Wall Street*, New York: McGraw-Hill, 1996, p. 273.

2. Charles D. Ellis, "The Loser's Game," *Financial Analysts Journal*, vol. 31, no. 4 (July/August 1975).

3. Fund data provided by Walter Lenhard of the Vanguard Group. See John C. Bogle, *Bogle on Mutual Funds*, Burr Ridge, IL: Irwin Professional Publishing, 1994, for a fuller description of these data.

4. Burton G. Malkiel, *A Random Walk Down Wall Street: The Time-Tested Strategy for Successful Investing*, 5th ed., New York: Norton, 1990, p. 362.

5. The standard deviation of the Magellan Fund over Lynch's period was 21.38 percent, compared with 13.88 percent for the Wilshire 5000, while its correlation coefficient with the Wilshire was .86.

6. "The Superinvestors of Graham-and-Doddsville," *Hermes, the Columbia Business School Magazine*, 1984 (reprinted 2004).

7. Money managers are assumed to expose their clients to the same risk as would the market, and the money managers have a correlation coefficient of .88 with market returns, which has been typical of equity mutual funds since 1971.

8. Darryll Hendricks, Jayendu Patel, and Richard Zeckhauser, "Hot Hands in Mutual Funds: Short-Run Persistence of Relative Performance, 1974–1988," *Journal of Finance*, vol. 48, no. 1 (March 1993), pp. 93–130.

9. Edwin J. Elton, Martin J. Gruber, and Christopher R. Blake, "The Persistence of Risk-Adjusted Mutual Fund Performance," *Journal of Business*, vol. 69, no. 2 (April 1996), pp. 133–157.

10. Burton G. Malkiel, *A Random Walk Down Wall Street*, 8th ed., New York: Norton, 2003, pp. 372–274.

11. John C. Bogle, *The Little Book of Common Sense Investing*, Hoboken, NJ: Wiley, 2007, Chap. 9.

12. Ellis, "The Loser's Game," *Financial Analysts Journal*, p. 19.

13. Five years before the Vanguard 500 Index Fund, Wells Fargo created an equally weighted index fund called "Samsonite," but its assets remained relatively small.

14. Heather Bell, "Vanguard 500 Turns 25, Legacy in Passive Investing," *Journal of Index Issues*, Fourth Quarter 2001, pp. 8–10.

15. The Vanguard Institutional Index Fund Plus shares, with a minimum investment of $200 million, have outperformed the S&P 500 Index by 3 basis points over the 10 years ending June 30, 2013.

16. Roger J. Bos, *Event Study: Quantifying the Effect of Being Added to an S&P Index*, New York: McGraw-Hill, Standard & Poor's, September 2000.

17. See David Blitzer and Srikant Dash, "Index Effect Revisited," *Standard & Poor's*, September 20, 2004.

18. Practically, there is no bright line between those shares "readily available" and those that are not. Holdings by index funds may actually be less available than those of close family members.

19. As a matter of full disclosure, I am a senior investment strategy advisor at WisdomTree Investment, Inc., a company that issues fundamentally weighted ETFs.

20. Robert D. Arnott, Jason C. Hsu, and Philip Moore, "Fundamental Indexation," *Financial Analysts Journal*, vol. 61, no. 2 (March/April 2005). Also Social Science Research Network (SSRN).

21. Henry Fernandez, "Straight Talk," *Journal of Indexes*, July/August 2007.
22. Robert Jones, "Earnings Basis for Weighting Stock Portfolios," *Pensions and Investments*, August 6, 1990.
23. Paul C. Wood and Richard E. Evans, "Fundamental Profit-Based Equity Indexation," *Journal of Indexes*, Second Quarter 2003.
24. Arnott, Hsu, and Moore, "Fundamental Indexation." *Financial Analysts Journal*.

Chapter 24

1. John Maynard Keynes, *A Tract on Monetary Reform*, London: Macmillan, 1924, p. 80.
2. Linda Grant, "Striking Out at Wall Street," *U.S. News & World Report*, June 20, 1994, p. 58.
3. John Maynard Keynes, *The General Theory of Employment, Interest, and Money*, New York: Harcourt, Brace & World, 1965, First Harbinger Edition, p. 158.

INDEX

ABOUT THE AUTHOR

Jeremy J. Siegel is the Russell E. Palmer Professor of Finance at The Wharton School of the University of Pennsylvania, the academic director of the Securities Industry Institute, and a senior investment strategy advisor to WisdomTree Investments, which creates and markets exchange-traded funds.